Queer Roots for the Diaspora

Queer Roots for the Diaspora

Ghosts in the Family Tree

✦ ✦ ✦

JARROD HAYES

University of Michigan Press
Ann Arbor

Published in the United States of America by the
University of Michigan Press
Manufactured in the United States of America
♾ Printed on acid-free paper

2019   2018   2017   2016   4   3   2   1

A CIP catalog record for this book is available from the British Library.

ISBN: 978-0-472-07316-0 (hardcover)
ISBN: 978-0-472-05316-2 (paperback)
ISBN: 978-0-472-12206-6 (ebook)

in memoriam
Mason Cooley
dear friend and mentor

✦ ✦ ✦

Acknowledgments

✦ ✦ ✦

A project such as this one, which has taken well over a decade to complete, owes much gratitude to the many who have offered their assistance along the way. Peggy McCracken generously read the entire manuscript and offered numerous suggestions and feedback. An invaluable mentor since she arrived at the University of Michigan, she chaired both my tenure and promotion committees. While such professional moments can often be quite stressful, under her leadership they felt much more like times of intense mentoring. My professional life—not just this book—owes much to her kindness, friendship, support, and guidance.

Over twenty years after my years as a graduate student, I still find myself thanking my dissertation advisers Nancy K. Miller and Francesca Canadé Sautman for their years of mentoring and guidance. Many of my colleagues would be envious to have had just one adviser like them; I was blessed with two. I was auditing Francesca's course on African literature when I first presented some of the ideas that would become chapter 1 herein. Her encouragement from early on did much to keep me pursuing this project, and her invitation to speak at a conference entitled Migration, Memory, and Trace: Writing in French outside of the Hexagon, cosponsored by the CUNY Graduate Center and New York University in 2001, gave me the opportunity to share the earliest parts of this project with a wider audience. She continues to this day to be one of the strongest connections I maintain with my alma mater.

Nancy has continued to provide letters of reference long after the end of my studies, as well as frequent advice on professional matters such as the job market and grant applications. She, too, invited me to share a later version of this work at a conference entitled Rites of Return: Poetics and Politics, cosponsored by Columbia University and the CUNY Graduate Center in 2008. She and Marianne Hirsch then included a revised version of this talk in their collection *Rites of Return: Diaspora Poetics and the Politics of Memory*. In my trips back to New York, frequent at times, less so at others, both Francesca and Nancy have always made time to catch up and renew their unending support.

Ross Chambers, Timothy J. Reiss, and Lawrence D. Kritzman read the earliest proposals for this project and provided valuable feedback from the very beginning, not only on the project as a whole but also on a number of its chapters. Others have read more than one chapter and offered extensive feedback: David Caron, Frieda Ekotto, and Aaron Boalick. Many friends and colleagues have read a chapter or part thereof and offered valuable suggestions: Jossianna Arroyo, Ralph Bauer, Patricia Penn Hilden, Carina Yervasi, Shari M. Huhndorf, Marie-Hélène Huet, Sara Salih, Sharmilla Beezmohun, Claire Decoteau, Fatima Aslı Gür, Ulrike Peters, Michael Rahfaldt, Jesse Hoffnung-Garskof, Janet Carol Hart, Aslı Iğsız, Tobin Siebers, Madeleine Dobie, Marianne Hirsch, Yannick Viers, and Céline Portet. A number of friends and colleagues brought their valuable expertise to specific chapters: Bénédicte Boisseron, Luc Boisseron, Guy Kabile, and John Stiles (for chapter 1); Neville Hoad, Brenna Munro, and Charles Gueboguo (for chapter 2); Ryan Szpiech and Kate Jenckes (for chapter 3); and Roger Grant and Nadine Hubbs (for chapter 4).

Others helped in myriad ways, after talks or during conversations, by making crucial observations and suggestions: Patrick Cullen, Marc Schachter, Helen Solterer, Richard Watts, Aliko Songolo, J. Michael Dash, Patricia Yaeger, Joseph A. Massad, Royal S. Brown, Lynne Huffer, Elisabeth Ladenson, Nilo Couret, Lawrence La Fountain-Stokes, Jack Halberstam, Gema Pérez-Sánchez, Martine Antle, Sahar Amer, Dominique Fisher, Carla Freccero, Esther Gabara, Francisco-J. Hernández Adrián, Michèle Longino, Lawrence R. Schehr, Tina M. Campt, Rudolf P. Gaudio, Steven Blevins, Steven F. Butterman, Moulie Vidas, and Peggy Kamuf. And in addition to being the chair of the Department of Romance Languages and Literatures at Michigan when I was hired, William Paulson has been an important mentor throughout my career.

Of course I owe much gratitude to the institution where I have spent my entire professional career. The University of Michigan has

granted me one nurturance leave, two sabbaticals, a Michigan Humanities Award, a Global Ethnic Literatures Seminar Fellowship, and a
fellowship year at the Institute for the Humanities. Most recently, the
University of Michigan Office of Research offered me a Publication
Subvention to help offset the publication costs of this book. In addition, both the university as a whole and my own department have provided funding to attend numerous conferences at which I presented
many parts of this book. An early fellowship from the American Council of Learned Societies (1999–2000) allowed me to turn that first
nurturance leave into a full year devoted largely to the first stage of
this project. Finally, a number of institutions, through invited lectures,
often accompanied by honoraria, helped finance this project in less
obvious ways: the CUNY Graduate Center, New York University, the
University of North Carolina (Chapel Hill), Tulane University, Duke
University, the University of Pittsburgh, the University of Maryland
(College Park), Columbia University, the University of Miami, and the
University of California (Davis).

This book represents my first foray into archival research. Colleagues
in French studies have regaled me with horror stories of their own experiences in the French archives. My own experiences on this side of the
Atlantic were, on the contrary, quite pleasant. For this I wish to thank the
librarians and staff of Duke University's David M. Rubenstein Rare Book
and Manuscript Library (for their assistance in consulting the Jim Grimsley Papers), as well as the Stanly County Public Library and its Margaret
Johnson Heritage Room (where I did much of the research for chapter 6).

Finally, my acknowledgments would not be complete without an expression of gratitude to my sister, Audra Hayes Tombült, and parents Wanda
West Hayes and Jesse Lee Hayes, who not only performed the function of
archivists in their own right by clipping relevant articles from local papers
and saving other materials but also, especially in my parents' case, hosted
me during long periods in the summer and while on leave. Without this
"financial" and emotional support, this project might still be ongoing.

Previous versions of various parts of this book have appeared elsewhere as the following:

"Looking for Roots among the Mangroves: *Errances enracinées* and
Migratory Identities." *Centennial Review* 42.3 (1998): 459–74.
"*Créolité*'s Queer Mangrove." *Music, Writing, and Cultural Unity in
the Caribbean.* Ed. Timothy J. Reiss. Trenton, NJ: Africa World P,
2005. 307–32.

"Circumcising Zionism, Queering Diaspora: Reviving Albert
Memmi's Penis." *Wasafiri* 22.1 (2007): 6–11.
"Queer Roots in Africa." *Topographies of Race and Gender: Mapping
Cultural Representations.* Ed. Patricia Penn Hilden, Shari M.
Huhndorf, and Timothy J. Reiss. 2 vols. Spec. issue of *Annals of
Scholarship* 17.3/18.1–18.2/3 (2009): vol. 2, 151–82.
"Queering Roots, Queering Diaspora." *Rites of Return: Diaspora Poetics
and the Politics of Memory.* Ed. Marianne Hirsch and Nancy K.
Miller. New York: Columbia UP, 2011. 72–87.

They are reprinted here with the permission of the publishers.

Note on Translations

✦ ✦ ✦

To avoid burdening my text with unnecessary translations, I have only provided the French originals for quotations from my key primary texts for which a translation alone would be insufficient to communicate the full meaning of the passage. Translations of texts for which no published translations are listed among the works cited are my own. Translations without page references for which the original is also cited are also my own. For modified published translations for which the original is not given, the first page reference is to the translation and the second to the French original.

Contents

✦ ✦ ✦

Introduction

✦ ✦ ✦

You know, honey, us colored folks is
branches without roots and that makes
things come round in queer ways.
     —Zora Neale Hurston, *Their Eyes Were Watching God*

"To be rooted," wrote Simone Weil, "is perhaps the most important and least recognized need of the human soul" (43). Why this "need for roots"? How does knowing where we come from help us know who we are? If identity is rooted (and I increasingly think that it must be), what does the notion of roots tell us about identity? Roots, after all, are planted—they nourish and provide sustenance. They define the affective attachment to a geographic site of origins as organic and biological. I search for my roots, then, as I search for myself. As a comparative study in queer diaspora studies, *Queer Roots for the Diaspora: Ghosts in the Family Tree* takes as its primary object of study this desire for rooted identity—a desire to find and become one with one's roots—as well as the problems that inevitably arise when one sets out on such a journey. *Queer Roots* is thus about a certain obsession with beginnings and origins and the impossibility of returning to those origins with any certainty, or of knowing that the beginnings one has returned to are the true beginnings and not just the product of the fiction making that is the telling of the story of that return. It is a book about the writtenness of roots, the impossibility of roots, and the importance of recognizing both.

1

As a way of understanding identity, rootedness has increasingly been subjected to acerbic critiques, both political and theoretical. Politically, roots narratives have been criticized for attempting to police identity through a politics of purity that uses roots to exclude anyone who does not share them. Theoretically, a critique of essentialism has led to a suspicion of essence and origins regardless of their political implications. My argument is that, in spite of these conceptual debates around the concept of roots, ultimately the desire for roots contains the "roots" of its own deconstruction. To demonstrate this point, I carry out my own search for alternative roots that offer models of collective identity that are heterogeneous instead of homogeneous, acknowledge their own fictionality, and deploy family trees haunted by the queer others that patrilineal genealogy seems to marginalize. Frequently, therefore, these alternative roots narratives welcome sexual diversity, acknowledge that even a single collective identity can be rooted in multiple ways, and challenge the patrilineal lines of descent implied by roots, in part by disrupting the linear storytelling that constitutes identity. These roots narratives thereby recognize the dangers of their desires, highlight their queerness, and turn this queerness against the dangers in order to disarm them, but not totally.

I may very well know that my roots have never existed except inasmuch as I "return" to them (i.e., write and create them) through autobiographical acts, but just the same I set out on this return as if they were already there. In this study, therefore, the expression "queer roots" constitutes a description of my object of study (roots that are queer), of my methodology (the queering of roots as a critical practice), and of its political implications (roots that queer also resist the normative, homogenizing imperatives of rooted identity). Yet, whereas the critical practice of queering is primarily a deconstructivist one here, *Queer Roots* far from engages in a simple undoing of paradigms of rooted identity; it also contributes to our understanding of the ethical implications and political possibilities of queering as a critical practice. Throughout this study I therefore use *queer* flexibly, not only as a noun or adjective but also as a verb. Such usage allows me to take advantage of the full potential the term has come to represent in LGBTQ studies, as well as to enrich it. My definition of *queer* also gradually emerges from the multiple readings that make up this study.

The implications of queering roots become especially clear when one situates roots narratives in the context of the diaspora in which they are produced. Though inspired by my previous research on North African literature, the study that follows marks a widening of interest into other regions of French and Francophone studies, such as the Caribbean and West and Central Africa, as well as into African and American cultures in English. This comparatist, interdisciplinary study thus brings Francophone studies into dialogue with the fields of history, anthropology, film studies, and music. Indeed, the narratives examined herein simultaneously assert and question rooted identities within a *number* of diasporas—African, Jewish, and Armenian—and this book explores the intersections among them. Without attempting to be encyclopedic, including these varied diasporas and their different configurations changes the stakes of their "queer roots" by theorizing strategies for queering roots that can transcend the specificity of any given diaspora. If there can be no roots without diaspora, and likewise no diaspora without roots, queering roots or diaspora must occur somewhere in the dialogic relation between the two.

Queering Roots

Several interrelated paradoxes have emerged through which I organize my principle thoughts on roots narratives. The first paradox is political: whereas a return to roots attempts to remedy the alienation resulting from a historical uprooting, an assertion of roots can just as easily justify authority and oppression by excluding those considered not to share them. The second is narrative: whereas roots narratives claim merely to discover an origin that preexists the search for and so-called discovery of roots, the telling of the story is actually what creates the origins and, indeed, the identity rooted in them. The third is sexual: whereas roots narratives frequently rely on a patrilineal family tree structured by heterosexual marriage and reproduction and would therefore seem to exclude queerness, African and Caribbean writers, among others, frequently find a diversity of sexual practices and identifications upon returning to their roots. While the *queer* of my title might seem to apply most directly to this third, sexual paradox, I argue that the queerness of roots might be most productively theorized in the interconnectedness of all three paradoxes and the way they reinforce one another.

In the early 1990s, I once saw a t-shirt that read, "The family tree stops with me." With this slogan, the wearer performed a coming out, albeit a coded one. Rendered intelligible by the frequent opposition between queerness and family, and in particular between queerness and the heterosexual descent visualized as the family tree, this t-shirt might be read as resisting the very kinship that structures *narratives* of return to the roots of identity. Conversely, the notion of roots has allowed a number of lesbian and gay writers to establish a connection to their "forebears" "hidden from history" (cf. Duberman et al.). What would a queer family tree look like? What would a study of roots tell us about queer identities? A particular tree common in tropical regions and Caribbean and African literatures usefully visualizes the queerness of roots as understood through the interrelatedness of the three paradoxes of roots narratives: the mangrove. In a mangrove swamp, the roots of many trees are interconnected, and roots do not necessarily precede the tree; indeed, it is often impossible to discern which roots belong to which trees. If the mangrove can send down new roots from its branches, and new branches from its roots, its roots are connected in a network that might be described as rhizomatic (mangroves belong to the genus *Rhizophora*, after all).

Since any given mangrove tree can have an unlimited number of roots, a genealogy structured like a mangrove can offer roots without asserting any single one as an absolute origin that would justify a monopoly over the definition of identity. The diverse imagined community resulting from the model of the mangrove swamp can then safeguard against the danger of deploying roots to disempower rather than empower as the multiple roots of the mangrove ground a collective identity that is heterogeneous rather than homogeneous. In addition, since origins are indistinguishable from effects in the mangrove swamp, stories structured along the lines of its tangled roots disrupt the linear, cause-and-effect structure of paradigmatic roots narratives, as well as the distinction between beginning and end, thereby making it just as likely that roots are the *result* of storytelling as its preexisting impetus. Finally, as we shall see in the examples examined in chapter 1, by allowing multiple roots, mangrove narratives also open up the family tree to "unauthorized" models of descent and, therefore, nonnormative sexualities.

In a US context, the most familiar roots narrative is undoubtedly Alex Haley's 1976 novel *Roots*. Amazingly, Haley was able to trace his family tree back to Africa from the traces of oral history that his family had retained in spite of centuries of uprootedness and slavery. This unparalleled example of cultural memory obviously struck a chord; when *Roots* was broadcast as a miniseries in 1977, seven of its ten episodes became the most-watched shows in television history at the time. Haley also set off a genealogical fervor, as almost everyone, or so it seemed, began looking for his or her roots. The impact of this work, which traced the roots of an African American family back to Africa, can still be felt today, as is attested by the popular interest in genealogy. That this interest continues to this very day is evidenced by the British television series *Who Do You Think You Are?*, which has inspired versions in the United States, Canada, Australia, Ireland, Sweden, Denmark, Norway, the Czech Republic, and France. After three seasons on NBC between 2010 and 2012, the American version was picked up by TLC, which continued to produce new seasons at least through 2015.

Although the NBC and TLC series may have a wider audience, in part because it focuses on celebrities who are frequently white, a more direct descendent of Haley's *Roots* was the PBS special *African American Lives*, hosted by Henry Louis Gates Jr. The 2006 DVD release of the special that was the fourth series in this project, *Finding Oprah's Roots: Finding Your Own*, succinctly expresses the desire for a rooted identity on the back cover: "When Alex Haley published his bestselling novel *Roots* in the mid-1970s it raised the hopes of many African Americans that one day they too could trace their own roots back to Africa. Today, dramatic developments in genealogical research techniques and breakthroughs in DNA analysis are making that dream a reality." Oprah Winfrey also appears as early as the first series, in which we see her tearing up upon discovering a slave ancestor. This visceral connection with the past, with ancestors in her family tree, is strengthened upon the discovery of a match between her mitochondrial DNA and the Kpelle "tribe" in Liberia, after which she states, "Alex Haley is somewhere doing a high-five."

Perhaps the most interesting aspect of Oprah's return is that it was facilitated by a scholar as anti-essentialist as Gates. Yet Gates, who retraces his own roots along with Oprah's, discovers not only that his DNA admixture is half European, half African but also that his mitochondrial DNA is most certainly European. In a humorous scene, he reveals what he calls a "big surprise for me, Captain Black Man himself," and jokes, "I'm going to have to give up my job as chairman of the Department of African American Studies." "I'm heart-broken," he admits, still laughing, explaining that he undertook the project expressly to find his own African roots. Yet, if he can admit that "[f]amily history is as much about process as about destination," has he not found African roots in a way? If Haley could assert, "My own ancestors' [*sic*] would automatically also be a symbolic saga of all African-descent people—who are without exception the seeds of someone like Kunta who was born and grew up in some black African village, someone who was captured and chained down in one of those slave ships that sailed them across the same ocean, into some succession of plantations, and since then a struggle for freedom" (*Roots* 722), does Gates not share Oprah's roots by writing and reading them?

The kind of return that Oprah realizes but remains elusive for Gates is literalized in *Roots* when Haley not only *finds* his roots but also becomes one with them. During his physical return to Africa at the end of *Roots*, as Haley approaches Juffure, Gambia, he writes, "I felt queasily, uncomfortably alien" (716). This alienation, however, is repaired after a griot tells the story of Kunta Kinte, Haley's "farthest-back" African forebear (704): "Later the men of Juffure took me into their mosque built of bamboo and thatch, and they prayed around me in Arabic. . . . Later the crux of their prayer was translated for me: 'Praise be to Allah for the one long lost from us whom Allah has returned'" (720). Villagers of all ages even exclaim, "Meester Kinte!" (722), thereby authenticating Haley's reconstituted genealogy (at least in his perception) and establishing an unbroken link between them and him. The entire experience is one of transcendence for him: "There is an expression called 'the peak experience'—that which emotionally, nothing in your life ever transcends. I've had mine, that first day in the back country of black West Africa" (717). Haley reconnects, here, much as Oprah would do decades later, with a time of collective plenitude and jouissance. Likewise, by recovering a similarly lost past, all roots narratives idealize a time when the community's home was supposedly located where its roots are planted. When individuals find their roots, they live in harmony—with themselves, with each other, and with their past—indeed, in the complete presence of the essence of their identity. Returning to one's roots after a long exile is to reconnect with that essence, bring it back from the past, and make it present again. When I find my roots, I find a certain truth about myself.

Part of what constitutes this "truth," however, is that it can be shared. As Haley points out in the passage quoted above, his reconstituted family tree structures a "saga" with collective implications that are underscored by his subtitle: *The Saga of an American Family*. *Family* in this context includes not only living relatives and all the ancestors with whom Haley manages to connect but also, figuratively, all those who collectively share similar family histories. Haley's roots thus represent, metonymically, those of all African Americans who also share a history *tout court*. Indeed, the title suggests that *all* Americans, regardless of race, share his story in one way or another. This assertion of collective memory thereby constitutes an act of community building or, to allude to Benedict Anderson's expression, community imagining, one that responds to racism by revalorizing and even glorifying the African origins that are denigrated by the discourses that accompany and justify forced migration.[1] Such a response is based on the premise that searching for and then finding one's roots can cure uprootedness and the resulting alienation by retracing the steps of the initial uprooting: capture, enslavement, and transport across the Middle Passage. In their very structure, therefore, roots narratives reverse the trajectory of uprooting and, we could say, undo it. Yet the disconnectedness that roots narratives purport to cure is synchronic as well as diachronic; it afflicts not only the relation between individuals of a diaspora and their past but also the relations *among* individuals at any given time within this diaspora. While the cause of uprootedness is historical, in other words, its cure is all about the present (about the branches, one could say).

If another way of understanding this cure is as a recovery of a lost truth, being disconnected from one's roots results in a number of falsehoods: a false understanding (a misunderstanding) of the past resulting in a false (or alienated) identity. Correcting such falsehoods would thus require not only finding the truth but also telling it, a claim Haley devoted no small effort toward asserting. The term he used to describe *Roots* was *faction*; although he admitted having invented the details of narration and dialogue, he maintained that the basic outline and main events of his story were based on true facts. This truth claim of *Roots* is inscribed within the novel itself, as a part of its ending.[2] Most people, at least at first, believed that Haley not only had found a kind of truth but also was telling the truth. In spite of such claims, however, not everyone jumped on the bandwagon; a group of critics gradually emerged who began digging around for possible errors. As a result, and as chapter 3 elaborates, no potential factual basis for *Roots* has remained unchallenged. Though accused of telling lies by some, however, Haley has been defended by others as telling the truth even as they acknowledge the validity of the accusations they are defending him against. In other words, even if all the accusations are true, *Roots* still tells a kind of "truth" about roots.

Uprootings

In contrast to Haley's detractors, and perhaps even his defenders, I would suggest that it is important to consider the accusations along with the defense; the former are important not because they help us get to the "truth" about *Roots* but because they tell us something about the nature of roots. Through them, we can understand how, to a certain extent, roots are always inventions or fictions. Although Haley always denied the lies he was accused of telling, there is a way in which the text of *Roots* acknowledges a different kind of fabrication. For Haley's novel actually consists of *two* parallel narratives, both of which take the form of trajectories or journeys. The first begins in Africa and is the story of Kunta Kinte and his descendants, a story whose structure could be visualized as a family tree. This trajectory is that of the Middle Passage, of the enslavement of a Mandinka man and his forcible removal from African soil to be transported to America. This narrative is one of an uprooting, and, at the allegorical level, Kunta Kinte's story is the history of the African diaspora in the New World. This narrative begins in the past and ends in the present, in America. In contrast, the second narrative proceeds in the opposite direction, both geographically and temporally. It begins in America and is the story of retracing the family tree and telling Kunta Kinte's story; it is the story of the *writing* of *Roots*. Its trajectory is one of a return—to Africa, Haley's African roots, and the site of the first story's beginning. The second story is one of a quest for, then discovery of, roots; it is the story of a rerooting through the writing of a narrative. At the allegorical level, this story is that of a collective African American identity. In this second narrative, then, origins are an end not a beginning; they are the result of the search (or the story of the search), not its starting point or cause. In its very narrative structure, therefore, Haley's *Roots* acknowledges its own fictionality and reveals the narrative paradox that identity is a story that links a subject to his or her identification by creating its origin in this way.

Understanding roots in this way, however, implies that there can be no rerooting without an initial uprooting and that looking for one's roots presumes that they were somehow lost. Why else would they need to be found, and if they must be lost before they can be found, can roots even make sense outside of diaspora (or the cultural disruption produced by colonialism)? Bringing about rootedness (as opposed to desiring roots as a project or goal), then, would entail the death of diaspora, and if there can be no roots without diaspora, rerooting runs the risk of carrying out an uprooting as well. There have certainly been entire movements based on the promise of rerooting as a political and/or cultural solution to racism, forced migration, and colonial alienation. Such movements include the Back to Africa movement as well as the Rastafari movement and other forms of Afrocentrism or Afrocentricity. Afrocentrism has been frequently criticized and sometimes ridiculed, often perhaps prematurely so, since if there can be no roots without diaspora there can likewise be no diaspora without roots. Afrocentrism's parallel in Francophone Africa and its American and European diaspora, Négritude, associated with writers such as Aimé Césaire from Martinique, Léopold Sédar Senghor from Senegal, and Léon-Gontran Damas from Guyane, countered the colonial denigration of everything African by espousing a return to African civilization and values and valorizing a "Black soul" or essence. Négritude has withstood an ongoing critique for over half a century now (which itself suggests that what the critiques denigrate must be more powerful than they would let on).

A common denominator among critiques of Négritude is an argument (or one of a number of related arguments) that can be boiled down to the second, political paradox of roots narratives. In spite of the stated intention of countering the racializing mythmaking of colonial discourse, many roots-based paradigms simply reverse the values of racial oppositions and thereby attribute a positive valence to the stereotypes deployed in racial othering and racist violence. In other words, they might contribute as much to the "structures of violence" that accompany uprooting as to the cure for that uprooting; racial difference (the key product of racist discourse) remains firmly rooted.[3] But does this critique mean that one might simply reject notions of rooted identity? The answer to this question, much diasporic literature suggests, depends on the way one narrates the relation between roots and diaspora. One might say, in fact, that the answer lies in the realization that roots are a story, a narrative process, and not an end. And since ends are intimately connected with origins, the realization that roots are not an end entails a simultaneous realization that they are not an origin that has been there from the beginning. The narrative and the political paradoxes are thus intertwined to such an extent that acknowledging the narrative paradox can also have the political benefit of disarming the potential of roots narratives to justify domination and oppression.

Yet, regardless of how Haley's bidirectional narrative structure acknowledges the fact that *Roots* creates roots as opposed to returning to preexisting ones, it might still be said to naturalize another kind of origin, the one resulting from *pro*creation. While *Roots* reveals the writtenness of African roots, the roots of a family tree that reconnects an uprooted people to their origins are still firmly planted in heterosexual reproduction. In other words, in the face of dispersion, *Roots* uses family history to provide the continuity that connects African Americans to one another as a kind of family. This cohesion, however, relies on a model of kinship that excludes alternative forms of affiliation and descent. And while this exclusion remains implicit in Haley's version of African roots, it has become an explicit aspect of a certain trend in both pan-African nationalism and US black nationalism, a trend that claims that homosexuality is a white disease imposed on black peoples by colonialism and/or slavery. In other words, according to this position, homosexuality cannot have African roots. Such a notion of roots disconnects gay African Americans and both Africans and African Americans engaging in any sort of same-sex desire from any African past or tradition. It uproots them, in short, and in so doing excludes questions of gender and sexuality from the concerns of antiracist movements and national liberation struggles. Furthermore, by denying the blackness or Africanness of same-sex eroticism, desires, and sexual acts, it also reinforces sexual and gender hierarchies (themselves often imposed by colonialism as opposed to constituting a part of a so-called African tradition). Unlike Haley, then, this political deployment of roots denies that it invents the roots it claims to be founded on, thereby grounding a masculinist vision of black liberation and actively shutting out demands that often question dominant articulations of the roots of identity within these movements.

If this exclusionary practice were limited to the discourses of resistance movements, it might raise less concern. Resistance movements, however, are such because of their opposition to regimes in power. They therefore usually seek to transform or even overturn the regimes they oppose, and they occasionally realize their goals. And it is at the moment of success, of coming to power, that a previously empowering move can become the basis of a new (or perhaps not so new) form of power (see Chambers, *Room* xii). Furthermore, it is not only through sexuality that the empowering potential of roots can be converted into a tool of oppression, exclusion, and marginalization; African and Caribbean dictators such as François Duvalier (in Haiti) and Mobutu Sese Seko (in what was, at the time, Zaïre) used concepts such as *noirisme* and the return to a black essence or African authenticity to consolidate their power and maintain their totalitarian regimes by policing racial and/or national identity, as well as through political marginalization and even physical violence. Many African and Caribbean writers, fully aware of the danger of this kind of exclusion, have, in contrast, sought ways to harness the empowering potential of roots without increasing the danger of their deployment to reinforce the very oppression one seeks to resist.

Rerootings, Reroutings

From the late 1970s through the early 1990s, Francophone Caribbean writers, in particular, found a solution to this double bind in the image of the mangrove, which offers an alternative to rooting Caribbean identity in African origins by rerouting its roots to places along the migrations that have led to the Caribbean. During approximately the same period, Martiniquan writer Édouard Glissant began to articulate a more abstract theoretical notion that would play a role similar to that of the concrete image of the mangrove. In *Caribbean Discourse* (1981), he first proposed a model of rhizomatic identity inspired by Gilles Deleuze and Félix Guattari's *A Thousand Plateaus*. Glissant elaborates further on this concept in *Poetics of Relation* (1990), in which, perhaps in part because this theorization was beginning to resonate with more frequent uses of the mangrove in Francophone Caribbean fiction, the rhizomatic finds its most succinct and quotable elaboration: "The root is unique, a stock taking all upon itself and killing all around it. . . . [T]he rhizome [is] an enmeshed root system, a network spreading either in the ground or in the air, with no predatory rootstock taking over permanently. The notion of the rhizome maintains, therefore, the idea of rootedness but challenges that of a totalitarian root" (11). Whereas the single root would be totalitarian in its prescription, even legislation, of a homogeneous identity, like the roots of the mangrove, rhizomes offer a multiplicity of roots that defines Caribbean identity as heterogeneous and acknowledges the many *métissages* that have resulted in Caribbean identities. For Glissant, therefore, rhizomes represent one way around the political paradox of roots.

Glissant's concept of rhizomes carries additional implications of movement, which he considers in relation to the concept of nomadism à la Deleuze and Guattari. In Glissant's writing, nomadic *errance* ("wandering," often translated as "errantry"), as opposed to exile, can thus be *enracinée* (rooted), and leaving home need not entail a deracinated identity. According to this model, one may still take along one's roots when one chooses or is forced to leave "home," when one is separated from the land where one's roots are planted. In spite of the fact that Glissant's notion of the rhizomatic was inspired by Deleuze and Guattari, his version not only is attached to a specific geocultural context—the Caribbean—but also allows for an identity rooted in that place. Like Deleuze and Guattari, Glissant rejects the root; unlike them, he keeps rootedness. Like their abstract nomads, his Caribbean subject is on the move. It is nonetheless a subject and not a schizo, though both may very well find their ideal "position" on a walk and not as an analysand on the couch.

Just a few years after the publication of *Poetics of Relation*, as the English translation of *Caribbean Discourse* was becoming better known among Anglophone Caribbeanists, the rhizomatic would become a key component of the title concept in *The Black Atlantic: Modernity and Double Consciousness* (1993), by the British sociologist and cultural critic Paul Gilroy. Here Gilroy draws attention to what he considers to be "conceptual problems common to English and African-American versions of cultural studies which, [he] argue[s], share a nationalistic focus that is antithetical to the rhizomorphic, fractal structure of the transcultural, international formation [he] call[s] the black Atlantic" (4). Unlike most other English-language cultural critics, Gilroy acknowledges the intermediary role of Glissant in introducing Deleuze and Guattari's concept into Caribbean studies, even if his acknowledgments are often embedded in footnotes and one must piece them together by tracing a different kind of rhizomatic connection (see esp. 28, 30). Like Glissant, Gilroy, as a self-labeled anti-anti-essentialist, recognizes the political importance of recovering African roots; by reconnecting with these roots, many were able to resist the Eurocentrism that denigrates them. Yet in *The Black Atlantic*, he stresses the importance of both roots and routes—of African origins and the crisscrossing of the Atlantic—in defining black identity: "Dealing equally with the significance of roots and routes . . . should undermine the purified appeal of either Afrocentrism or the Eurocentrisms it struggles to answer" (190). While "roots" ground identity in an essentialist understanding of origins, Gilroy leaves them in a suspended state of tension with "routes." Gilroy's *The Black Atlantic* thus parallels Glissant's retention of rootedness in the alternative concept of rhizomes in spite of the immobility roots imply.

Gilroy complements his rerouting of black identity through the Atlantic with the concept of diaspora, and he references Glissant as a key predecessor for theorizing this concept (80, 236n16). Gilroy himself had already begun using the term *diaspora* in *"There Ain't No Black in the Union Jack": The Cultural Politics of Race and Nation* (1987) to counter racial nationalism along the same lines as Glissant in his first use of the term. Indeed, since the late 1980s, the concept of diaspora has become a productive catalyst for theorizing identities in movement both to and from the sites of origins for these identities. From its original uses in describing Jewish (or Greek or Armenian) dispersal, it has been expanded to include, in addition to the African diaspora, other "expatriate minority communities whose members . . . , or their ancestors, have been dispersed from a specific original 'center' to two or more 'peripheral,' or foreign, regions [and] retain a collective memory, vision, or myth about their original homeland" (Safran 83). Furthermore, since the beginning of the 1990s, uses of the term *diaspora* have exploded, and a field known as diaspora studies has emerged whose most visible sign is the journal *Diaspora: A Journal of Transnational Studies*, which began publication in 1991. As Jana Evans Braziel and Anita Mannur write in their introduction to *Theorizing Diaspora*, the use of the term *diaspora* established itself in relation to a number of critical terms that had already become productive within postcolonial studies "[l]ike . . . *rhizome, créole, creolization, hybridity, heterogeneity, métis* and *métissage*" (4). Whereas *The Black Atlantic* would become one of the most frequently cited texts in the emerging field of diaspora studies, therefore, it was published in the midst a significant body of work that set the stage and provided a context for this reception.

One of the key arenas for an elaboration of the notion of diaspora that would drive this emerging field was what some have called black British cultural studies. For example, Kobena Mercer's "Diaspora Culture and the Dialogic Imagination" shortly followed Gilroy's *There Ain't No Black* in 1988. In this essay, Mercer deploys the "diaspora perspective" because of its "potential to expose and illuminate the sheer heterogeneity of the diverse social forces always repressed by the monologism of dominant discourse—discourses of domination" (257–58). Stuart Hall would add an additional layer of complexity to this emerging picture of the African diaspora in "Cultural Identity and Diaspora" (1990), in which he invokes the concept of diaspora to emphasize "not the rediscovery but the *production* of identity. Not an identity grounded in the archeology, but in the *re-telling* of the past. . . . Not an essence but a *positioning*. Hence, there is always a politics of identity, a politics of position, which has no absolute guarantee in an unproblematic, transcendental 'law of origin'" (22, 24). While he opposes diaspora to such movements as Négritude and pan-Africanism, Hall keeps with his predecessors in acknowledging that, "because this New World is constituted for us as a place, a narrative of displacement, . . . it gives rise so profoundly to a certain imaginary plenitude, recreating the endless desire to return to 'lost origins,' to be one again with the mother, to go back to the beginning" (32).

Only a year after the publication of *The Black Atlantic*, James Clifford would provide an excellent overview of the field of diaspora studies up to that point in "Diasporas" (1994).[4] In this essay, he not only asks "what is at stake, politically and intellectually, in contemporary invocations of diaspora" (302) but also brings diaspora studies back to its roots, so to speak, by offering a comparative analysis "of diasporism from contemporary black Britain and from anti-Zionist Judaism" (302). In addition, he outlines "important differences between Mercer's and Gilroy's conceptions of diaspora" regarding the place of roots within African diaspora studies (319). Nonetheless, regardless of differences between Mercer's and Gilroy's take on essentialism, Clifford acknowledges that within black cultural studies, the African diaspora is characterized by the retention of a place for roots: "Diaspora cultures thus mediate, in a lived tension, the experiences of separation and entanglement, of living here and remembering/desiring another place" (311).

Yet in spite of the fact that, within their understandings of diaspora, Gilroy, Mercer, and Hall all retain an important place for roots (albeit to differing degrees), the term *diaspora* has frequently been understood as doing away with roots. Yet such an understanding denies the continuity between theorizations of diaspora in black British cultural studies and the earlier development of the concept in African American studies "between the mid-1950s and the mid-1960s [when] the expression *African diaspora* began to be used increasingly by writers and thinkers who were concerned with the status and prospects of persons of African descent around the world as well as at home" (Shepperson 41). In this earlier career, *diaspora* was used to stress connections between African Americans and their African roots in a pan-African approach to African American studies, connections foreshadowed by the African American identification with the *Jewish* diaspora in such classics as the African American spiritual "Go Down Moses (Let My People Go)," about the captivity of the Israelites in Egypt. Previously, in other words, diaspora was entirely about roots. But as we have seen, to a certain extent we could say that it still is, since in the most widely cited works in diaspora studies roots usually remain crucial to the very theorizations of diaspora that challenge them. In other words, regardless of how much diaspora involves displacement of and away from roots, as a practice and a concept it is eternally returning to roots.

Furthermore, if there can be no diaspora without roots and no roots without diaspora, it is possible to go back and recover the rhizomatic nature of the seemingly most straightforward roots narratives. After all, even in the very title of Aimé Césaire's *Notebook of a Return to the Native Land*—the text that, indeed, is often considered to have invented the term *Négritude* in 1939—we can see that African roots are inseparable from the routes that must be traveled to reconnect with them. In fact, David Chioni Moore has made just this point in defending Haley's *Roots* against its detractors:

> *Roots* profoundly argues, in some sense against itself, that we need to talk not about *roots* but about *routes*: trajectories, paths, interactions, links. . . . The recovery of a root—as in Haley's *Roots*—serves an especially important function when a major chunk of the tangle of one's identity has been either erased or systematically denigrated. . . . Yet once that origin is recovered, that nobility restored, the next important, and, I would argue, moral task is to recognize that purities can only ever be tentative. . . . We are . . . a *rhizome*, a network with no one center, with nodes of temporary concentration but with no absolute origin; with power, but without absolute logic. The metaphor for human culture should be more the mangrove than the tree. ("Routes" 21)

Haley's roots, after all, are inseparable from the routes of both intellectual pursuit and his physical return to Africa; they are, in short, traveling roots. And if there are routes in *Roots*, we can also find rhizomes and mangroves there. Like Moore, and using Gilroy as a prompt, we might thus deploy concepts like diaspora and rhizomes less to value some texts at the expense of others than to find diasporic and/or rhizomatic elements in the most paradigmatic of roots narratives. Furthermore, *Queer Roots* argues, discerning rhizomes within *Roots* will constitute a key component of queering both roots and diaspora.

Queer Diasporas

In 1994 Mercer published a collection of essays entitled *Welcome to the Jungle: New Positions in Black Cultural Studies*, an intervention not only in studies of the African diaspora but also in queer theory:

> [D]iaspora, as the domain of disseminated and dispersed identities originating from an initial loss of one, is also the field of desire; specifically, in this case, desires that have inspired the creativity of black lesbian and gay community-building practices, whose proliferation in Britain and the US has achieved a level of visibility that was unthinkable ten or fifteen years ago. (30)

Although Mercer is not often cited among the key thinkers associated with queer diaspora studies, if one establishes a genealogy of the queer black cultural studies he outlines in this book, a genealogy going back to his contribution to the earliest redefinitions of diaspora in black British cultural studies, it starts to look like diaspora may very well have been queer all along.

In 1997, in fact, David L. Eng also juxtaposed *queer* and *diaspora* in "Out Here and Over There: Queerness and Diaspora in Asian American Studies." Here he considers potential tensions between queer studies and the increasing popularity of the concept of diaspora in Asian American studies by listing possible reasons why the home or roots on which diaspora as a concept relies might be inhospitable to queers:

> The often literal ejection of queers from their homes . . . coupled with their marginalization by pervasive structures of normative heterosexuality . . . , [t]raumatic displacement from a lost heterosexual "origin," questions of political membership, and the impossibilities of full social recognition dog the queer subject in a mainstream society impelled by the presumptions of compulsory heterosexuality. (32)

As a result, "queer entitlements to home and a nation-state remain doubtful" (32). Whereas Eng focuses on the home, origin, or nation-state from which dispersal radiates, in an earlier and oft-cited work in diaspora studies, "Kinship, Nation, and Paul Gilroy's Concept of Diaspora" (1992), Stefan Helmreich suggests that such inhospitality may also exist in the very structure of diaspora. Because the term *diaspora* "comes from the Greek διασπορα (dispersion), from δια (through) + σπειρειν (to sow or scatter)" (245), it carries sexual implications for Helmreich:

> The original meaning of diaspora summons up the image of scattered seeds, and we should remember that . . . seeds are metaphorical for the male "substance" that is traced in genealogical histories. . . . The word "sperm" is etymologically connected to diaspora. . . . Diaspora, in its traditional sense, thus refers us to a system of kinship reckoned through men and suggests the questions of legitimacy in paternity that patriarchy generates. (245)

Clifford's assertion that "[d]iasporic experiences are always gendered" thus becomes quite an understatement (313).[5] In other words, the very concept of diaspora can imply a heterosexual, masculinist, and patriarchal definition of the relation between a diasporic community and its roots. In its heterosexuality, therefore, the concept of diaspora may not differ that much from the concept of roots.

Nonetheless, very quickly after Eng's essay was published, the concept of diaspora became a productive one for an emerging body of work at the intersection of queer theory, on the one hand, and postcolonial studies on the other, as well as what some have called "queer of color critique." The term *queer diaspora* quickly followed, whose first use, as far as I can tell, was in Gayatri Gopinath's 1998 dissertation "Queer Diasporas: Gender, Sexuality, and Migration in Contemporary South Asian Literature and Cultural Production," of which a revised version was published in 2005 as *Impossible Desires: Queer Diasporas and South Asian Public Cultures*.[6] Herself drawing on Helmreich's work, Gopinath proposes the concept of queer diaspora to "challenge postcolonial diasporic narratives that imagine diaspora and nation through the tropes of home, family, and community that are invariably organized around heteronormative, patriarchal authority" (*Impossible* 68) and to enable "a simultaneous critique of heterosexuality and the nation form while exploding the binary oppositions between nation and diaspora, heterosexuality and homosexuality, original and copy" (11). Gopinath hereby offers what is perhaps the most sustained and elaborate theorization of the concept of queer diaspora, one that goes beyond the presence of same-sex desires and sexual practices in diasporic cultures not only to queer diaspora as a concept but also to diasporize, so to speak, as a mode of queering the nation. For Gopinath retrieving a queer South Asian diaspora leads directly to queering the nation because of the compatibility of nationalism and diaspora in the hegemonic models of diasporism she critiques, in which "queerness is to heterosexuality as the diaspora is to the nation." In other words, within the nationalist discourses of the South Asian diaspora elite, "If within heteronormative logic the queer is seen as the debased and inadequate copy of the heterosexual, so too is diaspora within nationalist logic positioned as the queer Other of the nation, its inauthentic imitation" (11).

In spite of the precedent of Gopinath's dissertation, however, Cindy Patton and Benigno Sánchez-Eppler used a similar title for their collection *Queer Diasporas* (2000), which offers the first *published* use of the term *queer diaspora* that I have found.[7] Although this collection could be more accurately entitled "Homosexualities from an International Perspective" (because most of its contributions consider contexts that cannot properly be called diasporas and are more interested in same-sex desires and sexual practices than in using *queer* as a critical and analytical tool),[8] in their introduction, Patton and Sánchez-Eppler offer a number of reflections that helped define some key concepts of the emerging subfield. Subtitled "With a Passport out of Eden," this introduction roots their account of queer diaspora in one of the earliest narrations of dispersals, that of Adam and Eve from Eden, by reading Genesis as a foundation myth for heterosexuality: "[T]he simultaneity of the expulsion from Eden and the installation of heterosexuality suggest that Western sexual and diasporal discourses are fundamentally, if anxiously related" (2). Furthermore, they simultaneously reread and queer Genesis by understanding Eve as disrupting a homosocial bond between Adam—that is, Man—and God. It is perhaps through a slip that Patton and Sánchez-Eppler conflate prelapsarian paradise with the promised land as the site of prediasporic origins, but this confusion might nonetheless serve as a productive reminder that "the biblical story is not one of autochthony but one of always already coming from somewhere else" (Boyarin and Boyarin, "Diaspora" 715). That is, every origin is always preceded by an even prior migration from somewhere else.

Whereas Gopinath's theorization of queer diaspora focuses on the nation as point of origin (due to the specific character of the South Asian diaspora), the study of other diasporas leads to a consideration of what queer diaspora means for roots in a more general sense. Published in the same year as Gopinath's book (2005), Jasbir K. Puar's "Queer Times, Queer Assemblages" would indeed speak of origins in such a more general way:

> The notion of queer diaspora retools diaspora to account for connectivity beyond or different from sharing a common ancestral homeland. That is, to shift away from origin for a moment allows other forms of diasporic affiliative and cathartic entities . . . to show their affiliative powers. Furthermore, an unsettling of the site of origin, that is, nation as one of the two binding terms of diaspora, de facto punctures the homeland-to-diaspora telos and wrenches ancestral progression out of the automatic purview of diaspora, allowing for queer narratives of kinship, belonging, and home. (135)

While this passage equates nation and the site of origin, a comparative approach to diaspora studies (as advocated by a number of scholars in the field) can highlight a certain instability with regard to the relation between roots and diaspora.⁹ Some diasporic discourses presume stable roots that can ground a stable identity. Others promote diaspora as a destabilization of any version of roots that might ground identity in a homogenized community whose purity could thereby be policed. This tension or discrepancy then leads to several questions that should be made central to the field of queer diaspora studies. Where, for example, is the queer in queer diaspora or roots? Does one have to queer roots in order to queer diaspora or vice versa? Does the one necessarily lead to the other? Will queering diaspora entail queering roots in every diasporic context? Is either diaspora or roots inherently queer in relation to the other? It is to such a comparative approach to diaspora studies that *Queer Roots* seeks to contribute. In addition to the African diaspora understood more conventionally (chapters 1, 2, and 6), *Queer Roots* returns to the roots of diaspora as a concept, so to speak, by bringing into comparison the Armenian (chapter 5) and Jewish diasporas (chapters 3 and 4), which exemplify the most conventional understandings of diaspora as a concept. In particular, this book will look to doubly diasporic Jewish writings from North Africa as examples of "overlapping diasporas" (Lewis 772) that are both African and Jewish and as an exemplary site for bringing diasporas into comparison while still paying careful attention to the specificities of individual diasporic cultures.

If queering either roots or diaspora occurs in the dialogic relation between the two, this queering is related to a structural peculiarity of the narrative moves necessary to connect a diaspora to its roots, a peculiarity that is in fact precisely what I have called the narrative paradox: roots narratives narrate a "return" to a "prior" "origin" that is actually *not* prior since it is an *effect* of the narration, not its cause, and thus not actually an origin. The narrative itself can therefore only be considered a return if the notion of return is queered, along with the notions of priorness, origins, and roots. Queer roots, in other words, are origins that are not original; queer diasporas exist through "returns" to these origins-that-are-not-origins. This defining aporia at the heart of roots narratives can also be likened to the deconstruction of origins most succinctly articulated by Jacques Derrida in *Of Grammatology*: "The trace is not only the disappearance of origin . . . [for] it means that the origin did not even disappear, that it was never constituted except reciprocally by a nonorigin, the trace, which thus becomes the origin of the origin" (61).¹⁰ Chapters 3 and 4 further explore such connections between queering the roots of diaspora and deconstruction.

Queer Roots

As Eng suggests in his essay on queerness and diaspora, it has not always seemed possible to queer roots through or in relation to diaspora. The same might be said for the genealogical narrative structure on which roots rely, the one resisted by "The family tree stops with me" t-shirt. Furthermore, the political implications of roots narratives intersect with sexuality in a way that goes beyond the policing of sexuality justified by certain versions of, say, African roots; getting to the root of homosexuality has often been used as an attempt to eliminate it. It is precisely because of the history of scientific experimentation on lesbian and gay peoples—to make them heterosexual by discovering the "origins" of their homosexuality and thereby curing it—that Eve Kosofsky Sedgwick warns against similar, but pro-gay, efforts to pinpoint a single gay origin (such as a so-called gay gene): "In this unstable balance of assumptions between nature and culture . . . , under the overarching, relatively unchallenged aegis of a culture's desire that gay people *not be,* there is no unthreatened, unthreatening conceptual home for a concept of gay origins. We have all the more reason, then, to keep our understanding of gay origins, of gay cultural and material reproduction, plural, multi-capillaried, argus-eyed, respectful, and endlessly cherished" (43–44). Sedgwick hereby draws attention to the fact that the heterosexual hegemony reinforced by family trees is not the only danger of using the concept of roots to articulate accounts of lesbian and gay identities.

For to be useful a notion of queer roots must allow for the kinds of diversity, multiplicity, and contradiction that Sedgwick advocates. They must, in short, be rhizomatic or mangrovelike. In other words, they have a lesson or two to learn from the Caribbean fiction that I consider in chapter 1, which not only queers the notion of African roots through mangrove novels but also offers an opportunity to queer non-Caribbean queers and queer theory even further.[11] Indeed, precisely such an engagement with Caribbean fiction is what will reveal the sexual implications of the narrative and political paradoxes (and their interconnectedness) as well as the *sexual* paradox itself. While most writers discussed in *Queer Roots* are *not* homosexual, their return narratives queer the relation between diasporic identity and its roots by acknowledging their own fictionality. They simultaneously challenge the heterosexuality of the family tree that typically structures return narratives and propose alternative, multiple roots that ground an identity based not only on sexual diversity but also on diversity in general. Queer roots, in these accounts, thereby challenge the patrilineal lines of descent implied by roots by disrupting the linear process of storytelling that constitutes identity.

Readers will remark that, while a number of my chapters include both men and women writers, most of the examples of same-sex desire explored by these writers occur between men. I do not, however, wish to propose a male-centered model of queering. When I reflect, as I finish this project, on the choice of texts that have attracted me over its course, I realize that it was frequently less my putative identification with male homoeroticism that inspired my engagement (though this "attraction" certainly played a role) than the instability of *hetero*sexual masculinity in the writings of a number of supposedly "straight" writers. The experience of the symbolic (and not just symbolic) violence of masculinity is indeed a major part of my own roots narrative, and the desire to respond to that violence with no small amount of critical hubris has frequently been the source of much verve in my writing since well before I began this project. This passion is most evident in my fourth chapter, and as this book comes to a close in the sixth, I theorize the relation between a desire for gender treason and that for the racial treason suggested in white southern lesbian feminist Mab Segrest's title *Memoir of a Race Traitor*.

To return to the sexual paradox, then, the fact that the heteronormativity of roots might make them a problematic concept in telling stories of lesbian and gay identity has not prevented precisely such a use of them. Analogies to the uprootedness resulting from diaspora have helped many lesbians and gay men propose ancestors for a rooted history as the following titles attest: "Must We Deracinate Indians to Find Gay Roots?" (Gutiérrez), which I discuss at greater length in chapter 2; the section "Remembering Our Roots" in the anthology *The New Lesbian Studies* (Zimmerman and McNaron); *Gay Roots: Twenty Years of Gay Sunshine* (Leyland); "'They Wonder to Which Sex I Belong': The Historical Roots of the Modern Lesbian Identity" (Vicinus); and my favorite discovery, "African Roots, American Fruits: The Queerness of Afrocentricity" (Smith), which I discuss at more length in chapter 2. These "queer" roots also raise the question of whether the *family* in *family tree* might be similarly queered.

Commonplace knowledge in the United States frequently situates gay men and lesbians as somehow outsiders in relation to the family. Coming out to one's "family," for example, is often considered an especially difficult act, one fraught with fears of rejection, exclusion, and disavowal. Gay and lesbian minors kicked out of their homes by homophobic parents are far from unheard of. Holidays traditionally spent with one's "family" are considered by some queer folk to be especially stressful; gay bars often open later on these days for precisely this reason. One could also say that such holiday openings allow gay men and lesbians to be with a different kind of family. The t-shirt described earlier notwithstanding, the word *family* also has another, distinctly queer use in gayspeak. "She's family" can also mean "he is gay." Sister Sledge's 1979 "We Are Family" has often served as an anthem of gay solidarity in which kinship relations stand in for political and/or community affiliation. It is precisely in relation to this kind of tension that one should situate Kate Weston's 1991 *Families We Choose: Lesbians, Gays, Kinship*, whose title refers to alternative kinship structures created by lesbians and gay men constituting support networks—families, in other words, based on affiliation rather than filiation.

Interestingly, the question of affiliation (the queering of family) versus filiation (family as heteronormative kinship) may have its own narrative implications in a further crossing of the sexual and narrative paradoxes of roots narratives. In *The World, the Text, and the Critic* (1983), Edward M. Said describes the "turn from filiation to affiliation" (18) to examine a crisis in filiation: "Childless couples, orphaned children, aborted childbirths, and unregenerately celibate men and women populate the world of high modernism with remarkable insistence, all of them suggesting the difficulties of filiation" (17). Two years later, in the preface to the 1985 edition of *Beginnings: Intention and Method* (1975), he would connect such an opposition between affiliation and filiation with his earlier discussion of the narrative role of beginnings: "[M]odernism was an aesthetic and ideological phenomenon that was a response to the crisis of what could be called *filiation*—linear, biologically grounded process, that which ties children to their parents—which produced the counter-crisis within modernism of affiliation, that is, those creeds, philosophies, and visions re-assembling the world in new non-familial ways" (xiii). The opposition between filiation and affiliation should thus be considered inseparable from Said's other key distinction, "the notion of *beginning* as opposed to *origin*, the latter divine, mythical and privileged, the former secular, humanly produced, and ceaselessly re-examined" (xii–xiii). Although in *Beginnings*, Said had distinguished "between *author* (origin) and *beginning intention* (purpose and interpretation)" (174), beginnings also authorize (17), and "[a]uthority . . . and its molestations are at the root of the fictional process" (84). Nonetheless, because "a beginning might as well be a necessary fiction" (50), this authority should be considered the effect of the narrative role of beginnings, not its cause and certainly not its origin. To paraphrase Said through the critical vocabulary I have used thus far, beginnings acknowledge the narrative paradox whereas origins deny them. In fact, because "beginning is basically an activity which ultimately implies return and repetition rather than simple linear accomplishment" (xvii), the function Said assigns to beginnings within fiction in general begins to look a lot like that of origins within the structure of roots narratives.

If all narrative beginnings authorize the story that follows, according to Said, they are also created through "active" narrative endeavors (in spite of the fact that part of such endeavors involve covering up this intention). Since beginnings do not determine what follows, they are a moment of freedom in which the outcome of a narrative remains open. Part of the project of *this* study is the search for a way to privilege this freedom over the authority that roots narratives imply. Said offers a hint as to how such freedom might be found in the relation between narrative and kinship structures implied in the connection he suggests between his two studies in the 1985 preface to the earlier one. Indeed, we might now reread *Beginnings* through the later discussion of filiation and affiliation, especially since Said suggests in *The World, the Text, and the Critic* that the distinction between filiation and affiliation may not be as clear as it might seem at first: "Affiliation becomes a form of representing the filiative processes to be found in nature, although affiliation takes validated nonbiological social and cultural forms" (23); "affiliation sometimes reproduces filiation, sometimes makes its own forms" (24). In other words, filiation may be nothing more than the naturalization of affiliation as kinship. Whereas Said might be said to have later deconstructed the opposition between filiation and affiliation that helped him to distinguish between origins and beginnings in *Beginnings*, one of the premises of this study is that all origins, even as Said understands them, are always merely beginnings. They become origins by means of their own mythification, by hiding the fact that they are asserted by narratives that create them as their beginnings *after the fact.*

Furthermore, Said's associations of filiation and origins, on the one hand, and affiliation and beginnings on the other might be further mined to elaborate on the interconnectedness of the sexual and narrative paradoxes. A model of rooted identity is a linear one: identity is a story that links a subject to his or her identification by creating an origin, which it claims to have merely discovered (hence my use of the term *fiction*), an origin that becomes the story's beginning. The double, bidirectional structure of narratives like *Roots* therefore resembles that of detective novels in which the quest to solve a mystery is also a return to the scene of the crime, the story's beginning and source of its plot. The work of the detective parallels that of interpretation in that the search for clues (the equivalent of the second story of a roots narrative) also constitutes a reading of the crime narrative (which is like the first story of a roots narrative). This is, in part, the way roots narratives function as allegories of their own reading: they, like the detective story, turn their reader into a kind of detective who is given an incentive to return to a beginning through the very return that the story recounts. Furthermore, in carrying out the work of the "detective," interpretations of roots narratives like the ones this study proposes, become their own kind of detective narratives. What, then, do they look for, exactly?

Ghosts

Although affiliations invisible to the family tree might seem external to it, kinship structures defined through patrilineal filiation nonetheless depend on what they exclude. Furthermore, all families (in both the literal and metaphorical sense) are haunted by the traces of such exclusions. By looking for ghosts lurking within the family tree and conjuring them up, *Queer Roots* seeks to foster the potential disruption and subversion that can happen when the otherness disavowed by the sameness that *family* presumes is understood as *central* to the definition of *family* itself. Bringing these ghosts into the light of day, that is, acknowledging the difference they represent instead of repressing it, this book carries out a "ghost busting" that embraces its discoveries as opposed to imprisoning or even annihilating them. Such a queer equivalent of *Ghost Hunters* also has its theoretical precedents in a Derridean understanding of hauntology. Yet Derrida's 1993 *Specters of Marx* itself emerged as part of a conversation with the psychoanalytic understanding of haunting that Nicolas Abraham and Maria Torok began to articulate in the mid-1970s.[12]

For Abraham and Torok, the phantom appears as the trace of a family secret reproduced from generation to generation. By locating the phantom squarely within the reproduction of kinship structures, they therefore offer a model of haunting whose roots can be found within the family tree. These roots, in fact, might be considered the equal of those named in the first part of my title, *Queer Roots*; understanding this equivalence will become the starting point for making "ghosts in the family tree" central to "queering the roots of diaspora" and vice versa. Indeed, even the most rooted (i.e., geographically stable) genealogies conceal forms of dispersion and diaspora in that "family" always extends outward toward its others. In fact, by examining narratives of identity in diaspora, *Queer Roots* proposes that roots narratives can tell us a lot about identities not usually associated with diaspora and theorize the formative role that both narratives of origin and a certain kind of family romance play in the construction of identity as diasporic. By understanding family as diasporic,[13] therefore, it will be possible to read family romances—in the strictly Freudian sense, as well as in a larger understanding of the term, as saying something about how families in general are structured by this particular Freudian fantasy—as allegories of diasporic histories in which the sexual allegorizes the political and offers answers to the questions asked by Molly McGarry in her 2008 *Ghosts of Futures Past: Spiritualism and the Cultural Politics of Nineteenth-Century America*: "What is the relationship between mourning and militancy? How might a single death be transformed from an individual occurrence into an occasion for collective praxis? How can the dead speak through the living as something other than the haunting, seething presence of absence?" (7).

Indeed, the ghosts conjured up herein result from repressions that are not only psychological but also political; although they haunt the family tree, their significance extends far beyond their individual families into the realm of the collective, both past and present. Sociologist Avery F. Gordon, in fact, has used the concept of haunting to theorize precisely such a relationship between kinship and the political. In *Ghostly Matters: Haunting and the Sociological Imagination* (1997), she explores "the ghost as a social figure" (25), with the result that haunting becomes not just a way to understand the relation between the individual and the collective—how each haunts the other—but also an interdisciplinary methodology for theorizing that relation. For in addition to exploring the haunted gap between sociology and psychoanalysis, Gordon also accords an important role to literary texts because "they enable other kinds of sociological information to emerge" (25). Because "sociology is wedded to facticity as its special truth, it must continually police and expel its margin—the margin of error—which is the fictive" (26). Like the psychoanalytic, therefore, the literary haunts the social.

The most important of the literary texts that Gordon considers to arrive at these conclusions is Toni Morrison's *Beloved*, which is, more than anything else, the story of a haunting. The eponymous ghost of Morrison's novel represents, of course, the trace of slavery in the form of the daughter that Sethe killed. Though abolished, in other words, slavery continues to exert its effects in the present, and haunting is the phenomenon by which these effects reveal themselves. Furthermore, by reading Morrison alongside the memoirs of Levi Coffin, a white abolitionist, Gordon shows how the ghosts of slavery haunt even the family trees of white families. And if the tree of scars on Sethe's back might be understood as the visible marks of violence done by slavery to African American kinship (a kind of family tree beaten into her flesh), the ghosts in white family trees represent a different repression—the disavowal of complicity in the violence that left and leaves those very marks. Rather than repudiating this genealogy, however, by conjuring *up* its ghosts instead of attempting to conjure them *away*, *Queer Roots* brings them, too, into the light of day to embrace the haunting they represent. For to acknowledge such ghosts is to remember and acknowledge the violence whose traces they represent, violence often omitted (or at least deindividualized) from dominant versions of history. Indeed, this book argues, remembering such violence is a necessary first step toward offering reparations for it.

Since the publication of *Ghostly Matters*, a considerable body of theoretical work has followed suit in drawing on *Specters of Marx* (as well as Abraham and Torok in some cases) to explore the conjuring of ghosts as the basis for additional strategies for understanding the traces of the past in the present, particularly present identities and/or subjectivities, as well as the relation between the individual and the collective. A complete review of that corpus is beyond the scope of this introduction, but two additional works are worth mentioning here for their contribution to my own ghost hunting: Christopher Peterson's elaboration on Gordon's connection of slavery, haunting, and kinship in *Kindred Specters: Death, Mourning, and American Affinity* (2007), which understands kinship structures in general as haunted and adds the expression *kindred spirits* to the critical vocabulary on haunting; and Ross Chambers's *Untimely Interventions: AIDS Writing, Testimonial, and the Rhetoric of Haunting* (2004), which adds another critical concept to the theorization of haunting— "phantom pain" (the persistent sensation of pain in an amputated limb)—as a metaphor for the collective memory of a different kind of trauma. In a trauma as collective as the Holocaust, Chambers argues, a person can experience the memory of trauma as a kind of phantom pain, "real events and historically lived traumas that are made available, but in an elusive, hard to situate, and uncanny way, to those who might not otherwise have grasped the nightmare in their heads" (32). In other words, we could also say, it is not just the case that witnessing the Holocaust is an effect of trauma; memory of trauma is also the effect of the collective discursive phenomenon that is witnessing. Witnessing, then, might be said to have a bidirectional narrative structure similar to that of roots narratives, and Chambers's notion of phantom pain is thus another means of understanding how individual pasts "haunt the social" in a parallel way to that described by Gordon.[14]

Queering the Roots of Deconstruction

If "queering the roots of diaspora" and conjuring up "ghosts in the family tree" are such interrelated projects, then, situating hauntology within the development of Derridean deconstruction can help us to further theorize the relation between deconstruction and queering as a critical move. Like Abraham and Torok, Derrida's *Specters of Marx* draws on Shakespeare's *Hamlet* as a key pre-text in the form of the ghost of Hamlet's father, to which Derrida adds the ghosts of Marx: the ways in which Marx continues to haunt us after the so-called death of communism (as the specter of communism haunts Europe in the *Communist Manifesto*) and the ghosts that haunted him (the spectrality of money as simulacrum, of the exchange value it represents, of the commodity as fetish, and of a past that repeats itself). Derrida would even ensure that the ghost of Marx will continue to haunt (thereby conjuring him up) as a way to keep deconstruction faithful to Marxism. If the etymological root of the word *radical* is *root* itself, Derrida makes a claim for the radical roots of deconstruction. In its double affinity to both Marxism and deconstruction, *Queer Roots* undertakes a search for similarly radical roots, for accounts of roots that suggest that roots are never without their glitches and might, in fact, always already be queer.

In "Letter to a Japanese Friend," Derrida responded to a question about how to translate *deconstruction* into Japanese by asserting that it,

> like all other words, acquires its value only from its inscription in a chain of possible substitutions, in what is too blithely called a "context." For me, for what I have tried and still try to write, the word has interest only within a certain context, where it replaces and lets itself be determined by such other words as "écriture," "trace," "differance," "supplement," "hymen," "pharmakon," "marge," "entame," "parergon," etc. By definition, the list can never be closed. (275)

We could add *hauntology* to this list, and if every ontology is a hauntology, every essence haunted by an absence, we might further understand deconstruction itself as haunted; conjuring up *its* ghosts is another major component of this project. And one of the ghosts that haunt deconstruction is that of the origins Derrida deconstructs from his earliest writings. In *Writing and Difference*, he would articulate this deconstruction as follows:

> The writing of the origin, the writing that retraces the origin, tracking down the signs of its disappearance, the lost writing of the origin. . . . But what disposes it in this way, we now know, is not the origin, but that which takes its place; which is not, moreover, the opposite of an origin. It is not absence instead of presence, but a trace which replaces a presence which has never been present, an origin by means of which nothing has begun. (295)

It might seem that, from this perspective, a roots narrative would be impossible or, at least, an act of bad faith.

In fact, in *Monolingualism of the Other*, Derrida would extend his earlier deconstruction of origins to implicate the roots narrative implied by any autobiographical act:

> In its common concept, autobiographical anamnesis presupposes *identification*. And precisely not identity. No, an identity is never given, received, or attained; only the interminable and indefinitely phantasmatic process of identification endures. Whatever the story of a return to oneself or to *one's home* [*chez-soi*], into the "hut" ["case"] of one's home (*chez* is the *casa*), no matter what an odyssey or bildungsroman it might be, in whatever manner one invents the story of a construction of the *self*, the *autos*, or the *ipse*, it is always *imagined* that the one who writes should know how to say *I*. (28; translator's brackets)

Indeed, autobiographical writing requires a return to roots whose deconstruction means that writing the life of the self necessarily involves writing fiction. Nonetheless, in spite of the fact that return narratives create their origins retrospectively, in *Monolingualism* Derrida engages in the very autobiographical act he simultaneously deconstructs. Through an account of his relation to the French language, he returns to Algerian Jewish roots that must preexist his narration of that return in contradiction to the above passage. In spite of Derrida's deconstruction of origins, therefore, origins keep coming back. If roots as a sign of essence are haunted in Derrida's hauntology, we could also say that they haunt deconstruction; deconstruction is haunted by the very origins it deconstructs. In fact, in this impossibility of eliminating the obsession with origins that haunts deconstruction lies part of its potential as a queer maneuver.

Strategically Queer

If Derridean deconstruction has so often been obsessed with aporias, here we can see that, to the extent that it can ever be defined, it might be defined through the aporia described above: origins are impossible; deconstruction depends on origins. How is it that deconstruction can continue to exist, justify itself, and desire the very thing whose impossibility it delights in? The answer to this question might be summed up with a simple formula: "Je sais bien . . . mais tout de même." It is with this formula that, in *The Pleasure of the Text*, Roland Barthes defined a paradox at the heart of a certain reading practice: "Of all readings, that of tragedy is the most perverse: I take pleasure in hearing myself tell a story *whose end I know*: I know and I don't know, I act toward myself as though I did not know: I know perfectly well Oedipus will be unmasked, that Danton will be guillotined, *but all the same...*" (47–48). In *On Autobiography*, Philippe Lejeune uses another citation from Barthes to define autobiography with a similarly paradoxical formula: "'In the field of the subject, there is no referent.' . . . We *indeed know* all this; we are not so dumb, but once this precaution has been taken, we go on as if we did not know it. Telling the truth about the self, constituting the self as complete subject—it is a fantasy. In spite of the fact that autobiography is impossible, this in no way prevents it from existing" (131–32). Lejeune hereby sets his autobiographical desires *against* Barthes's writing on the subject; he seeks to study what Barthes would characterize as impossible. Yet the very syntax Lejeune uses to justify what he presents as a contradiction uses the same paradoxical syntax that Barthes uses to characterize perversion as a reading practice; at the heart of both accounts is a desiring subject that I argue is an ideal reader, indeed an implied reader, of queer roots narratives.

Even if I acknowledge the writtenness of roots, I must strategically assume their prior existence if I am to set off on a productive return, that is, to begin to tell the story that writes them. A deconstruction of essence might lead to identity's tragic end, yet even though I know my reading practice might put to death the very identity that enables it, I keep on deconstructing as if I did not know, for I desire the very identity I ritually put to death with each deconstruction, which brings so much queer pleasure. This experience of identity, I suggest, is not nearly as naive as it may seem (even among those who have not discovered the joys of deconstruction, which can themselves be quite perverse and queer). Understood in this way, identity begins to look more like a practice and even a strategy. In *Roland Barthes by Roland Barthes*, he defines perversion as, quite simply, a way of being happy, as that which serves no purpose in relation to economic production or social or sexual reproduction (63–64); as exemplary perversions, he would name hashish, homosexuality, and . . . love (*Grain* 232). And love, according to Derrida, is at the root of every deconstructivist practice: "I love very much everything that I deconstruct in my own manner; the texts I want to read from the deconstructive point of view are texts I love, with that impulse of identification which is indispensable for reading. They are texts whose future, I think, will not be exhausted for a long time" (*Ear* 87). Is deconstruction itself, then, an act of critical perversion? And if Barthesian perversion coincides nicely with what is referred to as queer in Anglo-American critical discourses, is not deconstruction itself a queer strategy? Would it not be a rather perverse kind of deconstruction that, even as it deconstructs identity, nonetheless offers the possibility of an anti-identitarian identity (a contradiction in terms, an impossibility), an identity that nonetheless threatens to dissolve the very subversiveness that defines it and makes it so attractive?

If I have already promised that *Queer Roots* will offer strategies for dealing with identity (which I have also described as being a kind of strategy in itself) and for dealing with the dangers of the essentialism that identity requires, as well as for understanding the recalcitrance of that essentialism, a discussion of Gayatri Chakravorty Spivak's oft-cited concept of strategic essentialism is unavoidable. About this concept, Spivak herself has stated, "I have certainly reconsidered my cry to a strategic use of essentialism because it is too deliberate. The idea of a *strategy* in a personalist culture, among people within the humanities who are generally wordsmiths, has been forgotten. The strategic really is taken as a kind of self-differentiation from the poor essentialists" ("In a Word" 156–57). In fact, Spivak has pointed out, many deployments of this concept merely offer "a counter-essence disguised under the alibi of a strategy" (155). Spivak even seems perplexed that this expression had been so widely quoted (154). With the term *deliberate*, she hints at a common understanding of the expression *strategic essentialism* by which many have implied something like a decision to advance essentialist arguments, a decision consciously made by intellectually anti-essentialist feminists for its supposedly expedient political efficacy.

An example of this understanding of the expression can be found in Alice Jardine's contribution to the debate that culminated in a volume she coedited with Paul Smith—*Men in Feminism* (1987): "But this now rather familiar argument against 'essentialism' does not go further; for example, it cannot work with and through what I find to be one of the most thought-provoking statements of recent date by a feminist theorist: Gayatri Spivak's suggestion (echoing Heath) that women today may *have* to take 'the risk of essence' in order to think really different-ly" ("Men" 58). Never mind that the expression "the risk of essence" is solely Heath's and was never "echoed" by Spivak, and never mind that Spivak's supposed statements in favor of strategic essentialism never turn out to be as clear-cut as those who "echo" her position have implied. Many activists *and* critics have contributed to a collective understanding of Spivak's notion of strategic essentialism that, I would argue, cannot be supported by her words alone.[15]

An interview that is often cited as a source for Spivak's position contains the following key passage:

> [T]he choice of universality there was a sort of strategic choice. I spoke of universality because universality was in the air on the other side in the talk of female discourse. . . . [S]trategically I suggested that perhaps rather than woman inhabiting the spaces of absence, perhaps here was an item which could be used as a universal signifier. I was asking myself the question . . . how can the unexamined univer-salizing discourse of a certain sort of feminism become useful for us since this is the hegemonic space of feminist discourse. . . . I think we have to choose again strategically, not universal discourse but essen-tialist discourse. I think that since as a deconstructivist,—see, I just took a label upon myself—I cannot in fact clean my hands and say I'm specific. In fact I must say I am an essentialist from time to time. There is, for example, the strategic choice of a genitalist essentialism in anti-sexist work today. . . . I think it's absolutely on target to take a stand against the discourses of essentialism, universalism as it comes in terms of the universal—of classical German philosophy or the uni-versal as the white upper class male . . . etc. But *strategically* we cannot. (Gross 183–84; second ellipsis Spivak's)

Unlike the partisans of strategic essentialism whom she critiques in "In a Word," Spivak not once in this passage puts the words *strategic* and *essentialism* next to each other. The emphasis, here, is indeed on strategy, and essentialism is as much a problem to be addressed by this strategy as something that can or should be chosen as a result of it. In this passage, then, strategy involves less a decision to be essentialist than a begrudging acknowledgment that, to a certain extent, it is impossible not to be one.

Indeed, although the concept she supposedly created is rarely traced back this far, I would argue for a continuity between the oft-cited sources for strategic essentialism and Spivak's earliest engagement with Derrida's writing, her translation of *Of Grammatology*, published ten years before her essay on subaltern studies and her interview with Gross. Here Derrida himself describes a particular strategic move that, for him, characterizes the very concept of deconstruction:

> The movements of deconstruction do not destroy structures from the outside. They are not possible and effective, nor can they take accurate aim, except by inhabiting those structures. Inhabiting them *in a certain way*, because one always inhabits, and all the more when one does not suspect it. Operating necessarily from the inside, borrowing all the strategic and economic resources of subversion from the old structure, borrowing them structurally, that is to say without being able to isolate their elements and atoms, the enterprise of deconstruction always in a certain way falls prey to its own work. (24)

If deconstruction directs its critique at one or another manifestation of essentialism, then, the strategy used to deal with this essentialism would come from within that essentialism itself. Strategic essentialism here is thus more aligned with deconstruction than something that would be in opposition to or contradict it. That deconstruction can never be final or complete, that it never fulfills its goals, constitutes part of its pleasure. The deconstruction of essence is not only perpetually deferred (because, yes, *différance* characterizes the meaning produced by deconstructivists no less than any other textual production), but it also necessarily involves essentialism. Indeed, deconstruction applies this strategy not only outward—to the object of its critique—but also inward to itself.

For a more concrete description of what this strategy entails one may look to Derrida's more straightforward definitions of *deconstruction*. In one of the interviews that make up *Positions*, for example, he suggests that a provisional acceptance of an essentialist position is the prerequisite for any deconstructivist move:

> [W]hat is the strategic necessity (and why do we still call *strategic* an operation that in the last analysis refuses to be governed by a teleo-eschatalogical horizon? Up to what point is this refusal possible and how does it *negotiate* its effects? Why must it negotiate these effects, including the effect of this *why* itself? Why does *strategy* refer to the *play* of the strategem rather than to the hierarchical organization of the means and the ends? etc. These questions will not be quickly reduced.), what then, is the "strategic" necessity that requires the occasional maintenance of an *old name* in order to launch a new concept? (71)

This "'strategic' necessity" might then be equated with the moves that make up deconstruction in one of its more common definitions, which presents it as, first, overturning the hierarchy that structures the two terms in a binary opposition, and then undoing that hierarchy, in part by demonstrating how the dominant term relies on (defers to) the weaker term present within itself if only as the trace left by its exclusion: "What interested me then, that I am attempting to pursue along other lines now, was, at the same time as a 'general economy,' a kind of *general strategy of deconstruction*. The latter is to avoid both simply *neutralizing* the binary oppositions of metaphysics and simply *residing* within the closed field of these oppositions, thereby confirming it" (41). In other words, the overturning of the opposition does not result in its elimination. In part the binary remains after its own deconstruction because there is no "after its deconstruction." The strategy that is deconstruction is in part internal to the hierarchy it deconstructs. If the binaries that deconstruction critiques are what structure essentialist thinking, deconstruction requires taking a provisional metaphysical position in order to deconstruct it. (One cannot deconstruct something whose very existence one denies; one must first, if only provisionally, acknowledge its existence in order to deconstruct it.) Yet this provisional move cannot be overcome or surpassed because it has no "after"; there is no end to or teleology of deconstruction. Nonetheless, I would argue, this "provisional" move might be understood as an equivalent to the strategic essentialism that many have attributed to Spivak. Indeed, strategic essentialism might be most productively understood as an alternative expression for deconstruction itself.

If this book examines a specific set of identity practices that seem to revel in their own queerness even when sexuality is marginalized within the collective articulation of identity on which these practices depend, it confronts an impossibility similar to the one through which Derrida defines deconstruction: "[T]he impossible is deconstruction's affair" (*Resistances* 48). And if deconstruction might be thought of as the move that causes so much trouble for metaphysics, it is also troubled by the very origins it deconstructs. If even diasporic writers critical of essence have found ways to hang onto it, they are not trying to have their cake and eat it too (though what is the point of having cake if you cannot eat it?); rather their articulations of diasporic identity reflect not just the dialogic relation between roots and routes but also the paradoxes that structure the very narratives required to assert diasporic identity as rooted. While it is commonly assumed that diaspora results from uprooting, roots and diaspora are in fact interdependent; identities are narrated as diasporic through a desire for the very roots that diaspora as a concept has come to challenge. This perverse desire that creates its own object is one mode of queering identity. If roots are defined by paradoxes that would place them *sous rature*, those roots that persist in spite of and beyond that strategic move are at the root of another strategy, that of identity as resistance to uprootedness, which can comfortably coexist with resistance to any politics of identity that can only root its particular struggles in a politics of purity policed through homogenization and exclusion. These are the queer roots, the roots that queer, and the queering of roots that will follow.

Yet, while my working understanding of queering as a critical move is closely aligned with deconstruction, readers of this introduction may have already noticed aspects of my theoretical toolbox that do not fit neatly within this alignment. There is certainly a tradition of setting the works of Derrida and Deleuze against each other; early on in their careers, Derrida was unable to endorse the acerbic critique of Freudian psychoanalysis on such full display in Deleuze and Guattari's *Anti-Oedipus*. In contrast, Freud would become one of Derrida's important pre-texts in such works as "Freud and the Scene of Writing" (1966; in *Writing and Difference*), "To Speculate—on 'Freud'" (in *The Post Card* [1980]), *Psyche* (1987), *Resistances of Psychoanalysis* (1996), *Archive Fever: A Freudian Impression* (1995), and *États-d'âme de la psychanalyse* (2000). Yet in Derrida's much more recent "The Transcendental 'Stupidity' (Bêtise') of Man and the Becoming-Animal According to Deleuze" (2007), Deleuze becomes a more suitable pre-text for deconstruction and therefore an object of love for Derrida (see also Schwab).

In this essay, all the while noting remaining divergences from Deleuze, Derrida nonetheless acknowledges that the two may very well have more in common than previously thought, especially in terms of what many have begun to call animality studies. The very title of Derrida's essay draws attention to Deleuze's notion of becoming-animal, elaborated in the chapter of *A Thousand Plateaus* entitled "1730: Becoming-Intense, Becoming-Animal, Becoming Imperceptible . . . ," and Derrida's *The Animal That Therefore I Am* is also a foundational text for the theorization of animality (see also Derrida, *Beast*). While Deleuze initially figured in *Queer Roots* only through Glissant's recuperation (and, I argue, significant rewriting) of the rhizomatic, I have come to realize that Deleuze (and Guattari) might have more to contribute to a theorization of queering than I initially believed, especially when one considers the importance of their two-volume *Capitalism and Schizophrenia*, and especially its *first* volume, *Anti-Oedipus* (i.e., *not* the volume in which one finds their theorization of the rhizomatic), in Guy Hocquenghem's decentering of the phallic in his theorization of desire and recentering of sexuality around the anus in *Homosexual Desire* (1972).[16] In my previous work, I had already been interested in their critique of "the imperialism of Oedipus" (*Anti-Oedipus* 106)—which Hocquenghem also takes up—in my critique of the colonial implications of coming-out models of lesbian and gay history. Like Freudian narratives of development, these models constitute narratives of progress that cast nonwestern sexualities as more primitive (there is more on this point in chapter 4). We shall also see how Glissant's rejection of Oedipus (considered in chapter 1), when understood in relation to his own taking up of Derridean deconstruction of origins as traces (in chapter 3), prefigures the rapprochement between Derrida and Deleuze explored in such collections as Gabriele Schwab's *Derrida, Deleuze, Psychoanalysis* (2007).

In its pursuit of a deconstructive critical practice of queering, this project thus continues this work of retroactive rapprochement between Derrida and Deleuze. And it is precisely in furthering the implications of their work for both diaspora studies, specifically, and postcolonial studies more generally that one might understand a Deleuzoguattarian conceptualization of the rhizomatic (again, especially as reworked by Glissant) and Derridean dissemination as allegory of diasporic belonging. According to Patricia T. Clough, "When in the early to mid-1990s, critical theorists and cultural critics invited a turn to affect, they often did so in response to what they argued were limitations of poststructuralism and deconstruction" (206). *The Affect Theory Reader*, which reprinted her essay "The Affective Turn" (Gregg and Seigworth), contains numerous references to Deleuze and almost none to Derrida, yet the branch of "affect theory" that concerns itself with "queer affect" might also turn to *The Animal That Therefore I Am* and particularly to Derrida's experience of being ashamed of his nudity before his cat in its continued theorization of gay shame. In my own exploration of the affective experience of roots, I likewise consider the possibility of a connection to origins as one possible manifestation of queer affect.

The Route Ahead

If up to this point references to subsequent chapters have seemed haphazard or out of order, it is because reading narratives whose structures resemble mangrove swamps has often required structuring this book in a similarly rhizomatic way. Although I sketch out a narrative that connects them below, readers of this book might actually trace a number of overlapping moves behind the structure of *Queer Roots*. The first move is signaled by the two parts of my title: a shift from diaspora and its roots toward a greater emphasis on family and the family tree. This move is toward an increasing hauntedness to the extent that this study even ends by conjuring up the ghosts within my own family tree. Furthermore, in that later chapters become increasingly haunted, *Queer Roots* might also be read as an extended engagement with deconstruction qua hauntology. And in its move from roots and diaspora to the family tree, as well as the one from the Caribbean and Africa to North Carolina, *Queer Roots* also tells the story of my own roots, a sort of homecoming, even if only in a rather abstract way. By working toward my own personal affective connection with roots, therefore, each chapter represents a different aspect of queering to end with a challenge to the critical subject who engages in a search for queer roots.

Another move is the particularly disciplinary journey that *Queer Roots* represents in relation to my "home" field, French and Francophone studies. My previous project was a firmly disciplinary study that began as a dissertation in French studies. More specifically, it was situated within what is usually called Francophone studies. In practice, Francophone studies tends (or at least tended) to focus on its four most commonly recognized regional divisions—the Maghreb, sub-Saharan Africa, the Caribbean, and Québec/French Canada—all of which sometimes stand as semi-autonomous subfields. True, my *Queer Nations* was just as firmly situated in queer theory and postcolonial studies, and it was the intersection between these two interdisciplinary fields that it sought to explore. Indeed, the emergence of a subfield that has sometimes been called queer postcolonial studies coincided with the years I spent working on *Queer Nations*. In addition, the very notion of the national allegory requires an intimate relation between the literary (fictional narratives of identity) and history (the story of emerging nations). Nonetheless, institutional and professional affiliation, not to mention formal training, meant that, regardless of how interdisciplinary the desires behind *Queer Nations* were, it came to embody a fairly conventionally disciplinary project. As part of my professionalization as a Francophonist who was also expected to teach even French Canadian culture, I looked for examples of queerness in the other literatures of the Francophone world. Focusing on the same dynamic that interested me in Maghrebian literature while broadening my repertory in Caribbean, African, and Québec/French Canadian studies offered a point of entry into the literature of (the rest of) Africa and its diaspora. As a result, what at first was a simple application to other regions of the theoretical intersection between postcolonial and queer studies that I had worked through in *Queer Nations* allowed me to discover that the queer nations of the Francophone world were not limited to the Maghreb.

The first two chapters of this book are a direct result of this cross-pollination between my teaching and my research. The first chapter is exclusively focused on mangrove literature in French from the Caribbean. In moving to African literature, the second chapter includes African novels written in English. The third and fourth chapters, while both concerned in part with Sephardic writing from North Africa, simultaneously move toward a more detailed consideration of African and Jewish diasporic cultures in English. The fifth chapter (on the Armenian diaspora) and the sixth (on North Carolina) might seem totally divorced from French were it not for their engagement with French-language psychoanalytic theorists (Jean Laplanche and Jean-Baptiste Pontalis in the fifth chapter, Abraham and Torok in the sixth). This third move is thus toward an increasingly comparative approach to Francophone studies, postcolonial studies, and diaspora studies, the last of which has engaged in the internal process of theorizing its own comparativeness. As it becomes more and more comparative, it also becomes more interdisciplinary in its engagement with anthropology (chapters 1 and 2), music (chapter 4), film (chapter 5), and folklore (chapter 6).

Chapter 1, "Looking for Roots among the Mangroves," follows

through on my earlier discussion of Caribbean deployments of the image of the mangrove. By examining specific literary and theoretical texts that use the mangrove as a metaphor for the multiple origins of Caribbean identity (namely, Maryse Condé's *Traversée de la mangrove* and a number of texts by Raphaël Confiant and Patrick Chamoiseau), I consider what happens when the mangrove becomes an explicit model for roots. In particular, I focus on the intertwining of the sexual paradox with the narrative and political ones among the twisted roots of mangrove narratives, which also make room for the figure of the *makoumè* (Creole for "sissy faggot"). Furthermore, when the *makoumè* gets tangled up in the mangrove roots of the family tree, he or she elicits a rethinking of the intellectual genealogy that has conventionally been used to structure histories of Caribbean thought in relation to the question of identity.

Likewise chapter 2, "Queer Roots in Africa," returns to African roots in novels that uncover same-sex desire through a return narrative that challenges claims that homosexuality is a white disease or colonial imposition. Through readings of Ken Bugul's *Le baobab fou* [published in English as *The Abandoned Baobab*], Mariama Bâ's *Un chant écarlate* [*Scarlet Song*], V. Y. Mudimbe's *Entre les eaux* [Between the Waters], Ama Ata Aidoo's *Our Sister Killjoy*, and Wole Soyinka's, *The Interpreters*, I argue that many African writers return to roots in order to articulate an alternative, indeed queer, Afrocentricity. Furthermore, in addition to queering Afrocentricity and Négritude, Soyinka offers an allegory of interdisciplinarity that allows me to theorize the interdisciplinary approaches that make up *Queer Roots*.

In the third chapter, "Scandals and Lies: The Truth about Roots," I reread the lies Alex Haley was accused of telling through the novel *Un mensonge* [A Lie], by the Jewish Moroccan singer, actress, and writer Sapho. The lie of her title refers first of all to the novel's alpha character— Alph, the very personification of origins—who denies his Jewish Moroccan origins. But the novel goes even further to suggest that, when Alph rectifies these lies and begins to "tell the truth" about his identity, these "real" roots are also the product of fiction making. The novel thereby acknowledges the fictionality of all roots narratives, and as a rewriting of the Zohar, or key text of Kabbalah, *Un mensonge* even emphasizes the writtenness of more theological understandings of origins, such as those found in Genesis. Furthermore, although *Un mensonge* has an explicitly homosexual character, Sapho's examination of its main characters' *het-erosexuality* is what queers the relation between diasporic identity and its roots, for Alph's communion with his origins coincides with his heterosexual union with Bette, which suggests a link between the narrative paradox and the sexual one. By highlighting the lie of heterosexuality that structures family trees such as Haley's, Sapho thereby challenges the patrilineal lines of descent implied by roots. Finally, Sapho's foundational lies constitute an affinity between her writing and that of other North African Sephardic writers such as the Egyptian poet Edmond Jabès and his understanding of beginning as both *commencement* and *comment se ment* (how it lies to itself), as well as Derrida's use of Jabès as a theoretical pre-text for his deconstruction of origins.

In chapter 4, "From Roots That Uproot to Queer Diasporas," I examine the dangers of planting roots where others already live. The Jewish American composer Steve Reich's work of musical theater *The Cave* demonstrates the disastrous consequences of competing claims to the same roots in the Middle East. This minimalist opera provides a unique musical narrative about a specific return to roots (the establishment of the state of Israel) and the uprooting that resulted (because Palestinians were removed from the site where Israeli roots were to be planted). Even though *The Cave* only hints at violence in subtle ways, the resulting conflict in the Middle East is a vivid example of the dangers of roots. By retelling Israeli, Palestinian, and American accounts of the burial of Abraham and Sarah in the Cave of Machpelah in Hebron, Reich also suggests a more complex understanding of diaspora in which communities previously assumed to be homogeneous exist "in relation" with their others à la Glissant. This understanding comes out of a shared mythical kinship with Abraham on the part of what some (including Derrida) refer to as the Abrahamic religions. Furthermore, as the father of Jews *and* Arabs, Abraham is also the first male circumcised. It is in fact by remembering their circumcisions that both Derrida and the Jewish Tunisian writer Albert Memmi queer the return narratives that serve as the basis for a Zionist *right* of return. By turning this male *rite* of passage, which bestows masculinity, into an emasculating act of anamnesis, Memmi's novelistic roots narratives contradict his more explicitly pro-Zionist essays, and to similar political ends, Derrida reinforces his deconstruction of the metaphysical grounds on which much Zionist discourse relies.

Chapter 5, "The Seduction of Roots and the Roots of Seduction," analyzes the importance of desire (and the desire for roots) in the work of the Armenian Canadian filmmaker Atom Egoyan. In film after film, Armenian Canadian characters reinvent their genealogies and use their roots as catalysts for perverse diasporic desires. And nowhere is this perversion more visible than in Egoyan's casting of his own wife, Arsinée

Khanjian, who plays such roles as phone-sex operator and prostitute, strip-club owner, hotel worker hopelessly in love with a gigolo porn star, government pornography censor who pirates the very material she is paid to suppress, and the wife of a character played by Egoyan himself who leaves her husband for a native-born Armenian with whom she has an affair during their joint "return" to Armenia. Egoyan's films represent roots as seducing those who seek them, in both the sexual sense and the etymological sense of leading astray. Roots, that is, get roots seekers lost on their routes of return; roots even seduce readers into returning to their own roots. To theorize further the queer potential of roots, this chapter also considers a particular example of psychoanalytic roots narratives (which frequently seek to cure symptoms by getting to their root): Jean Laplanche and Jean-Baptiste Pontalis's work on seduction, fantasies of seduction, the origins of fantasy, and the primal fantasy of seduction as the origin of sexuality. The roots of sexuality, in their understanding of seduction, have the same queer *après-coup* narrative structure as the other roots narratives considered in *Queer Roots*. The roots of sexuality itself, in other words, also turn out to be queer.

Finally, by returning to my own North Carolina roots, *Queer Roots* ends with a consideration of texts that suggest ways of queering southern identity. Chapter 6, "Booger Hollar and Other Queer Sites: Ghosts in the Family Tree," examines two haunted North Carolina novels, Thomas Wolfe's *Look Homeward, Angel* and Jim Grimsley's *Dream Boy*, which conjure up ghosts that challenge the family tree's racial purity and haunt both southern and American identity. Here, southern identity (and by extension American identity, itself haunted by the South) is haunted by the history of its institutionalized violence of racial difference. How are we all haunted by our family histories? How might our roots and family trees always be haunted? I end with a consideration of how a southern white man might reclaim his origins in a way that does not glorify a history of racial violence. To do so, I turn to the published family history of my maternal grandmother's family, Oscar Agburn Efird's *History and Genealogy of the Efird Family*, and its account of the Anglicization of our forebear's German name. This mutilation of the Name of the Father leaves its traces in ghost stories of local lore, especially that of Booger Hollar, a site just down the hill from the Lutheran church founded by my forebear.

Looking for Roots
among the Mangroves

✦ ✦ ✦

In an article entitled "L'honneur des makoumès" [The *Makoumès'* Honor] and published in the gay French monthly *Têtu,* Joël Métreau describes men cruising one another on the beaches of Martinique. Behind one beach in particular, frequented by heterosexual families on weekends, saltwater marshes offer a perfect meeting place for gay men during the week: "All along the pathway, crabs, mongooses, and herons scatter when men approach. In the vicinity of the cape, called Catherine Point, men wander about among the mangroves, seemingly nonchalantly, staring at each other out of the corners of their eyes." Whereas Métreau uses the term *gay* to describe these men, the title of his article highlights the Creole word *makoumè*, which roughly means "sissy faggot." Considered insulting by most Martiniquan men regardless of their sexual orientation, this label nonetheless appears in a number of Caribbean texts in French. And, as on the beaches described above, these *makoumè* might often be discerned circulating among the mangroves. This chapter follows through on the introduction's discussion of the importance of the mangrove in Caribbean thought and fiction particularly as regards the interrelated political, narrative, and sexual paradoxes of roots as a concept. When the *makoumè* circulates among mangroves, he (or she, if one uses the transgender pronoun) therefore literalizes the sexual implications of roots narratives already visualized by mangroves as an image for a less patrilineal and repronormative family tree. Furthermore, the use of a Creole word for same-sex desire and cross-gendered identification puts the *makoumè* at the center of debates about the politics of language as it has played out in the history of French Caribbean thought and troubles the Oedipal genealogies that have often been used to write the history of this thought.

In 1989, Martiniquan writers Jean Bernabé, Patrick Chamoiseau, and Raphaël Confiant would make the mangrove image central to their articulation of Créolité, or Creoleness, as a model for understanding Caribbean identity: "Creoleness is our primitive soup and our continuation, our [original] chaos and our mangrove swamp of virtualities" (892; 28). This passage appeared in their manifesto *Éloge de la créolité* [In Praise of Creoleness], which announced Créolité as a movement that valorizes the multiple origins of Caribbean identity and the resulting diversity of Caribbean (and other) Creole cultures. Indeed, like Glissant before them, who opposed Négritude with Antillanité (Caribbeanness), the Créolistes refused to seek a model of identity in a "mythical elsewhere" and sought to define not their *racial* affinity to Africa but their *cultural* difference from both Africa and Europe. Bernabé and his colleagues thus rejected the politics of purity associated with Négritude, whose return to Africa they saw as just as alienating and as much an imposition of foreign values as those imposed by colonialism. Yet, whereas Glissant rooted his geopolitical notion of Antillanité in the Caribbean archipelago, the Créolistes chose a more linguistic paradigm exemplified by the confrontation of multiple languages (and therefore the cultures that spoke them and were spoken through them) that produced not only Caribbean Creoles but all the Creole languages and cultures on the planet.

Nonetheless, although the mangrove, here, challenges what Glissant calls the "racine unique," as the words *primitive* and *original* attest, it still stands as a figure for origins. The Créolistes' theoretical deployment of this image, like Glissant's reworking of the rhizomatic outlined in my introduction, finds fictional parallels in a substantial body of Caribbean novels in French. Glissant himself would name the very same tree in most of his novels, from *La Lézarde* (1958) through *Ormerod* (2003). *Tout-monde* (1993), the first novel published after *Poetics of Relation*, is particularly notable in its use of the word *mangrove* along with French synonyms for it, including *mangle* and *paletuvier*.[1] Furthermore, taken together, Glissant's novels might be characterized as a mangrove text, for they all offer parts of the story of four intertwined (and therefore mangrovelike) family trees: those of the Longoué family, whose ancestor marooned upon arriving in Martinique from Africa; the Béluse family, whose ancestors remained in slavery; and the Targin and Celat families. Their story spans the years from 500 BCE to the present; one novel— *Sartorius: Le roman des Batoutos* (1999)—even tells the story of the Batoutos, the fictional ethnic group to which Odono (the ancestor of a number of characters) belongs.[2] Odono thus parallels Haley's "farthest-back" Kunta Kinte except that, taken together, these novels read as if the pages of *Roots* had been torn apart, scrambled, and rebound "out of order." In addition, the interlocking roots of these families' genealogies allegorize the dialogic relation between resistance and submission in Glissant's epic story of Martiniquan identity. Finally, as Glissant has authored an essay that rereads the novels of William Faulkner from a Caribbean perspective (see *Faulkner*), his mangrove novels provide a counterpoint to Faulkner's Yoknapatawpha County and rhizomatic family trees in the form of the re-creation of a world of slaves' descendants instead of one of slave owners' descendants.

The Créolistes, too, have authored a number of mangrove novels, ones whose plots are often just as twisted as the roots of a mangrove. More literally, the eponymous neighborhood of Chamoiseau's novel *Texaco*, which won the Prix Goncourt in 1992, is described as an urban mangrove constructed on the site of a former mangrove swamp (just like Terres-Sainvilles, the neighborhood setting of Confiant's 1994 novel *L'allée des soupirs* [Avenue of Sighs], as well as Fort-de-France as a whole in Chamoiseau's 1986 *Chronique des sept misères* [*Chronicle of the Seven Sorrows*]). Instead of offering a complete survey of Caribbean mangrove novels, however, this chapter opens with a single mangrove novel, Maryse Condé's 1989 *Traversée de la mangrove* [*Crossing the Mangrove*], which begins in a Guadeloupan village with the discovery of Francis Sancher's body. Francis's story is told retrospectively by different villagers in a jumble of competing versions that are as hard to untangle as the roots of a mangrove. Furthermore, Condé gives this mangrove a queer twist in the rumors spread by other characters about a homosexual relationship between Francis and a Haitian buddy. *Makoumè*, the word that Condé uses to describe these rumors, is also the word for a gossiping woman and therefore binds questions of sexuality in the novel to its gossiplike structure in which there is no beginning or end to the story of Francis's life, no cause-and-effect explanations that could fit into and be strengthened by such a chronological order. *Traversée de la mangrove* is thus a prime example of how queering roots affects the *structure* of roots narratives as much as their representations of sexuality.

Condé's novel takes its title from that of the fictional novel Francis was writing when he died (or more accurately not writing, since he had not gotten any farther than the title). When one villager learns of this novel, she objects, "On ne traverse pas la mangrove. On s'empale sur les racines des palétuviers. On s'enterre et on étouffe dans la boue saumâtre" (192) [You don't cross a mangrove. You'd spike yourself on the roots of the mangrove trees. You'd be sucked down and suffocated in the brackish mud (158)]. In other words, the very title *Traversée de la mangrove* signals a difficulty that I suggest might be read as an allegory for reading other Caribbean novels, particularly those of the Créolistes. Whereas the latter have been criticized by a number of feminist and antihomophobic scholars for their representations of female characters and the propensity on the part of their male characters to hurl *makoumè* as an insult, the difficulty announced by Condé's villager can be put to productive use as a strategy for dragging their sexual politics across the roots of their own mangroves. In spite of the homophobia several critics have accused them of, queerness lurks as much among the roots of *their* mangroves as among Condé's. If, as Malena writes, "*Traversée de la Mangrove* can be seen as a thoughtful 'mise en scène' of the concept of 'créolité,' inscribing its undoing within the performance itself" (*Negotiated Self* 68), the *makoumè* who serve as figures for this queerness, then, will also prompt a rereading of the Créolistes' intellectual genealogy and their so-called Oedipal revolt against the founding father(s) of Négritude. In *Homosexual Desire*, Hocquenghem writes, "The cruising homosexual, on the look-out for anything that might come and plug in to his own desire, is reminiscent of the ['schizophrenic on a walk'] described in *L'Anti-Œdipe*" (131; 151). Like Deleuze and Guattari's "schizophrenic on a walk," then, the homosexual cruising through a mangrove swamp described by Métreau similarly offers a countergenealogy for Caribbean identity, one that decenters Oedipus as much as Oedipal structures marginalize nonnormative sexualities and desires.

Makoumès *in the Mangrove*

Like Négritude and Antillanité before it, Créolité was developed as a model for understanding Caribbean identity by men, and Martiniquan men at that (cf. Burton, "*Ki moun nou ye?*" 8, 17). In her 1993 feminist history of Caribbean writing, "Order, Disorder, Freedom, and the West

Indian Writer," Maryse Condé situates Créolité within a male-centered tradition of Caribbean thought, which she traces back to Haitian writer Jacques Roumain's 1946 novel *Gouverneurs de la rosée* [*Master of the Dew*] (126). Regarding Roumain's representation of sexuality, Condé writes, "Although [his characters] produce children, no reference should be made to sex. If any, it will be to male sexuality. . . . Of course, heterosexuality is the absolute rule" (126). She goes on to argue that the Créolistes' literary practices do not substantially alter this paradigm: "[W]e see only minor changes. . . . Sexuality (especially in Confiant's novel [*Le nègre et l'amiral*]) is no longer absent, but is exclusively male sexuality" (129). A number of other critics have also argued that the account of Caribbean cultural unity articulated in the *Éloge* and other writings by the Créolistes "is not only masculine but masculinist" (Arnold, "Gendering" 21). Thomas C. Spear adds, "Implicit in the exaggeration of male sexuality and the glorification of men "who have balls" is a flourishing heterosexuality that is often extremely homophobic. Homosexuality is only exceptionally evoked by Caribbean novelists, as a joke for example, when a character is called a *makoumè*" (141). A. James Arnold similarly argues, "[H]omophobia in the French West Indies is linked dialectically to the representation of the island male as a superstud. In literature this extreme form of gendering the masculine has resulted in the effective suppression of any homosexual discourse in the culture" ("Créolité" 39). These critics have singled out the Créolistes as being especially homophobic, thereby suggesting that they share a politics of sexual purity with many black nationalists in spite of their critique of Négritude's politics of racial purity.

About Confiant's novel *Eau de Café* (1991), named after its narrator's godmother, Arnold writes, "Confiant has two *majors*—toughest of super-males—insult one another with the term *makoumè* in ritual boasts" ("Gendering" 34). In this fresco of life in an Atlantic Coast town, such verbal duels are the way *majors* jockey for the recognition of their masculinity. The *major* (*majò* in Creole) is a frequent archetype in Créolité novels, and has been defined by Chamoiseau as a "[s]orte de héros de quartier. Chaque quartier avait le sien" (*Chronique* 88) [kind of neighborhood hero. Each neighborhood had one]. On two occasions in *Eau de Café*, the Frenchified version of *makoumè* (*ma-commère*) is shouted during the daily drag races between Major Bérard, driver of the taxi "Bourreau du Nord" [Executioner of the North], and Maître Salvie, who only picks up hooligans in his taxi, the "Golem":

Lorsque ce dernier, rempli bien avant lui comme d'habitude (que voulez-vous, les nègres vagabonds n'ont pas d'occupations si tôt le matin !), stoppa à sa hauteur et que Major Bérard lui lança le même défi vieux de quinze ans: «Si tu arrives sur le pont du Galion avant moi, je suis un petit ma-commère !» Maître Salvie n'en fut pas humilié. (166)

[When the latter, filled before it as usual (what can you say, vagabond Negroes have nothing to do so early in the morning!), stopped beside him and Major Bérard hurled the same challenge he has used for the past fifteen years ("If you get to Galion Bridge before I do, I am a little *ma-commère!*"). Maître Salvie wasn't humiliated by it.][3]

The arrival of Charles de Gaulle for a visit in Martinique is the occasion for another verbal joust; one of Maître Salvie's passengers chides him along: "Si tu permets à ces ma-commères du 'Golem' d'atteindre le Gros-Morne avant nous, je ne voyagerai plus avec toi, mon nègre. C'est fini ! fit une voix au bord de l'hystérie" (297) [If you let those Golem *ma-commères* get to Big-Hill before we do, I'll never ride in your taxi again, old buddy. It's all over, said a voice on the verge of hysteria].

Anthropologist David Murray describes such verbal jousts as central to Martiniquan masculinity: "The Creole pejorative 'macoumé' is a dangerous and highly volatile insult if slung by one man at another, as it challenges the very foundation of masculinity. Yet it is a term which helps to ground the ethic of hypermasculinity in its creation of an opposite anti-male" (14–15). Furthermore, "Extending the analogy, the homosexual was thus fundamentally implicated in the constitution of official constructions of a Martiniquais Cultural identity" (11). During the drag races in *Eau de Café*, however, the sexual implications of the term *makoumè* seem far from the intentions of those who use it, which is perhaps why, when the Creole equivalent is used in the same context, its French translation is given merely as *sissy*, not *faggot*: "A l'instant du doublement, les nègres-Golem criaient à l'endroit des nègres-Bourreau : 'Sakré bann makoumè ki zôt yé !' (Tas de femmelettes !)" (296) [When Bérard passed Salvie, the Golem-gang shouted at the Bourreau-gang: Sakré bann makoumè ki zôt yé! (Tas de femmelettes!)]. (The Creole expression translates roughly as "You bunch of goddamned faggots!" whereas its French translation is more like "Bunch of sissies!") Indeed, in the first passage from *Eau de Café* cited above, *makoumè* is used as a hypothetical self-labeling, which implies that the loser, hopefully Salvie (in the eyes of Bérard), will be a *ma-commère* instead. But then again, this passenger's wagering of his own masculinity seems perilous. What if Salvie wins? Would that really make the passenger a faggot? Is masculinity in such short supply that one man must deny another's masculinity to assert his own? Furthermore, in the heat of calling each other faggots to confirm their own masculinity, these male characters falter on the verge of hysteria, a malady usually associated with femininity. Although many have described such passages as a glorification of masculinity, what is often missed is the irony with which these displays of male bravura are parodied. Instead of glorifying masculinity, therefore, the *makoumè*'s numerous guises and the frequency with which the term recurs in the Créolistes' novels may indicate an analytical understanding of the complexity of masculinity and even its deconstruction.

Confiant's 1994 novel *L'allée des soupirs* [Avenue of Sighs], set during riots in Fort-de-France at the end of 1959, contains similar rituals of verbal jousts in which the *makoumè* plays a central role. Here, two Pieds-Noirs, or European settlers from Algeria, occupy the public bench habitually used by Fils-du-Diable-en-Personne and Bec-en-Or. When the latter fail to react, "Eugène Lamour . . . se mit à les traiter de ma-commères" [Eugène Lamour began to call them *ma-commères*]. This insult spurs the two Martiniquans into action as they prove their manhood by chasing the Pieds-Noirs away from the bench. The Pieds-Noirs respond in kind: "[V]a te faire voir chez les Grecs, bicot !" (155) [Fuck off with the Greeks, Nigger!].[4] Within a few pages, one of these same Pieds-Noirs calls Charles de Gaulle an *enculé* (someone who has been fucked in the ass) (158). Thus, for Eugène Lamour a *makoumè* is someone who allows Europeans to dominate him, and for the Pieds-Noirs homosexuality is associated with a weak commitment to French colonial rule in Algeria. In both cases, political strength is seen as masculine and passivity is a sign of queerness. *Makoumè* is thus applied here less as a sign of sexual otherness than to signal political, cultural, or even racial difference. Such is the case when the Hôtel de l'Europe's European boss is similarly labeled because he wears an apron: "Il était pour nous tout-à-faitement honteux qu'un homme, à moins qu'il soit un ma-commère, s'affichât dans cette tenue" (187) [For us it was completely absolutely disgraceful for a man, unless he was a *ma-commère*, to display himself dressed in this way].

These political associations are echoed in the description of the event that sets off the riots constituting the novel's main event—the fight that breaks out after a French man backs over a Martiniquan's Vespa without apologizing: "Heureusement, le docker n'a pas accepté ça, c'est un nègre qui a du sentiment dans son corps, il n'est pas prêt à baisser sa culotte face à un étranger" (188) [Fortunately, the docker didn't take that sitting down; he's a black man with pride who is unwilling to lower his britches for a foreigner]. Bending over for the colonizer, therefore, entails being not only colonized but also unmanned; colonized men are screwed, literally and figuratively, by the colonizer. Even Martiniquan men who go too far in adapting French manners become suspect; the more-French-than-the-French journalist Romule Casoar is thus designated in an association of Frenchness with a lack of masculinity:

> Ainsi donc, comme d'aucuns le soupçonnaient, Romule Casoar n'était qu'un vulgaire ma-commère, un homme qui aimait les hommes et voilà pourquoi il demeurait avec obstination célibataire. Pour bailler le change, Casoar se proclamait "célibertin" afin qu'on s'imaginât qu'il était aussi coureur de donzelles qu'Eugène Lamour mais la preuve venait d'être faite. Bec-en-Or en fut à nouveau statufié. Des braillards le dérisionnaient avec une méchanceté revancharde :
> "Ta concubine te cocufie avec un ma-commère ! Ouaille, man-man, foutre que c'est triste pour toi !" (385)

[Thus, as some suspected, Romule Casoar was nothing but a vulgar *ma-commère*, a man who loved men, and that's why he obstinately remained a bachelor (*célibataire*). To hide his intentions, Casoar proclaimed himself a "bachelibertine" (*célibertin*) so that everyone would think he was as much of a skirt chaser as Eugène Lamour, but the proof was just given. Bec-en-Or was frozen from shock once again. Loudmouths mocked him with a vengeful cruelty:
"Your woman is fooling around on you with a *ma-commère!* I'll be damned, it's a fucking sad day for you."]

Such associations of homosexuality with the colonizer are far from rare in political discourses of Africa and its diaspora. They are, for example, central to the oft-quoted discussion of homosexuality in Frantz Fanon's *Peau noire, masques blancs* (1952) [*Black Skin, White Masks*], which contains an explicit claim that all male racists are repressed homosexuals and all female racists secretly desire black men (127). In a lengthy footnote, Fanon elaborates:

> Mentionnons rapidement qu'il ne nous a pas été donné de constater la présence manifeste de pédérastie en Martinique. Il faut y voir la

conséquence de l'absence de l'Œdipe aux Antilles. On connaît en effet le schéma de l'homosexualité. Rappelons toutefois l'existence de ce qu'on appelle là-bas "des hommes habillés en dames" ou "Ma Commère". Ils ont la plupart du temps une veste et une jupe. Mais nous restons persuadé qu'ils ont une vie sexuelle normale. Ils prennent le punch comme n'importe quel gaillard et ne sont pas insensibles aux charmes des femmes,–marchandes de poissons, de légumes. Par contre en Europe nous avons trouvé quelques camarades qui sont devenus pédérastes, toujours passifs. Mais ce n'était point là homosexualité névrotique, c'était pour eux un expédient comme pour d'autres celui de souteneur. (146)

[Let me observe at once that I had no opportunity to establish the overt presence of homosexuality in Martinique. This must be viewed as the result of the absence of the Oedipus complex in the Antilles. The schema of homosexuality is well enough known. We should not overlook, however, the existence of what are called there "men dressed like women" or "godmothers." Generally they wear shirts and skirts. But I am convinced that they lead normal sex lives. They can take a punch like any "he-man" and they are not impervious to the allures of women—fish and vegetable merchants. In Europe, on the other hand, I have known several Martinicans who became homosexuals, always passive. But this was by no means a neurotic homosexuality: For them it was a means to a livelihood, as pimping is for others. (*Black Skin* 180)][5]

When Martiniquan men succumb to homosexuality in Europe, he claims, it is because such neurotic, abnormal practices are imposed by the colonizer, characterized, unlike Martiniquans, by the Oedipus complex. Martiniquan men become homosexual when screwed by Europeans; when Confiant's Vespa operator challenges the colonial privilege of the Metropolitan French man who damaged his scooter, other characters characterize him as refusing to be screwed in a like manner. If, for Martiniquan men, homosexuality can only arise in relations with the colonizers, a "truly" Martiniquan homosexuality cannot exist. Yet, as the footnote attests, in spite of his initial denial of Martiniquan homosexuality, Fanon knows quite a bit about and expands at great length on something that supposedly does not exist.[6]

Interestingly, in the French version of this passage, instead of *makoumè* Fanon uses its corresponding French words, which do not carry the same meaning, hence the original translator's rendition as "godmother" as opposed to the more accurate "sissy faggot."[7] In a French-language text, *Ma Commère* might seem out of place since using this term to address the godmother (on the part of the godfather) is no longer even current in French (although in Caribbean texts one may still see respected women addressed as *ma commère* in a more general use of the original meaning). Had Fanon given the Creole version, he would have had a harder time denying the existence of Martiniquan homosexuality, since a distinct Creole word for such practices would seem to imply a culturally specific way of understanding them. Fanon's language choice in this footnote thus connects his assertions with parallel ones that use as part of their evidence the claim that there is no word for homosexual in the indigenous languages of non-European cultures.

In spite of their affirmation of the *makoumè*'s centrality to Martiniquan culture, in many passages the Créolistes seem to share Fanon's language politics as well as the homophobia it implies. In the passages of *Eau de Café* and *L'allée des soupirs* quoted above, either most references to the *makoumè* are given as *ma-commère* without suggesting that it is a French translation of a Creole word or the Creole is given with no transcription/translation or one that gives no indication of the word's homosexual implication (which to a non-Creolophone reader might seem to represent a similar denial). In the case of the Créolistes, the relation between sexuality on the one hand and their use and translation of Creole words and expressions on the other has resulted in much spilling of ink. Indeed, the extensive replacement of *makoumè* with *ma-commère* in Créoliste novels, while perhaps sometimes making the homosexual implications of the Creole term invisible to "outsiders," is also quite consistent with the Créolistes' project of Creolization of the French language in their novels, particularly as regards the topic of sexuality. This linguistic procedure has been the topic of a number of essays, but most focus on how Creole words for *heterosexual* acts are used to make literary French more Creole. Creole words (or their Frenchified versions) for female genitalia (*coucoune*), penis (*kal*), to have sex (*coquer*), testicles (*graines*), and buttocks (*bonda*) abound in their novels, and the Créolistes' use of *ma-commère* is inseparable from their use of Creole in relation to sexuality. Arnold regards this language politics as an important component of the masculinist aspect of Créoliste fiction:

> The eroticism that has so titillated European readers of Chamoiseau and Confiant is couched in one or the other of these linguistic tech-

niques. The local names of human sexual organs are written both in a frenchified form, to make them more recognizable, and, elsewhere in the same text, in their creole form, presumably for purposes of authenticity. . . . [T]he sexual terms used are ones that women novelists avoid because they find them invasive and potentially violent. ("Créolité" 40)

While quick to defend themselves against such accusations, the Créolistes nonetheless often seem to ignore the sexual politics of the language position at the heart of Créolité.

Scholars studying gender divisions in the use of Creole corroborate Arnold's assertion. Both David Murray and Schnepel have described taboos against speaking Creole faced by women in certain contexts. Furthermore, Schnepel associates Creole use with an affirmation of masculinity:

[I]n order to signal their masculinity and sound more "macho," men tended to identify with lower-status groups by imitating their speech, while women of all class backgrounds (except the lowest) were known to reproduce the speech of the dominant group or "hypercorrect" towards the standard. . . . [I]t was more acceptable for a little boy to speak Creole than for a little girl. . . . Furthermore, swearing in Creole was the marker of being "on ti-mal," part of the cult of masculinity. (251, 254)[8]

Although Confiant and Chamoiseau implicitly recognize this gendered tension between French and Creole in the numerous passages in which women faint upon hearing proper French, their specific use of Creole in novels may be unavailable to women writers. Thus, even when they might be read as ridiculing the *major*'s male bravura, they imitate his use of sexual language as an exercise of male privilege.

The sexual politics of language choice in Créoliste novels has also become the justification for a substantial body of criticism of women writers on the part of the Créolistes: "[T]he official *créolistes* have denounced, both publicly and privately, women writers—usually from Guadeloupe—whose use of creole they deem inadequate. . . . Language is both the major focus of the *créolistes'* polemical writings and the club with which they batter those whose fiction they don't like" (Arnold, "Créolité" 37, 39). The question of how Creole words are used in French-language Caribbean novels has thus been the object of a rather persnickety debate.

In "Reflections on Maryse Condé's *Traversée de la mangrove*," Chamoiseau takes the Guadeloupan writer to task for providing footnote definitions for the Creole words she includes in her 1989 novel: "[A]ll the footnotes that explain what we already know make us think, dear Maryse, that you are not addressing us, but some other people. Self-explication is not, it seems to me, appropriate. Why not leave that task to editors and translators if they deem it necessary?" (394). Likewise, Confiant has claimed in an interview, "Before Créolité, most Antillean authors would agree to add glossaries or footnotes explaining Creole words. So you'd see '*Morne*: low-lying hill in the Antilles,' or '*Chabin*: mixed-race, black and white,' and so on. Patrick [Chamoiseau] and I were the first to refuse to explicate the Creole in our writing" (Taylor 148). No doubt catching on to the equivocal nature of this assertion, the interviewer modified Confiant's response to make it more accurate: "Sometimes you do provide such 'tools,' but you turn the whole idea on its head, poking fun at the idea of cross-cultural dictionary definitions by playing with the language—making puns or rebuking the reader for his or her ignorance" (148). Chamoiseau, however, does not admit that Condé's use of footnotes might be just as playful or parodic. Furthermore, *chabin* is precisely the word that he defines (incompletely, I might add) in a footnote in *Chronique des sept misères* with the following definition: "Métis blanc-nègre" (31) [Black-white mix]. It is thus around the question of footnotes that Chamoiseau articulates a position of nationalist "insiderism" that one might view as contradicting the assertion of Créolité as enabling multiple solidarities.

Queering the Mangrove

Makoumè is another Creole word that the Créolistes frequently feel the need to translate for their Francophone readers. Unlike them, however, Condé neither Frenchifies the word nor glosses over its homosexual meaning.[9] In *Traversée de la mangrove*, when one of the villagers of Rivière au Sel describes a rumor concerning the nature of Francis's friendship with Moïse, Condé writes:

> [C]e fut Moïse qui vint y dormir et y boire des nuits entières. Faut-il le dire ? Les méchants ricanèrent. Cette amitié-là avait sale odeur et les deux hommes étaient des makoumé ! Pour sûr !

Nombreux étaient ceux dans ce village guère dévot, mais perdu au fin fond des bois et de ce fait ignorant des vices courants dans les villes, qui n'avaient jamais vu de makoumé, à part Sirop Batterie qui s'habillait en femme les jours de Carnaval à Petit Bourg. Ils examinèrent les compères avec incrédulité. Moïse, passe encore ! Mais Francis ! Il n'en avait pas l'air ! Néanmoins la plante malfaisante de cette médisance crût et fleurit dans le terreau du village et ne s'étiola que lorsque éclata la nouvelle de l'affaire avec Mira. Un violeur de femmes peut-il en même temps être un makoumé ? Peut-on avoir goût aux femmes et en même temps aux hommes ? (36–37)

[There were some wicked sneers. There was something fishy about that friendship and the two men were makoumeh! That's for sure.

Many of the inhabitants of this hardly God-fearing village, buried in the back of beyond, were ignorant of the vices common in towns and had never seen a makoumeh except for Sirop Batterie who dressed up as a woman at carnival time in Petit-Bourg. They inspected the two in disbelief. Moïse, perhaps! But Francis! He didn't look like one. The poisonous plant of mischief, however, grew and flourished in the compost of the village and only wilted once the news of the affair with Mira broke out. Can a rapist of women be a makoumeh as well? Can one have a liking for both men and women? (20)]

On the one hand, Condé's passage could be said to go along with Fanon in some respects. Both texts mention a tradition of cross-dressing, and Condé's use of the word *compère* recalls Fanon's *commère*. Both Fanon and Condé seem to associate homosexuality with foreigners like, in Condé's case, Francis (of elusive but probably Hispanic origins) or the two Haitian buddies Désinor and Carlos:

Un jour, las de se heurter aux refus de ces [femmes] sans-cœur, ils s'étaient enfourchés l'un l'autre et surprise, au bout de l'étreinte, ils avaient trouvé la même fulgurance de plaisir. Alors, ils avaient recommencé. (199)

[One day, tired of being refused by these heartless women, they climbed on each other, and to their surprise found the same flash of pleasure at the end of their lovemaking. So they had started all over again. (165)]

As in Fanon, a description of what supposedly does not exist immediately follows its denial, and like Fanon, the villagers claim to be ignorant of the practices of *makoumè*, even though they occur in broad daylight during Carnival.

What Fanon describes as a Caribbean/Metropolitan France dichotomy, however, becomes a rural/urban one in Condé's novel. Presumably, the cities to which the *makoumè* are confined are subjected to a much greater French influence. Perhaps, however, it is because homosexuality (and its transgender associations) can only be seen during Carnival that its existence can be denied during the rest of the year. Indeed, Carnival has often been described as a time when reversals in the social order are allowed so that this order may be maintained throughout the rest of the year. Furthermore, other aspects of Condé's passage almost seem as if they were written to refute Fanon. Condé contradicts the villagers' association of homosexuality with urban vice through the presence of Sirop Batterie, the very rural *makoumè*. She replaces Fanon's French expression "Ma Commère" with the Creole original he translates and even glosses it as "homosexual" in a note. She dislodges *makoumè* from its association with femininity by applying it equally to both active and passive partners and by attaching it to its gendered opposite, *compère*. Why use the Creole *makoumè* in a novel in French when, in fact, any number of French equivalents would have worked just fine? It is as if the homosexuality she describes is so Caribbean that only a Creole word will do. The Creole word, in fact, asserts the Caribbeanness of homosexuality. For Fanon, there are no queers at "home" in Martinique, and homosexuality represents a false or alienated identity for Martiniquans; for Condé, there must be a "home" for queers in Guadeloupe. Her fiction, in fact, asserts the "truth" of this necessity.

When one considers that the word Condé glosses as "homosexual" is related to that for a gossiping woman (*une commère* in French), her discussion of homosexuality becomes much more central to the concerns of the novel: the homosexuality in question is a subject of gossip, and this in a novel whose plot consists entirely of gossip. To the extent one can say that *Traversée de la mangrove* has a plot, its plot is fairly simple. As Leah Hewitt has written, Condé's novel "is structured around the death of one character, Francis Sancher, whose shadowy identity and enigmatic death are presented as two puzzles to be solved" (84). Francis, alias Francisco Alvarez-Sanchez, came to the small Guadeloupan village Rivière au Sel and had affairs with at least two village women. Through the stories told by villagers at his wake, the novel attempts to reconstruct Francis's origins, his past, his reasons for moving to Rivière au Sel, and the circumstances surrounding his death.[10] Its narrative consists solely of these different and conflicting versions of Francis's story, and, although the novel resembles a "popular detective story" (Hewitt 84), it never provides definite answers to the questions it asks. Indeed, Hewitt has also compared Condé's novel (as opposed to Francis's) to a mangrove swamp:

> The mangrove of the title . . . provides a metaphor for the reader's situation. . . . The mangrove's tree branches . . . are a physical equivalent to the jumble of stories that overlap, intersect and crisscross one another. In the mangrove's thick growth it is difficult to tell roots from trunks and branches, origins from effects, beginnings from ends. Similarly, the entanglement of contradictory facts, beliefs and attitudes undermines the reader's desire to get to a univocal truth concerning the "root" or "origin" of Sancher's identity and the cause of his death. (85)

The gossip about Francis Sancher—the various versions of his story that Hewitt compares to the jumble of roots and branches of the mangrove tree—makes up the narrative structure of *Traversée*, so that finding truth amid all this gossip or establishing a definitive version of the plot is just as impossible as the eponymous endeavor of crossing the mangrove.

Renée Larrier has argued that what I call the novel's gossipy structure calls Francis's masculinity into question. If "male characters are associated with trees and tree roots with which they have special communication" (137), "the roving *Is*, through multiple perspectives, reconstruct the life of a migrating central character whose masculinity . . . is undermined" (129). In addition to his masculinity, I would argue, since "Francis Sancher remains a mysterious figure, emblematic of Caribbean identity" (Larrier 144), Condé also interrogates the roots of Caribbean identity in offering an alternative model of roots to the patrilineal family tree through the mangrove as an image of genealogical accounts of identity. Furthermore, since the *makoumè* figures as one of the many roots of the mangrove, Condé simultaneously highlights the sexual paradox of all roots narratives. In showing that roots can also be rewritten in sexually subversive ways, Condé therefore queers not only the roots paradigm but also the structure of return narratives. For the expression Condé uses to describe the spread of gossip about Sancher's homosexuality, "the evil-doing plant of malicious gossip,"[11] associates gossip with roots in the image of rumor taking root in Rivière au Sel. This equivalence between gossip and narrative, both of which are like roots of the mangrove, means that in Condé's mangrove the narrative paradox is intertwined with the sexual one. In *Traversée de la mangrove*, the *makoumè* in the mangrove thus literalizes the queering of Caribbean roots that can happen when the mangrove structures alternative versions of roots narratives and highlights the political, narrative, and sexual paradoxes inherent therein. Condé's novel thus queers the model represented by Haley and can also prompt a rereading of the Créolistes' own mangrove novels, in relation to which the agency for the critical maneuver of queering lies more squarely with the reader.

Queering Créolité

While the critics cited above have elaborated an accurate understanding of the way gender infuses Créoliste novels, I would also argue that antihomophobic criticism can gain even more by paying careful attention to the insight the Créolistes provide into the workings of gender and sexuality in the Caribbean. While one may find in the Créolistes' novels many male characters who fit Spear's and Arnold's descriptions of their homophobia, it would be hasty to assume that homophobic characters are sufficient to make a novel homophobic. The Créoliste novelists Chamoiseau and Confiant (especially the latter) are also unique in the openness with which they deal with topics related to homosexuality, and the sheer frequency with which they use *makoumè* or *ma-commère* merits further consideration. What some critics have seen as a glorification of supermasculine characters is often treated with a great deal of irony by Chamoiseau and Confiant, and even characters who seem to represent the Créolistes' anti-Négritude position can be subjected to a significant amount of ridicule. It is therefore necessary to carry out close readings of the so-called homophobic passages (including their language politics) to contextualize them within each novel's general presentation of its characters.

To return to Confiant's *L'allée des soupirs*, for example, in spite of journalist Romule Casoar's reputation as a "godmother," he did manage to steal Bec-en-Or's mistress. When loudmouths then tease the latter by referring to the former's alleged homosexuality, the insult *makoumè* is used to attack not Romule but Bec-en-Or, whose masculinity suffers from this defeat at the hands of a sellout. The fact that the rumor about

Romule is wrong does not prevent other Martiniquan men from using it to shore up their own masculinities at the expense of Bec-en-Or's (not to mention Romule's). Thus, while Fanon used the term *Ma Commère* to name a homosexuality that supposedly does not exist, Confiant, while making reference to the existence of homosexuality, uses *ma-commère* in a context far removed from its actual practice. Furthermore, in spite of Confiant's general adherence to Fanon's language politics, a single passage in *L'allée des soupirs* disrupts them by giving the French translation of *makoumè* as "*pédéraste*" or "faggot." When the young Jean, one of the novel's most important characters, pays more attention to a film than the girl he is watching it with, "'*Ou sé an makoumè oben ki sa ?*' (T'es pédéraste ou quoi ?) s'énervait Lamour" (117) [Are you a faggot or what?" said Lamour impatiently]. One might even argue that, in contradistinction to an avoidance of using the Creole word in other passages, this passage proclaims the Créolité of the *makoumè*.

Published one year before *Traversée*, Patrick Chamoiseau's *Solibo Magnifique* (1988) [*Solibo Magnificent*] resembles Condé's novel in a number of interesting ways. Detailing the investigation that follows the eponymous storyteller's death during Carnival from choking on his own words, it begins like Condé's novel with a dead man. Solibo falls dead into the roots of a tamarind tree, and, as one of the characters, Chamoiseau is also a witness to Solibo's death. Chamoiseau's novel also disrupts Fanon's association of homosexuality with the colonizer, as well as the gender politics described by Murray of using *makoumè* as an insult. In this novel, *makoumè* occurs in a confrontation not between two men but between a man and a woman. In a confrontation between the *major* Diab-Anba-Feuilles and the *majorine* Lolita Boidevan, nicknamed Doudou-Ménar, the latter says, "J'ai des outils pour toi !" (92) [I have some tools for you]. He interprets this remark as an accusation and an insult:

[T]u me vois avec le bleu de la Loi, tu te dis : aye, c'est un ma-commère ! . . . , je ne suis pas un ma-commère han, je ne suis pas une commère, regarde si je suis une commère . . .—et il porte flap ! le poing à la bouche, se mord hanm ! (93)

[You see me in a police uniform and you say to yourself, My God! he's a *ma-commère!* . . . I'm not a *ma-commère,* no way, I'm not a *commère,* you'll see whether I'm a *commère.* And wham, he sticks his fist in his mouth and, crunch, bites it.]

By bleeding for her, the passage implies, he is threatening to kill her (see Plumecocq 131).

Doudou's perceived insult then elicits a barrage of words that can only be transmitted in Creole. The following passage is exclaimed by Diab-Anba-Feuilles during the bloody fight that ensues:

> Man sé an makoumê ? ès man sé an makoumê ? mi oala ou défol-manté akôdi sé koko siklon fésé, han ! man sé pilonnen'w atê-a là, wi ! man sé grajé'w kon an bi manyôk ek pijé'w anba plat' pyé mwen pou fè'w ladÿé sos fyel-ou ! ou modi ! oala man menyen'w ou modi ! pon labé pé ké tiré'y ba'w é dyab ké ayé oute zo'w yonn aprélot ! mé ansé an jan mentsiyen, man grafyen'w ou pwézonnen ! fwa'w pwézonnen ! koukoun-ou pwézonnen ! dréséguidup anpé ba'w fifin bout'la. (94)

The French translation of this passage is given in a footnote as follows:

> Je suis un pleutre ? suis-je un pleutre ? te voilà comme un cocotier dévasté par un cyclone ! oh, j'aimerai te détruire, te piétiner ! tu es maudite ! maintenant que je t'ai touchée, ton corps, ton foie, ton sexe sont soumis à ma malédiction ! aucun sacrement n'y pourra rien désormais ! tu es maudite ! relève-toi pour que je puisse t'achever ! . . . (Chamoiseau's ellipsis)

> [I'm a coward? am I a coward? there you are like a coconut tree blown down by a cyclone! oh how I would love to destroy you, trample on you! curses to you! now that I have touched you, your body, your liver, your sexual organs are under my curse! no sacrament will do anything for you from now on! get up so I can finish you off! . . .]

Here the French translation of the Creole gives no indication of *makoumè*'s homosexual implications; the word is simply translated as "*pleutre*" or "coward." Yet the way *makoumè* is translated is not the only discrepancy between the two versions. Many of the Creole original's sexual implications are lost, as are culturally specific references such as cassava, manzanita, and suggestions of popular religious practices and/or beliefs. A more accurate translation of the Creole passage would yield something more like:

> I'm a faggot? am I a faggot? goodness, you are as scattered as coconuts spanked to the ground by a cyclone! I feel like trampling *you* into the

ground! I'll grate you and squeeze you like a piece of cassava under my foot to purge the juice from your bile! curses to you! curses! no priest can take them away so the devil will take out your bones one by one! I'm a sort of manzanita, I'll scratch you to poison you! your liver is poisoned! your punani is poisoned! I've got a rise out of something to give you the finest from the tip. . . .[12]

In addition, although some critics have made much of the use of the term *makoumè* by *majors* in their jousts, the fact that one partner here is a *majorine* complicates readings that argue that these passages glorify the masculinity of their characters. Yes, it is true that Doudou is wounded in the violence that a male character deploys in the name of masculinity, but she responds to this attack with a formidable amount of resistance. At first the police-squad chief Bouafesse does not let the rescue squad take the wounded Doudou to the hospital simply because she is a witness to Solibo's death. After the ambulance attendants persuade him to change his mind, Doudou regains consciousness en route to the hospital and sees Nono-Bec-en-Or. She knocks out all his teeth (forcing the ambulance to veer off course) and throws him against the back window, breaking it, before falling back into a coma. Upon awaking once more, she again attacks Nono before escaping from the hospital. When she returns to the scene of Solibo's death, she attacks Diab again, knocks him out, and then turns to Bouafesse. Two of his subordinates beat her to death before they can be stopped. Only the combined forces of five armed police officers, one of whom is a *major*, can subdue what might be read as this female character's resistance to masculinity.

Doudou's tragic end, a result of police brutality, occurs after a heroic battle during which she usurps the male position, and she pays for this gendered revolt with her life. Yet one might also argue that she has usurped no one but is merely playing out a role available to Martiniquan women and that this sequence is a minor variation on previous ones involving two male *majors*. Doudou would thus, like the *major*, constitute an archetypal figure, one that Chamoiseau himself has discussed in describing his own mother: "She's a woman with balls (*femme-à-graines*), a mannish woman; all Caribbean women are like that" (McCusker 731). Ellen M. Schnepel articulates a different view of this archetype: "[T]he Creole expression *on mal-fanm* . . . means literally a 'male-woman.' The phrase refers to a strong-willed woman and has a pejorative significance, implying that the woman doesn't know her place" (252). Whereas Chamoiseau describes the archetype in an effort to defend himself against accusations of sexism, Schnepel sees the archetype itself as a product of sexist social forces that attempt to keep women "in their place."

While Chamoiseau seems to see the archetype as evidence of a lack of sexism in Caribbean societies, his own self-defense relies less on the value of the archetype than on the fact that he is accurately representing a "real" aspect of Caribbean cultures:

> I've never been able to understand the "masculinist" critique of our work; it seems completely unfounded. In fact, I am astonished at how many of my novels have been about women. But not "Western" women—this is the big error in the Western masculinist critique, they always imagine women as Western women. My novels are about Creole women, *matadoras*—women who come from matrifocal families and have always had to fight, to develop strategies of survival and resistance. (Taylor 154)

Although Chamoiseau echoes the critique of western feminism's cultural biases articulated by a number of nonwestern feminists, his notion of representation as value neutral and politically unmotivated has long been discredited. Arnold dismisses such defenses and links issues of representation to questions of sexuality, as well as those of gender: "[T]he *créolistes* reproduce . . . an aggressive heterosexual eroticism, envisaged from the perspective of a more or less predatory philandering male whose activities can be justified—if need be—through the claim of verisimilitude" ("Gendering" 37). Contra Chamoiseau, however, I would argue that it is not the Créolistes' representations of mannish women that offer something useful for gender studies but their representation of mannish men as objects of ridicule. Contra Arnold, I would point out that, while gender and sexuality are certainly intertwined here, even if one could maintain that the overabundance of supermale characters constitutes a glorification rather than a critique of masculinity, the abundance of *makoumè* cannot be treated as a strict parallel. While sexism may be reproduced through displays (representations) of male bravura, as one can see from the example of Fanon, homophobia often works by hiding (refusing to represent) what it attempts to repress. It is precisely the latter rule that the Créolistes refuse to follow. A truly antihomophobic criticism, I feel, should guard against critiquing sexual representations in ways suggesting that *de*sexualized representations are the best alternative to either sexism or homophobia.

The entire battle between Doudou and the forces of masculinity, as well as those of social order, intercut with the investigation that continues during her trip to the hospital, is also imbued with a significant amount of ridicule. The entire sequence of events not only displays the police force as being inept but also exaggerates reactions by attributing monstrous effects to innocuous causes. Diab's reaction to Doudou is one such monstrosity; since Doudou does not pronounce the word *makoumè*, one must recognize that it is inferred or imagined by Diab. The cop creates the homophobic insult himself and then responds in a homophobic manner. Whereas Fanon associated the imposition of homosexuality with French colonization, in this passage at least, Chamoiseau associates *homophobia* with the French-run police force (which he explicitly treats as a representative of the Republic itself). While Diab assumes that his police uniform makes him more vulnerable to being called a *makoumè* (presumably because he has already bent over for the French Republic!), ridiculing Diab's masculinity is part and parcel of a Créoliste's political critique of colonial violence. Chamoiseau describes this tactic in an interview in response to a question about precisely this sequence of police brutality: "Because the Creole storyteller has used laughter, irony, mockery, derision—in short, the whole effect of mocking distanciation—in an exemplary manner, I can only situate myself in the same tradition. In fact, laughter allows me to make fun of myself, in other words, not to take myself seriously, to maintain an amused distance with what I am, what I do, my ambitions, my worries" (McCusker 728). Although Arnold has argued that this identification with the male storyteller is another aspect of the Créolistes' masculinist bias ("Gendering" 30), in *Solibo*, Chamoiseau actually appears as a writer-character who is clearly differentiated from the oral storyteller and of whom other characters occasionally make fun. Thus, not only is the ridicule of burlesque masculinity a frequent aspect of these novels, but it is also an integral aspect of a self-critique firmly embedded within the Créolistes' fictional writing.

One passage in Confiant's 1988 novel *Le nègre et l'amiral* [The Negro and the Admiral] actually identifies this practice with an antisexist politics explicitly. In this novel about life in Martinique during World War II under the pro-Vichy Admiral Robert (referred to in the novel's title), the former Latin teacher Amédée Mauville describes how his beloved, the prostitute Philomène, teaches him to appreciate the subtleties of the word *coucoune* (written by Chamoiseau in more a standard Creole as *koukoun*):

C'est Philomène qui m'apprend à aimer, dans un même balan, et son corps et le créole car elle fait l'amour dans cette langue, déployant des paroles d'une doucine inouïe, incomparable, qui ébranle mon être tout entier. Aussi, dans nos babils post-coïtaux, je ressens un bien-être physique à habiter chaque mot, même le plus banal, et à être habité par lui. . . . Je m'avise avec incrédulité que la langue de nos tuteurs blancs n'a pas de mot aussi beau que "coucoune" pour désigner le sexe de la femme et que tous les vocables dont elle dispose, "chatte," "con," "choune" ou "fente," recèlent une verdeur insultante pour nos compagnes. (127)

[Philomène is the one who is teaching me how to love both her body and Creole at the same time, because this is the language she makes love in, using words of unequaled, incomparable sweetness that shake up my entire being. Also, during our postcoital chatter, I sense a physical well-being in inhabiting each word, even the most banal, and in being inhabited by it. . . . I realize with disbelief that the language of our white teachers has no word as beautiful as *coucoune* to designate a woman's sexual organs, and that all the terms it uses—*pussy, cunt, snatch, slit*—contain a crudeness insulting to our female companions.]

According to this passage, therefore, Creole's sexual vocabulary is less vulgar than that of French, and its valences are the opposite of those described by Arnold, Murray, and Schnepel. In addition, Amédée's praise of the antisexist valences of Creole's sexual vocabulary coincides with his condemnation of misogyny on the part of Rigobert (the *nègre* of the title) (267).[13] While the novel obviously valorizes Rigobert's resistance to the Vichy government, Amédée is more representative of the Créoliste position on language. Amédée thus accuses the *major* Rigobert of being sexist as part of a Créoliste position on language politics. It is probably also fair to say that the novel embraces his critique of misogyny even though (or perhaps because) this critique remains inherently male. The sexual politics of the Créolistes' use of Creolized French is thus harder to pin down than some critics have suggested.

In addition to the Créolistes' use of *makoumè* as part of a Creolization of both sexuality and French linguistic hegemony, a Creolization that demarginalizes not only Creole but also a specifically Creole vision of sexuality, Confiant's *Le nègre et l'amiral* further brings the *makoumè* into public view, even if only during Carnival. In a mixture of French and Creole, an announcement for Carnival's funeral is diffused over the radio on behalf of a list of characters, including *makoumè*:

Les obsèques de Vaval, roi bwabwa
Vaval le plus grand majô
surnommé nonm a bonm
Ses obsèques auront lieu à partir de deux heures cet
après-midi dans tout le pays et en ville menm parèy.
Le cortège se réunira la zôt ka wè anlo moun ki ka mô ri.
l'inhumation aura lieu ansanm nwè fèt
en même temps que l'incinération.
Cet avis est diffusé de la part
des actuellement en Métropole
des yichkôn
des boulé, des bwètzouti, des gôlbo
des soubawou, des nègmawon
des soukouyan, des totoblo, des vagabonds
des bitako, des pété'y man ka pété'y
des désherbants, des matadô
des makoumè, des malélivé
An tout bagay-tala, si nou obliyé condoléances aux
parents, amis et alliés
Après la cérémonie, toute la famille sera heureuse de
vous recevoir, mizik par-devant, dans les zouk les bals,
les diri san kriyé, les dékalé mangous, les touféyenyen
kon lidé zôt di zôt. (75–76)

In the following translation, I have left in the words that are in Creole in the original with a translation in parentheses (or in the notes for longer ones):

The funeral for *Vaval*,[14] king *bwabwa*[15]
Vaval the greatest *majô*
nicknamed *nonm a bonm* (party man)
His funeral will begin at two this
afternoon throughout the country and in town *menm parèy* (in the
same way).
The procession will gather *la zôt ka wè anlo moun ki ka mô ri* (where
people are dying laughing).

The burial will occur *ansanm nwè fèt* (at nightfall)
at the same time as the cremation.
This announcement comes from
those who have moved to France
yichkôn (sons of bitches)
boulé (drunkards), *bwètzouti*,[16] *gôlbo*[17]
soubawou (wild men), *nègmawon* (maroons)[18]
soukouyan (bloodsuckers), *totoblo* (musicians), vagabonds/good-for-
    nothings
bitako (rednecks),[19] *pété'y man ka pété'y* (revelers)
weed killers, *matadõ*[20]
makoumè, malélivé (misbehavers)
An tout bagay-tala, si nou obliyé (In all this affair, if we forget)
    condolences for
parents, friends, and allies
After the ceremony, the family invites
you for *mizik* (music) up front, in *zouk* (big parties with music), balls,
diri san kriyé (dishes of rice that has not been sorted), *dékalé mangous*
    (mongoose killings), *touféyenyen* (dirty dancing)[21]
kon lidé zôt di zôt (to do as you like).[22]

The list of sponsors for this announcement reads somewhat like a Carnival procession in itself, and, although it contains several labels that might
be considered pejorative (the first among which is *makoumè* but also *bitako* and, in some contexts, *nègmawon*), a number of the characters they
describe (such as the *vakabon* and *nègmawon*) have been valorized by the
Créolistes as Creole supermale heroes, often seemingly at the expense
of the *makoumè*. So, although one might read the passage as describing a
group of marginalized figures sending out a funeral announcement for
their enemy Vaval, represented here as a *major*, it is precisely this *major*
who brings these figures out of the margins during Carnival. During Carnival, then, the *major* can parade side by side with the *makoumè*. On the
one hand, there might be nothing unusual about giving the *makoumè* a
platform equal to that of the *major* during Carnival; as soon as Carnival
is over, the *makoumè* can be whisked quickly back to the margins. On the
other, the distinction between Carnival and the rest of the year is consciously blurred in the Créolistes' novels, in which Carnival seems to last
all year. In other words, this funeral announcement could just as easily
be the list of characters in a Créoliste novel.

In addition, the announcement occurs not as part of the narration of the novel's events but during a digression, a flashback that recounts the meeting of Rigobert and Julien Dorival, nicknamed Lapin Échaudé (Scalded Rabbit), the head *crieur*, a person paid to entice customers into a store. The announcement is heard on the radio in the second version of their meeting. The existence of competing versions of the same event signals that the *makoumè* enters narrative as the object of gossip as in Condé's *Traversée*. Indeed, the plots of Créoliste novels are often driven by gossip or the *radio-bois-patate* (the grapevine or rumor-mill), and, as we have seen, it is often as the object of this gossip that the *makoumè* disrupts the masculinity of the most super-male characters. Using Condé to queer the mangrove of the Créolistes' novels can thus lead us back to the passage in Confiant's *L'allée des soupirs* in which the Indian undertaker Ziguinote could not bear to see an animal killed as a child: "On l'affubla très tôt du sobriquet de "Petit Ma-commère," le plus infamant dont on disposât dans nos contrées en ce début de siècle" (252–53) [He was immediately saddled with the nickname Little *Ma-commère*, the most slanderous one available in our region at the beginning of this century]. As an adult, he falls in love with a woman, the notions store (*mercerie*) keeper Sylvanise: "Dans une première mouture, il est dit que Ziguinote, alias Petit Ma-commère, espéra la mulâtresse au sortir de la messe" (255) [In a first version, it is said that Ziguinote, alias Little *Ma-commère*, waited for the mulatta to come out after mass]. A reference to the first *mouture*—usually the first version of a written text before it is revised but used here to describe the first *oral* version of a story—implies that later versions will be different, precisely the kind of transformation that characterizes gossip.

The etymological association between the *makoumè* and gossip is thus also a thematic one in many Créoliste novels. In *L'allée*, for example, Hilaire Tersinien gains the title of *major* by defeating Maxime Saint-Prix, the legendary "danseur de damiers" (checkerboard dancer or fighter/wrestler), in a fight. When the "checkerboard dance" is outlawed (except when it actually consists of dancing),[23] Maxime is delighted: "'Divertissement pour ma-commères!' lâchait Saint-Prix avec morgue quand on l'invitait à rejoindre les jeunes mâles nègres dans le cercle des danseurs" (308) [That's a pastime for *ma-commères*! Saint-Prix scoffed when invited to join the young black males among the circle of dancers]. From that point on, Maxime was able to live off the reputation of his masculinity without having to prove it, until, that is, Hilaire took that reputation from him. Masculinity, like homosexuality, is therefore often more a matter of rumor than fact. And since it is so frequently fought over (i.e., in high demand), it also seems to be in rather short supply. We have also seen how, in *Eau de Café*, the *nègmawon* Julien Thémistocle asserted his own masculinity by calling others *makoumè*. Yet, as far as using *makoumè* as an insult goes, *what goes around comes around!* The following insult was supposedly pronounced by Franciane, Eau de Café's mother, but it is related by Man Doris, who has dubious motives: "'Julien est un ma-commère,' clame-t-elle partout" (368) ["Julien is a *ma-commère*," she declared everywhere she went].

The supermale's comeuppance, however, is much greater than hearsay; Julien and Bérard (the *major* whose masculinity is also established at the expense of the *makoumè*) are the only ones who are also actually sodomized during the course of the novel. The character referred to as the Syrian (because none of the other characters can pronounce his Arabic name) carries out his threat to punish Major Bérard for sleeping with his wife by sodomizing him, first with a gun, then with his penis:

> Lentement mais sûrement, il enfonça le canon de son arme dans le trou-caca de Major Bérard qui mordit un oreiller pour ne pas meugler. . . . Puis Syrien retira brusquement l'arme et l'encula à grands coups de reins qui arrachèrent au nègre des cris déchirants. Et de lui dire : "Après ça, je te mets au défi d'aller claironner que tu as coqué la femme d'Abdelhamid Tanin. Je veux qu'à chaque fois que tu t'avises de faire ça, tu sentes tes fesses te brûler, mon bougre." (346)

> [Slowly but surely, he pushed the barrel of his weapon into the arsehole of Chief Bérard, who bit a pillow so as not to make a mooing sound. . . . Then Syrian suddenly pulled out his weapon and buggered the black man with great thrusts, which drew excruciating screams from him. And then he said: "After this, I challenge you to go and spread it about that you fucked Abdelhamid Tanin's wife. Each time you're tempted to say anything, I want you to feel your buttocks burning, my friend. (266–67)][24]

Julien Thémistocle apparently even brags about being sodomized by the hermaphroditic snake god(dess) Bothrops (whom he also penetrates while being penetrated) because this act of sexual initiation is the source of his sexual prowess and spiritual power (cf. Spear 146; Arnold, "Gendering" 38).[25] Is this the way the male writer gets the upper hand over his most masculine characters? Confiant could be read here as engaging in the same kind of verbal joust as his characters in order to position himself, the writer, as a male hero above all the *majors* and *nègmawon* of his novel. Is he, in turn, sodomizing his *majô* characters?

Oedipus among the Mangroves

Beyond the possibility that the Créolistes are screwing their male characters, there is another way in which the *makoumè* comes out of the mangroves to screw the Créolistes by overturning the patrilineal intellectual genealogy that they have deployed in situating Créolité within the history of Caribbean thought. This genealogy is neatly presented by the dedication of the *Éloge*:

Pour
AIMÉ CÉSAIRE
Pour
ÉDOUARD GLISSANT
ba
FRANKÉTYÈN

It reads, first in French, "for Aimé Césaire, for Édouard Glissant," then in Creole, "for Frankétyèn," the Haitian author who writes in Creole. If one reads this passage as a family tree, Négritude begat Antillanité, which in turn begat Créolité, asserted by the Créolistes as the teleological culmination of Caribbean literary history. No genealogy could be less like a mangrove and more dependent on a strictly patrilineal structure; as in biblical trees of begats, each movement is sired solely by a father, which means that each is also personified by a male writer. Heather Smyth writes, "It is clear in the *Éloge* which gender is the agent of culture in their program for creoleness: in order to return to oral Creole culture they must 'inseminate Creole in the new writing.' The male figure is responsible for the insemination of this reborn culture, and the male writer suffers a metaphorical 'castration' when cut off from Creole culture" (15).

In the *Éloge*, the Créolistes also explicitly posit Césaire as an intellectual father: "Nous sommes à jamais fils d'Aimé Césaire" (18) [We are forever Césaire's sons" (888)]. Likewise, in *Aimé Césaire*, Confiant describes his critique of Césaire's politics and poetics as "le cri sincère d'un fils qui estime avoir été trahi par ses pères et en l'occurence par le premier d'entre eux" (37) [the sincere cry of a son who considers himself betrayed by his fathers and, in this case, by the first and foremost among them]. It would therefore be the duty of these betrayed sons to rebel against their father's treason. Créolité, then, comes into existence through what Richard D. E. Burton has called the Créolistes' "attack on the Father" ("Two Views" 143); the roots of Créolité are thus not only patrilineal but also Oedipal. Yet in the *Éloge* the Créolistes also claim to rescue Césaire from the Oedipal tendencies of *other* critics: "Nous voilà sommés d'affranchir Aimé Césaire de l'accusation—aux relents œdipiens—d'hostilité à la langue créole" (17) [This brings us to free Aimé Césaire of the accusation—with Oedipal overtones—of hostility to the Creole language" (888)]. As Burton describes it, "the father-son bond is affirmed, denied and then reaffirmed" ("Two Views" 143) in a peculiar kind of flip-flopping.

Condé's queer mangrove can also be used to overturn this patrilineal genealogy. As Chamoiseau himself has suggested, the tangled roots of the mangrove also describe Francis's family tree: "The character of Francisco Sanchez has an unclear genealogy; he isn't transparent, and we do not know where he comes from, where he was born, what he wants, what he fears" (391–92). Since the characters' genealogies are intertwined but only become obvious bit by bit, reading this novel and making sense of it are like retracing one's family tree in a mangrove swamp, where it is impossible to isolate one's family tree from all the others. And since it is never clear which branches belong to which roots in the mangrove, a family tree structured like a mangrove also casts doubt on the paternity of individual family members. Finally, because Condé's mangrove opens up the lines of descent to allow for nonheterosexual roots in *Traversée*, the specter of homosexuality also interferes with the heterosexual purity of the novel's genealogy.

If Fanon attributed a lack of homosexuality in the Caribbean to an absence of the Oedipus complex there, rereading the Créolistes through Condé can bring their literary deployment of Oedipus into conflict with the more explicit denial of Oedipus in their essays. For example, at the end of Confiant's *Eau de Café*, one finds a fictional example of reversing Oedipal accusations when the narrator sees the character Bec-en-Or masturbating at the foot of the statue of Napoleon's wife Joséphine in Fort-de-France and hears him shout:[26]

> Crevez tous, bandes de couillons ! Vous avez forniqué avec vos propres mères, vous avez enseveli sous des laves de béton vos terres à ignames, vous avez prostitué vos femmes et vos sœurs, vous avez sacrifié la langue patiemment édifiée par les ancêtres, vous vous êtes

déculottés jour après jour, maintenant crevez ! . . . Ah, je revois . . . vos discours lamentables de maires et de députés véreux et verrats, vos bavasseries risibles de littérateurs de la Négritude et j'en passe. Alors crevez maintenant ! (377–78)

[Die, dumbasses! all of you. You've fornicated with your own mothers, you've buried your yam gardens under concrete slabs, you've prostituted your wives and sisters, you've sacrificed the language patiently elaborated by the ancestors, you've lowered your britches day after day, so die now. You crooked pigs, I can still hear your pitiful speeches as mayors and deputies, your laughable chatter as *Négritude littérateurs*. Just die now!]

It would be hard not to read this passage as targeting Césaire, who has had a long political career as mayor of Fort-de-France and deputy to the French National Assembly, especially since the political speeches condemned here are so clearly associated with the literary discourse of Négritude. Since Césaire, though unnamed, is associated with those who have betrayed the Creole language and culture, as well as fornicated with their mothers, he becomes the Oedipus figure here. The sons, however, are the ones who harbor a death wish for him, which is an Oedipal desire as well. And since the Oedipal father lowers his pants for the colonizer, what are we to think of the Créolistes who proffer this insult when the very same insult comes back to them?

In *Caribbean Discourse*, Glissant questions the relevance of the Oedipus complex in the Caribbean. He also argues (albeit in a much more nuanced fashion than Fanon) that "here, the Oedipus complex should be approached with caution, at least with the will to avoid imposing on the psychic reality of Martiniquans stereotypes that have been developed in the West" (99; my trans.). As reasons he cites "women's traditional energy, men's practice of avoiding responsibility, the 'historically' non-binding nature of family structures, and the ambiguous way in which they are lived" (98–99; my trans.). Thus, "Oedipal relations with the mother have not been a problem here (or more generally, Oedipus *as a problem* is a western invention) inasmuch as Martiniquan society has not really been required to adopt the western (triangular) model of family organization. In the extended family, the Oedipal relation is not problematic" (286; my trans.). In other words, in addition to his explicit acknowledgment of Deleuze and Guattari in taking up their theorization of the rhizomatic, he also shares their association of Oedipus with colonization.

Unlike Fanon, however, Glissant does not assert that homosexuality is impossible outside of an Oedipal kinship structure. In one passage, he even refers to female homosexuality as a rather positive indication of resistance to *machisme* and as a logical consequence of the matrifocal tendencies of the Caribbean family (298). Like Hocquenghem before him, therefore, Glissant explores the possibility of a homosexual desire decoupled from Oedipus. Furthermore, following Glissant's argument, one might say that, in the mangrovelike family trees of the Caribbean, Oedipus can only get bogged down where he can do no harm. Furthermore, in spite of the Oedipal structure inherent in the articulation of Créolité's descent, Oedipus gets lost in the Créolistes' fiction as well. Unlike the *major*, the *nègmawon*, and even the *makoumè*, Oedipus is not a Créoliste character.

Even if Confiant seems to get the upper hand over his *major* characters, however, the insult *makoumè* also comes back to him in *L'allée des soupirs* through the character of Jacquou Chartier. Chartier clearly verbalizes the theories of Créolité; he praises the Creole language (206), criticizes Césaire (209–10), and proclaims, "La Martinique est un grand pays parce qu'elle est diverselle" (149) [Martinique is a great country because it is diversal.] (*Diversel* is obtained by combining the French adjectives for *diverse* and *universal.* Taking their cue from Glissant, Confiant implies with this neologism that an anti-essentialist notion of diversity is a universal value.) Chartier is even writing a novel that strangely resembles those of Confiant (264). Yet his name associates him more with the European colonization of the New World than with the Creolization that occurred once the Caribbean was populated with people with diverse origins. He is also a Blanc-France, a European-born Frenchman whom none of the locals understands. When he speaks French, women faint, and he defends Créolité while people are being shot in the street. As J. Michael Dash writes, "In Chartier's incessant babbling, all the main ideas of créolité are parodied" (122). In one scene, he is even subjected to a litany of insults not unlike those in which other characters are called *makoumè*:

> D'après Mathilde, il fallait à tout prix dérisionner l'habitude qu'avait Chartier de parler comme un perroquet-répéteur : Un soir plein de fraîcheur, on se réunit donc place de l'Abbé Grégoire et l'on mit son intelligence en commun afin de le sobriqueter. Chacun eut son mot à proposer que l'on examina avec le plus grand soin : blablateur (la logeuse de monsieur Jean), jaspineur (la mère-maquerelle), hâbleur (la

pacotilleuse), baragouineur (Jojo Coiffeur), bavardeur (Ziguinote), paroleur (Ho-Chen-Sang, dit Chine), jargonneur (le Syrien Mehdi Aboubaker . . .), jacoteur (Bec-en-Or), bagoulard (Siméon, le fils de la logeuse de monsieur Jean), brimborioneur (Ancinelle Bertrand), plaidoyeur (Cicéron . . .) et puis clapotier, caquetier, et des mots par grappes, des dévalaisons de mots à dormir dehors—car le Martiniquais est un grand fabriqueur de mots, oui ! (212)

[According to Mathilde, we had to mock at all costs Chartier's habit of talking like a miming parrot, so one cool evening, we got together at L'Abbé Grégoire Square, and we pooled our intelligence so we could nickname him. Each person had a word to propose, which we examined with the greatest care: blablabla (Mr. Jean's tenant), chatterbox (the brothel madam), talker (the odds-and-ends seller), yack-yack (Jojo the Hairdresser), babbler (Ziguinote), windbag (Ho-Cheng-Sang, aka China), jiver (the Syrian Mehdi Aboubaker), driveler (Bec-en-Or), prattler (Siméon, Mr. Jean's tenant's son), gibber-jabberer (Ancinelle Bertrand), whiner (Cicéron . . .), and then twaddler, cackler, and words by the bunches, an avalanche of words that would put you to sleep—because Martiniquans are great word manufacturers, yes they are!]

In this passage, a long list of Creole characters ridicule the white Créoliste, and it would be difficult not to read this critique as somehow affecting the real-life Créoliste writers as well. By Confiant's own admission, it is the Créoliste writer (in Chartier) who has most thoroughly assimilated the psychological paradigms of the colonizer. If, in the same novel, Romule Casoar and the hotel boss are treated as *makoumè* because of their behavior, what are we to think of Chartier and through him the Créolistes? Are they not likewise implicitly accused of bending over for the colonizer?

While Bec-en-Or may accuse Césaire of bending over for the French in *L'allée des soupirs*, in Chamoiseau's *Chronique des sept misères*, the character similarly accused embraces a cultural politics that are considerably more ambiguous. In this portrait of the lives of the *djobeurs* (odd-jobs men for hire at the Fort-de-France market), the protagonist and head *djobeur* Pierre Philomène, nicknamed Pipi, is accused of being a *makoumè*:

Quelques gens du marché lui demandaient s'il n'était pas devenu macoumê (homosexuel). Sans rire de la blague, Pipi se réfugiait dans une gravité raide et murmurait en s'en allant : Congos, Bambaras, Mandingues, tous fils d'Afrique . . . (149; Chamoiseau's ellipsis)

[Several folks from the market asked him whether he had become a *makoumè*, or homosexual. Without laughing at the joke, Pipi sought refuge in a somber rigidity and mumbled as he walked away, "Bakongo, Bambara, Mandingo, all sons of Africa . . ."]

A quick glance at this passage might lead one to believe that Pipi responds to one insult (*makoumè*) with another (*nèg Kongo*).[27] Carefully contextualizing this passage, however, leads to another reading. The *djobeurs* are disappearing as a result of economic transformations brought about by departmentalization. (Césaire proposed the law that turned French Caribbean territories into *départements* in 1946.) Pipi is thus a Creole archetype and hero, and like the *djobeurs* he literally disappears from the marketplace (in the end, he is never heard from again) as he spends more and more time in search of the gold of a former master who killed the slave who helped him bury it. Afoukal, the ghost/zombi of that slave, guards the treasure, speaks to Pipi in dreams after being dug up, and becomes Pipi's connection with his past, his history, and therefore his identity rooted in that history.

Pipi's regular visits to Afoukal and his subsequent deep meditations on the African past lead those who know him to confuse his distraction with the behavior of a *makoumè*. Instead of responding to this epithet with more insults, he escapes into a reflection on the history of slavery; the word *Congo* is uttered not to label his detractors but to list the peoples deported from Africa to the Caribbean, peoples with whom he establishes a family tree (tous fils d'Afrique). Pipi is thus protected from the insult *makoumè* by embracing his Négritude. While at first it may seem that Afoukal leads Pipi back to *African* roots, when Pipi wants to "return" to Africa the zombi laughs at him and tells him that this is impossible. Although Pipi is a victim of Césaire's politics, he is temporarily "duped" (from the Créoliste point of view) by Césaire's cultural ideology (Négritude), which Confiant has argued is intertwined with his politics. Yet the tensions between Créolité and Négritude are never resolved for Pipi. Though treated as a *makoumè*, Pipi is unfazed and thus is an anti-*major*; and it is unclear whether Créolité or Négritude makes his masculinity immune to such attacks (although on one occasion he is practically reduced to a state of hysteria upon meeting Césaire and being addressed by him in French). Perhaps, rather, it is the symbiotic relation between Créolité and Négritude that leads Pipi to reject the call to a violent masculinity implied in the epithet. The critique of Négritude is thus much more ambivalent here than in the Créolistes' nonfiction writings.

Yet, rather than argue that these blind spots represent a shortcoming in the Créolité model, I would argue that the Créolistes' complex reliance on a genealogical notion of filiation, yet also an almost Oedipal revolt against the forefathers acknowledged through this genealogy, might best be visualized as the roots of the mangrove, where Pipi is surprised to wake up one morning and whose image has been deployed by the writers of all three movements, Négritude, Antillanité, and Créolité. Even Aimé Césaire deployed the image of the mangrove in the service of Négritude. More specifically, his collection of poems *moi, laminaire...* contains two poems, "Mangrove" and "La condition-mangrove" [The Mangrove Condition], in which the mangrove figures prominently (*Poésie* 9, 30). Although Richard D. E. Burton has argued that "the mangrove frequently suggests torpor and stagnation in Césaire's poetry" ("*Ki moun*" 29n11), Césaire counters (in advance), "La mangrove respire" [The Mangrove Breathes] (30). To use the title of a poem by Césaire, identity, according to this model, is a "condition-mangrove." The mangrove in Césaire's poetry also serves as a reminder of the line from the *Cahier d'un retour au pays natal*, forgotten by so many of those who accuse Césaire of being an essentialist: "[M]a négritude n'est pas une pierre" (46) [My negritude is not a stone (35)]. Négritude had its anti-essentialist tendencies all along; both Antillanité and Créolité have developed these, reflected on them, and strengthened them. J. Michael Dash has described Chamoiseau's *Solibo Magnifique* as "a better manifesto of the créolité movement than the polemical *Éloge de la Créolité*" (12), and one might generalize this statement to include other Chamoiseau novels and perhaps those of Confiant as well. Pipi certainly demonstrates the complexity of Créolité's relation to Négritude better than the *Éloge* or Confiant's and Bernabé's essays on Césaire. In comparison with the *Éloge*, Pipi embodies an alternative genealogy, one not structured by Oedipal conflicts between father and sons and in which the term *makoumè* loses its role of enforcing masculinity through violence.

Créolité becomes even more accepting of nonnormative sexualities in Confiant's *Le nègre et l'amiral* after Amédée's praise of the Creole word *coucoune* (quoted above). This passage leads to a reflection on a conversation with his intellectual friend Dalmeida:

Dans les moments fusionnels de l'amour créole, je mets enfin un sens sur les propos de Dalmeida se méfiant de la valorisation excessive de la race noire par les jeunes intellectuels martiniquais.

"Être créole, me disait-il, c'est être une manière de compromis entre le Blanc et le Noir, entre le Noir et l'Indien, entre l'Indien et le bâtard-Chinois ou le Syrien. Au fond, que sommes-nous d'autre que des bâtards ? Et bien revendiquons notre bâtardise comme un honneur et ne recherchons pas, à l'instar des békés, des ancêtres héroïques dans une Guinée de chimère ou dans l'Inde éternelle. Voyez-vous, mon cher Amédée, tout ce mélange a produit une race nouvelle, une langue neuve, souple, serpentine, tout en étant conviviale et charnelle. Je suis trop vieux pour espérer voir le jour où notre peuple se dressera face au monde dans sa créolité. . . ." (127–28; Confiant's ellipsis)

[. . . I finally understood what Dalmeida said in suspicion of the excessive valorization of the black race by young Martiniquan intellectuals.

"To be Creole," he told me, "is a sort of compromise between White and Black, between Black and Indian, between Indian and mongrel Chinese or Syrian. In fact, what are we if we're not bastards/mongrels? So let's reclaim our bastard/mongrel nature as an honor and let us not seek, following the honky's example, ancestors in an imaginary Africa or eternal India. You see, dear Amédée, all this mixing has produced a new race, a brand new language, one that is supple and serpentine all the while being convivial and sensual. I'm too old to hope to see the day when our people will stand up to the world by affirming their Creoleness . . ."]

In this simultaneous critique of Négritude and praise of Creoleness, the descent of Créolité's intellectual genealogy spills out of western kinship structures altogether, first by separating the roles of pater and genitor (combined in the person of the father in nuclear families). (A less euphemistic description would acknowledge that the "father" is treated here as a cuckold.) While the family romance (a fantasy involving, among other things, denying the paternity of one's father) is not incompatible with an Oedipal family structure, this passage does more than deny the very paternity that is affirmed in the *Éloge*. More than inventing an alternative set of nuclear parents, this passage multiplies lines of descent; more than replacing one family tree with another, it proposes a mangrove.

Furthermore, as another kind of *Créoliste avant la lettre* (because he articulates his Créolité in the 1940s), Dalmeida stands out even more than Jacquou Chartier. This perfectly tailored character (92) is quite a dandy (101) and one of ambiguous race at that. In this Dalmeida is truly unique as a Créoliste character. Although Créoliste novels celebrate the racial diversity of the Caribbean, their usual mode of doing so involves carefully cataloging their characters' racial affiliation through such labels as *chabin, échappé-couli, câpresse,* and so on. Dalmeida has tried to convince Amédée to stop hanging out in Morne Pichevin, a kind of slumming that, in addition to bringing Amédée into solidarity with the most disfavored classes of Fort-de-France, also leads him to bond with its most supermale inhabitants. Furthermore, Dalmeida has taught Alcide (a fellow teacher and resistance comrade of Amédée's) how to abstain from sexual relations with women (91). Though not labeled a *makoumè*, Dalmeida is certainly not a supermale, and we might even say that his ambiguous race parallels an ambiguous sexuality. Yet he articulates a cultural position that is most indicative of the Créolistes'. Since the *makoumè* may be a heterosexual misconception of homosexuality, the fact that Dalmeida is not called a *makoumè* may be one indication of his queerness. (Murray carefully points out that the term *makoumè* is not used by homosexual men in Martinique to label themselves; rather they prefer the term *branché,* which in Metropolitan French means "hip," or "in the know." Murray also describes scenes of violent reaction to being called *makoumè*—such as those written by the Créolistes—among homosexual men.)

Following Dash, then, I suggest that the Créolistes' fiction proposes a much more mangrovelike theorization of Créolité than their so-called theoretical essays do. While they may seem at first glance to hurl *makoumè* as an insult even more vociferously than their most obnoxious *major* characters, on closer examination their representations of *makoumè* are rich with the possibility of challenging the very masculinity that many readings have accused the Créolistes of glorifying. In *Lettres créoles* (1991), Chamoiseau and Confiant write, "Dans la culture créole chaque Moi contient une part ouverte des Autres, et au bordage de chaque Moi se maintient frisonnante la part d'opacité irréductible des Autres" (51) [In Creole culture, each Self contains an open portion of the Other, and on the border of each Self, the Other's portion of opacity stands shivering from excitement]. This admittedly very male Creole self or subject (*Moi*) might therefore be read as being more open to his sexual other, the *makoumè,* than has been assumed. Perhaps, then, the many passages considered above produce similar states of excitement on the part of their Créoliste writers, for whom contact with the *makoumè* results in a distinctly sexual frisson. In short, instead of rejecting the African roots with which Négritude sought to ground black identity as the Créolistes frequently claim in their essays, manifestos, and interviews, Créoliste fiction, like Condé's writing in general, may be read as queering them.

CHAPTER 2

Queer Roots in Africa

✦ ✦ ✦

In the previous chapter, I focused more on the literary and discursive implications of resisting a politics of purity through articulations of identity modeled on the mangrove than on the political implications of such a discursive strategy. Nonetheless, the political is never far removed from these questions. In the Caribbean, François Duvalier used *noirisme* to buttress his dictatorship in Haiti. In Zaïre, as it was then called, Mobutu Sese Seko used a similar return to African authenticity in the 1970s to justify attempts to homogenize Zaïrean identity and thereby maintain his totalitarian regime. After the organization Gays and Lesbians of Zimbabwe (GALZ) was barred from participating in its country's international book fair in 1995, Zimbabwean president Robert Mugabe became well known for his discursive attacks on lesbians and gay men, whom he described as being "worse than dogs and pigs" (cited in Phillips, "Zimbabwe" 52). In his New Year's 2000 address, Mugabe stated, "We cannot have a man marrying a man or a woman marrying a woman here. What an abomination, a rottenness of culture, real decadence of culture. Once you impose a foreign culture on us then you naturally evoke the devil in us" ("Zimbabwe's Mugabe").

That there is no such thing as homosexuality in Africa is a common cliché of certain African nationalist discourses. According to this argument, any manifestation of homosexuality would be the result of a colonial imposition of foreign practices (as Mugabe suggests). The cliché might be considered partially valid if homosexuality were understood in a strictly Foucauldian sense as a modern phenomenon of industrial societies. In this case, it is true that homosexuality "as we know it today" first appeared in western countries. The cliché is rarely understood as such, however, because such a use of the term should also argue that heterosexuality as well is a western phenomenon and has been equally imposed on Africa. Arguments such as Mugabe's, therefore, fail to acknowledge how they themselves also reproduce a fully colonial discourse, a homophobic discourse that troped Africans as possessing a bestial sexuality, even as it claimed that Africa was not bound by the fetters of civilization (as Europe was) and had thus maintained a state of natural purity (see Epprecht, *Heterosexual Africa?*). As Neville Hoad writes, "President Mugabe is obviously less worried about Western cultural imperialism when he puts on a suit and tie in the morning, and no one accuses monogamous heterosexuality of being a decadent Western import (which, given the historical polygamy of many sub-Saharan African societies, it clearly is)" (*African Intimacies* 73). In addition, the Foucauldian argument concerning the modern construction of homosexuality in no way means that no sexual activity previously occurred between members of the same sex. Yet anti-homosexual postindependence rulers distort a constructionist logic in this way to consolidate their own power by claiming to represent a return to precolonial roots that would resurrect an African authenticity free of European influence. In contrast, however, a number of African writers narrate alternative returns to African roots, ones that uncover same-sex sexual practices that colonial powers attempted to eradicate and postindependence elites have attempted to deny and, sometimes, following the lead of their colonial predecessors, even annihilate.

The effects of troping same-sex sexual practices as foreign or imposed by colonialism are not limited to the discursive level of political speeches but also translate into a very physical violence deployed against many Africans today. On 30 October 1999, while Mugabe was traveling in England for personal reasons, OutRage!, a British gay activist group, performed a citizen's arrest and demanded that the British government try him for torture. When charges were dropped against the "arresting officers," Mugabe accused the Blair government of "using gangster gays" (Mogale) to carry out its neocolonial policies. In a letter to Blair, one of the arresting members, Peter Tatchell, claimed, "Since his inflammatory comments, homosexuals in Zimbabwe have been beaten, arrested, framed on trumped up charges, fire bombed and threatened with death." After the incident, GALZ's statement concerning the "citizen's arrest" stated that, "though GALZ had no prior knowledge of Out-

rage's intention to arrest President Mugabe and did not order it, innocent black gay men [in Zimbabwe] have been targeted for revenge. . . .
[O]ne man was threatened and falsely arrested and imprisoned; another
was beaten and insulted by two plain-clothes policemen. Both were blamed
for the humiliation of the President in London even though it was clear
that neither of them had any knowledge of the incident" (Goddard).[1]

In his attempt to hold on to power, then, Mugabe has resorted to
homophobic violence in a supposedly anticolonial campaign to rid
Zimbabwe of all that is foreign.[2] Likewise, his support of black squatters
occupying white-owned farms has used an anticolonial discourse to mask
antidemocratic moves (Swarns, "Mugabe's Real Foes"). Although squatters have voiced quite legitimate demands,[3] one of the greatest obstacles
to land reform has been Mugabe himself, who has been promising it
since 1980, particularly at election time. Previous redistributions were
too modest, did not succeed because of a lack of follow-up support, or
gave land to Mugabe's supporters and political associates. Britain (as well
as other donors) has subsequently used such cronyism as an excuse to
withhold compensation to white farmers for land that was stolen from
blacks during British colonial rule. In addition, Mugabe seized on the climate created by the land seizures to intimidate his political opponents;
in the period leading up to the June 2000 parliamentary elections, at
least twenty-six people were killed, mostly members of the opposition
(Swarns, "Political Shift") in a cycle that would continue throughout the
presidential elections of 2001.[4] A similar cycle of violence accompanied
the 2008 elections, when the opposition party of Morgan Tsvangirai won
the general elections. Upon winning the first round of the presidential
elections, Tsvangirai was forced to withdraw after the murder of at least
two hundred of his party supporters. Since 2009 Mugabe has been in
a power-sharing agreement with Tsvangirai as prime minister.[5] To date,
however, this agreement has not resulted in a significant loosening of
Mugabe's hold on power. The economy is still in shambles, and the racial
divide in landownership persists in spite of continued invasions of white-
owned farms. Yet his reign of political terror has eased somewhat, at least
for now.[6]

Male Wives and Female Husbands

Even if one confines oneself to a Zimbabwean context, Mugabe's claim
that same-sex sexual behavior, desires, and institutions are not indig-

enous to Africa is not borne out by ethnographic literature. Paradoxically, Mugabe has chosen same-sex marriage as the target of his diatribe, a practice that traditionally exists in many African societies. In Zimbabwe itself, there is a tradition of a "heterosexual type of temporary marriage known in chiShona as *mapoto*."[7] A cross-generational version of this practice among men is known as the *ngotshana*.[8] Marriage between women has a long tradition in many societies in all regions of Africa; Denise O'Brien states that it occurs in "over 30 African populations" (109). It can be undertaken for a number of reasons and varies from society to society. Krige defines it as "the institution by which it is possible for a woman to give bridewealth for, and marry, a woman over whom and whose offspring she has full control, delegating to a male genitor the duties of procreation" (11). Such marriages thus imply that the "wife" will take on male lovers so as to provide children for the female husband. O'Brien distinguishes between the "surrogate female husband . . . who acts as a substitute for a male kinsman in order to provide heirs for his agnatic lineage" (112) and the "autonomous female husband . . . who is always pater to children borne by her wife or wives" (113). For example, in the first case, the daughter of a sonless father may contract a marriage to ensure the continuation of the patrilineage. Some marriages of the second type are undertaken to ensure a powerful or wealthy woman's independence or her control over her or her father's property. Barrenness may also be a factor in the second case, in addition to "a desire to improve or maintain her own status socially (by becoming a father), economically, or politically" (113). Political motivations become most evident when female rulers take on one or more wives. In some cases, the "husband" in a woman-woman marriage may also be married to a man. In addition to woman-woman marriages, male-male marriages are not uncommon (see Evans-Pritchard). Perhaps the best-known example is that of men who take boy-wives in southern African mining communities. So, although Mugabe incorporates a diatribe against same-sex marriage into his attacks on lesbian and gay Zimbabweans, perhaps nowhere else on earth is there a stronger tradition of same-sex marriages than in Africa.

In the case of woman-woman marriages, however, ethnographers have gone out of their way to deny any lesbian implications, in spite of suggestions to the contrary by an earlier commentator on the institution, Melville J. Herskovits (1937). According to him, woman marriage in Dahomey "does not imply a homosexual relationship between 'husband' and 'wife,' though it is not to be doubted that occasionally homo-

sexual women who have inherited wealth or have prospered economically establish compounds of their own and at the same time utilize the
relationship in which they stand to the women whom they 'marry' to
satisfy themselves" ("Note" 338). Since Herskovits wrote these lines, he
has been criticized for not substantiating his claims. Krige argued, for
example, that "Herskovits imputed to it sexual overtones that are foreign
to the institution" (11). In contrast, Carrier and Murray have questioned
these criticisms of Herskovits: "A careful reading of Herskovits, however,
shows that Krige, O'Brien, and Obbo exaggerate his remarks" (264).[9]
They point out that in his later book-length study, *Dahomey: An Ancient
West African Kingdom* (1938), Herskovits provided evidence of female
homosexuality in other contexts: "Given the broader context of Daho-
mean sexual behavior, no great leap of the imagination is required to
suggest, as did Herskovits, that some of the females involved in woman-
woman marriage in Dahomey might also use the relationship as a means
of obtaining sexual satisfaction" (Carrier and Murray 265). They also
point out that "no one questions whether men and women in manda-
tory, arranged marriages have or desire sex with each other or, indeed,
even 'prefer' the opposite sex in general" (266). Indeed, Krige's association of the foreign with homosexuality reiterates the tropes of homophobic nationalism. When she writes that "woman-marriage is no aberrant,
quaint custom[, n]or has it any sexual connotation for the two women
concerned" (34), whereas she seems to criticize ethnographers who
romanticize the institution by imposing their own Eurocentric bias, it is
actually she who reveals a western bias by writing of "the two women concerned" even though her own research shows that woman-woman marriage is often polygamous. Furthermore, Evans-Pritchard suggests that,
even in polygamous marriages with male husbands, women are able to
negotiate patriarchal institutions so as to create the possibility of having
sexual relations among themselves.[10]

Toward a Queer Interdisciplinarity

The debate between Herskovits and his detractors, however, is an important reminder as to why ethnography alone, though quite adequate for
pointing out the fallacies of political discourses such as Mugabe's, is not
sufficient to queer Afrocentric, US black nationalist, or African nationalist discourses. Indeed, pointing out the queerness of Africa is hardly new;
both Christian and "scientific" discourses postulated Africans' sexuality,

perverse by European standards, as a sign of their primitiveness. It was therefore the "white man's burden" to civilize them and convert them to the missionary position. Ethnographers such as Herskovits, who pay special attention to "queer" African sexualities, might thus be seen as following in this tradition. Yet many critiques of this parallel to orientalism in western discourses on Africa silence Africans with nonnormative sexualities.[11] African literatures nonetheless offer a great diversity of cultural representations of same-sex desires, eroticisms, and sexual acts. To engage with them, however, I suggest that one must look beyond literary studies altogether to such fields as anthropology and history.

The importance of reading African literature alongside anthropology is a major part of Christopher L. Miller's key argument in *Theories of Africans: Francophone Literature and Anthropology in Africa* (1990): "[A] fair Western reading of African literatures demands engagement with, and even dependence on, anthropology" (4). I have engaged at length elsewhere with this argument, often by pointing out that history, particularly in the kinds of allegorical readings of African novels I tend to articulate, can be just as important as anthropology (if not more so). I have also pointed out that, especially since the 1960s, African literature has often had an antagonistic relation with anthropology, even resisting the ethnographic gaze of western readers (*Queer Nations* 266–77). But Miller is far from articulating an uncritical embrace of anthropological readings of African literature: "This is not intended to place anthropology in a position of dominance or let it block out other concerns, which I hope will find adequate attention here. Rather my desire is to blend disciplines together in a hybrid approach befitting the complexity of cultural questions in Africa and their translation into Western understanding" (5). In other words, Miller is far from arguing that anthropology should be the *only* other disciplinary discourse considered in relation to African literature, or even the most important one.

Furthermore, when Miller asserts that he will "be trying to fill a gap" (5), he is referring to a lacuna in African literary studies, but we might also consider the gaps that remain even after interdisciplinary encounters in literary criticism. Likewise, in *African Intimacies: Race, Homosexuality, Globalization* (2007), Neville Hoad outlines the potential contribution of literary studies to interdisciplinary approaches to African studies: "[I]maginative fiction, as a site for investigation of questions of race, sex, and decolonization, is useful for me because it allows the horizons of the imaginable to become visible. In fiction, one can find an archive for the complex lived and felt experience of never completely determining social abstractions" (22). Hoad's model, "in which readers may work to being othered by the text by watching their enabling abstractions and assumptions come under pressure" (22), as I suggest throughout this chapter, allows for literature to fill in gaps left in the study of African cultures in other disciplines. It elaborates on the importance that Miller already accords to close reading in both theory (in terms of his paradigm of reading) and practice (his own readings of African literary texts). Indeed, if we take Miller's reading of Camara Laye's *L'enfant noir* as exemplary of his reading practice, it becomes clear that he just as often uses literary texts to challenge anthropological models (as well as psychoanalytic ones based on anthropology, e.g., Freud's understanding of totemism).

Such reading into the gaps, or between the lines, may be related to an important essay in postcolonial theory. In "Can the Subaltern Speak?"—about the ways Indian women have been silenced in both British and male Indian writings on *sati*, or widow immolation—Gayatri Chakravorty Spivak writes, "Part of our 'unlearning' project is to articulate that ideological formation—by *measuring* silences, if necessary—into the *object* of investigation" (296). Simply attempting to speak for those who have been silenced does not necessarily eliminate the silences; as some ethnographic literature demonstrates, speaking openly about homosexual acts may create other silences regarding the colonial relation between ethnographer and informants. One way to measure silences, I would suggest, is to stage a conversation between the various discourses on African homosexualities to allow their different silences to be mismatched and thrown out of whack in order to challenge one another. Such a conversation would not combine these discourses to fill in their silences or gaps, so to speak, for these discourses cannot be said to fit together like a puzzle in any sense. Their overlaps will produce contradictions, which present even further complications, but it is precisely into these complications, into the fissures that reading one discourse against the others can reveal, that queer roots might be able to wedge themselves, further disrupting official discourses on African identity such as Mugabe's.

First of all, one reason why ethnographic studies of "homosexualities" specific to African societies rarely match up neatly with literary representations is that anthropologists and novelists frequently seem to be interested in totally different phenomena. When anthropology and literature do manage to be on the same page, the former often consists of an outdated, descriptive ethnography of the sort that has come under question within anthropology's self-critique of the past several decades. And as part of a general trend toward challenging the ethnographic gaze of the western reader since the 1960s, African novels also frequently question any totalizing differences between western and African sexualities of the sort an older anthropology might emphasize. I, however, have come to view such mismatches as blessings in disguise, since they force us to reflect on the role of literary criticism in interdisciplinary approaches to the study of sexuality.

Second, interdisciplinary approaches to literary studies often turn literature into a mere illustration of the theories produced by other discourses; what are supposed to be the "primary" sources (i.e., literary works) are thus considered inadequate as pre-texts for theorizing in and of themselves. Paradoxically, the "secondary" texts are treated as more primary than the primary ones, which are thereby devalorized. In such approaches, literary critics often demean the object of study specific to their field and relinquish what, as Hoad suggests, is potentially their greatest contribution to the interdisciplinary encounter: the ability to read carefully and critically between the lines. I have thus come to see the gaps between various disciplinary discourses as a far more interesting object of study than what obtains when "other" disciplines are used as master discourses that might explain literary passages whose meaning is treated as elusive. Another contribution literary critics can make to interdisciplinarity is extending their skill in reading between the lines to read between the disciplines that get together in interdisciplinary approaches to sexuality. Such a reading between the disciplines also encourages a theorization of interdisciplinarity in which all disciplines called on are allowed to challenge and question one another. In this understanding of interdisciplinary analysis, the interdisciplinary influence goes both ways. History and anthropology, say, are not just consulted to elucidate literature; literature is also allowed to reflect on the disciplinary constraints of other fields.

An unlikely candidate for an alternate discourse on African homosexuality (as least as far as scholarly inquiry is concerned) is a discussion of homosexuality by an African newsgroup (afrique@univ-lyon1.fr) around the time of GALZ's exclusion from its country's book fair. A number of participants discussed Mugabe's remarks, and some even used his remarks as evidence of the dictatorial aspect of his regime. This discussion demonstrates how cultural codes and *idées reçues* concerning the supposed nonexistence of African homosexuality can filter into informal, semiacademic discussions. The Internet provides an interesting window onto such discussions because it facilitates "conversations" that might not otherwise occur due to geographic distance. (Indeed, although the newsgroup was centered in Lyon, the discussants partici- pated from university sites in the United States, Canada, Belgium, Ger- many, Switzerland, and elsewhere in France.) In addition, unlike face- to-face conversations, e-mail discussions leave "written" traces.[12] Using a newsgroup discussion as a cultural text creates its own interpretive dif- ficulties, such as the danger of turning participants into "native infor- mants" or overestimating what such texts can tell us about homosexuality in Africa. While most of the participants (though not all) have (or at least use) African names, they were by definition limited to a certain class of Africans (living in the metropolis) whose economic situation (fairly privileged, especially at that time) allowed them access to computers. This does not imply that their views are any more or less "authentic" (itself a problematic category) than those of the "typical villager" (also problematic), who is often assumed to be the best "native informant" by a more conventional anthropological discourse. As will become clear below, discussants held a wide variety of positions from the denial of African homosexuality to its affirmation.

One discussant writes, "Yes, there have been homosexuals in Africa since colonization. This practice is imported."[13] A respondent adds, "I don't see what this discussion on homosexuality is doing in an African newsgroup. Homosexuality or pederasty or the gay lifestyle, whatever you choose to call it, is essentially a white problem."[14] Similar clichés of a heterosexual African purity appear in Camara Laye's 1966 novel *Dra- mouss* [*A Dream of Africa*] during an exchange between Fatomane (the narrator) and Liliane (a Frenchwoman) about a Frenchman who has just made a pass at him:

—Mais tu as peur, ma parole ! . . . Tu ne sais pas que cet homme est un p . . . ?

Et elle m'expliqua longuement ce que ce mot signifiait.

—Ah ça, non ! protestai-je. Il n'y a pas de cela dans mon pays. Là- bas, un homme est fait pour vivre avec une femme. Un homme est fait pour se marier et pour avoir des enfants.

—Tu ne nous connaîtras jamais assez, toi ! dit-elle. Nous avons des vices, ici ! Vous êtes purs, vous, les Africains. Vous ignorez les artifices et les perversions. C'est bien mieux ainsi. (82; Camara's ellipses)

["My! You're really frightened, aren't you! . . . Don't you know he's queer?"

And she then gave me a lengthy explanation about what that word meant.

"Oh, no!" I protested. "There's nothing like that goes on in my country. Out there, a man is made to live with a woman. A man is supposed to marry in order to produce children."

"You'll never get the hang of things here!" she said. "We all have our vices over here! You Africans are pure. You know nothing about our tricks and perversions. So much the better, too." (64)]

Yet it is also in the newsgroup discussion that one can find a refutation of Fatomane's argument. One discussant calmly points out the political implications of the assertion that no "authentic" African homosexuality existed prior to colonization:

> The debate on homosexuality reveals in certain people a stubborn attempt to hold onto a pure image of precolonial Africa and even of contemporary Africa. I'm sorry but this can quite simply only be due to a lack of anthropological and sociological knowledge of current and previous realities in Africa. The way some approach homosexuality reminds me of the polemic that the origin of the AIDS virus set off . . .
>
> It's useless to try to maintain at any cost a falsely pure image of a mythical Africa, which only exists in the heads of a few dreamers in our times.
>
> This false image of Africa is transmitted by Africans who cannot yet tell the difference between the continent's actual characteristics before the conquerors' arrival and what they left us.
>
> So before anyone begins to attack homosexuals, let's seriously verify whether this behavior is African or imported. In fact, the anthropological literature shows that this behavior is not only present among westerners. It is present in a number of Latin American and African societies.
>
> Contemporary Africa is the product of numerous cultural *métissages* both internal and external. From this point of view, it is currently difficult to hold onto a discourse that maintains a pure image of Africa.[15]

He thus challenges notions of an African essence that resists change and cross-cultural pollination. Such a notion of African purity would in fact merely reproduce colonial stereotypes of primitiveness. When read closely, the passage from *Dramouss* also contextualizes the nationalist denial of the existence of "authentic" African homosexualities; while Fatomane reproduces a homophobic discourse of homosexuality as a crime against nature, Camara himself places the image of a pure Africa in the response of a Frenchwoman (representative of the former colonizer). Both characters, however, reinforce the notion that Africa is purer and closer to nature (i.e., more primitive) than Europe, although the Frenchwoman is certainly more infantilizing in her characterization of African purity.

Although many African novels reproduce the politics of purity exemplified by Mugabe, a number of other sub-Saharan novelists return to African roots in order to queer them. Their representations of African "traditions" are remarkably inclusive, and the heterogeneity they discover in precolonial origins also includes sexual diversity. In this way, literature constitutes another discourse that might help us measure the silences around homosexuality in Africa. For literary representations and their referents are often in self-consciously complex relationships with one another. This is not to say that such complexity never obtains in ethnography, but ethnography has traditionally claimed to provide an accurate representation of its referents. Reading literature *against* ethnography, then, can help to emphasize the fact that ethnography, like literature, is often engaged in the writing of fiction. It is precisely in literature that the silences to which Spivak refers become laden with meaning. As we have seen, history, as it contextualizes representations of sexuality (or its denial) with respect to colonialism, is also crucial to an interdisciplinary project of reading various discourses on African homosexualities against each other. But, as history is always already *written* and constantly in the process of being *re*written, examples of the (mis)use of history to justify violence abound. Again, literature, self-conscious of its writtenness and imaginative possibilities, also offers ways to reread history that can sometimes draw attention to the silences left in both colonial and anticolonial versions of the same events. In spite of my stake in the discipline of literary criticism, however, I shall not propose literature as a panacea for the colonial ills of other discourses; literary criticism, as we shall also see, has its own history of fabricating silences.

Men-Women in Senegal

One of the arguments often used to disclaim an indigenous African homosexuality is that no word exists in African languages for same-sex sexual behaviors. One member of the newsgroup wrote, "I'm basing myself on, among other things, the absence of any 'African' term designating homosexuality. In addition, among all of my acquaintances, there isn't a single member of my tribe who practices homosexuality. This practice is exclusively urban in Africa; it is an imported practice."[16] This argument blatantly contradicts all the anthropological literature. Murray and Roscoe list seventy-seven such terms (279–82), including the Wolof term *gôr-diguen* (as they spell it), which also occurs in *Le baobab fou* [*The Abandoned Baobab*] by Ken Bugul (1984).[17] When Ken, the narrator/protagonist studying in Europe, meets and moves in with a Belgian homosexual, Jean Wermer, instead of asserting the uniquely western nature of same-sex desire, she compares western homosexuality to a Wolof practice:

> Je savais que les homosexuels existaient, il y en avait dans mon pays. J'avais eu moi-même un esclave homosexuel hérité de longue tradition. "*Gor Djigen*," on l'appelait ainsi. Cela restait abstrait pour moi. Mais Jean Wermer avait été marié, avait des enfants, et n'avait pas les manières des Gor-Djigen. (72)

> [I knew there were homosexuals, we had them in my country. I myself had had a homosexual slave, inherited from long tradition. "Gor Djigen" they called him. It had always remained an abstract idea for me. But Jean Wermer had been married, had children, and he didn't act like the Gor Djigens. (58)]

In this passage, Ken returns, figuratively, to the village where she was born and grew up (and therefore to her roots) to make a cross-cultural comparison that brings out similarities, as well as differences, between African and European same-sex sexual behaviors. She directly contradicts the oft-used argument that there is no word in African languages for homosexuality (and therefore that homosexuality cannot be African), by inserting a Wolof term for men who, if not exactly like European homosexuals, are at least comparable in her opinion. Furthermore, whereas constructionist accounts of the uniqueness of western homosexuality often rely on its supposed exclusiveness, in this passage it is the *gôr-djiguen* who is exclusively homosexual and the western homosexual who is not (because he was once married). Bugul thus disrupts the clichés of western homosexuality as exceptional and reliant on a nonwestern and/or precontemporary Other.

Several Europeans have mentioned the *gôr-djiguen* in their accounts of their travels in West Africa. In *Africa Dances: A Book about West African Negroes* (1935), for example, Geoffrey Gorer observes:

> It is said that homosexuality is recent among the Wolof, at any rate in any frequency; but it now receives, and has for some years received, such extremely august and almost publicly exhibited patronage, that pathics are a common sight. They are called in Wolof men-women, gor-digen, and do their best to deserve the epithet by their mannerisms, their dress and their make-up; some even dress their hair like women. They do not suffer in any way socially, though the Mohammedans refuse them religious burial; on the contrary they are sought after as the best conversationalists and the best dancers. This phase is usually transitory, finishing with the departure of the European who has been keeping the boy; but a certain number from taste, interest, or for economic reasons continue their practices and there is now quite a large pederastic society. If I am right in ascribing the increase in European homosexuality to a neurotic fear of life and responsibility the conditions of urban life in Africa lead to the prognosis that this society will greatly increase. (36;1935 edition)

Gorer leaves unquestioned the assumption that African homosexuality occurs only in contact with Europeans and that it is a recent phenomenon. In addition, he uses his discussion of African same-sex practices to pathologize European homosexuality. In contrast, however, and perhaps surprisingly, he argues that the *gôr-djiguen* are tolerated in Senegal, perhaps more so than in the Europe of his day.

In *Pagans and Politicians* (1959), Michael Crowder makes similar observations concerning the tolerance of the *gôr-djiguen*:

> [H]omosexuality had a much freer rein [than prostitution], being prevalent amongst Africans, Mauretanians and Europeans alike. In Place Prôtet, the main square of Dakar, young African boys, more often than not Jollofs, could be seen waiting to be picked up. Under the Code Napoleon it is, of course, legal, and in theory presents no problem, though many people are worried by its spread in the city.
>
> Of course, to many of these boys with no work, it is one way of making money. But amongst the Jollofs it seems to be more deeply *rooted*. Contact with Frenchmen in St. Louis, who often preferred

black boys to black mistresses and contact with the Mauretanians may provide an explanation.

Today one can even see Jollof men dressed in women's clothes. I once met one in a small bar outside Dakar. He was obviously pathetically feminine. The Jollof must be used to this since they even have a word for them—Gor-Digen. The elders and faithful Muslims condemn men for this, but it is typical of African tolerance that they are left very much alone by the rest of the people. (68; emphasis added)[18]

Like Gorer, Crowder treats homosexuality as a contagious disease that can only be transmitted by foreigners; rulers like Mugabe are thus far from being the first to make such arguments. Both Gorer and Crowder, in opposition to the Africans they encounter, consider the sight of cross-dressed men to be a pathetic one. One e-mail discussant, Alioune Deme, presumably Senegalese himself, similarly argued in 1995 that there is more tolerance for homosexuality in Senegal than in the West:

In contemporary Senegal, and in contrast with what you might think, homosexuality exists and is more tolerated than in the West. Homosexuals are also transvestites. They are called "man-woman" (Goorjiguen). There is a special, well-liked dish (because it is spicy and very succulent) that carries their name; in fact, this dish is called "Mbaxaal goor-jiguen"; it's a special dish reserved for prestigious guests or for special events. Today, for baptisms, homosexuals are more and more invited by women to do the cooking. They also participate in ceremonies such as marriage.[19]

In its affectionate tone, this discussant's intimate representation of the gôr-djiguen's quotidian integration into Senegalese life provides an important counterpoint to the accounts of these self-styled ethnographers. Whereas the travelers were only able to see public displays of the gôr-djiguen, Deme shows how they can also be integrated into a domestic economy within the home.

In "Homosexuality in Dakar: Is the Bed the Heart of a Sexual Subculture?" (1996), based on research conducted in 1990, Niels Teunis also provides an intimate account of the life of the gordjiguène (as he spells it). His account of this role, however, more recent and *supposedly* more scholarly than those of Gorer and Crowder, is based not on research conducted inside the home but on conversations with patrons in a Dakar bar frequented by men who consider themselves to be gôr-djiguen:

The men whom I met there referred to themselves as *homosexuèles* [*sic*], homosexuals in French (my communication language with them), and *gordjiguène* in Wolof, their own language. . . . The word is used among Senegalese homosexuals and by others, in which case it is meant as an insult. One of the members of the milieu explained to me that one can distinguish two separate groups in the community of *gordjiguène*. First, there are men who play the inserter role in anal intercourse. The other group comprises those who are the insertees. Wolof terms for these groups exist, but they have no French equivalent. The ones who act as inserter are called *yauss*. . . . The insertee men are called *oubi*, which literally means "open". . . . One is either a *yauss* or an *oubi*—changing from one group to the other is not possible. Leon, the man who explained this to me, said that the latter group was composed of what he called "we the women." This included me, too. (160)

Although Teunis is not Senegalese, his informants do not hesitate to apply a Wolof term, with the specifically Senegalese construction of sexuality that it implies, to the ethnographer (whom they did not acknowledge as such).[20] The difference between European and Senegalese constructions of homosexual identities, therefore, does not prevent them—as Ken in Bugul's novel—from translating a European sexual identity into Wolof. In fact, this translation might be read as a countertranslation; whereas usually it is the European ethnographer who translates the "native" culture into a language his European readers will understand, here the "natives" are the ones who translate the ethnographer through a Senegalese concept.

Whereas all the accounts considered above assume that the *gôr-djiguen* is necessarily transgendered, according to Teunis *gôr-djiguen* include not only the "femmes" but also the "butches." In other words, unlike other accounts, though the term refers to a feminized male for Teunis, it can also refer to those who are considered to play the man's role, even though "[m]en considered as *yauss* did not really form a distinguishable group" (160). This is one way Teunis contradicts earlier travel accounts, but in so doing, he also contradicts himself; for later in the article, he writes, "The cultural model of the . . . *gordjiguène* . . . distinguishes between two categories: *yauss* and *oubi*. . . . In practice, the *oubi* identify themselves as *gordjiguène*; *yauss* in general, do not. . . . Those who identify as *gordjiguène*, the *oubi*, come together in a bar. There they recognize each other as fellow *oubi*, and, contrary to the *yauss*, they form a social group" (166–

67). In other words, the *yauss* both are and are not *gôr-djiguen*. Teunis does tell the story of one *yauss* who identifies as a *gôr-djiguen*, but his story is complicated by the fact that, although he was a *yauss* in practice, his "type" was "lightskinned (not white) men, with big chests and huge muscles, like Rambo" (164), who—were he ever to find such a man!—would play the role of the inserter. This example, embedded within Teunis's account, disrupts the generalizations he makes about the mutually exclusive aspects of the two roles and the lack of ambiguity or impermeability of the boundary that separates them. Interestingly (and contra usual expectations), Teunis also discovers that *oubi* can have sex with each other, although it is not considered "sex" but "playing" (165–66). He does not give either the French or the Wolof term for such activity, nor is he able to tell us exactly what it consists of, since he turned down his only opportunity to engage in it!

The major way in which Teunis contradicts both the travel accounts and Deme, is that the former claims that *gôr-djiguen* are not accepted; according to him, the term is one of insult. In *Un chant écarlate* [*Scarlet Song*] (1981), the Senegalese novelist Mariama Bâ also suggests that the *gôr-djiguen* is less tolerated than others suggest:

Dans son nouveau quartier, le couple d'en face avait un fils, un fils bien drôle ! Cet adolescent d'une quinzaine d'années refusait obstinément la compagnie et les jeux des garçons de son âge, pour rechercher la compagnie et les jeux des petites filles ! Bien drôle cet adolescent qui imitait les filles, dans leur allure, leur langage traînant et leurs occupations !

Son père, quand il le surprenait à jacasser parmi les commères, ou à faire mijoter les plats dans les goûters, entrait dans de folles colères, la cravache à la main. En vain.

En vain, sa mère le rasait-elle pour l'enlaidir. On le prendrait pour l'une des fillettes qu'il fréquentait. Il roulait les yeux en parlant. Mais il ne roulait pas que les yeux. Il roulait avec perversité ses hanches et lançait ses fesses en arrière quand il se déplaçait. Dès qu'il était hors de portée du regard de sa mère, il s'entourait d'un pagne et se dandinait.

"Sauf miracle, ce garçonnet deviendrait un 'gôr djiguène' destiné à passer sa vie, accroupi aux pieds d'une courtisane dont il demeurait l'homme de main. Ce serait son rôle de dénicher les amants généreux pour l'entretient coûteux de ce genre de maisonnée. Ce serait à lui d'ordonner les menus des repas. Et il lui arriverait quelquefois d'être préféré à sa patronne . . ."

Yaye Khady plaignait sincèrement la mère de cet échantillon. (106–7; Bâ's ellipsis)

[In their new neighbourhood the couple opposite had a son, a very [odd] youngster! This fifteen-year-old obstinately refused the company and games of boys of his own age and sought the company and games of little girls! A funny sort of boy this was, who modeled his bearing, drawling speech and activities on those of girls!

When his father came upon him, gossiping away with the old women, or cooking up dishes [for afternoon snacks], he went wild with rage and took a whip to him. But to no avail.

It was to no avail that his mother shaved all his hair off to make him ugly. You could still mistake him for one of the little girls he played with. He rolled his eyes as he spoke. And it wasn't only his eyes that rolled. He wantonly wiggled his hips and stuck out his bottom as he walked. As soon as he was out of his mother's sight, he draped himself in a pagne and strutted about.

"Nothing short of a miracle will stop that youngster [from] turning into a *gôr djiguène*, a pansy destined to spend his life at the feet of a courtesan, doing all her dirty work. His job would be to procure generous lovers to keep that type of pricey household going. His would be the job of settling the accounts for the meals. And sometimes it might happen that the clients would fancy him rather than his mistress . . ."

Yaye Khady was sincerely sorry for the mother of this specimen. (69–70)]

On one level, this passage constitutes a description of the scorn with which the *gôr-djiguen* is sometimes viewed. Yet it must be said that, in a society in which the actions of any family member may dishonor the entire family (which may also depend on a son for assuring patrilineal descendants), a parent's reaction to a son's becoming a *gôr-djiguen* might be very different from that of society as a whole. On another level, this passage is an eloquent description of how, even in spite of parental violence, a boy affirms a gender identity, which seems to develop "naturally," far removed from any foreign influence. This *gôr-djiguen* in the making parades his identity freely, being a bit more discreet only when in the presence of his parents. Although parts of this passage recall details from other descriptions, such as the association with the art of cooking (Deme), the role of domestic servant (Bugul), and of course the common element of transgender identity, this boy—not (yet) a *gôr-djiguen*—serves as the catalyst for a lengthy ethnographic description of the *gôr-djiguen*'s social role that includes many details not mentioned in other accounts. The speaker behind the ethnographic paragraph (enclosed within quotation marks), however, is not clearly identified. Is it Yaye Khady, the boy's mother, or merely the prevailing, collective gossip of the neighborhood? The tone of this passage does suggest that it presents an "insider's" view (like that of Bugul or Deme as opposed to that of Gorer, Crowder, or Teunis).

Unlike Bâ's *gôr-djiguen* and those described by everyone except Teunis, who claims that all his informants led closeted lives, Teunis, at least as long as he was in Senegal, was in the closet as both a homosexual and an ethnographer.[21] Even though he describes the openness with which "many streetboys" operate on Dakar's main street (160)—and here he echoes Crowder—he also describes blackmail (163) and the tendency of police to target the bar for ID checks (162). Is there not a contradiction between the obviousness implied in the term *man-woman* and the invisibility Teunis attributes to them? How accurate can we consider his observations to be when his closetedness (as he understood it) prevented him from asking "heterosexual" informants about their own feelings toward *gôr-djiguen*? Although one might be tempted to suspect that travel accounts will be more prejudiced by the clichés of colonial discourse (because written by amateurs?), Teunis's account demonstrates that even the gay ethnographer can project *idées reçues* onto his "homosexual" informants and even antihomophobic ethnography can produce its own closets.[22]

The Civilizing Mission and the Missionary Position

The motif of travel is a common one when the topic of homosexuality arises in African literature. It is often upon leaving Africa that characters are first confronted with the issue of homosexuality. Yet, as we have seen in Ken's example, this trip abroad is often balanced by a parallel return to the native land, which contradicts the initial tendency to link same-sex sexual behavior and desires with Europe or the United States. Although Ken first mentions homosexuality in conjunction with her experience in Europe, her encounter with a Belgian homosexual leads her not to assert a European monopoly on same-sex sexual behaviors and desires but to affirm a Senegalese counterpart. Likewise, in Ama Ata Aidoo's *Our Sister Killjoy* (1977), when the Ghanaian protagonist Sissie encounters homosexuality in Europe (this time in the form of sexual advances made to her by a married German woman, Marija), she returns, figuratively, to her native village: "[O]ne evening the woman seizes you in her embrace, her cold fingers on your breasts, warm tears on your face, hot lips on your lips, do you go back to your village in Africa" (65). What she reveals in this memorative return to her origins is the story of a missionary to the Guinea coast who, "on one of her regular nocturnal inspections . . . found two girls in bed together" (66). On the one hand, Sissie's response to Marija's desire to plan a surprise going-away dinner could be said to fit into the formula of homosexual desire as *contra naturam*: "Besides, it is not sound for a woman to enjoy cooking for another woman. Not under any circumstances. It is not done. It is not possible. Special meals are for men. They are the only sex to whom the Maker gave a mouth with which to enjoy eating" (77). If one replaced the culinary vocabulary with a sexual one, the passage exactly fits the model of one homophobic argument against homosexuality, even though the absurdity of the image it conjures up—that of women without mouths!—might be said to disrupt that homophobia. On the other hand, Aidoo historicizes this response by associating it with the missionary's characterization of two African girls in bed as "a/C-r-i-m-e/A Sin/S-o-d-o-m-y" (67).[23]

After an initial discussion of homosexuality in sub-Saharan African novels, "L'homophilie dans le roman négro-africain d'expression anglaise et française" (1983), in which Daniel Vignal divides the novels he reads into homophobic and nonhomophobic camps, Chris Dunton articulated more nuanced readings of the same and other novels in "'Wheyting Be Dat?': The Treatment of Homosexuality in African Literature" (1989).[24] Since for a long time essays that deal with homosexuality in African literature were few and far between, both articles articulate useful readings of often neglected passages, or passages that have provoked homophobic readings on the part of many critics. Dunton, however, who provides a three-page analysis of Marija's pass at Sissie (431–34), does not mention the novel's representation of the repression of homosexuality by a European missionary. Although he argues that "Aidoo's treatment of homosexuality is not unsympathetic" (432), his reading of Aidoo and other novelists allows him to conclude:

What remains conspicuous in all these works is the abstention among African writers, and even among the most searching and responsive of these, from a fully characterized and nonschematic depiction of a homosexual relationship between Africans. . . . [T]he practice of homosexuality within African society remains an area of experience that has not been granted a history by African writers, but has been greeted, rather, with a sustained outburst of silence. Whether this has been carried out within or beyond the limits of the stereotype, the identification of homosexuality with the West has helped defend that silence. An "official" history has concealed the reluctance of African writers to admit homosexuality into the bounds of a different kind of discussion. (445)

In his reading of Aidoo, which leads him to argue that her novelistic representations of African homosexualities are ahistorical, Dunton does not consider the novel's reference to colonial history. Although he argues that the African novel's approach to homosexuality produces silences, by failing to read the intertextual connection between history and African literary representations of homosexuality, Dunton creates silences of his own. In his discussion of Camara's *Dramouss*, for example, Dunton only remarks that Fatomane "protests angrily that nothing like that could happen in his own country" (426). He fails to point out how the novel situates his comments with Liliane's reproduction of colonial discourse. Reading Bâ, he writes, "Yet even if homosexual practice is acknowledged in these passages to have been allocated a specialized, legitimate role in traditional society, it still is stigmatized" (423). Again, he does not consider how the novel itself *contextualizes* this stigmatization.[25]

Dunton thus provides an important example of how even antihomophobic literary criticism can fail to read between the lines in order to uncover meaning within silences. In so doing, he clearly demonstrates the dangers, within literary *criticism*, of ignoring history. For it is not the African novel that fails to grant a history to African homosexuality but its critics. Clearly, then, it is not only that literature can help read silences in the writing of history but that history must also be studied by the literary critic (who must also be on the lookout for the ways novels participate in the writing of history) to avoid silencing historical references in the works he or she reads. In contrast to Dunton, Aidoo's novel suggests that Sissie's reaction to the possibility of homosexual desire is a product less of African tradition than of the imposition of Christianity that accompanied colonial conquest. *Our Sister Killjoy* (regardless of any intention on the author's part) thus historicizes the deployment of homophobia by colonial discourse and suggests that, rather than homosexuality, hetero-sexuality was the more significant imposition of colonialism. Aidoo thus provides the historical background that allows us to understand further Liliane's comments in Camara's *Dramouss*. Aidoo also draws attention to another important consideration in any discussion of African discourses on homosexuality, the influence of missionaries. Although the novel's protagonist rejects homosexuality as un-African, the novel historicizes this rejection and suggests that Sissie, rather than defending a preco-lonial African purity, may actually only be repeating a discourse that she learned from European missionaries. While the African sexualities encountered by missionaries may have been diverse, their response was quite uniform. In her work in Lesotho on mummie-baby relationships (a terminology used to describe institutionalized romantic relationships between women), Judith Gay (1985) describes a similar Christian repres-sion of homosexual or homoerotic behaviors accepted by Africans: "Although informants experienced these relationships as normal and enjoyable, and said their mothers usually permitted them if they knew, girls who had attended mission schools said that the nuns and matrons strongly disapproved and attempted to prevent them" (106).

Whereas Aidoo situates clichés concerning a so-called absence of African homosexuality within a colonial history, V. Y. Mudimbe's *Entre les eaux* (1973) [Between the Waters], confronts the aftermath of colonial homophobia in postindependence Africa in very subtle ways. Although the author is from what was called Zaïre when the novel was published, its setting is an unnamed African country in which the government is being challenged by armed resistance. Because of its fictional setting, the novel (as is common in postindependence novels) defies a "straight"-forward association with ethnography; it also resists comparison with would-be historical references in any simple way. I would argue, however, that history can be crucial in understanding the novel's representation of homosexuality through a reading that might tease out the novel's sexual politics by bringing to the fore the ironic and paradoxical ways in which the novel deploys sexuality and perverts Christian missionary discourse.

Cannibals and Queers

Entre les eaux tells the story of Pierre, who resigns from his position as a Catholic priest to join a revolutionary militia. Because of what it reveals to his superiors, Pierre's letter of resignation is considered to be an act of treason by his comrades in the militia, who subsequently condemn him to death. After government forces attack their unit, thereby dismantling it and killing many of its members, the execution is not carried out. Before the letter is discovered, however, in conversation with the "Chef" (leader of the unit), the latter reveals to Pierre that he has pederastic tendencies:

> Moi, je suis un vicieux. Oui, vicieux. J'adore le chanvre, la boisson forte, les grosses femmes. Oui, les grosses. Elles sont tendres comme de gros fruits mûrs, bien juteux. Elles saignent de l'or. Les beaux garçons aussi, bien entendu. Je suis, comme vous dites dans votre langage de savants. . . . Oui, merci, c'est cela, polyvalent. J'adore aussi le sang. Une passion que je porte en moi. J'aurais dû être un fauve. Voyez-vous ? Pierre, je suis un être foncièrement immoral. Tenez, il y a un mois, j'ai mangé de la chair humaine. . . . (51; Mudimbe's ellipses)

> [I am a man of vice. Yes, vice. I adore hemp, strong drink, fat women. Yes, fat ones; they are as tender as plump, ripe, very juicy fruit. They bleed gold. Beautiful boys as well, of course. I am, as you say in your learned language. . . . Yes, thanks, that's it, polyvalent. A passion I carry within. I should have been a wild animal. Do you see? Pierre, I am a fundamentally immoral being. In fact, a month ago, I ate human flesh. . . . .]

Here resistance to a neocolonial regime is embodied by a pervert. The Chef seems to fit perfectly with Catholic descriptions of perversion as bestial ("J'aurais dû être un fauve"), descriptions that also link sexual deviance with political aberration. The comparison between pederasty and cannibalism found in this passage would *not* be unusual in colonial Christian propaganda. In early modern colonial discourse, cannibals (more a figure of the Christian imagination than a historical reality) epitomized all that was un-Christian and, therefore, uncivilized. As W. Arens points out in his demystification of cannibalism, *The Man-Eating Myth*, the Spanish often claimed that the Aztecs "practiced both cannibalism and sodomy" (77). He also mentions "titillating descriptions of often-combined cannibalistic and sexual acts" (99). In his introduction to *Cannibalism and the Colonial World*, Peter Hulme describes a tendency to represent cannibalism (particularly in nonanthropological discourses) "as an orgy of limb-tearing violence, possibly accompanied by excesses of other sorts, from infanticide to sodomy" (Barker, Hulme, and Iversen 24).

While awaiting his execution, Pierre not only wonders whether he can describe his experience in terms of martyrdom; he also speculates about being canonized. The question of martyrdom, particularly in relation to a death sentence meted out by a polysexual leader, recalls an incident from the annals of history—that of the so-called Uganda holocaust.[26] The "martyrs" in this incident were royal pages (Christian converts, beatified in 1920 and canonized in 1964) who were killed between 1885 and 1887 by the Kabaka (king) Mwanga of Buganda (a part of present-day Uganda) because their religion led them to defy his traditional power and because they supposedly refused his homosexual advances. Christian accounts of these "human sacrifices" made much use of the second explanation to demonize the Kabaka and emphasize his bestiality. ("Human sacrifices" thus play a role in colonial discourse similar to that of "cannibalism"; in fact, the two were often linked [Arens 64, 68, 70].) The *New Catholic Encyclopedia* describes Mwanga in terms remarkably similar to the Chef's self-description: "The persecution occurred early in the reign of Mwanga, a *vicious, perverse* youth, after his Christian page boys refused to submit to his homosexual advances" ("Uganda, Martyr's of" 363; emphasis added). J. F. Faupel's *African Holocaust: The Story of the Uganda Martyrs* (1962), which carries the *nihil obstat* and *imprimatur* of the Catholic Church, likewise demonizes the Kabaka in the service of hagiography, which in this case passes for history.[27] What is rarely suggested, however, is that the "martyrs" were killed less because they were defending an African (and therefore natural) purity than because they were the advocates of a Christian notion of purity foreign to the traditions of the Baganda.[28] Furthermore, Christianity was actively attacking and destroying traditional African social structures, and the presence of Christian missionaries in Buganda directly paved the way for the establishment of the British protectorate in 1894.

Mwanga's "purge of Christians," however, has not only been deployed in the production of colonial homophobia in Catholic discourse; he is also used to justify homophobic nationalism from an anticolonial perspective. To deny the existence of homosexuality in Africa, participants in the newsgroup discussion dismissed accounts of the Kabaka's pederasty as lies invented by missionaries. The issue was raised by a non-African discussant:[29] "But I remember hearing at the time about the canonization of 22 Uganda Saints martyred long ago because they refused the homosexual advances of a Kabaka. Perhaps someone could tell us whether it is completely false."[30] And an African participant replied, "It's commonplace to accuse Negroes of being sodomites. It's pure Christian propaganda. It was one of the arguments used to justify slavery."[31] The first participant seemed to agree: "It's precisely because I was suspicious of Christian propaganda that I wondered whether the account of the homosexual Kabaka was true."[32] Some western gay scholars, in an equally disturbing move, have used the incident as proof of a precolonial African homosexuality without questioning the colonial implications of the Christian accounts (see Dynes 206).

Although *chef* means "leader" in French, it is also the word used to describe so-called tribal chiefs. This association also links Mudimbe's Chef with representations of precolonial African rulers in colonial discourse, which often labeled kings "chiefs" because it could not conceive of "advanced" forms of statehood in Africa prior to colonization. Therefore, in conjunction with Mudimbe's parody of the colonial clichés of Christian discourse, the Chef might be a representation of rulers such as the Kabaka. The novel's mention of cannibalism might make it easy to demonize the Chef, and homosexuality along with him. In spite of Pierre's romance with a female guerrilla, however, he questions any way in which the novel might distance itself from the Chef by confessing his own homosexual tendencies: "'Mon vieux Pierre, me suis-je dit, tu as des tendances bien prononcées pour ton propre sexe.' La honte m'a envahi" (120) ["My good old Pierre," I said to myself, "you have a rather pronounced tendency for your own sex." Shame invaded me]. While he might be read as a personification of the cliché that all priests are driven to pederasty by their celibacy or that they entered the priesthood to hide their pederastic tendencies, Mudimbe suggests that both Catholic priests and revolutionary nationalists can have homosexual tendencies. *Entre les eaux* thus brings back what hagiography and homophobic nationalism have attempted to repress. Whereas the detail of Pierre's possible martyrdom means that his imminent execution might be said to recall that of the Ugandan "martyrs," unlike those martyrs, Pierre asserts his affinity with the revolutionary Chef and his homosexual tendencies. By reading the historical incident through Mudimbe, then, one can understand *Entre les eaux* as challenging the demonization of homosexuality through a move not unlike Bugul's and Aidoo's returns to queer roots in Africa. In Mudimbe, however, it is the repressed roots of an Africa constructed as queer by missionary discourse that return with such force. Reading Mudimbe through and against history, however, also reveals that one must sometimes look to historical events *not* represented in the literary texts under analysis to articulate interdisciplinary readings in a way that measures silences in the gaps between disciplinary discourses on homosexuality in Africa.

Even more recently, Uganda has continued to be a site of debate over African homosexualities. Ugandan President Yoweri Museveni is often cited, along with Mugabe, Kenya's Daniel arap Moi, and Namibia's Sam Nujoma, as one of Africa's most vehemently homophobic leaders. Around the time of Zimbabwe's book fair controversy, Museveni was calling for arrests of homosexuals under the country's sodomy law.[33] What he never admits, however, is that the law whose enforcement he has polemically called for was written not by Ugandans but by the British colonial rulers. As in Zimbabwe, Museveni's homophobic rhetoric is not merely discursive, but has resulted in the arrests of many Ugandans (see IGLHRC). In continuing to enforce homophobic colonial laws (not to mention just leaving them on the books), Museveni demonstrates that, when it comes to homosexuality in Uganda, decolonization has yet to begin. Furthermore, like Mugabe, he masks his homophobic attacks with anticolonial rhetoric, even stating that "the Universal Declaration of Human Rights . . . had not been drawn up with the participation of African countries and therefore was 'not universal to Africa'" ("Uganda to Arrest Gays" 22). Museveni's implied critique of the enlightenment ideals behind human rights conventions is understandable when one considers that these very ideals were used as a justification for colonialism. The abolition of slavery *among Africans,* for example, was often paradoxically given as a reason for colonial invasion. Yet this critique is not the one performed by Museveni in his attacks on human rights; for his justifications of state-sponsored homophobic terror rely on the same colonial discourse he pretends to condemn. It is an irony of history, however, that, after the inauguration of homophobic discourse in Uganda by Christian missionaries, resistance to Museveni's homophobia would first take the form of the Anglican lesbian and gay organization Integrity. On 7 July 2000, the formation of the first African chapter of Integrity in Kampala, Uganda, was announced (Integrity USA). We may also thank Mugabe for transforming GALZ from a small, mostly white organization into a larger one with a substantial black membership.

Queer Interpretations

When GALZ's exclusion from Zimbabwe's book fair set off Mugabe's homophobic campaign, the Nigerian writer Wole Soyinka, winner of the

1986 Nobel Prize in literature, publicly condemned this exclusion in the name of freedom of expression (Patron 22).[34] Even earlier his 1965 novel *The Interpreters* included a major gay African American character—Joe Golder, a concert singer, writer, and history lecturer at the university. In his extensive reading of Soyinka in *African Intimacies*, Neville Hoad writes, "In 1965, *The Interpreters* stages a version of the 'no homosexuality in African culture' debate that will follow a series of pronouncements by 1990s African presidents, with much more attention to the mutually constitutive categories of race, gender, and sexuality under conditions of decolonization and postcoloniality" (21). And at the center of Soyinka's version of this debate is the Golder character. The interpreters referred to in the novel's title are usually considered to be the following characters: Egbo, a civil servant who has also inherited a position of traditional ruler; Biodun Sagoe, a journalist and former philosophy student; Sekoni, an engineer turned sculptor; Kola, an art teacher and painter; and Bandele, also a lecturer at the university. The novel intertwines their personal stories and conversations into a complex structure of flashbacks, which often are not clearly marked. *What*, exactly, they are interpreting is open to interpretation however. A conventional reading might understand them to be interpreting the role of western-educated intellectuals in postindependence Nigeria. A certain kind of politicized reading might compare the eponymous interpreters with the philosophers Marx criticized for merely seeking to understand the world not change it. Regardless of how one understands the interpretation signaled by the title, however, most criticism excludes Golder from the rank of "interpreter" in spite of his importance and professional activities.[35]

There is no shortage, in fact, of readings (both homophobic and anti-homophobic) that argue that the novel condemns Golder because of his homosexuality. Since one character, the Christian convert Noah, jumps to his death after Golder makes a pass at him, critics often blame Noah's death on Golder's homosexuality as opposed to the sexual interdictions imposed by Christianity.[36] Indeed, Egbo himself has such a reaction, as Hoad describes: "In the most powerfully homophobic scene in the novel, Egbo comforts the distraught Joe Golder after the death of Noah by patting his knee. However, upon being told that Golder is 'queer,' he experiences strong feelings of contamination and revulsion" (43). The following passage from the novel describes this reaction on Egbo's part:

As from vileness below human imagining Egbo snatched his hand away, his face distorted with revulsion and a sense of the degrading contamination. He threw himself forward, away even from the back seat, staring into the sagging figure at the back as at some noxious insect, and he felt his entire body crawl in disgust. His hand which had touched Joe Golder suddenly felt foreign to his body and he got out of the car and wiped it on grass dew. Bandele and Kola stared at him, isolated from this hatred they had not known in Egbo, and the sudden angry spasms that seemed to overtake each motion of his body. (236–37)

When L. R. Early suggests that "Noah is a tragic sacrifice to the fundamental cannibalism of society (represented by Joe Golder)" (172), thereby implying that Golder himself is a cannibal, he not only reproduces Egbo's reaction but also fully reproduces colonial clichés of the sexually perverse cannibal, the same clichés Mudimbe parodies in the character of the Chef. We might also state that blaming Golder for Noah's suicide reproduces the very homophobic assumptions—instilled by western Christianity—that propel this character to his death. But such readings of this scene fail to take into account the fact that, in the above passage from *The Interpreters*, for the one character who offers a homophobic interpretation, Soyinka offers two who counter it. Furthermore, in a move that will be repeated in the novel (as we will see below), Egbo performs his reading *from behind*, "throwing himself forward," in the direction of Golder's backside in a way that perhaps suggests that his revulsion is an abjection that attempts to expel what is in fact partially internal, partially a part of himself. Indeed, it is his own hand, the one that touched Golder, that becomes foreign to him. It is little wonder, then, that several critics have argued that Golder is Egbo's double (Houbein 98; Morrison, K. 756). Since in traditional society Egbo would have been a hereditary ruler, the novel also links Golder (through the "couple" he forms with Egbo) with traditional political structures, as I explain below. In other words, in spite of attempts on the part of many critics to attribute Golder's homosexuality to his alienation from Africanness due to both his *métissage* and the fact that, sexually, he represents a Euro-American contamination of African purity, the novel actually connects Golder's sexual marginality to the most traditional aspect of Nigerian culture, religious practices that predate the advent of both Islam and Christianity. Indeed, it is around the question of how to interpret Golder's Afrocentricity, I would argue, that his character becomes central to a reading of *The Interpreters* as an allegory of reading or interpretation in which heteronormative versions of Afrocentricity are deconstructed and queered.

Nonetheless, as Gaurav Desai writes in "Out in Africa" (1997), "Gold-er remains to this day in the criticism of this text, the homosexual—and therefore—the accused" (142). In his assessment of criticism on the novel, he adds:

> Herein, then, lies Joe Golder's tragedy—attempting to escape both the homophobia within the African American community at home and the insistent hypersexuality ascribed to the black man by the larg-er predominantly white American society, Joe finds that in Africa, too, he is no more than a sexual body. Yet, if the possibility of this reading is left open by the narrative, it is one that few critics have pursued. Instead, the critics *replay* the textual tragedy in their own criticism. (142)

According to Desai, then, most critics fail to understand Golder as the embodiment of the intersectionality of racial and sexual identities. Implied in Desai's commentary is a suggestion that in spite of the anti-colonial positioning of most Soyinka scholarship, critics often tend to deploy colonial stereotypes about black sexuality, though projected onto (a supposedly white) *homo*sexuality.

Furthermore, critics often argue that, since Golder is only "one-fourth black," he is ashamed of not being more purely African; for them his inability to become one with his African roots (because he is ashamed of not being more purely African) is a sign of his inauthenticity (Ojo-Ade 748; Jeyifo 176). As Desai also writes, "Joe . . . has consistently been read . . . as Soyinka's emblem of everything that is wrong with a Western-based, romanticized Afrocentricity" (141). Interestingly, such a reading of Golder preexists criticism of the novel, since Soyinka himself already provides a parody of it in the pronouncements of another interpreter, Sagoe, who most openly mocks Golder's Afrocentricity: "Look, the truth is that I get rather sick of self-love. Even nationalism is a kind of self-love but that can be defended. It is this cult of black beauty which sickens me. Are albinos supposed to go and drown themselves, for instance" (195–96). Sagoe has even accused Golder of being "mentally white," to which the latter responds:

> "Black is something I like to be, that I have every right to be. There is no reason at all why I shouldn't have been born jet black."
> "You would have died of over-masturbation, I am sure."
> "You enjoy being vulgar?" (195)

Soyinka has long been a critic of Négritude; his famous sentence, "A tiger does not go around proclaiming its tigritude," amply demonstrates that he does not hesitate to resort to mockery to get his point across. (Négritude is, after all, an Afrocentric movement.) Neither can one deny that Soyinka often directs a similar criticism against Golder, such is the multiplicity of positions he stages on this question, as on others.

It would, however, be simplistic to take all of this mockery at face value. For there is no one the novel mocks more than Sagoe, who on occasion even seems to border on mental instability. The novel is even harsher on him than Bandele and Kola are on Egbo. Sagoe spends much of the novel trying to convert his pidgin-speaking messenger Mathias to his personal philosophy, which he calls Voidancy, "the philosophy of shit" (71). He is also quite a misogynist, arguing on occasion that women who behave in certain ways should be beaten (67) or raped (105). (By denying Dehinwe, an important female character, the status of interpreter in much the same way that they treat Golder, many critics may be said to share this misogyny.) Few critics, however, would argue that the *novel* espouses Sagoe's misogyny or his "*voidante*" philosophy, yet when it comes to his homophobia, for many critics, Sagoe suddenly becomes the novel's (and Soyinka's) mouthpiece. Why not, in contrast, understand the novel as suggesting that, by association, Sagoe's misogyny and his homophobia are likewise "philosophies of shit"? Furthermore, when critics take up Sagoe's opinion of Golder, they fail to mention that Sagoe acquired his philosophy as a student in the United States and that older characters refer to him as "that boy from America" (94). Sagoe is thus hardly in any position to defend African purity of any kind. In fact, one might argue that the greatest American influence on Sagoe was the formation of his homophobia.

Although Dunton, like many other critics, argues that "Golder is not one of the interpreters" (442), like Desai he integrates Golder into an antihomophobic reading of the novel: "Soyinka's characterization of Golder can hardly be said to be sympathetic. Yet there is a concern with Golder's social psychology that finally does distinguish his characterization from the stereotype and that suggests that his role bears a complex relationship to the novel's thematic development" (440). He also suggests a connection between Golder's racial and sexual identities: "[W]hile Soyinka is hardly concerned with projecting a metaphorical identification of the stigmatization of homosexuality with that of blackness, he does establish such an identification as integral to Joe Golder's psychological make-up. He shows how Golder advertises his blackness as a means of displacing the alienation he suffers because of his homosexuality" (440). Desai, however, interestingly takes a totally opposite stance from not only Dunton but also most other critics on the subject of how likable Soyinka's portrayal of Golder is:

> [I]t is precisely in addressing [Golder's] simultaneous negotiations of racial and sexual identities that Soyinka presents Golder as a profoundly sympathetic character. Golder is an individual who has had to claim actively at least two identities that continually threaten to escape him—he is at once a light-skinned black man capable of "passing" as a white man and a homosexual capable of passing as straight. His choice not to pass—his choice to reaffirm at once two identities not only at odds with the hegemonic order of things but also, more importantly, at odds with one another—is a choice that must sober even the most unsympathetic of readers. Furthermore, Joe's decision to study African history and his move to Nigeria, despite its potentially romanticizing implications, is presented by Soyinka as his continual attempt to negotiate the different demands placed upon his identities. (142–43)

In an approach to Golder that is profoundly different from the ones taken by many readers of Soyinka's novel, Desai puts a more positive spin on the way Golder's racial and sexual identities work in nexus with each other, their intersectionality in other words.

Hoad's reading of Soyinka's novel, however, takes issue with the notion that an antihomophobic criticism, especially an anticolonial one, would need to defend Golder against his detractors, both the novel's characters and its literary critics. In fact, he is the only antihomophobic reader who offers a somewhat critical view of Golder's behavior; for this reason, I consider his analysis of this character in greater depth.[37] He describes Golder as "a very complicated kind of Pan-Africanist sex tourist" (43) and adds, contra Desai, "I do not think the essentially predatory Golder is a figure available for heroic sublimation" (44). Although Hoad qualifies his assessment, like Dunton, with an acknowledgment of how Soyinka complicates the cliché of homosexuality as a white man's disease—"What is remarkable about *The Interpreters'* understanding of Golder's homosexuality is its refusal of psychogenetic narratives of homosexuality, which must be described rather than explained" (42)—he nonetheless reads him as a symptom of the complications that arise when western constructions of sexuality are imbricated in the flows and exchanges that make up global-

ization. Whereas I will be reading Golder as a personification of queer
roots (in the form of a queering of the Afrocentrism he espouses), I view
Hoad's reading as a possible corrective to my own potentially celebratory
one. (For, as I pointed out above, none of Soyinka's characters escapes
mockery and/or criticism.) And, although our readings of the character
of Golder and the relation between him and Sagoe constitute the area
where Hoad and I diverge the most, both our readings serve the broader
concerns of our individual studies, Hoad's focus being on globalization,
mine on queering African roots as a discursive strategy. That Golder is
available for such diverse and seemingly mutually exclusive interpretations, in fact, might have as much to do with the polysemic nature of
Soyinka's novel as an allegory for precisely the kind of interpretative strategies I have been developing in this chapter as with the "rightness" or
"wrongness" of any given reading. As a matter of fact, in the context of his
own interpretative narrative, I can find no fault with Hoad's reading; it is
not, however, the reading I perform here.

Regarding the relation between Golder and Sagoe, the latter begins
to learn of the former's homosexuality in the discussion that begins in
the passage quoted above during which Sagoe mocks Golder's Ameri-
canness and American notions of racial belonging. At one point in this
conversation, Golder asks whether Sagoe is afraid of him:

> "Do you think . . . are you afraid I might molest you? Is that it? Do you
> think I am a homo?"
> "Good God, no." The suggestion startled Sagoe and he did not
> even think before he rejected it. "You have some rather effeminate
> mannerisms, but that is all."
> "Come come, be quite frank now." (199)

As Hoad writes of this passage, Golder actually misreads Sagoe's statement: "Golder begins by imputing homosexual panic where none has
been expressed by Sagoe" (40). Nonetheless, egged on by Golder, Sagoe
goes on to deny the existence of a vaguely expressed "perversion" in his
own society: "Listen you, it is true I have spent some time in places where
every possible perversion is practised, but I do not on that account jump
to hasty conclusions. I happen to be born into a comparatively healthy
society . . ." (199; Soyinka's ellipsis). In response, Golder not only points
out the homosexual practices of certain traditional rulers but also gets
Sagoe to reveal that, in spite of his mockery of Afrocentrism, he shares
the claim it stakes to the purity of African roots:

"Don't give me that? Comparatively healthy society my foot. Do you
think I know nothing of your Emirs and their little boys? You forget
history is my subject. And what about those exclusive coteries in Lagos?"

Sagoe gestured defeat. "You seem better informed than I am. But
if you don't mind I'll persist in my delusion. (199)

Although Dunton's five-and-a-half-page discussion of Soyinka (439–44)
does not mention this reference to history (and recall that he is the one
who argues that the African novel denies homosexuality a history), it is
through an assertion of his knowledge of African history that Golder
reveals the fallacies of nationalist denials of African homosexualities.[38]
Indeed, at one point Golder says to Sagoe, "I am writing my second
book, a historical novel set in Africa" (190). Golder thus carries out
a move similar to Aidoo's in *Our Sister Killjoy*, which, unlike Sissie in
her response to Marija, gives a history to matters of sexuality in Africa.
We might even take his lead to reread seemingly simplistic representations, such as the one by Camara in *Dramouss* with which I began this
chapter, to point out that after the protagonist asserts the absence of
homosexuality in Africa it is the Frenchwoman who voices the colonial
cliché of Africa's sexual purity. In so doing, she might be read as the representative of colonial power who embodies precisely the history that
Aidoo and Soyinka recall. Like Aidoo's Sissie at first, one interpreter
of Soyinka's novel (Dunton), like at least one interpreter *in* it (Sagoe),
ignores this connection between the novel and a colonial history of sexual normalization.

Nonetheless, in his reading of this passage, Hoad does not find
Sagoe's statement to be homophobic, at least not in any simplistic
way (42). And, as Hoad wisely points out, Golder's examples may be
far from asserting an "authentically" African same-sex desire or sexual practices: "The reference to 'Emirs and their little boys' further
engages two colonial-era stereotypes. One depicts Islam as a religion
of sexual license and a corrupting influence on Africans. In the other,
the reference to little boys marks the infantilizing of, and concomitant
denial of masculinity to, African men in colonial racist ideology" (41).
The same holds true for the second example of same-sex desire that
Golder offers: "Both the milieus that Golder mentions in his argument
with Sagoe—'the Emirs and their little boys' and 'those exclusive coteries in Lagos'—reveal different strategies of 'homosexual' othering for
our Bohemian protagonists: the Emirs with the taint of Islam and the

North, the little boys bearing the infantilizing and emasculating charge of racism, and the exclusive coteries as class enemies of sorts" (41). Whereas I would agree with this assertion, I am more interested here in the binary opposition Sagoe asserts between "perversion" (presumably western) and a "comparatively healthy society" (which must be African or Nigerian or Yoruba).

Indeed, in spite of Golder's qualifications as a historian, it is actually anthropology more than history that provides the interdisciplinary intertext for a thick reading of this passage. In fact, it is possible to understand *The Interpreters* itself as a model of interdisciplinarity in that each of the interpreters interprets from a different discipline, the very kind of queer interdisciplinarity I pointed to at the beginning of this chapter, a model of interdisciplinarity that involves much more than using history or anthropology to clarify or elucidate literary texts and, instead, brings various discourses into confrontation to read them not only for their contradictions but also for their silences, including those of the literary text. For, as in previous novels examined in this chapter, the ethnographic literature does not match up with these allusions on Golder's part in any simple way. Regarding "those exclusive coteries in Lagos," I have found only two references to anything similar in either the historical or the anthropological literature, the first of which is in a personal communication by sociolinguist Rudolf P. Gaudio to Stephen O. Murray and/or Will Roscoe:

> I met at least two Yoruba self-identified "gay" men in Kano, neither of whom had ever lived abroad, who told me about the many other "gays" they knew in such cities as Ilorin, Ibadan, and, of course, Lagos where there is a "Gentleman's Alliance" with pan-Southern membership. My Kano Yoruba contacts told me that GA members have private parties at each other's homes, and that there is a division of Yoruba gay male social circles into "kings" and "queens." . . . When I asked one of these Yoruba "queens" whether there was any Yoruba equivalent to the Hausa 'yan daudu, he said that no, Yoruba queens had more "respect" than the 'yan daudu, insofar as Yoruba queens keep their outrageous, feminine behaviors a secret from other people. (qtd. in Murray and Roscoe 101)

Of course it might be a stretch to equate the GA Gaudio describes with the "exclusive coteries" Golder mentions; over thirty years separate their mention. According to Daniel Vangroenweghe, the GA was founded in

1989 (223), which does not exclude the possibility of earlier precursors. But if such a connection could be established, Gaudio's account here offers an alternative to Hoad's class-based associations. Reading Golder's reference to the "exclusive" nature of the Lagos coteries as referring not to a socioeconomic elite but to a closed organization in which terms of royalty are used as coded references to gendered distinctions between men who have sex with men would lessen the likelihood of an association between homosexuality and so-called bourgeois decadence or the "class enemies" mentioned by Hoad.

In relation to Golder's other example, the "Emirs and their little boys," the novel is presumably referring to Hausa and Muslim northern Nigeria. Here again, the novel seems to draw attention to the very problematic nature Hoad highlights by offering examples that do *not* match up with the anthropological literature on Nigerian "homosexualities." Most such literature focuses on the Hausa figure of the *'dan daudu*, to whom Gaudio compares the queens of the Lagos GA in the passage cited above. In "Masculine Power and Gender Ambiguity in Urban Hausa Society," for example, Gerald W. Kleis and Salisu A. Abdullahi define this figure as follows:

> The *'yan daudu* (sing. *'dan daudu*) form a strikingly distinctive social category of males associated with female prostitution in the Hausa-speaking areas of northern Nigeria and Niger Republic. The most conspicuous aspect of the *'dan daudu*'s status is his rejection of conventional masculine identity and adoption of feminine dress, speech, and mannerisms.[39] This behavior seems especially incongruous in Hausa society, which insists on a strict separation of the male and female domains. However, on further analysis it is evident that the sharp definition and segregation of gender roles are crucial in explaining the *daudu* phenomenon. Viewed in this light it becomes clear that, while the *daudu* is deviant, his deviance illuminates and actually reinforces the boundary between the male and female worlds, while contributing to the maintenance of patriarchal authority. (39)[40]

Regarding the *'dan daudu*'s sexuality, Kleis and Abdullahi add, "Many *'yan daudu* are assumed also to be homosexuals, although this does not seem to be the major feature of their social status, which hinges more on their self-identification as females" (44).[41] As we can see from this anthropological account, therefore, the phenomenon bears some resemblance to that of the Senegalese *gôr-djiguen* discussed above.

In addition to being associated with *female* prostitution, the *'yan dau-*

du are often associated with another specifically Hausa cultural practice, the *bori* cult of spirit possession. In *Horses, Musicians, and Gods: The Hausa Cult of Possession-Trance*, for example, Fremont E. Besmer describes the role of *'yan daudu* in relation to the Hausa *bori* cult: "They appear at public bori performances where they dance in an effeminate manner. 'Yan daudu do not fall into trance at these events and confine their participation to the giving of small gifts of money to cult-adepts who do enter possession-trance, especially when the spirit, *Dan Galadima*, is present" (18). What characterizes *bori* cult practices, however, is their *distance* from orthodox Islam; they are usually considered to be remnants of pre-Islamic socioreligious practices often in conflict with more orthodox manifestations of Islam in Hausaland. So, while Hoad may be absolutely right on the mark regarding Golder's association of "the Emirs with the taint of Islam and the North" (41), measuring the silences that emerge when the novel is read in conjunction with the anthropological literature highlights specifically *Nigerian* same-sex practices, not ones introduced from the outside. Furthermore, perhaps Golder's examples (as read by Hoad) are related to his problematic embodiment of an Afrocentrism that the novel clearly criticizes.

Nonetheless, I would suggest, the novel hints simultaneously at queer possibilities for Golder's Afrocentrism and black nationalism and at a queer roots narrative exemplified by this particular return to African origins on his part. This model, in fact, is actually rather diasporic, for in addition to Golder's profession as a history lecturer and concert singer, he is an avid reader (i.e., an interpreter), and in spite of his desire to reconnect with his African roots, he displays a particular fondness not for African literature but for a specific African American writer: James Baldwin. In fact, Baldwin becomes a focal point in one of Sagoe's most homophobic exchanges with Golder. In the following passage, Golder discusses a Baldwin novel with Sagoe, to whom he has offered a ride:

GOLDER: "It's *Another Country*, the latest Baldwin. Have you read it?"
SAGOE: "I spell it Another Cuntry, C-U-N-T."
GOLDER: "You don't like it?"
SAGOE: "It reminded me somehow of another title, *Eric, or Little by Little!* Said with an anal gasp, if you get my meaning."
"You enjoy being vulgar," [Golder] said again.
SAGOE: "And you? Why is this lying on the car seat? So when you give lifts to students you can find an easy opening for exploring?"
GOLDER: "You are trying to hurt me?" (200)[42]

Although Sagoe expresses views shared by many critics, this passage is rarely quoted, perhaps because it would be difficult even for many homophobes to sympathize with Sagoe here (given his vivid imagining of anal sex!) and even harder to argue that Sagoe expresses the view of the entire novel, let alone Soyinka himself. When Femi Ojo-Ade writes, "A homosexual, Golder has a field day making passes at students and colleagues" (748), he echoes Sagoe's position. Like Sagoe, Ojo-Ade also does not care how often Joe has been robbed or blackmailed as a result of his attempts at intimacy. One might even say that Ojo-Ade has been tricked by Soyinka into playing the role of one of the more ridiculous "interpreters," more specifically Sagoe.

Sagoe's literary reference is to a 1858 novel written by Frederic W. Farrar, a preacher, headmaster, and theological writer. It tells the tale of Eric Williams, a well-born and -raised boy sent to board at school while his parents are in the employ of the British colonial system in India. Under the bad influence of some of his schoolmates the virtuous young man spirals into a moral decline, which leads to delinquency (consisting of cheating and bullying, as well as such supposedly equally horrendous acts as cursing, smoking, and drinking!) and, ultimately, his death. The homosocial setting of the all-boys school, however, lends much to possible queer readings of the novel. From the prelapsarian Eric's being the "loving friend" (32) of the virtuous Russell to the kiss Eric gives Russell on the latter's deathbed (120–21) to the system of "taking up" (which consists of older boys taking younger ones under their wings and often leads the younger boys "to sink into the effeminate condition which usually grows on the young delectables who have the misfortune to be 'taken up'" [58]), the novel is ripe with innuendo even as it condemns the very delinquency that invites a campy interpretation: "May every schoolboy who reads this page be warned by the waving of their wasted hands, from that burning marle of passion, where they found nothing but shame and ruin, polluted affections, and an early grave" (69). That the African Sagoe reads the title of this Anglican morality tale (a title that most immediately refers to the gradual nature of Eric's *moral* decline) as referring to a penis slowly penetrating a man's tight anus suggests that, in spite of his professed homophobia, he displays his own talents for queer interpretation. In so doing, he suggests that it is not just the case that Britain imposed Christianity on Nigeria but also that Africans are quite capable of queering that cultural import. In Sagoe's queer reading of Farrar, therefore, Soyinka not only reflects on the long history of collaboration between Christian missionaries and colonialism around the matter of sexuality along the same lines we saw with Aidoo and Mudimbe, but he also queers it.

Queering Afrocentricity

In an essay published in the New York queer weekly *Outweek* in the early 1990s, "African Roots, American Fruits: The Queerness of Afrocentricity," Michael S. Smith analyzes the prevalence of homophobia in three examples of Afrocentric discourse—Eldridge Cleaver's *Soul on Ice* (1968), Molefi Kete Asante's *Afrocentricity* (1988), and Frances Cress Welsing's *The Isis (Yssis) Papers* (1991)—with the project of articulating a queer alternative: "Though Afrocentricity may not be anti-white, it is anti-queer. Still that is not sufficient enough reason to reject the theory. . . . There is nothing about Afrocentricity . . . that necessitates homophobia" (31). In that he applies his analysis of Afrocentricity to Cleaver, a member of the Black Panther Party, Smith also suggests that a common logic unites Afrocentricity and black nationalism in their use of homophobia to police a male-centered model of black identity: "It is as if . . . Blackness and/or manhood is reaffirmed and strengthened by taking a stand against the faggot. Gay sexuality, it is claimed, is symptomatic of Black moral and cultural degradation" (31). As a result, homosexuality constitutes an inauthentic mode of being for African Americans, being cut off from one's roots.

With a play on the literal and slang meanings of the word *fruit* (of which the latter means "queer"), Smith's title suggests the possibility of a queer Afrocentricity through the image of African American "fruits" growing on trees whose roots are planted in Africa. Smith's essay, however, does not quite realize the potential of its title; while he criticizes the homophobia of straight models of Afrocentricity, he does little to propose an alternative, *queer* model. Nor does he mention the counterdiscourse to Cleaver's that arose within the Black Panther Party itself. Huey Newton's 1970 statement entitled "A Letter from Huey to the Revolutionary Brothers and Sisters about the Women's Liberation and Gay Liberation Movements" (reprinted in Teal 169–71) was a manifesto of solidarity among black, feminist, and gay activists and came out of a history of supporting the Black Panther Party on the part of the Gay Liberation Front.

I would argue, however, that the queer model suggested in Smith's title might even be said to have preexisted the earliest homophobic text he considers, Cleaver's, which was published three years *after The Interpreters*. For, in relation to Soyinka's allusions to *Another Country* and other texts by Baldwin, one may tease out an intertext that includes precisely the kind of discourse Cleaver exemplifies. There is, in fact, much for Golder to identify with in Baldwin's authorial persona: like Golder, Baldwin was gay, and his blackness has similarly been questioned by some Black nationalists; and, like Baldwin, Golder resists being labeled as homosexual or gay (Field 458). Of these, none more bitterly attacked Baldwin than Cleaver, who singled out *Another Country* in *Soul on Ice* to make many of the same comments about Baldwin that some Soyinka critics have made about Golder. According to Cleaver, the black homosexual is the epitome of an Uncle Tom:

> He becomes a white man in a black body. A self-willed, automated slave, he becomes the white man's most valuable tool in oppressing other blacks.
>
> The black homosexual, when his twist has a racial nexus, is an extreme embodiment of this contradiction. The white man has deprived him of his masculinity, castrated him in the center of his burning skull, and when he submits to this change and takes the white man for his lover as well as Big Daddy, he focuses on "whiteness" all the love in his pent up soul and turns the razor edge of hatred against "blackness"—upon himself, what he is, and all those who look like him, remind him of himself. (103)

Furthermore, for Cleaver, Baldwin becomes a very model of the black man who has sold out his race to serve the interests of the white "man" (99); homosexuality, then, becomes a form of racial suicide (102). If, as described in the previous chapter, the Créolistes accuse Europeanized men of bending over for the French, Cleaver accuses Baldwin of bending over for white men by mere dint of being a homosexual, which becomes the ultimate sign of his racial self-hatred. Cleaver calls Baldwin's African American character Rufus Scott in *Another Country* "a pathetic wretch who indulged in the white man's pastime of committing suicide, who let a white bisexual fuck him in the ass . . . [and] was the epitome of a black eunuch who has completely submitted to a white man" (107). Sagoe, it should be noted, is far from the Cleaver we see in this passage. First of all, he distances himself from black nationalism à la Cleaver. Second, he rejects Golder's desire for an authentic blackness. Sagoe nonetheless shares Cleaver's abjection of anal sex between men. Yet the novel, as I asserted above, is far from embracing Sagoe's views on this matter in any unambiguous way. Although *The Interpreters* was published three years prior to *Soul on Ice*, in other words, and in spite of Sagoe's sarcastic indictments of Afrocentricity, Soyinka mocks the very reading of Baldwin and his work that Cleaver would later articulate and foreshadows debates about the Africanness or blackness of homosexuality that continue to this day. In short, although Cleaver's version of Afrocentricity was predicated on turning James Baldwin into a scapegoat, the gay African American writer plays a major role in Golder's queerer version of Afrocentricity.

Furthermore, *Another Country* is not the only reference to Baldwin in Soyinka's novel. While Golder is preparing to pose in the nude for Kola's painting of the Yoruba pantheon, the painter remembers their first meeting:

> Joe Golder, ugly on a stool, confessing, "Do you remember that first time I asked you for drinks? That afternoon when . . ."
>
> How could he forget? Entering the flat, he was astonished to see Joe lying on the sofa, naked with a scant towel on the small of his back and pretending to read *Giovanni's Room*.
>
> "It is so terribly hot, isn't it? What time is it? I was just going to have a bath." (217; Soyinka's ellipsis)

Kola, here, actually picks up on something quite subtle in Golder's use of Baldwin as a coded pick-up technique. And in spite of what some critics have described as predatory or lewd, Golder's literary references actually seem intended only for those in the know. Receiving visitors in the nude notwithstanding, the lewdness, if lewdness there is, lies less in Golder's messages or actions than in the interpretations of them that, it must also be repeated, are articulated by a minority of the eponymous interpreters even when Golder and Dehinwe are excluded from this group.

In the above allusion to *Giovanni's Room*, Soyinka also makes subtle references to the kinds of interpretations hinted at in his own novel's title. Baldwin's protagonist, David, a penniless American in Paris who is waiting for money and his fiancée to arrive, rooms and has an affair with the eponymous ne'er-do-well, whom he later abandons. Unable to recover from this abandonment, Giovanni kills his former boss and lover Guillaume after the latter refuses to give him his job back even after tricking with him. The account of this outcome, however, is not presented as an eyewitness one in the novel. "I could hear the conversation" (225), the narrator David comments, which suggests that he conjures up this conversation between murderer and victim. When David states that Giovanni "is actually facing Guillaume, not conjuring him up in his mind" (226), he contrasts his own "interpretation" of Giovanni's actions with the supposed realness of the actual conversation (again, as *imagined* by the narrator). The narrator then imagines that Guillaume conceals his "real" reasons for not rehiring Giovanni: "Beneath whatever reasons Guillaume invents the real one lies hidden and they both, dimly, in their different fashions, see it" (228). Thus, in the narrator's reading of his past relation with Giovanni (one that also haunts him in the present), there are multiple levels of interpretation that are imagined as being layered vertically, not between the lines but "beneath" them in a kind of "bottom" reading, or reading from the bottom,[43] of exactly the sort that Sagoe performs in his imagining of anal penetration, articulated with the gasp of a bottom, one that also recalls, though from the opposite sexual positioning, Egbo's reading Golder from behind.

Baldwin's narrator conjures up Giovanni's death in a similar way when, after imagining his beheading, he sees his ghost in the mirror (245). The mirror, in which one usually sees one*self*, returns an image of the self as haunted. This haunting troubles David, and as his fiancée Hella attempts to resolve issues resulting from this haunting she discovers his secret, his homosexual love for Giovanni. But before this realization, she offers to abandon some of her feminist objections to the gendered hierarchy he wishes to impose in defining their relationship. "I'll throw away the books" (237), she states, thereby characterizing reading as antithetical to the heterosexual gender norms that would define their marriage. By coming out of the closet that such a relationship would require, David provides a model for a different kind of reading from the one implied by Hella's rejection of books, a kind of reading I would characterize as queer. And it is precisely such a reading that Soyinka stages in the relation between his interpreters, for Soyinka reveals himself to be a much better reader of Baldwin than Sagoe and perhaps even Golder; it goes without saying that he is a much better reader of Baldwin than Cleaver.

As Desai suggests, the song Golder sings in concert, "I Sometimes Feel Like a Motherless Child," might also be read as an allusion to Baldwin's mention of the same song in an essay entitled "Encounter on the Seine: Black Meets Brown," included in *Notes of a Native Son* (Desai 143; Baldwin 89), which, like the title essay of that collection, is obviously a reference to Richard Wright's *Native Son*, the very novel Cleaver defends against Baldwin in *Soul on Ice*. Yet in defending Wright's character, Bigger Thomas, it is actually Cleaver who bends Baldwin over for Wright: "O.K., Sugar, but isn't it true that Rufus Scott, the weak, craven-hearted ghost of *Another Country*, bears the same relation to Bigger Thomas of *Native Son*, the black rebel of the ghetto and a man, as you yourself bore to the fallen giant, Richard Wright, a rebel and a man?" (106). He bends Baldwin's character over for Wright's and therefore one writer for the other. Although the "Sugar" is presumably ironic or sarcastic, what prevents us from reading it against the grain as affectionate? And if we compare Cleaver's reading to Egbo's and Sagoe's, whose would it resemble more? Is it a "bottom" reading like Sagoe's (as I have read him through David of *Giovanni's Room*) or is it a reading from behind (a "top" reading") like Egbo's?

Interestingly, I am not the first to "mess (around) with" Cleaver in this way; in a reading of him in *Black Macho and the Myth of the Superwoman* (1990) that has often been cited in queer black studies, Michele Wallace writes:

> If one is to take Cleaver at his word, the black homosexual is counter-revolutionary (1) because he's being fucked and (2) because he's being fucked by a white man. By so doing he reduces himself to the status of our black grandmothers who, as everyone knows, were fucked by white men all the time.
>
> However, it would follow that if *a black man were doing the fucking* and the one being fucked were a white man, the black male homosexual would be just as good a revolutionary as a black heterosexual male, if not a better one. Black Macho would have to lead to this conclusion. If whom you fuck indicates your power, then obviously the greatest power would be gained by fucking a white man first, a black man second, a white woman third and a black woman not at all. The important rule is that *nobody* fucks you.
>
> Finally, if homosexuals are put down, even though they're males, because they get fucked, where does that leave women in terms of revolution? (68)

Wallace later adds, "And when the black man went as far as the adoration of his own genitals could carry him, his revolution stopped. A big Afro, a rifle, and a penis in good working order were not enough to lick the white man's world after all" (69). Although she positions Cleaver as the top in any intercourse he might have with Baldwin (social or sexual), this last passage suggests not only that Cleaver is not quite up to the task of such a top reading but also that he likes to rim (with Baldwin being first in line to receive such a pleasure).

In "Tearing the Goat's Flesh," Robert F. Reid-Pharr goes a bit further by arguing that Cleaver's homophobia must be read in the context of the prison in which *Soul on Ice* was written, where homoeroticism would have been too close for comfort (104–12). He thereby not only contributes to the queering of Cleaver that Wallace began—admittedly, quite a difficult task—but also suggests that Cleaver's greater fear is that of becoming a bottom. In fact, if we read Baldwin's Giovanni as a queering of Wright's Bigger Thomas (and therefore of Cleaver's defense of both Wright and his character), is it not more appropriate to see Baldwin as bending Cleaver over in what, according to Wallace, would be one of the most revolutionary nationalist acts of black masculinity? Indeed, in *James Baldwin's Turkish Decade: Erotics of Exile*, Magdalena J. Zaborowska seconds the suggestions of both Wallace and Reid-Pharr:

> A misogynist, self-acknowledged rapist, and bombastically anxious heterosexist whose sexual ambivalences have been probed by many critics, Cleaver "lusted" after Baldwin's books in *Soul on Ice*, on the one hand, and reduced him to his "little jive ass," a despised fag's body, on the other. Amiri Baraka, who struggled with his own sexual identification, and undoubtedly many of Cleaver's Black Power peers similarly defined their aggressively heterosexist, homophobic, and inevitably misogynistic masculinity against Baldwin's much more complex configurations of gender, race, sexuality, class, and power. (199)

The difference between Zaborowska's reading and those of her predecessors, however, is that here Cleaver is the one who is "probed," that is, bent over in the encounter with Baldwin.

To return to Golder, when read through the intertextual web I have just woven, which includes African *American* writers as diverse as Baldwin, Cleaver, and Wright, *The Interpreters* roots its representations of homosexuality in Africa. Golder, in other words, who has come to Africa to find his roots, also asserts their queer aspect. Indeed, his wish to become blacker is actually granted by Kola, who includes him in his painting of the Yoruba pantheon, for which Golder poses as the god Erinle, defined in the novel's glossary merely as "an animal spirit" (259). Although Erinle is not the most frequently discussed Yoruba *orisha*, or divinity, it seems that Erinle's gender identity is far from clear. In his work on Yoruba religious practices in the nineteenth century, Peter McKenzie includes an entire section on changes of gender among the *orisha* (490–96), including that of Erinle: "Another 'god of stream,' Eyinle or Erinle was worshipped as a male *orisha* at Lagos and as a goddess at Otta" (29). Soyinka's novel as well discusses precisely this kind of gender variability: "[Golder] had said once, You should paint me as one of those Indian gods, hermaphrodite. Kola laughed and said, You'd be surprised, we have a few Gods like that. In one area they are male, in another female" (215).[44] Reflecting on this passage from the novel, Kinkead-Weeks writes:

> Golder is a man apparently caught in hopeless opposition, but to measure him against *Erinle* is to reinforce the sense of what he could be, transformed in the crucible of clashing forces from within. For *Erinle* is bisexual and contradictory. . . . For Soyinka, it is intrinsic to the Yoruba sense of deity that there is a vital connection between opposites; there is, for example, healing in violence and violence in healing. To fix on one aspect of the exclusion of the opposite is to distort the nature, and inhibit the potential, of the god-like power that is in man, and can transform him. To *be* both fully is to explode contraries into power and progression; to tap the divine forces in the universe, and to become more godlike. (232)

In *The Invention of Women: Making an African Sense of Western Gender Discourses* (1997), Oyeronke Oyewumi argues that gender as we know it in the West did not exist in precolonial Yoruba societies:

> [T]he fundamental category "woman"—which is foundational in Western gender discourses—simply did not exist in Yorubaland prior to its sustained contact with the West. There was no such preexisting group characterized by shared interests, desires, or social position. The cultural logic of Western social categories is based on an ideology of biological determinism: the conception that biology provides the rationale for the organization of the social world. (ix)

She offers as supporting evidence the facts that "Yoruba kinship terms did not denote gender, and other nonfamilial social categories were not gender-specific either" (13), that "most Yoruba names are gender-free" (43), and that "[u]nlike European languages, Yoruba does not 'do gender,' it 'does seniority' instead. . . . Seniority, unlike gender, is only comprehensible as part of relationships. Thus it is neither rigidly fixated on the body nor dichotomized" (42). Indeed, "Seniority as the foundation of Yoruba social intercourse is relational and dynamic; unlike gender, it is not focused on the body" (14). Seniority was patricentric in this patrilocal society; that is, wives begin to accrue seniority upon joining their husband's household, whereas paternal relatives begin to accrue seniority at birth. For example, a husband's younger sister would have the status of "husband" in relation to his wives and the latter that of "wives" in relation to his younger sister, even when they were older than his sister (unless they were married to him before she was born). In such a context, therefore, does it even make sense to discuss the gender of gods or, for that matter, that of female "husbands"? Oyewumi's work should thus also lead us to cast debates considered earlier in this chapter about homosexual relations between female husbands and their wives in an entirely different light; whereas most western observers focus on the female couple in "woman-woman" marriages (an expression that would only make sense in a context in which gender exists), any "woman" can have the status of husband in an extended family joined by additional "women."

Kola's "reading" of Golder, then, his painting of him into the Yoruba pantheon, or Kola's reading of Golder's relation to the African diaspora and its roots in precolonial religious beliefs, associates him with a pre-gender society that would seem as queer to many westerners as it does to Golder. This is also the reading that reconciles him to his blackness, which he has found defective throughout the novel. Right after the passage quoted above in which Kola remembers meeting Golder for the first time while the latter was wearing only a towel and pretending to read *Giovanni's Room*, Golder at first tries to seduce him (as he tries to seduce Sagoe during their first meeting). In spite of the fact that the novel describes Golder as "ugly on a stool" (217), and although Kola is not interested in a sexual encounter, when Golder takes off the towel, Kola finds him beautiful: "He had a hard-sprung body, truly beautiful. 'You see,' he said, 'my body is fully negro; it is simply an act of perverseness that I turn out mostly white.' And then he leapt up suddenly ran round to look at the first brush strokes" (217). As Kola begins to paint the *orisha* Golder is posing for, the latter requests, "For God's sake, blacken me. Make me the blackest black blackness in your pantheon" (217).

In spite of the fact that Golder's racial self-hatred prevents him from being able to recognize his own beauty, a beauty that requires the rejection of a politics of purity in order to be seen, it is only upon "returning" to Africa that this beauty can be appreciated in the eyes of an African artist. The fact that Kola paints him blacker than he sees him is not what creates this beauty; instead, his aesthetics relies on an appreciation of diversity that is also sexual. In spite of wanting to be purer in his Africanness, upon returning to his African roots, Golder asserts that they are actually quite queer by pointing to the local existence of same-sex desires. In this sense, his return to origins parallels those of Ken in Bugul's *Le baobab fou* and Sissie in Aidoo's *Our Sister Killjoy*. Although Sagoe characterizes Afrocentricity as a form of masturbation (which is, when one thinks about it, a rather queer way to describe Afrocentricity), Golder is the character who points out to Sagoe that he is more nationalistic than he lets on: "You Africans are so damned nationalistic" (194). Golder thus represents a version of Afrocentricity that questions nationalism, an antinationalist nationalism, a rather queer nationalism since, as the slogan goes, "the Queer Nation has no borders." He reiterates a trope of nationalist discourse (the desire to return to a precolonial Africa), but what he finds there contests the sexual purity that this very same nationalism attempts to enforce.

It is perhaps an irony of history that it took a straight African writer to create a queer model of American Afrocentricity, a model that queer Americans have yet to surpass. As it has been the task of this chapter to demonstrate, such a queer Afrocentricity requires an interdisciplinary quest for queer African roots, whether the "fruits" of these roots are African or American. Given the history of homophobic criticism of Soyinka's novel (and even, in some cases, antihomophobic criticism that denies a history to same-sex desire in Africa), as well as the curious fact that certain interpreters *of* the novel echo certain interpreters *in* the novel, one might also say that Soyinka's novel constitutes an allegory of literary criticism in that it has somehow managed to get its critics to illustrate what it criticizes. Soyinka's novel still manages to mock its own readers over forty-five years after its first publication; literary critics who fail to recognize the model of literary criticism *The Interpreters* proposes end up embodying the kind of interpretation it makes fun of. Soyinka thus has much to teach western queer studies, for through him one might say that the roots of the African diaspora are indeed always already queer.

CHAPTER 3

Scandals and Lies

The Truth about Roots

✦ ✦ ✦

Le mensonge a d'innombrables racines.
[The lie has numberless roots.]
  —Edmond Jabès

The Scandal of Roots

Many detractors have dug up reasons for challenging the factuality of Alex Haley's *Roots*. He has been accused of and sued twice for plagiarizing parts of the novel (Reuter; Boyd, H.; Nobile 32–33).[1] The so-called griot who told Haley the story of Kunta Kinte not only was accused of being a fake but also had perhaps told him only what he had paid to hear (Nobile 34–35; Wright 208–12; Ottaway). Kinte's village, Juffure, where he was supposedly kidnapped, was actually involved in selling *neighboring* peoples to white slavers, which makes it unlikely that anyone from there would have been enslaved (Rose 3; Ottaway).[2] Historians have pointed out numerous anachronisms and questioned the existence of the slave ship that Haley claims brought Kinte to America (Rose 4; Nobile 35–36; Ottaway). American genealogical records contradict Haley's account of the American portion of his family tree (Mills, "*Roots*" and "Genealogist's Assessment"). And Haley's editor at *Playboy* magazine made such drastic corrections that some have argued he might more appropriately be considered the writer of *Roots* (Nobile 37–38; Haley, *Roots* 9). To these accusations, Philip Nobile added a sort of coup de grace in his 1993 *Village Voice* article "Uncovering Roots," proposing that Haley had perhaps even invented the oral history that supposedly retained the few Mandinka words that provided the bridge back to Africa (35). As David Chioni Moore writes, "[I]t had been concluded by many that *Roots* was, in some sense, a 'lie'" ("Routes" 9). To those who sought to expose this lie, *Roots* was nothing short of scandalous.

Chief among *Roots*' defenders has been Moore himself. To counter the lawsuits' challenges to the novel's integrity, he argues that "the distinction between originality and plagiarism, like that between fact and fiction, has been attacked as recent, historically variable, and theoretically untenable" ("Revisiting" 197–98; "Routes" 9). Others have also defended Haley against various specific charges. For example, when Mark Ottaway pointed out that Juffure's collaboration with slavers made it highly unlikely that any of its villagers would have been enslaved, as Kunta Kinte is supposed to have been, "Most American historians, when contacted, said that regardless of errors, the historical essence of the book was truthful" (McFadden 29; see also Shenker 29). And in response to Ottaway's accusation that Haley's griot was a fake, Robin Law wrote:

> Implicit in Ottaway's critique is the assumption that if Haley had consulted a genuine *griot* rather than a charlatan he would have been offered genuine traditions rather than being told what he wished to hear. Now, it may be that in this particular context this view is correct, but as a judgment of the historicity of the accounts of *griots* in general it would be absurd. . . . If a *parvenu* king needed respectable ancestors to legitimise his rule, his *griot* supplied them. Fofana of Juffure, though not a *griot* by heredity or training, was therefore true to the spirit of the *griot* calling when he obligingly provided Alex Haley with the ancestor he was seeking. His patron was a black American visitor rather than an African king, but that is a minor difference. The black American, like the African kings, wanted ancestors, and it was the business of the *griot* to give the rich and powerful what they want. (132–33)

It might be argued, then, that the challenges to *Roots*' veracity could apply to even the most historically accurate, good-faith roots narrative that involves returning to a predominantly oral culture.

In contrast to the scandal that Haley's novel set off and his denial of the lies he was accused of, *Un mensonge* [A Lie], published in 1990 and written by the Jewish, Moroccan-born actress, singer, and writer Sapho, more explicitly examines the connection between lies and origins by narrating a quest for truth in origins, which turn out to be a fiction. In its very title, *Un mensonge* suggests an entirely different approach to the truth claims of roots narratives; by openly associating lies and roots, Sapho highlights the narrative paradox at the heart of all roots narratives. While most literary critics today would not consider fictitious genres to be composed of lies, the difference between the two was less clear and thus a source of anxiety in earlier periods of literary history. Sapho seems to confuse the two in a similar manner. Although some narrative genres (such as history and legal testimony) present their representations as factual and others (such as the novel) acknowledge that their representations are fictitious or at least other than factual (regardless of how plausible they might seem), using the term *fiction* to describe roots emphasizes that, in all of these discourses and in spite of their claims, truth is a narrative construct.

At first the actor/protagonist of *Un mensonge*, Alph Hade, lies about his Jewish Moroccan origins. The return to these roots that he carries out in an attempt to rectify his lies, however, ends not with the retrieval of a "true" or "authentic" Sephardic identity but rather with an assertion of the writtenness of this identity. For Alph also turns out to be the main "character" (or letter) in an allegory of Genesis read as an act of divine fiction making in Kabbalistic readings of the Creation story, which can then become the origin of a rabbinical tradition of exegesis as much as of humanity. Furthermore, *Un mensonge* follows up on the *Zohar*'s sexualization of the male scholar engaged in holy intercourse with his beloved Torah by exploring the paradox of its own sexualized allegory of Creation in Alph's lovemaking with Bette, another of Sapho's main characters/letters. By bringing Sapho into comparison with Haley, this chapter takes up the task of using the overlapping diasporas of Jewish North Africa to queer both the roots of diaspora and diaspora studies as a field. For the roots Alph returns to in his multiple trips to Morocco turn out to be always already deconstructed. And even the heterosexual sexual allegory of origins proposed by the *Zohar* and Sapho's Kabbalistic rabbi come undone in her novel's "climax." When read as an allegory of reading roots narratives like Haley's, Sapho's novel also offers an allegory of deconstruction as a narrative about diasporic identity in the writings of other French-language Sephardic writers such as Jacques Derrida and Edmond Jabès.

A *Lie about Roots*

In denying his own roots as the son of a Moroccan Jewish mother, Alph actually tells multiple lies, which are integrated into his very name. For he even attempted to officialize his fictional name by erasing the letter *E* from the beginning of his original name, Ehade, on his passport: "Il avait tenu à déformer légèrement [son nom] jusqu'à commettre cet acte fou, un jour, d'utiliser du corrector sur son passeport, pour retirer une lettre à son nom qu'il trouvait imprononçable" (32) [He insisted on slightly deforming his name, even committing the insanity, one day, of using white-out to remove a letter from his name that he found unpronounceable]. Since the novel states that *ehade* means "one" in Hebrew (160–61), Alph's passport not only denies his "true" origins, but also effaces his name as beginning in another kind of denial of origin. Alph first lied as a child in response to questions by Agnieska, a girl he was in love with, about why he never went to mass. Because "[o]n soupçonnait qu'il était juif[,] changeait de trottoir à sa vue [et] ne lui montrait plus les timbres rares et son dernier Meccano" (74) [he was suspected of being Jewish, and others crossed the street when they saw him coming and no longer showed him their rare stamps and their latest Meccano], he replied that he was Protestant and therefore went to the Protestant church.

Yet Alph begins to question the value of his lies after the event that sets off the novel's plot: his seemingly unexplainable, near-fatal fall during the last performance of a run of Molière's seventeenth-century play *Le misanthrope*, in which he plays the title role of Alceste, who refuses to submit to the social conventions of the time, which he openly condemns as hypocritical. Upon his recovery, he seeks to unravel the mystery of this incident. Was he pushed, and if so by whom, or did he want to die and therefore "pushed" himself? And in seeking to explain his fall, Alph turns to Albert Sarfate,[3] a filmmaking, skirt-chasing, Kabbalistic rabbi who has a very interesting method of finding an explanation: the actors in Molière's play have names that correspond to letters of the Hebrew alphabet. Each of these names also has a meaning, according to the rabbi, who directs Alph to ask the actors and the director to make a sentence with the words to which their names correspond (see tables 3.1 and 3.2). As part of this elaborate interpretative ploy, the rabbi leads Alph to Bette, the actress who plays the flirtatious Célimène, with whom Alceste falls in love in spite of the fact that she epitomizes everything he despises. Bette confirms the rabbi's interpretation of the sentences by describing how the play's director arranged to make him fall as a gag for

Table 3.1. Characters in Sapho's *Un mensonge*

Character in Sapho's Novel	Role in Molière's Play	Corresponding Hebrew Letter[a]	Meanings of Names[b]	Sentence Constructed from Words in the Previous Column
Alph Hade/ Ehade	Alceste	aleph	A, le chercheur	L'instrument existe: le mur entre le faussaire et le chercheur c'est l'arme dans la maison. La porte c'est le voyage.
Bette/Betty Duclos	Célimène	bet	maison	Le voyageur existe. L'instrument du faussaire c'est l'arme qui porte A loin de la maison par-dessus le mur.
Iseult Guimmel	Arsinoé	guimel	chameau, voyage	La porte de la maison est l'instrument ou l'arme du chercheur voyageant dans les murs du faussaire.
Philippe Dalette	Clitandre	daleth	porte	Armé jusqu'aux dents il chercha aux murs de la maison l'instrument, porte, voyage de son existence.
Jacques de la Haye	Philinte	hé	être, exister	Existe dans la maison un mur avec une porte, instrument du faussaire, c'est ce qui arme le chercheur pour le voyage.
Vava Carton	Éliante	vav	any conjunction, clou, instrument	Le faussaire est un chercheur dont l'arme est l'instrument du voyage hors de la maison après le mur.
Féodor Zaïne	Acaste	zaïn	arme	Son instrument entre les dents près d'une maison sans porte A le voyageur et son arme sont murs.[c]
Christian Hette	Oronte	het	mur	Sur la porte du mur, dans la maison du chercheur est une dent de chameau, une fausse arme.[d]

[a]As spelled in *Un mensonge*.
[b]These meanings are given by Albert (*Un mensonge* 194).
[c]The sentences of Alph through Christian Hette are in *Un mensonge*, 242–43.
[d]Hubert's sentence is in *Un mensonge*, 263.

the closing performance in order to ridicule Alph's character, the ever so serious Alceste, who is marked by a radical refusal to lie even, and especially, for the purposes of social decorum.[4] At the same time, Alph seduces and is seduced by Bette, and the novel ends as he ceases to lie and espouses "the truth." When Alph is joined with Bette, this heterosexual union symbolizes the decoding of the novel's mystery/crime and, as we shall see later in this chapter, it offers an allegory for reading all roots narratives as detective fiction. The heterosexual union of Alph and Bette thus serves as a metaphor for decoding the novel's mystery/crime.

Table 3.2. English Translations of the Meanings of Names in Sapho's *Un mensonge*

A, the seeker	The instrument exists: the wall between the forger and the seeker is the arm in the house. The door/gate is the journey.
House/home	The traveler exists. The forger's instrument is the arm that carries A far from the house over the wall.
Camel, journey	The door of the house is the instrument or arm of the seeker traveling within the forger's walls.
Door/gate	Armed to the teeth, he looked—on the walls of the house—for the instrument, door/gate, journey of his existence.
To be/exist	In the house, there exists a wall with a door, the forger's instrument, which is what arms the seeker for the journey.
Nail, instrument	The forger is a seeker whose arm is the instrument of the journey out of the house, beyond the wall.
Arm/weapon	Near a house without doors, with his instrument between this teeth, A the traveler and his arm are ripe.[a]
Wall	On the door in the wall, in the seeker's house, there is a camel's tooth, a false arm.
Tooth, falsifier	The forger, armed with a nail, carries A towards the house for a journey beyond the wall of being.

[a]Here Zaïne uses mur as its adjectival homophone, mûr(e), which means "ripe." It is written in his sentence, however, without its circumflex. Albert appreciates this play on words (260).

As part of seeking the truth about his fall, to a certain extent Alph recovers his identity through a return to his Moroccan roots. "Cette chute le ramenait à son origine" (61) [This fall led him back to his origins], writes Sapho, and these roots are found in memories—stimulated by his fall—memories of both his Moroccan childhood and a journey to Morocco that occurred just prior to the beginning of rehearsals for *Le misanthrope*, a journey narrated retroactively in the appropriately entitled chapter "Alph et l'Afrique" [Alph and Africa]. Alph also makes a second journey to Morocco as part of his efforts to explain the fall. His return to origins is quite literally a return to himself because Alph's *first* name is derived from the first letter of the Hebrew alphabet (*alef*). And, like Adam and Abraham (with whom the novel explicitly compares him), his name begins with the very letter it signifies. Taken as a whole, the name *Alph Hade* is itself a paradox. It both signifies origins (in the first name) and denies them (in the faked last name). The protagonist is named, therefore, with both an affirmation and a denial of origins. So, in contrast with his falsified last name, his first name marks him as the personification of beginnings and origins. One could say, then, that the "lie" is foundational to his identity; it is not just *about* his origins, it is his origins. His name tells the truth about his identity by naming him as the product of a lie and thereby exemplifies the narrative paradox of roots narratives.

In a further paradox, the origins of the character who personifies origins are themselves occulted not only by the lie he has been living by denying his own roots as the son of a Moroccan Jewish mother but also by his *mother*'s lies about his origins: "Elle avait tout accepté, que l'enfant soit baptisé, de considérer ses origines comme une honte" (47) [She gave in to everything, that her child be baptized, that he think of his origins as a source of shame]. And she told these lies in spite of having named him (or "baptized" him, as one could say in French) as origin, in spite of being his origin; she is thus also denying her self in an act of colonial alienation. Yet, when Alph ceases to lie about his origins and his name, he thereby returns to himself by reconciling his first name and his "true" last name, both of which signify a beginning. Telling the truth, in this reading, would constitute a remedy for colonial alienation. It would also be possible, therefore, to articulate a reading of *Un mensonge*, à la Haley's *Roots*, as a roots narrative that reconnects Alph with his "true" identity by correcting or repairing "the lie" and setting the story "straight," so to speak.

In the Beginning

Yet the first indication that such an organic reattachment to his roots might be problematic can be found in Alph's obsession with the beginning words of Genesis, which he repeats on several occasions in the novel: "'Au commencement étaient le tohu-bohu, le vide et le vague, disait la Genèse, et la lumière fut,' et le mensonge commença" (19) ["In the beginning were tohu-bohu,[5] emptiness, and formlessness," said Genesis, "and then there was light," and the lie began]. The notion of a foundational lie (the serpent's lie to Eve, who then lies to her husband) recurs in the novel as Alph again quotes the beginning of Genesis:

> Il écoutait parler en lui son "tohu-bohu," il aimait ces mots hébreux qui voulait dire le vide et le vague. N'était-ce pas vertigineux ? Le tohu-bohu, pas le chaos comme traduisent certaines Bibles françaises, "Au commencement étaient le tohu-bohu" et la lumière fut et le mensonge commença. (49)

> [He listened to his tohu-bohu speaking within him, he loved these Hebrew words which meant emptiness and formlessness. Wasn't it dizzying? The tohu-bohu, not chaos as certain French Bibles trans-

lated it, "In the beginning was tohu-bohu" and then there was light and the lie began.]

On one level, Alph's take on Genesis might be read as reiterating the biblical myth of the origins of humanity in sin. The lie would then be the serpent's lie to Eve, Eve's lie to Adam, and all the lies human beings have been telling (as a part of their sinfulness) ever since (lies reproduced heterosexually). In this sense, Alph's fall could be read as an allegory for the Fall of "Man," Bette would represent his heterosexual redemption, and his sexual union with her would be a return to a literally heterosexual paradise.

But again, as suggested by the unusual twist that the rabbi adds to Alph's association of Genesis and lies in his rather unorthodox take on the biblical myth of origins, the lies associated with the original heterosexual couple are more fundamental:

> Savez-vous que la Création commence par deux mensonges de Dieu lui-même ? Dans la Genèse, il prévient Adam et Ève : "Si vous mangez de l'arbre de vie, vous mourrez." Le serpent, lui, dit à Ève : "Si vous mangez (vouz saurez), vous serez comme Dieu." (248)

> [Did you know that the Creation begins with two lies on the part of God himself? In Genesis, he warns Adam and Eve, "If you eat of the tree of life, you shall die." As for the serpent, he tells Eve, "If you eat (you shall know), you shall be like God."]

The foundational lie is thus not just the lie told by serpent to woman, who reproduces it by retelling it to man. Rather, by pointing out that the first lie was told not by the serpent but by God himself, the rabbi suggests that the original lie was not the original sin but the *doctrine* of original sin. For, since the rabbi's assertion presupposes a slippage between God and Satan—if God told two lies, God and the serpent must be one and the same—the lies told by the creator precede the ones told by the original humans he created. In other words, this originating lie (the one told by "God"), this original, originary, or primal lie, founds not only humanity but also Alph's Moroccan roots. In fact, we could also say that it founds roots in general. For Alph finds his roots in a doubled diaspora, uprooted as he is (in part through his own lies) from his Moroccan homeland, itself the place of a Jewish identity already in diaspora. Furthermore, Sapho doubles even this original diaspora, for in *Un mensonge,* humanity begins as such with a still prior dispersal, that of Adam and Eve from paradise.

An additional part of the novel's recognition of its own fictionality is related to the way it points to itself as a novelistic version of the *Zohar*, or Book of Splendor. Written mostly in Aramaic toward the end of the thirteenth century in Spain,[6] this founding Kabbalistic text becomes a key point of reference for Sapho's rabbi:

> Dans le *Zohar*, le livre des lumières, on peut lire : ". . . Quand il [God] se décida à créer le monde, toutes les lettres se présentèrent à lui de la dernière à la première . . ." Bett [*sic*] a été choisie sans discussion : "C'est par toi (Bet) que je créerai le monde, tu seras l'inauguration de la création du monde." (*Mensonge* 166; second ellipsis Sapho's)

> [In the *Zohar*, the Book of Light, one reads: ". . . When God had resolved to create the world, all the letters presented themselves to him from the last to the first." *Bet* was chosen without discussion: "It's through you (*bet*) that I shall create the world: you shall be the inauguration of the creation of the world."]

The notion that "Bet was chosen without discussion" is somewhat misleading, however, since in the *Zohar* one finds a much more elaborate reading of the first four words of Genesis—*Bereshit bara Elohim et* (In the beginning God created)—and the account of Creation this reading is based on:

> Rav Hamnuna Sava said, "We find the letters backward: *Bet* first, followed by *bet: Bereshit, In the beginning*, followed by *bara*, created. Then *alef* first, followed by *alef: Elohim*, followed by *et*.
>
> "The reason is: When the blessed Holy One wished to fashion the world, all the letters were hidden away. For two thousand years before creating the world, the Blessed Holy One contemplated them and played with them. As He verged on creating the world, all the letters presented themselves before Him, from last to first.
>
> "The letter *tav* entered first of all. She said, 'Master of the worlds, may it please You to create the world by me, for I complete Your seal: *emet*, truth—and You are called Truth. It is fitting for the King of Truth to begin with a letter of truth and to create the world by me.'
>
> "The Blessed Holy One replied, 'You are seemly and worthy, but do not deserve to initiate Creation, since you are destined to be

marked on the foreheads of the faithful who fulfilled the Torah from *alef* to *tav*, and by your mark they will die. Furthermore you are the seal of *mavet*, death. So you do not deserve to serve as the instrument of Creation.' She immediately departed." (*The Zohar* 11–12)[7]

And this is just the discussion with the first letter to present herself (the letters are gendered feminine in the *Zohar*)—the Hebrew alphabet's last letter, *tav*. Each of the other letters likewise presents herself and offers a reason why Creation should begin with her; each then receives an explanation as to why she is unsuitable for this role.

Both the justifications and counterjustifications correspond to meanings produced by or through the letter itself—its shape, a word it is a part of, or a word similar to its own name. It is, in fact, its association of meaning with the various letters of the Hebrew alphabet (see tables 3.1 and 3.2) that allows the *Zohar* to provide the key for deciphering the mystery of Alph's fall. In this parade of letters, only to *bet* does God not have a retort, so He decides to begin Creation with her only to realize that one remaining letter was overlooked:

> The letter *alef* stood and did not enter. The Blessed Holy One said to her, "*Alef, alef*, why do you not enter My presence like all the other letters?"
>
> She replied, "Master of the world! Because I saw all letters leaving Your presence fruitlessly. What could I do there? Furthermore, look, You have given this enormous gift to the letter *bet*, and it is not fitting for the exalted King to take back a gift He has given to His servant and give it to another."
>
> The Blessed Holy One said, "*Alef, alef!* Although I will create the world with the letter *bet*, you will be the first of all the letters. Only through you do I become one. With you all counting begins and every deed in the world. No union is actualized except by *alef*." (16)

Genesis as read in the *Zohar* is thus quite literally conceived as an ordering of letters. Before the beginning, "*The earth was tohu va-bohu, chaos and void* (Gen. 1.2)—dregs of an inkwell in seepage" (*Zohar* 181), and out of this ink will come the Creation, written as if all of the world and humankind were a kind of fiction.

Since in the beginning God put *bet* and *alef* together as the initial letters of the first four words, when Alph and Bette have sex toward the end of Sapho's novel, this alpha-bet-ical union not only marks a return to Genesis but also reenacts its writing and recalls God's placing of the two together in the first words of Genesis (the beginning of the beginning). Unlike Eve, because *bet* begins Creation and precedes the Fall, when Alph (as Adam) returns to her he repairs not only his fall from the stage but also the Fall of Man. This heterosexualization of Genesis corresponds to the rabbi Albert's own vocal embrace of heterosexuality (though one that, at times, also embraces his sexual others). It also corresponds to the sexualized reading of Genesis articulated in Albert's most important textual reference, the *Zohar*. Furthermore, this instance of heterosexual intercourse parallels the *Zohar*'s description of Creation as a sexual act:

> When the world above was filled and impregnated, like a female impregnated by a male, it generated two children as one, male and female, who are *heaven* and *earth*, as above. *Earth* is nourished by the waters of *heaven*, released into her, though the upper are male and the lower female, the lower nourished by the male. The lower waters call to the upper, like a female opening to the male, pouring out water toward the water of the male to form seed. (177)

And the commentary of the Stanford translation, or Pritzker edition, describes heterosexual copulation as a reenactment of Creation: "When a human couple unites, they stimulate the union of *Shekinah* and Her partner, *Tif'eret*, thereby strengthening the entirety of the *sefirot*, the realm of faith" (*Zohar* 275n1290).[8] Likewise, even in its epigraph, *Un mensonge* gives sexual meaning to its Kabbalistic allusions:

> "Dès qu'une parole de la Torah est renouvelée par la bouche d'un homme . . . le Saint béni soit-il . . . recueille cette parole, lui donne un baiser et la pare de soixante-dix couronnes ornées et ciselées . . ."
>
> "La comprehension et le bien sont deux portes qui sont comme une. . . ."
>
> *Le Zohar, le livre de la Splendeur* (7; Sapho's ellipses)

> [As soon the word of the Torah is renewed by a man's mouth, the Holy One, blessed be he, receives this word, kisses it, and adorns it with seventy ornate, finely-crafted crowns.
>
> Understanding and the good are two gates that are as one.
>
> *The Zohar, Book of Splendor*]

Un mensonge thus retells Genesis to a certain extent, and reading the Torah is similarly a sexual act: "The moment a new word of Torah originates from the mouth of a human being, that word ascends and presents herself before the blessed Holy One, who lifts that word, kisses her, and adorns her with seventy crowns" (*Zohar* 25). Reading about origins in Genesis is thus to participate in the sexual act of Creation.

As a reading of the Torah (Genesis through Deuteronomy), therefore, the *Zohar* not only suggests that divine Creation was an act of writing, but it also suggests a parallel between the narrative act of creation and the tradition of exegesis and rabbinic commentary (including, e.g., the Talmud, the Midrash, and the Kabbalistic tradition) that expands on the Book—both the Torah and divinely authored Creation. In the *Zohar*, therefore, Genesis recognizes itself as an act of fiction.[9] In short, divine Creation might also be read as a founding moment for the mystical cryptography that the *Zohar* exemplifies and Sapho's novel picks up as a method of detection or crime solving. In fact, the meanings of the letters (and therefore the actors' names that correspond to them) in tables 3.1 and 3.2 are taken directly from the more ancient (and mystical) *Sefer Yetsirah* or *Book of Formation* (see Kaplan 8; Ben Joseph 19), "that ancient and prekabbalistic source from which the term *sefirah* itself is taken" (Green 54), part of

> the speculative-magical tradition that reached medieval Jewry through the little book called *Sefer Yetsirah* and various other small texts, mostly magical in content, that are associated with it. *Sefer Yetsirah* has been shown to be a very ancient work, close in spirit to aspects of Greek esotericism that flourished in the late Hellenistic era. While the practice associated with this school of thought is magical-theurgic, even including the attempt to make a *golem*, its chief text contains the most abstract worldview to be found within the legacy of ancient Judaism. (13–14)

The magical practice of fashioning a *golem* resonates with the passages from the *Zohar* quoted above and with the intertextual relationship between Sapho's novel and the *Zohar*. One of the most renowned experts of the Kabbalistic tradition, Gershom Scholem (1897–1982), describes the fashioning and unfashioning of a *golem* as follows: "According to other legends, the word *emet* ('truth'; 'the seal of the Holy One' . . .) was written on his forehead, and when the letter *alef* was erased there remained the word *met* ('dead')" (352).

On several occasions, Sapho's rabbi uses the same words, *emet* and *met*, to decode the mystery of Alph's fall:

Il y a dans votre présentation, dit Albert, un parallèle entre faussaire et chercheur, même si on les oppose (on les sépare d'un mur, Het, qui veut dire aussi péché), ils sont sur le même plan, Het, le péché qui les sépare, est apparu lorsque Adam et Ève ont mangé le fruit de l'arbre de vie, cette pomme, première transgression, et avec le péché est survenu le peu de connaissance dont nous disposions, une connaissance imparfaite de douleur et de frustration. Entre le faussaire et le chercheur, il y a ce savoir imparfait, ce péché. Du mensonge à la vérité, il y a "mort," "met," mais Adam a mangé de l'arbre de la connaissance, a commis le péché d'entrevoir et il n'est pas mort. Entre Chine et Aleph, il y a le péché qui est aussi l'arme dans la maison, cet instrument de mort. (251–52)

[In your account, said Albert, there is a parallel between the falsifier and the seeker; even if they are separated (separated by a wall, *het*, which also means sin), they are on the same plane; *het*, the sin that separates them, appeared when Adam and Eve ate fruit from the tree of life (the apple or first transgression), and with this sin came the bit of knowledge that we have at our disposal, an imperfect knowledge of pain and frustration. Between the falsifier and the seeker, there is this imperfect knowledge, this sin. From lie to truth, there is *death* (*met*), but Adam ate from the tree of knowledge, committed the sin of perception, and he did not die. Between *shin* and *alef*, there is sin, which is also the weapon in the house, that instrument of death.]

Another passage in *Un mensonge* more explicitly points out that *met* is *emet* without its initial *alef*:

Emet, Aleph est mort.
    Je vais vers Ité. La répétition.
    Vé   ver   ité
    La vérité, ce qui peut se répéter ? (271–72)
[*Emet*, Aleph is dead.
    I go toward Ité. Repetition.
    I go   toward/worm   ité
    Truth, that which repeats itself?]

Truth contains the *alef* and the *tav* (the alpha and the omega), the beginning and the end as death. Beginnings thus contain and depend on their endings. Truth (*emet*) consists of repeating letters and is destroyed by the removal of its beginning letter (*alef*), which turns *emet* into an ending (death or *met*).

Furthermore, the novel figures Alph as the personification of this narrative ordering of letters: "En hébreu, *Emet*, vérité, peut se décomposer en deux, *E/Met*, Aleph est mort, en araméen : je suis mort. Vous voyez bien que la vérité ne nous appartient pas" (248) [In Hebrew, *emet* (or truth) can be broken in half, *E/Met* (or *alef* is dead); in Aramaic, it means "I am dead." As you can very well see, truth does not belong to us]. Alph, as the personification of the first letter, *alef*, also separates truth (as founded in origins or roots) from the death of truth, or lies. He is the removable letter on which the creation of Adam depends: "Adam is called *golem*, meaning body without soul, in a Talmudic legend concerning the first 12 hours of his existence" (Scholem 351). Alph is thus Sapho's *golem* to a certain extent, for he is likewise fashioned out of letters, in particular the first one. And as such he is an iteration of Adam, with whom the novel has already explicitly compared him. The *golem*, that human perversion of divine Creation (except for the fact that divine Creation also begins with a *golem*), is thus described in Sapho (as in what Green calls the magical-theurgic school of thought) as an ordering of letters. Finally, as *golem*, Sapho's Alph is also a personification of the roots narrative *as an allegory of reading*, that is, as a narrative that offers its own way of reading origins and therefore has the potential to undo them.

Lying by the Book

After all, by partaking of both myths of origin (Genesis) and roots narratives (like *Roots*), *Un mensonge* opens up the possibility that all roots narratives might be read as reenactments of a kind of Genesis. The Hebrew title of the first book of the Torah, in fact, is the same as its first word—*Bereshit*—naming the book as beginning, not origin, which therefore reinforces my assertion in the introduction that Said's opposition between beginnings and origins in *Beginnings* is ripe for deconstruction. Furthermore, because narrative beginnings are, for Said, what authorize the story that follows but are ultimately arbitrary, they inevitably involve a falsehood: "The second special condition for generating narrative fiction is that the truth—whatever that may be—can only be approached indirectly, by means of a mediation that, paradoxically, because of its falseness makes the truth truer" (90). Put differently, we might understand the beginning's self-naming as a false naming, or at least an act of fiction making. In fact, the truth-generating effects of repetition described by Sapho might be seen as the mode of production by means of which fictions become truths and narratives become myth and identity. What Said adds to such an understanding of identity as fiction making is an analysis of the role of beginnings (and therefore, in my reading of Said, origins) in such a narrative production of identity:

> In this space [of the mind] certain fiction and certain reality come together as identity. Yet we can never be certain what part of identity is true, what part fictional. This will be true as long as part of the beginning eludes us, so long as we have language to help us and hinder us in finding it, and so long as language provides us with a word whose meaning must be *made* certain if it is not to be wholly obscure. (78)

For Said, then, beginnings mark the beginning of a hunch that identity is (only in part, in Said's formulation) an effect of narrative acts of identity rather than (again, only, for Said) being its cause. If identity is a fiction, then, Said begins the task of describing, understanding, and theorizing its narrative structure.

Another writer who can help us elaborate on such a narratology of identity is, paradoxically, a poet, the Jewish Egyptian Edmond Jabès, who has also explicitly explored the fictionality of origins and roots narratives by labeling them as lies. Consider the following passage from Jabès's *Le soupçon: Le désert* [*Intimations of the Desert*], vol. 2 of *Le livre des ressemblances* [*The Book of Resemblances*], which contains a section/poem entitled "Le mensonge des origines" [The Lie of Origins], whose first line reads, "L'origine ne serait, peut-être, que la brûlure de son effacement" (28) [Origins are perhaps only the burn of their erasure (*Book of Resemblances* II, 20)]. A few pages later, we read:

> *Commencement* : comment se ment ? Comment va mentir à soi-même le commencement afin de pouvoir s'imposer comme commencement ? Comment, se mentant, il va nous mentir, il va installer son mensonge au point de nous faire accroire que nous commençons avec lui ? (30)

[*Commencement,* "beginning": *comment se ment?* How does the beginning lie to itself in order to compel recognition as beginning? How does it, in lying to itself, lie to us and establish its lie so firmly it makes us believe we begin with it? (22)]

Since beginnings are only beginnings in the sense that by presenting themselves as such they come to be read as such, they are a kind of lie (asserting "I am a beginning") that tells the truth (because, therefore, its iteration—as in the passage from Sapho cited above—constitutes a self-fulfilling prophecy and, therefore, the truth). Like Sapho, Jabès understands truth claims as being fabricated from lies: "Il y a, parfois, une telle conviction dans le mensonge, que la vérité en est confondue" (*LQ* II, 194) [Sometimes there is such conviction in lies that truth is confounded (*LQ* III, 137)].[10] This lie is also a central part of the quest for truth: "Aucune quête de la vérité n'est possible hors de soi. / Le mensonge abrite une vérité que ses propres tourments dévorent" (*LQ* II, 159) [No quest [for] truth is possible outside yourself. / The lie shelters a truth [devoured] by its own torment (III, 110)]. And what are roots narratives if not a quest for truth? The end result, a narrative of identity, likewise depends on lies:

> Le mensonge est relié à la vérité, comme la corolle à la graine. L'image de soi qu'il exhibe inspire les interprétations les plus diverses que l'évidence entérine.
>
> Le mensonge nous souffle le moyen de nous réaliser, nous place dans la situation de nous contester, qui est la seule valable. (*LQ* II, 228)

> [Lies are bound to truth like the corolla to the seed. The self-image they show causes the most varied interpretations which evidence confirms.
>
> Lies prompt us, suggesting means of self-realization. They place us in the only valid position, that of challenging ourselves. (III, 160)]

And, like Sapho's rabbi, Jabès considers this lie as having originated with God himself: "Le mensonge de Dieu" (*LQ* II, 23) [The lie of God (III, 12)].

The fascination with identity as a narrative trajectory that Jabès shares with Sapho becomes less surprising when one considers that he shares, to a certain extent, her overlapping diasporas. Born in Cairo in 1912, he received an education entirely in French, one that culminated at the Lycée Français of Cairo. Although he maintained a long relationship with Max Jacob, met Paul Eluard early in his career, and has been loosely associated with the surrealists, he always kept a certain distance from them as a group. In 1957, due to increasing anti-Semitism in conjunction with Gamal Abdel Nasser's rise to power in Egypt, Jabès immigrated to France (Jabès, *Du désert* 187–90). In spite of a career spent mostly in exile there, Jabès's particularly Egyptian homeland remains at the center of his thematics. And in the figure of the desert Jabès makes of exile a specifically Jewish thematic concern. By focusing on the desert, in fact, he displaces the site of Jewish identity from Israel to Egypt in an implicit reworking of the biblical narrative of Egypt as a place of enslavement and therefore of an uprooted identity. Jabès is perhaps best known for a seven-volume collection of poems (or work in verse, since it is not always clear where one poem ends and another begins): *Le livre des questions* [*The Book of Questions*].[11] This work not only assembles a great number of questions, often in the form of rabbinic dialogues, but also questions the Book and all that comes with it, including God, who, having exiled himself after Creation, also authored Creation like a book as in the Kabbalistic tradition.

Jabès's God is thus a textual phenomenon similar to the author function, for like the author in literary studies, Jabès's God is dead. In fact, God's post-Creation exile or death (they seem to be quasi equivalents) is linked to his lies as in the understanding of the Creation story on the part of Sapho's rabbi:

Dieu S'exila, laissant à l'homme le soin de décacheter l'univers. Je serai tous les mensonges de Dieu pour mourir de Sa mort ;
    car Dieu est mort de mentir. Tout ce qui *est* ment. Être dans la vérité, c'est aspirer au Non-être. Dieu est Vérité. Ainsi Dieu est Conjonction, Dieu est Convergence. (*LQ* II, 129–30)

[God went into exile and left it to man to unseal the world. I shall be all the lies of God in order to die of His death.
    For God died of lying. All that *exists* lies. To be in the truth means wanting Not-To-Be. God is Truth. Thus God is Union, God is Convergence. (III, 91)]

And God's exile not only humanizes and textualizes him but also associates him with Jewishness understood as an exilic condition:

[C]ar être juif c'est, à la fois, s'exiler dans la parole et pleurer son exile.

Le retour au livre est retour aux sites oubliés.

L'héritage de Dieu ne pouvait se transmettre que dans la mort inaugurée avec Lui. (*LQ* II, 203)

[Because being Jewish means exiling yourself in the word and, at the same time, weeping for your exile

The return to the book is a return to forgotten sites.

God's heritage could only be handed on in the death He ushered.

(III, 143)]

In fact, the textualization of God is partly what makes him the God of the Jews, who are "une race issue du livre" (*LQ* I, 30) [a race born of the book (I, 25)], hence Jabès's diasporist understanding of the expression "people of the Book," by means of which "the Book" becomes both the homeland of the diaspora and the promised land to which return narratives can make "territorial" claims: "Je suis dans le livre. Le livre est mon univers, mon pays, mon toit et mon énigme. Le livre est ma respiration et mon repos" (*LQ* I, 36) [I am in the book. The book is my world, my country, my roof, and my riddle. The book is my breath and my rest (I, 31)].

Because a return to roots is a return to the Book (cf. the title of the third volume of the *Book of Questions, Le retour au livre*), it becomes a purely textual phenomenon for Jabès, an act of narration. Indeed, for Jabès, *all* writing is inextricably linked to the question of roots:

Écrire, c'est avoir la passion de l'origine ; c'est essayer d'atteindre le fond. Le fond est toujours le commencement. Dans la mort, sans doute aussi, une multitude de fonds constitue le tréfonds ; de sorte qu'écrire ne signifie pas s'arrêter au but, mais le dépasser sans cesse. (*LQ* I, 360)

[Writing means having a passion for origins. It means trying to go down to the roots. The roots are always the beginning. Even in death, no doubt, a host of roots form the deepest root bottom. So writing does not mean stopping at the goal, but always going beyond. (II, 159)]

Given that the thematics just described resonates with many of the concerns found within Derridean deconstruction, it should not come as a surprise that in two essays in *Writing and Difference*—"Edmond Jabès and the Question of the Book" and "Ellipsis"—Derrida would use Jabès as a pre-text for theorizing the deconstruction of origins. Indeed, Jabès's *Book of Questions* preceded Derrida in articulating what I have called the narrative paradox of roots narratives by questioning rootedness as signified by a site of origins and revealing the writtenness of roots. In fact, Jabès would even explicitly come to embrace the term *deconstruction*:

> Le livre ne se construit pas, mais se déconstruit. Dieu est mort par le livre.
> Livre, tombe abyssale de Dieu ?
> Cette déconstruction est retour à la parole initiale (*LQ* II, 312).

> [The book is not [constructed], but [deconstructed]. God dies of the book.
> The book, bottomless tomb of God?
> This [deconstruction] means a return to the initial word. (III, 218)]

Critics have often associated Jabès with deconstruction, not only, no doubt, because of Derrida's discussion of his work in *Writing and Difference* but also because of the recurrence of certain terms or themes in his work—*écriture*, traces, origins, *différance*, margins, absence/presence—as well as a certain undecidability regarding exactly what these terms mean, mark him as a sort of poet of deconstruction (cf. Kronick 968). Derrida would take up Jabès's passion for roots as well as his acknowledgment of their writtenness: "Writing, passion of the origin. . . . It is the origin itself which is impassioned, passive, and past, in that it is written. Which means inscribed. The inscription of the origin is doubtless its Being-as-writing, but it is also its Being-as-inscribed in a system in which it is only a function and a locus" (295–96). For Jabès, the figure of God fulfills some of the functions of a deconstructionist understanding of origins in the following verses: "Dans le livre, . . . l'écriture est absence et la page blanche, présence. / Ainsi Dieu qui est absence est présent dans le livre" (*LQ* II, 305) ["In the book," he said, "writing means absence, and the empty page, presence. / Thus God, who is absence, is present in the book" (III, 213)]. Indeed, Jabès characterizes the deconstruction of origins as a quintessentially Jewish relation to identity and in so doing provides a key for understanding Sapho's deconstruction of not only origins but also Jewish identity.

Derrida would echo Jabès's understanding of the absence/presence binary in defining the aporia that is roots, as the following passage, already quoted in the introduction, attests:

> The writing of the origin, the writing that retraces the origin, tracking down the signs of its disappearance, the lost writing of the origin. . . . But what disposes it in this way, we now know, is not the origin, but that which takes its place; which is not, moreover, the opposite of an origin. It is not absence instead of presence, but a trace which replaces a presence which has never been present, an origin by means of which nothing has begun. (*Writing* 295)

And here the trace—often understood as the trace of the Other within the dominant term of a binary pair whose self-definition thereby relies on the other that it others or as a manifestation of *différance* through which traces of difference contaminate essence—comes also to define roots.

Tracing Roots

Mensonge de Dieu, je te suis à la trace.
[Lie of God's, I am on your trail.]
　—Edmond Jabès

In another passage quoted in my introduction, this one from *Of Grammatology*, Derrida reinforces the association between traces and origins, as well as the characterization of origins as the trace left behind by their disappearance: "The trace is not only the disappearance of origin . . . it means that the origin did not even disappear, that it was never constituted except reciprocally by a nonorigin, the trace, which thus becomes the origin of the origin" (61). At first this Derridean concept of trace might seem to have nothing in common with the specifically Caribbean meaning of the word *trace* as "path" that we saw in chapter 1, especially the *trace* in which Francis Sancher is discovered dead in Condé's *Traversée de la mangrove*. In the more recent theoretical work of Édouard Glissant, however, these two meanings come together in a specifically Caribbean understanding of the trace as a concept for theorizing both diaspora and deconstruction as an allegory for diasporic identity. In *Introduction à une poétique du divers* (1996) [Introduction to a Poetics of the Diverse] and *Traité du tout-monde* (1997) [Treatise on the World as Totality],[12] Glissant develops what he calls a "pensée de la trace" [trace-thinking] as a way of thinking about the notion of origins or roots in relation to identities in the present. In a "pensée de la trace," the "roots" of Caribbean identity are accessible only as traces; one cannot "return" to these roots as Haley returns to Africa in *Roots*, although Glissant may very well offer a rereading of Haley that demonstrates how seemingly straightforward roots can be about traces as well. Whereas Glissant does not often acknowledge the similarities between his notion of the trace and Derrida's, the former prompts a rereading of the latter, one that teases out the relation between Glissantian traces and a deconstructionist conception of origins.

In *Introduction à une poétique du divers*, Glissant introduces the notion of a "pensée de la trace" in a three-paragraph passage that contrasts the trace with an essentialist understanding of identity and uses the trace to define a kind of identity-in-movement: "The trace assumes and carries not being-thought but the ramblings of the existent" (69). He then links the "pensée de la trace" with his conceptualization of the rhizome from earlier writings (in spite of the differences one might point out between Deleuze and Guattari on the one hand and Derrida on the other): "Remember that the single root has the pretention of depth and that the rhizomatic root extends into the expanse" (69). Like the rhizome, therefore, the trace is one particular manifestation of a "poetics of relation" that defines identity *in relation*—to others, to the Other—and values this relation with other cultures and peoples over an internal essence, a point Glissant clarifies in *Traité du tout-monde*, published a year later: "Let trace-thinking posit itself, in opposition to system-thinking, as a wandering that orients. We understand that the trace is what puts us, all of us, regardless of our origins, in Relation" (18).

Although the poetics of this relationality often seems to consist of relationality with other *contemporary* cultures, it also suggests a relation with the past in historical terms, for already in *Introduction à une poétique du divers*, Glissant was providing more concrete *historical* examples of what he means by traces:

> Africans traded in the Americas brought with them from beyond the Great Waters the trace of their gods, their customs, and their languages. Confronted with the colonizer's harsh disorder, they had the genius, linked to the suffering they endured, to nourish these traces, thereby creating, even better than syntheses, results whose secret they held. These Creole languages are the traces/pathways cleared through the waters of the Caribbean and the Indian Ocean. (70)

The syncretic religions and Creole languages of the Caribbean, as cultural artifacts often said to have African roots, are thus specific manifestations of traces of African roots, or, better, of African roots as traces. Furthermore, if Caribbean culture results from the ability to "fertilize these traces in order to create resulting ones" as Glissant specified in a lecture delivered in 2000, traces are not a residue left by the past but an act of creation (Keynote). In other words, roots as traces are not discovered but created by narratives of identity. As an alternative to rootedness, the trace thus offers connectedness with the past and the possibility of movement along the lines of the *errance enracincée* discussed in chapter 1.

In addition, the trace becomes a way of thinking about the *rewriting* of history as relation: "The white spaces on planetary maps are now woven with opacity, which has broken forever with the absolute of History, which initially was project and projection. Hereafter, History is undone as a concept at the same time as it dwells on these returns of the identitarian, the national, the fundamental, all the more sectarian since they have become obsolete" (69). In a reference to pathways, then, Glissant brings the abstract theoretical concept of the trace back to its concrete Caribbean specificity: "The trace does not repeat the uncompleted path where one stumbles, nor the carefully tended path that closes on a territory or a large estate" (70). Furthermore, in addition to resulting from a creative relation with history, the trace keeps the celebration of identity implied by roots: "The trace is to the route as revolt is to injunction and jubilation to the garrote" (69). In other words, the trace is both a revolt and a jubilation and is capable of accounting for the coexistence of contradictions. It is "a wandering that orients" as in one of the passages quoted above, or origins that are not origins, as discussed in my introduction. The trace, a revolt against the forced migrations of the past, also recognizes that those migrations are constitutive of identity in ways that are not determined by that oppression (i.e., there is an element of agency in the creative act that is identity).

In addition, here is also the place where we can see how Glissant differs slightly from Gilroy in his double emphasis on roots and routes; for Glissant routes are too restrictive, too mapped out; they leave too little room for detours, ramblings. Like the *trame*, or narrative pathways, in Condé's novel, these *traces* are just as likely to lead us away from our roots as toward them (think again of Haley as an example of a roots narrative that follows a straight path that leads unequivocally to its point, the point being "roots"). Traces offer *another, different* way of thinking about identity, a model of identity woven (*tramé*) with opacity. In French, *trame* means "weft" (as opposed to "warp," the set of threads attached to the loom); it is the thread carried by the shuttle as it passes between the threads of the warp. Though often translated as "framework" in addition to "weft," *trame* is also a word used when speaking of *plot*, which has no exact equivalent in French. We might say, therefore, that this *trame* is at once a plotting through narrative and the weaving (*tissage*) at the heart of *métissage* (see Lionnet 29). This *métissage* of the origins of Caribbean identity is visualized through the tangled roots of Glissant's rhizomes or Condé's mangrove (whose scientific name, again, is *rhizophora*). So, while one finds in Derrida's earlier work a notion of the trace that Glissant does not really contradict, the latter offers a more concrete understanding of how the trace relates to identity, particularly the diasporic identities that obtain in the Caribbean. In addition to the routes that, Paul Gilroy argues, are just as important as roots in the constitution of identity, Glissantian traces encompass more than grand historical narratives and great voyages across the seas; traces are also day-to-day walks on a more modest and local scale, walks that crisscross individual islands in a kind of topography of identity.

Lie Detectors

Furthermore, Glissant writes in *Traité du tout-monde,* "Cette trace, de l'Être à l'étant, aux miséricordieux étants ! Nous la suivons sans la défigurer" (239) [This trace/path from Being to beings, to merciful beings! We follow it without disfiguring it]. *Suivre à la trace* is to be hot on the trail of someone or something, like a detective in pursuit of a criminal. Although Jabès claims, "[L]es methods d'investigation des policiers me sont inconnues (*LQ* II, 98) [I am unfamiliar with the detective's investigative methods (my trans.)], in other passages he suggests the opposite, that diasporic identity is pieced together like clues in a detective novel: "J'ai relu les pages rédigées après le crime. . . . Machinalement, en les rangeant, je les ai posées au-dessus du récit de mon crime et de mon Journal" (*LQ* II, 164) [I have reread the pages written after my crime. . . . Mechanically I put them in order on top of the story of my crime and of my journal (III, 114)]. In the passage quoted as the epigraph to the previous section, Jabès is also always hot on the trail of God's lies ("Mensonge de Dieu, je te suis à la trace" [*LQ* II, 89]).

At several points in this study, I have compared the search for roots to the work of the detective and roots narratives to detective fiction. Condé's reader must piece together Francis Sancher's story from contradictory fragments. *Un mensonge* is also structured like a detective novel; its alpha character—Alph, the very personification of origins—reconnects with his roots upon solving the crime of his having been pushed off a theater stage. Furthermore, in Sapho's novel, searching for clues requires producing a text (the set of sentences produced by the actors in *Le misanthrope*), which must then be interpreted in an act of literary criticism (which here more closely resembles mystical cryptography). *Un mensonge* might also lead us back to reread Haley as a detective novel. In such a reading, the crime would be Kunta Kinte's kidnapping, enslavement, and transport to the New World for sale to the highest bidder, that is, his uprooting and the family tree that sprouts out of it; the search for clues in *Roots* would then be Haley's metanarrative return to Africa, as well as the reading of his uprooting as crime. In rerooting his identity, Haley not only "solves the crime" to a certain extent, but he also obtains a certain kind of justice and even reparation.[13] If as John G. Cawelti writes, "In the detective story, when we arrive at the detective's solution, we have arrived at the truth, the single right perspective and ordering of events" (89), solving the "crime" in a roots narrative, that is, finding roots, involves arriving at the truth of identity.

In fact, it is in relation to detective fiction that, in "Philosophy of the *Série Noire*" (1996), Deleuze takes up Nietzsche's notion of "powers of the false" to describe precisely the kind of production of truth-value that I have attributed to Sapho's *Un mensonge*, that is, the very fabrication that produces the truth as true. Describing "Sophocles' *Oedipus* [a]s a detective story" (7), he goes on to argue that "the detective novel has remained Oedipal" (6–7). Regarding the French detective novel series that inspired the essay, he maintains that "the power of the false became the detective-story element par excellence" (8).

By now a large body of work critical work has been produced on detective fiction, even after the 1970s as many of the phenomena that inspired it recede into the past: Borges and the Latin American Boom, the French New Novel, Umberto Eco's *The Name of the Rose*, and structuralism in general. In "The Adaptation of Detective Story Techniques in the French New Novel," Erica Mendelson Eisenger describes the narrative structure of detective fiction in a way that might enhance our understanding of the structure of the roots narrative as articulated in this study up to now: "Time is a forward moving line which culminates in death—a murder. Time in a detective novel, however, is retrospective. The detective story begins with the crime and works backwards from consequence to cause. 'Le travail policier consiste à combler à rebours le temps fascinant et insupportable qui sépare l'événement de sa cause'" (53).[14] In Michel Butor's *L'emploi du temps* (1956) [*Passing Time*], the narrator, Jacques Revel, goes into even greater detail regarding the detective novel's narrative structure and the French New Novel's interest in detective fiction as defined by this structure:

> [I]n detective fiction the story goes against the stream, beginning with the crime, the climax of all the dramatic events which the detective has to rediscover gradually, and that this is in many respects more natural than the narrative proceeding without a backward look, where the first day of the story is followed by the second and then by subsequent days in their calendar order, as I myself at that time had been describing my October experiences; in detective fiction the narrative gradually explores events anterior to the event with which it begins. . . . [D]etective fiction . . . superimposes two temporal sequences, the days of the inquiry which start at the crime, and the days of the drama which lead up to it, and . . . this is quite natural, since in real life one's mental analysis of past events takes place while other events are accumulating. (178–79)

Butor himself uses the tracing of origins here to describe the work of both the reader and the detective, for the end of the detective novel is in fact a return to its beginning, which is only explained (in the sense that its cause is "discovered" upon solving the crime) at the end of the story.[15] In other words, the detective novel shares the bidirectional narrative structure that I attribute to Haley's *Roots* since the roots narrative works by "retrospectively" (to use Eisenger's term) positing its own beginning (as a story) as the origin of identity. In short, the roots in roots narratives are thus first and foremost the beginning of a story, a narrative beginning.

Furthermore, if the roots narrative (including Haley's) can be understood as detective fiction, solving the crime is also an allegory for interpretation (reading for clues). In no other genre, perhaps, is the reader more encouraged to enter into a competition with the detective/protagonist in a race to solve the crime and be the first to reach the finish line (the beginning of the novel). In detective fiction, therefore, the reader reads the narrative being written. We might say, therefore, that since all roots narratives resemble detective fiction, reading them involves the same impulse to return to a beginning, a return that the story itself recounts. And if the work of the detective parallels that of interpreting the detective novel, the parallel of the reader as detective for roots narratives consists of the reader's returning to roots through the search for meaning in origins. In other words, roots narratives are allegories of their own reading, and interpretations of them, such as the ones this study proposes, become their own narratives of origin and of the deconstruction of origins.

Indeed, the eponymous lie of Sapho's title has its own connection to the detective genre, for in Eisenger's description of the genre, lies also play a central role in detective fiction: "The detective exists because people lie. False testimony is assumed, not only on the part of the murderer, but from all the suspects. Everyone has something to hide in a detective story—the author most of all. For he must willfully deceive his readers by withholding essential information from them, or by confusing them with 'unreliable narrators'" (96). By acknowledging similar lies at the heart of roots narratives as detective fiction, then, Sapho allows us to reread Haley in order to complicate our understanding of roots narratives and uncover the ways in which *Roots* embraces its lies even as it simultaneously denies them. For it is not just the case that Sapho's protagonist lies about his roots; Alph's role of staging fiction as an actor is marked as being a lie *by profession*: "[I]l exerçait là non seulement son métier de comédien, mais encore son métier de menteur . . ." (30; Sapho's ellipsis) [He practiced not only the trade of an actor, but furthermore that of a liar]. Yet only by being a professional liar is Alph able to tell the truth:

Il était un extraordinaire comédien, long à s'épanouir. Peu de gens savaient jusqu'où. Jusqu'où il pouvait porter la vérité d'un rôle. La vérité était sa passion. Il lui avait fallu s'exiler dans le mensonge pour cela. (18–19)

[He was an extraordinary actor who took a long time to mature. Few people knew just how far. How far he could take the truth of a role. Truth was his passion. For that he had to exile himself in lies.]

Likewise, one of the tasks that Sapho undertakes in *Un mensonge* is the deconstruction of the binary that distinguishes truth from lies:

Bien sûr la vérité fuit, insaisissable, et s'il n'y a pas de vérité comment peut-il y avoir mensonge, le mensonge n'est-il pas lui-même matière à vérité, matériau précieux du regard ? Quel faux débat il y avait là. Un homme coupable, voilà tout. Fermé dans des axes inventés mensonge-vérité. (122)

[Of course truth, evasive, eludes us, and if there were no truth, how could there be lies; are lies not the very stuff truth is made of, the precious matter of the gaze? What a false debate it was. A guilty man, that's all. Closed up in the made-up axes of lies and truth.]

For Sapho, then, lies tell the truth:

Tout y est vrai, même le mensonge. Et chaque mensonge n'est-il pas si marqué de celui qui l'énonce qu'il ne raconte que des vérités indispensables, plus troublantes encore, plus dignes d'intérêt, plus informatives que la "vérité" ? (178)

[Everything is true, even lies. And is each lie not so marked by the person who enunciates it that it tells only essential truths, more troubling ones, ones more worthy of interest, more informative than the "truth"?]

Truth and lies thus constitute a couple in the way Alph and Bette and Adam and Eve do.

If Sapho deconstructs roots as fictions of origins, Haley offers the clearest example of how all roots narratives are allegories of their own deconstruction in the de Manian sense. While on one level, the novel presents the return to origins as a quest for truth, its bidirectional structure can be read as drawing attention to the narrativity and fictionality of this return. If Haley's detractors accused him of lying about his family history and history *tout court*, the structure of his novel reveals "lies" to be just as much at the heart of his roots narrative as of Sapho's. The lie of Sapho's title, then, is not merely the one (or ones) set "straight" by the end of the novel; it is also the fabrication at the heart of any roots narrative, the lie that tells the truth about roots, so to speak, by acknowledging itself as such, by acknowledging that, to a certain extent, roots are always inventions or fictions. If Judith Roof writes in *Come as You Are: Sexuality and Narrative* (1996), "As a site of mastery, origins are a product of narrative rather than narrative's source; explaining narrative via its oedipal 'origin' is to try to account for narrative via narrative" (67), the slippage between lies and fiction in *Un mensonge* suggests that fictions (such as roots narratives) that deny their fictionality are also telling a lie. Truth may be a fiction, but a lie occurs when it claims that it is not. In revealing the roots narrative to be a lie that tells the truth about roots as the fiction of identity, Sapho reveals the narrativity of roots.

A Lie That Tells the Truth; or, The Queer Truth about Heterosexuality

Camp: The Lie That Tells the Truth is the title Philip Core gives to his book-length description of one particular manifestation of gay sensibility. If we take Core at his word, telling the truth by lying is one way many queer people give expression to their identities. A lie that tells the truth would thus be a queer sort of lie indeed. Likewise, the lie of Sapho's title involves an acknowledgment of not only the narrative paradox but, as we shall also see, the sexual one as well. Indeed, the lie that tells the truth also turns out to be the assertion of truth as heterosexual union at the end of *Un mensonge*, where Sapho at first seems to set the story "straight" by rooting Alph's identity in a heterosexual foundation. In a "straight"-forward, teleological reading of *Un mensonge*, in other words, Alph's roots narrative reaches its ending by establishing that ends are not only divine but also heterosexual. Such a reading, however, would fail to take into account the ways in which the novel itself destabilizes this very reading by treating its heterosexual ending as a lie and destabilizing the truth of roots as based in a heterosexual family tree. If, on a basic level, *Un mensonge* seems to confirm the heterosexuality of roots as evidenced by Haley's reliance on the patrilineal family tree and asserted by "The family tree stops with me" t-shirt mentioned in the introduction, when Alph and Bette come together as alphabet in an act of writing the truth of origins, the very writtenness of this conjoining is acknowledged to be fictional. Acknowledging the assertion of heterosexuality as the truth of roots to be a lie, then, also constitutes a queering of the genealogical structure of the roots narrative.

At the most basic level, the first suggestion that *Un mensonge* denies a heterosexual monopoly on roots consists of the inclusion of a gay character, Philippe, "[u]n homosexuel pas du tout féminin qui . . . se travestissait parfois et chantait avec une voix d'homme des chansons néoréalistes" (25) [a homosexual who wasn't the least bit feminine and who occasionally dressed in drag and sang neorealist songs in a man's voice].[16] This drag queen is a great source of consternation because he/she is simultaneously quite masculine:

[Q]uand il était en homme, c'était un solide garçon de trente-cinq ans qui, en débardeur, effrayait plus d'une frappe ou d'un allumé qui menaçait de traîner après la représentation, ou, d'une haleine avinée, de se répandre sur le décolleté de Célimène. (25)

[When he was dressed as a man, he was a stout fellow of 35 years who, in a tank top, scared off many a bum or horny guy who was liable to hang around after the show, or, with wine-smelling breath, to go on and on about Célimène's low-cut dress.]

However, any alternative Philippe might represent to the heterosexual myth of origins reenacted by Alph and Bette seems to be harnessed to heterosexual ends because the rabbi "a trouvé dans ce voyage transsexuel une connaissance profonde des choses inexplorées en l'homme-femme qui aparut–Dieu créa Adam homme-femme" (172) [discovered in this transsexual journey a profound knowledge of the unexplored regions of the man-woman who appeared. God created Adam man-woman]. While it might seem odd to refer to Adam as an androgyne, which is often considered to be a figure of gender *non*conformity, Albert's take is actually quite faithful to the biblical text; to quote the King James version, "Male and female created he them . . . and called their name Adam" (Gen. 5.2).

As we remember from Aristophanes's creation myth in Plato's *Symposium*, the androgyne is a figure that stands for the origins of sexual desire for the opposite sex. Philippe is thus explained away through transformation into an androgyne. While many cultural critics have attempted to carve out a subversive space for androgyny, they all too often fail to return to the origins of the figure, so to speak, and account for its heterosexual roots. Privileging the androgyne may thus be a way of effacing the parallel homosexual creation myths of the man-man and the woman-woman that accompany the androgyne in Aristophanes's myth and are conspicuously absent from Genesis. Yet, by turning the Adam-Eve couple into a similar androgyne, the rabbi gives Aristophanes's androgyne a further Judeo-Christian twist. The novel's only gay character thus leads back to decidedly heterosexual origins, back to the androgynous Adam Alph becomes by rejoining with Bette.

Such closure through the consolidation of a heterosexual relationship is certainly not unique to Sapho's ending. Many a comedy of manners ends with the announcement of a marriage. Interestingly, *Le misanthrope* does not have such an ending; Alceste is unable to enter into a relationship with Célimène precisely because he refuses to lie or accept her lies. In contrast, *Un mensonge* at first seems to canonize the heterosexuality of origins through its ending. Like the multiple narratives Roof describes in *Come As You Are*, Sapho's novel is a "coming story" (3). Ends come for Roof; narrative creates ending and a sense of fulfillment of meaning through closure as a male orgasm in a heterosexual relationship; they are related to what Paul Morrison calls "the teleology of 'discharge,' which Freud calls 'end-pleasure.' . . . Like the well-made narrative, normative sexual activity issues in climax, from which comes, as it were, quiescence" (55). This teleology is a key concept in his argument that "traditional narrative is at once heterosexual and heterosexualizing" (68).

This orgasm is quite literal in Sapho's novel, as can be discerned from the passage that describes Alph and Bette's first lovemaking:

> Son bustier part, la gloire de ses seins paraît. . . . Alph arrache sa chemise, se défait, entre avec elle, lui tire le bout de dentelle qui lui tient lieu de juste-aux-fesses, il embrasse ses seins, son ventre, la mord, lui lèche les cuisses, elle le prend, lui baise les reins et le creux de l'aine, elle le fait frissonner, elle le laboure et le frôle et le tempête, il lui prend les cheveux et l'embrasse et la mord et sa langue s'attendrit, et ils sont moitié évanouis l'un dans l'autre, mon amour, il est en elle sans y penser, et ils oublient les murs, il ne peut pas croire qu'il s'est oublié. Il ne sait pas si elle a joui. Oui, elle a joui. Pardon, il ne s'en est même pas assuré. Lui, une technique imparable, il a vu plus haut que lui, plus loin de lui, plus antique que lui. (240)

> [Her bra flies off, the glory of her breasts appears. . . . Alph rips off her shirt, undoes his pants, goes in with her, pulls her by the bit of lace that serves as her thong, he kisses her breasts, her abdomen, bites her, licks her thighs, she takes him, kisses his loins and the hollow of his groin, she makes him shiver, she works him over, brushes against him, works him into a tempest, he takes her hair, kisses her and bites her, and his tongue becomes tender, and they are practically swooning in each other, my love, he is inside her without even knowing it, and they forget the walls, he can't believe that he has abandoned himself. He doesn't know whether she came. Yes, she came. Excuse me, he didn't think to ask. He, with his unequaled technique, he saw higher than himself, farther than himself, more ancient than himself.]

When Alph ejaculates inside Bette, he has ceased to lie and has espoused "the truth." The passage mystifies (hetero)sexual union as the communion not only of kindred spirits but also with a higher being and meaning ("plus haut que lui," in this passage, "higher than himself"). Pronouns become instable, thereby marking self-shattering bliss. In addition, the joining of man and woman, here, returns Alph to a prelapsarian entity ("plus antique que lui" or "more ancient than himself"). The full implications of this heterosexual return become more explicit when one recalls Sapho's previous description of Alph with his former fiancée Elisabeth: "il était entre les bras de sa Genèse" (147) [he was in the arms of his Genesis]. So in addition to bringing the narrative to its end, therefore, heterosexual intercourse in Sapho's novel is described as a return to a kind of beginning or origins. For in *Un mensonge* Bette becomes the archetypal Woman, a sort of Eve if you will: "Bette, dans cette configuration, c'est la femme" (166) [In this configuration, Bette is Woman]. By uniting with Bette in sex, Alph not only repeats the Creation myth as told in Genesis, but he also returns to paradise.

Against such a reading, however, I argue that in *Un mensonge* queer roots lie less with its only gay character than within its simultaneous participation *in* and challenge *to* the genre of the roots narrative. This is also where the novel begins to queer Alph's Moroccan origins, Genesis, and origins in general. Although the union of Alph and Bette seems to suggest that truth is produced through heterosexual intercourse, the novel's final sentence hints that this heterosexual, divinely ordained "truth" is also a lie. Sapho writes in the novel's final sentence, "Comme vous le savez, ô lecteur, tout cela est un tissu de mensonges, mais dans tout mensonge, il y a de la vérité" (273) [As you know, reader, all of this is a fabric of lies, but in every lie, there is truth]. While a story that joins Alph and Bette and in which there is so much ado about the letters of the alphabet might seem overly gimmicky, the representation of their budding romance is no less so; the novel ultimately suggests that there is no heteroromance that is not just as corny. The Harlequin-Romance-like dialogues that accompany Alph and Bette's sexual communion suggest that their relationship is no less a "lie" than the illusion they are paid to produce onstage. If their first sex scene is composed of clichés, right after Alph admits his love to Bette she responds in a similarly cliché manner:

> Par pitié, restez, restez mais taisez-vous. Trois secondes. Je ne comprends rien à tout cela. Non, c'est faux. Trop d'informations me vien-

nent, Alph. Je vous savais emporté, surprenant. Mais j'ai le souffle
coupé. Qu'est-ce que vous me faites là ? Prenez garde. Je ne suis pas si
forte. Par pitié, protégez-moi. (222)

[Have pity, stay, stay, but say nothing. Just a moment. I don't understand what's happening. No, that's not true. I'm overwhelmed, Alph.
I knew you could get carried away, that you could be unpredictable.
But it just takes my breath away. What are you doing to me? Be careful. I'm not so strong. Have pity, protect me.]

It is a cliché that men lie to women: I'm not married, I really love you,
You can trust me. Alph told just this sort of lie when he changed the age
on his passport to make it easier to seduce the older women who are his
"type." And in the realm of such clichés, men do not hold a monopoly
on lies: Yes, honey, it was good for me, too.

In *Un mensonge*, the first time Alph mentions Albert to Bette, she asks,
"Mais qui est Albert, un . . . ami ?" [But who is this Albert, a . . . (boy)
friend?]. Alph replies, "Mais non, pas un amant ! Je préfère les filles . . .
les femmes" [Of course not, not a lover! I prefer girls . . . women]. When
Bette replies in turn, "Ah ! Je me suis demandé" [Oh! I was wondering],
she confirms his suspicion of her suspicion that he might be gay (230).
As Paul Morrison writes about such questions,

> And as with the class that would not, so too with the love that need
> not, speak its name. I mean, of course, heterosexuality, which both
> goes without saying and is the privilege of never having to say; the
> privilege, in fact, rarely emerges unscathed from the saying. "I am
> straight": to be forced or feel compelled to articulate one's hetero-
> sexual credentials is already to protest too much; the performative
> belies the declarative. If, then, heterosexuality need not, it also dare
> not, speak its name, which is why a straight coming-out narrative, no
> less than a good man, is hard to find. (68–69)

Alph's response to Bette's question about his sexual orientation, then,
is a lie, not because he is "really" gay but because he repeats the fiction
that heterosexuality is not its Other. The "truth" about his sexuality is a
fiction, the fiction created when lies are repeated to such an extent that
they become truth: "La vérité, ce qui peut se répéter ?" (272) [Truth,
that which can be repeated?]. Truth would be the fiction created when
lies are repeated to such an extent that they are *taken* as truth. Narratives

of origin come to constitute the truth about identity when their ritualized reiteration turns them into myth (or, we could also say, history). We might also say that the founding lie of heterosexuality is the reproduction of the fiction that heterosexuality is immune to queerness, that it can be separated from homosexuality.

If, therefore, a return to Genesis marks a return to heterosexual roots in the novel, because Creation begins with an originating lie on the part of God, the heterosexuality many see as founded in Genesis is also founded on this lie.[17] The lie of Sapho's title, therefore, is not only the lie Alph told *about* his origins, the one that is corrected by the end of the novel; it is also the origins themselves, the "authentic" (read "true") origins he finds and validates through heterosexuality. The lie could also be that Genesis has anything at all to do with heterosexuality to begin with. If we think of the fundamentalist cliché "God created Adam and Eve, not Adam and Steve," it is easy to understand how Genesis is currently used as a roots narrative that confuses the origins of humanity with those of heterosexuality. Perhaps the eponymous lie of Sapho's novel is thus the myth that humanity originated from a heterosexual couple, one that now serves to justify the institutionalization of heterosexuality in religious discourse. When read in this light, actually, theories of evolution that rely on heterosexual reproduction—and produce any other sexual activity as superfluous (e.g., how many high school biology texts propose an evolutionary justification for same-sex masturbation among dolphins?)—begin to resemble Genesis quite a bit.

This is the reason why queer roots, if they are not to *be* lies, must acknowledge their fictionality. In contrast, if the duplicity of compulsory heterosexuality were widely acknowledged, the institution would lose its authority. If Alph's lies can be said to come back to haunt him, how might other such ghosts be conjured up? Can these ghosts queer straight roots in addition to haunting them? Coming to queer roots at the end of a roots narrative would thus, indeed, result in "perverse end pleasure, pleasure taken the wrong end round, fucking or getting fucked in the ass" (Morrison, P. 61). Queering the concept of roots, therefore, cannot stop at deconstructing the truth claims of narratives of queer origins; they must deconstruct the truth claims of straight narratives of origins and narratives of straight origins as well.

CHAPTER 4

From Roots That Uproot
to Queer Diasporas

✦ ✦ ✦

Whereas accusations that *Roots* was a lie have been countered at every level, a different kind of accusation points toward another kind of danger with roots, the one implied, for example, in the title of Donald R. Wright's "Uprooting Kunta Kinte" (1981). In 1977 John Darnton wrote of how the village of Juffure had taken in Haley and accepted him as its child. Because of the many promises Haley had made, villagers' hopes were high. Indeed, the village would soon become a major destination for African American tourists returning to their own roots. Almost twenty years later, however, in "Gambians Criticize Noted *Roots* Author" (1995), Stephen Buckley wrote that Haley and his family broke promises to build a high school, provide scholarships for study in the United States, build a hotel and mosque, and provide villagers with new farming tools: "When Alex Haley first visited this village more than two decades ago, residents embraced the writer as more than a distant son returning home. They saw him as their savior. . . . [W]hile in Juffure, villagers say, Haley made a spate of promises. . . . Today Juffure, with 500 residents, has electricity and water and at least 10,000 tourists annually. But bitter villagers say they expected much more" (13A). Others have pointed out how Haley's representation of Africans in *Roots* redeploys Anglo-American stereotypes of a primitive Africa (Courlander) and the noble savage (Blayney). Furthermore, Wright argues that Haley irreparably contaminated Juffure's oral tradition, since oral epics now include Haley's version of Kunta Kinte's story, which may very well be an African American invention that now makes it impossible to recover the "true" oral tradition of Juffure.[1] While Haley portrayed his reconnections with African origins as the reestablishment of a kind of harmony, Juffure villagers' opinions suggest dissonance instead. What happens when other people live where we want to plant our roots? Do we have a responsibility toward them? Is it possible to uproot others as we plant our roots? If the reassertion of roots on the part of the uprooted can result in the policing and homogenization of identity *within* the collective identity, those from without may be subjected to an even more violent exclusion than my discussion of the political paradox has heretofore suggested.

These questions have a particular resonance with any consideration of queer roots because efforts to root contemporary lesbian and gay identities in a recovered past often attempt to "plant" roots in a similar way. Winston Leyland's *Gay Roots: Twenty Years of Gay Sunshine* (1991), for example, a collection of essays from the 1970s and 1980s, includes, under the heading "Gay History," Marc Daniel's "Arab Civilization and Male Love," which examines "gay love" from the seventh through the eleventh centuries; Winston Leyland's "Living in Truth: Akhenaten of Egypt (Reigned 1379–1362 B.C.)," which treats Akhenaten as a bisexual; Simon Karlinsky's "Russia's Gay History and Literature from the Eleventh to the Twentieth Centuries"; Rictor Norton's "Gay London in the 1720s: The Great Raid on Mother Clap's Molly House"; and Maurice Kenny's "Tinselled Bucks: An Historical Study in Indian Homosexuality." Just the titles of the last three essays should be enough to make social constructionists cringe. Like one of the founding texts of gay studies—John Boswell's *Christianity, Social Tolerance, and Homosexuality* (1980)—these texts assume that gay individuals can be found throughout history.

Such a notion of gay roots extending ad infinitum back through history has been almost entirely discredited through the lengthy debate in lesbian and gay studies between essentialism and social construction, which, coming to a head around Boswell and his critics, called into question such a notion of a "gay" past. According to the constructionist position, if it might be a stretch to say that homosexuality appears or is invented, it nonetheless develops in certain historical contexts, and the history of its "construction" can be written. Historical work from this perspective has added such constructions as heterosexuality (see Katz, J.), sexual identity, sexuality *tout court*, and even homophobia (see Chauncey) to the list of what could be similarly historicized. If I rehearse part of the history of lesbian and gay studies here, it is because certain constructionist narratives of history have been used to insidious political ends (witness the comments by Mugabe and Museveni discussed in chapter 2). At the other end of the spectrum from the homophobic antics of the likes of Mugabe, a version of antihomophobic constructionism created narratives of progress according to which the modern homosexual represents an evolution over his or her ancient, pre-, and early modern ancestors.

The colonial implications of such narratives of progress through which homosexuality was often historicized would be challenged toward the latter half of the 1990s in a parallel critique that emerged in the subfield that was increasingly becoming known as queer postcolonial studies. This critique revealed that other paradigms of same-sex eroticism, sexual behavior, and desire on the one hand and, on the other,

> "homosexuality as we know it today," as the cliché goes[,] are often ordered in a narrative sequence that looks a lot like a coming-out story. And in this coming-out story, even contemporary cultural others are associated with a prior time that is also thought of as being more primitive. In this model, queer history becomes a narrative of development, of civilization, and therefore of colonization. By coming out, the contemporary "lesbigay" subject leaves the dark continent of her past behind; by becoming homosexuality, same-sex desire does the same. A number of scholars have pointed out the parallel between the narratives of the civilizing mission and those of psychological development, but it should give one pause that in Freudian models of sexual development, nonnormative sexualities are what is relegated to this primitive past. In other words, in the coming-out model of lesbian and gay history, the homosexual has merely taken the place of the colonizer-heterosexual in narratives of both economic and psychosexual development. (Hayes, Higonnet, and Spurlin 16–17)

Gay roots, in other words, can share the same colonial implications as rooting as a political project.

Of the multiple essays from the *Gay Roots* anthology listed above, Kenny's "Tinselled Bucks: An Historical Study in Indian Homosexuality" stands out as having particular relevance to a theorization of the potential for one's roots to uproot others. Though about the work of Will Roscoe, Ramón A. Gutiérrez's "Must We Deracinate Indians to Find Gay Roots?" criticizes precisely the impulse Kenny's work exemplifies:

"By finding gay models where they do not exist, let us not perpetrate on We'wha or U'k yet another level of humiliation with our pens. For then, the 'conspiracy of silence' about the berdache which Harry Hay had hoped to shatter will only be shrouded once again in romantic obfuscations" (67). "Yet another level of humiliation," however, refers less to colonial violence here than to Gutiérrez's description of the social status of the so-called *berdache*: "Berdache status was one principally ascribed to defeated enemies. Among the insults and humiliations inflicted on prisoners of war were homosexual rape, castration, the wearing of women's clothes, and performing women's work" (62). In other words, what Evelyn Blackwood calls the "colonization of Native American transgender/lesbian/gay studies by predominantly white anthropologists" (197) is less an issue for Gutiérrez than the romantic idealization of such practices by those wishing to root contemporary lesbian and gay identities in a non-European past; he is interested less in violence done to Native Americans by Europeans than in the denial of violence done to *berdaches* by non-*berdaches*. I would suggest, however, that the idea suggested by Gutiérrez's title is also an important one to consider. What would it mean to plant roots that uproot others? In what kinds of contexts could such uprootings occur? How might they be avoided?

The primary example of roots that uproot under consideration in this chapter is the constitutive narrative of Zionism as exemplified in the contemporary Israeli state. The uprooting that occurred as a result of the very literal return to roots that characterizes Zionism (whether it could have been otherwise is a different question) seems to me to be quite different from the ones named in Wright's and Gutiérrez's titles. On the one hand, the uprooting Wright accuses Haley of cannot be separated from the latter's colonial and neocolonial privilege in relation to the actual inhabitants of the site of his African roots. Likewise, the uprooting Gutiérrez discerns in Will Roscoe's work on Native American two-spirit peoples (commonly referred to as berdaches by Europeans and Euro-Americans) is inseparable from the history of the genocide of Native Americans. On the other hand, however, Haley and Roscoe cannot be said to cause the physical uprooting of Africans and Native Americans in the way that Zionism (again, as institutionalized in the Israeli state) has uprooted Palestinians in another example of the political paradox of roots narratives.

Steve Reich's 1993 work of musical theater *The Cave* (which some have called an opera in spite of his own off-and-on resistance to the term) provides a unique narrative about the conflict resulting from a specific return to roots (the establishment of the state of Israel) and the uprooting that resulted (because Palestinians were removed from the site where Israeli roots were to be planted). In particular, *The Cave* makes amply clear that sharing a common ancestor—indeed, sharing a family tree—has not, as of yet, been able to pave the way toward peace in the Middle East. I will also be reading Reich in conjunction with two Jewish Maghrebian writers, Memmi and Derrida, whose writing (unlike their explicit political positionings in at least Memmi's case) can be read as exemplifying what James Clifford calls *"diasporist* anti-Zionism" ("Diasporas" 326).

Rooted in Zion

The Cave takes its name from the Cave of Machpelah in present-day Hebron, where in both biblical and Qur'anic traditions Abraham (Ibrahim in Arabic) and Sarah (Sirah) are buried in a cave. For a large portion of the world's population, the story of Abraham constitutes *the* founding narrative, and as the account of descendants from a common ancestor it provides a particular paradigm of the roots narrative. The three acts of Reich's work juxtapose Jewish, Palestinian, and American interpretations of the biblical story of Abraham and Sarah's burial site in the form of videotaped interviews conducted by video artist Beryl Korot (Reich's wife).[2] These videos serve, in lieu of a libretto, as the origin of the "opera's" text, and the three places where interviews were conducted—Israel, Palestine, and America—serve as the setting for the opera's three acts.[3] As Korot describes in an interview Jonathan Cott conducted with her and Reich, "[T]he work is a narrative told three times from the points of view of three different cultures" (13).[4] *The Cave's* composition consisted of isolated clips of Korot's videotaped interviews and superimposed music over dialogue, music that mimics the rhythms and tones of the interviewees' responses. Verses from the Hebrew Bible and passages from the Midrash are sung in English by members of the performing ensemble. Also included are recorded passages from the Torah and Surah from the Qur'an chanted in Hebrew and Arabic, recorded background noise from inside the cave (which Reich describes in the program notes as an "implied A minor") accompanied by an "A minor drone" (39), and "typing music"—a syncopated percussion "overture" whose programmatic reference (and the accompanying video images) suggests a mimetic relation with the rhythm of typing at a keyboard as texts appear on the giant video monitors that make up the set designed by Korot.[5]

The eponymous cave is thus a place where the roots of both Jewish and Muslim identities are planted, since Abraham/Ibrahim in both the biblical and Qur'anic traditions is the common ancestor of Jews and Arabs. In both traditions, his disinherited eldest son Ishmael (Ismail), borne of his wife's handmaid Hagar (Hajar), is considered to be the father of all Arabs, and his second son Isaac (Ishaq), borne of his wife, is considered to be the father of Israel. This familial relationship is eloquently evoked by one of the interviewees, Ephraim Isaac, for whom Abraham represents the originary figure of a family tree:

> Who is Abraham? Abraham, for me is my ancestor—my very own personal ancestor. . . . My father, when I was a young person, well, actually a child, used to count the names of our ancestors starting with Adam going all the way down to the Twelve Tribes. And I remember how we used to learn: Adam, Seth, Enosh, Kenan, Mahalalel, Yered, Enoch, Methuselah, Lamech, Noach, and then we would go on down, Noach, Shem, Arpachshad, Shelah, Peleg, Reu, Serug, Nahor, Terah, Abraham, and then we used to say, Abraham, Yitzhak, Ya'acov, and then we used to say the Twelve Tribes, our ancestors' names, just memorize all of them, Reuven, Shimon, Levi, Yehuda, Isaachar, Zebulun, Dan, Naftali, Gad, Asher, Josef, Benyamin, and then go all the way down and come down to my great, great grandfather whose name was Shimon, and then Shalom and then Shalam and Harun and Mesha, and Yizhak and myself. So for me there is a chain of ancestral relationship to Abraham. (30–31)

For Ephraim Isaac, this family tree structures a personal relationship with biblical narratives of Jewish history (Abraham is his "very own personal ancestor") and, in fact, goes all the way back to the creation myths told at the beginning of Genesis. The Cave of Machpelah itself is the site where this connection is rooted, since, as another interviewee points out, "The Midrash says that Adam and Eve were buried there" (38). Reich and Korot's opera also quotes the appropriate passage from the "Midrash, 'Chapters of R. Eliezer,' 36": "He ran to fetch a calf. But the calf ran before him and into the Cave of Machpelah. And he went in after it and found Adam and Eve on their biers, and they slept, and lights were kindled above them, and a sweet scent was upon them. (And Abraham returned to his guests)" (52). The cave is thus a site intimately connected with biblical trees of begats, which, as we saw in the previous chapter, begin with Adam and Eve. Ephraim Isaac thus provides a more detailed narrative, structured genealogically, by which we might understand Alph Hade's identity in *Un mensonge*, an identity simultaneously asserted and denied. For Isaac's family tree marks the perfect alignment of the familial and the collective, and his proper name names him as a son of Isaac, both Yizhak Isaac and Isaac, son of Abraham. Indeed, in the character and person of Ephraim Isaac (the documentarylike quality of *The Cave* makes the character a particularly vivid embodiment of personhood) a number of narratives collide (Genesis, Adam and Eve, Abraham's covenant with God) and mark him as a particularly acute example of identification with genealogy, of the embodiment of an identity structured genealogically, of an identity constructed through narrative.

Yet the seemingly straightforward and unbroken "chain of ancestral relationship to Abraham" is itself a family tree with its own ghosts. First, with the exception of a handful of generations extending back from the present, there is a huge, gaping hole in Ephraim Isaac's family tree. The names in the first part of this genealogy are nothing that cannot be found in Genesis; with a little time, anyone could become just as familiar with them as he. Even these familiar names hide their own ghosts. One name, Abraham, is the result of a divinely ordained name change from Abram at the moment of covenant. The other, Jacob (Ya'acov), was, again at God's orders, changed to Israel. It is interesting that in the case of Abraham the God-given name is used, whereas in the case of Jacob it is not. And the name elided in the latter case is the very one that would make this family tree a justification for the Israeli possession of Palestine. In other words, whereas both the biblical and Qur'anic roots of the Middle East crisis are explored in depth, the opera also explores alternative biblical and Qur'anic roots for a mediation to the conflict. In response to Cott's question in the interview quoted above, "So the seed for peace is already in the book of Genesis itself, isn't it?" Reich answers, "Yes—Isaac and Ishmael come together to bury Abraham" (15).

In the "libretto" itself, one Israeli interviewee describes Ishmael/Ismail as a "fighter" (34); another states, "But the children of Ishmael—we can see them in the streets" (34). Yet another states, "He's our relative" (34). Interviewee Francis E. Peters sums up the political implications of the biblical/Qur'anic narratives the interviews are based on: "You're talking about our common ancestor, so the stakes are fairly high in a place like that" (51). Indeed, even in the biblical version of this story (Gen. 21.13) in Reich's contextualization, God seems to justify a Palestinian state: "[F]rom the son of the slave woman / I will make a Nation, for he is your seed" (36). Likewise, Surah 3 of the Qur'an seems to promote a peaceful settlement inasmuch as it urges "people of the book" (i.e., Christians, Jews, and Muslims) not to dispute over Ibrahim, and one Palestinian interviewee notes that "Ibrahim or Abraham is this bridge between the two cultures" (40).

Although a rhizomatic model of rooted identity (at least as Glissant rereads it), which is both plural and singular, would suggest that the people of Israel could share origins and roots (and therefore territory) with Palestinians without uprooting them, the radical difference between the discursive possibilities suggested by *The Cave* and the political reality of violence in the Middle East demonstrates the practical limitations of a political project based on roots, queer as they may be. In other words, although roots narratives are always political, their politics can be constructive or destructive, and often a single narrative of roots, helpful to one group, may be harmful to another. Put differently, *The Cave* is thus a chthonic site of origins for two separate diasporas and provides an ample illustration of Glissant's description of the nature of roots.

Yet the cave is also a place where the tensions between conflicting versions of the same roots are very palpable. These tensions exploded in February 1994 when Baruch Goldstein walked into the mosque at this site (called the Ibrahimi Mosque by Muslims and the Tomb of the Patriarchs by Jews) and shot over 150 worshipping Palestinians, killing 29 of them, with a rifle issued by the Israeli army. He was subsequently beaten to death by survivors as he attempted to reload his gun. In response to the massacre, the site was closed for eight months, and a curfew was imposed on mostly Arab Hebron, a curfew that only applied to Arab residents, who complained that they were the ones who bore the brunt of these security measures even though they were the target of the violence that led to them. An Israeli inquiry on the massacre concluded that Goldstein acted alone; even though Israeli soldiers discharged weapons during the melee, they claimed that none was aimed at Palestinians.

This was not the first instance of interethnic violence in Hebron. In 1929, during the British Mandate, Arabs killed 69 Jews there. After the 1994 massacre, even the third point of what Noam Chomsky has called "the fateful triangle," the United States that is, was drawn into this history of conflict as resentment against Goldstein on the part of more secular Israeli Jews stoked anti-American sentiments (Haberman). But these events still lay in the future as Reich composed *The Cave*. Following the 1994 massacre, Reich and Korot reflected on the incident in a response entitled "Thoughts about the Madness in Abraham's Cave," in which they express skepticism regarding the potential for musical works to influence political change: "We do not think that *The Cave* or any other artwork can directly affect peace in the Middle East. Pablo Picasso's *Guernica* had no effect on the aerial bombing of civilians, nor did the works of Kurt Weill, Bertolt Brecht, and many other artists stop the rise of Hitler" (180).

This statement echoes an earlier interview with Reich regarding another composition, *Different Trains* (1988): "I want to make clear that no piece of music can have the slightest effect on any political reality, or rewrite history. I'm not going to change the Holocaust. I can't bring back six million people. I can't even affect the quality of train service on Amtrack!" (Schwarz, "Steve Reich" 35). Composed for string quartet and tape recorder, *Different Trains* makes use of compositional techniques similar to those of *The Cave*; instead of videotaped footage, however, the former takes as its point of departure *audiotapes* of the interviews on which the work is based. In his essay with the same title as the piece, Reich describes *Different Trains* as a recollection of traveling between New York and Los Angeles during his childhood after his parents' divorce. Since these trips occurred during World War II, he later realized, "[I]f I had been in Europe during this period, as a Jew I would have had to ride on very different trains" (151). The recordings themselves consist of the following:

1. Record my governess Virginia, now in her seventies, reminiscing about our train trips together.
2. Record a retired Pullman porter, Lawrence Davis, now in his eighties, who used to ride lines between New York and Los Angeles, reminiscing about his life.
3. Collect recordings of Holocaust survivors Rachella, Paul, and Rachel—all about my age and now living in America—speaking of their experiences.
4. Collect recorded American and European train sounds of the 1930s and '40s. (151–52)

Like *The Cave*, this piece imitates the "music" of the interviewees' spoken English, as well as using stringed instruments to imitate "train sounds," just as *The Cave* uses percussion instruments to make "typing sounds."

The compositional technique of imitating recorded sounds (whether

on video- or audiotape) dates back to some of Reich's earliest compositions, such as *It's Gonna Rain* (1965) and *Come Out* (1966), both of which
"took recordings of people speaking and searched within those recordings for moments when speech was, for various reasons, almost song—
when people speak, they sometimes sing" (Schwarz, "Steve Reich" 32).
It's Gonna Rain takes as its point of departure a recording of an African
American minister preaching in Union Square, San Francisco. Unlike
The Cave and *Different Trains, It's Gonna Rain* involves what Reich characterizes as "the process of gradually shifting phase relationships between
two or more identical repeating patterns as an extension of the idea of
infinite canon or round," and its performance consists of the following
process: "Two loops are lined up in unison and then gradually move completely out of phase with each other, and then back into unison" (Reich,
"It's Gonna Rain" 20). *Come Out* (1966) incorporates a taped interview
with Daniel Hamm, one of the African Americans (who became known
as the Harlem Six) arrested and convicted of murdering a white shop
owner during the 1964 Harlem riots. In this recording, Hamm describes
scratching a bruise inflicted during police torture so as to cause bleeding (to make the blood "come out") in order to be sent to the infirmary
and thereby avoid being further harmed or killed in custody. In these
earlier pieces, however, only a very small fragment of the recorded narrative is used, with the result that their narrative context might seem
neglected in favor of a more "purely" musical or aesthetic appreciation
of the recorded sounds (if one adheres to the frequent but problematic
division between the political and the aesthetic). While in and of itself
this piece might not seem political, therefore, it was composed and first
performed in a context that highly was.

In "Transethnicism and the American Experimental Tradition," musi-
cologist David Nicholls explicitly connects the political significance of
later works like *The Cave* to that of the aforementioned pieces (584).
Nonetheless, whereas Reich and Korot saw *The Cave* as being incapable
of exerting political influence, they nonetheless acknowledge that the
Cave of Machpelah "resonated not only with the events of the ancient
past but with the present Israeli-Arab conflict as well" ("Thoughts" 178–
79). Thus, while *The Cave* does not have a direct impact on the Middle
East crisis and certainly did not prevent the Hebron massacre, it can,
according to Reich and Korot, contribute to new ways of understanding
and contextualizing the conflict there: "The recent massacre of Muslim
worshipers . . . was also an attack on the legacy of Abraham, who fed
strangers, was not ensnared by the idols of his day, and deeply loved both

of his sons, Ishmael and Isaac" ("Thoughts" 179–80). And they remain optimistic about how much such works can reframe thinking about conflict in the Middle East: "With the aid of Muslim and Jewish advisers, we rooted *The Cave* in the biblical and koranic figures of Abraham/Ibrahim and his family, not only because they formed a classic story for music theater but also because we feel that without a spiritual rapprochement there can never be real peace in a land where these traditions run so deep" ("Thoughts" 180).

One often talks of the roots of the Middle East conflict but never of the roots of its resolution much less of how these two sets of roots might be intertwined. *The Cave*, however, suggests potential roots for thinking about how peace might become thinkable in the Middle East. In short, *The Cave* represents Reich's return to his own musical roots in the form of returning to both certain aspects of his earlier compositional techniques and his commitment to social commentary (even if it marks a more sophisticated awareness of the politics of appropriating the voices of other peoples).

Furthermore, if Paul Hillier can write about "[t]he Jewish element in Reich's music" (65), in "Steve Reich and Hebrew Cantillation," Antonella Puca writes that Reich's "interest in Hebrew cantillation dates from the mid-1970s and is accompanied by the rediscovery of his own Jewish background, by the study of the Hebrew language and of the Hebrew Bible, and by extended periods of residence in Israel" (537). She even argues that Reich's compositional techniques, described above, are related to this interest: "[I]n the works that Reich composed after his studies of Hebrew cantillation, the preservation of the semantic meaning of the words becomes for him a central concern, and . . . sound aspects of spoken language, such as intonation, timbre, melodic cadences, and metric accentuation become the defining elements of musical structure" (537). In other words, his return to Jewish roots has also played a role in the change in compositional techniques described above, so that semantic meaning is now kept when music imitates spoken language and the African and Jewish diasporas increasingly overlap. Furthermore, the Jewish influences on his music have their own connection to a different kind of roots, those articulated in Genesis and examined by Sapho: "While in Jerusalem, he pursued fieldwork research in the area of biblical cantillation, recording the first five verses of Bereshit (Genesis) chanted by older Jewish men from Baghdad, Yemen, Kurdistan, and India" (Puca 538–39). And, like Sapho, he has expressed an interest in the Kabbalah (Dadson 32). His most explicitly Jewish work in this regard is *Tehillim*

(1981), Reich's setting of Psalms to music. Nonetheless, in his interview with Hillier, Reich stresses the disconnect between his interest in the musical roots of Judaism and the thematic return to Jewish roots that occurs through the context of some works (Hillier 68). Indeed his interest in Psalm cantillation underscores a disconnect from roots:

> And the psalms are a musical text, we know that. Fortunately for me, the tradition in the West is totally unknown. What passes for psalm singing in synagogues today is basically very bad 19th-century Christian hymn-tunes that would make any self-respecting hymnist roll over in his grave. So the only Jews who have a tradition of singing Psalms are the Yemenites, and of course I'm not a Yemenite. The Yemenites are losing their tradition, having left Yemen and gone to Israel, where they've become westernized. (qtd. in Hillier, 66)

In short, Reich's return to Jewish roots through music often affects his composition in ways that are not straightforward. Indeed, one could say, often these roots more closely resemble rhizomes.

In addition, the Jewish roots of his diasporic identity might also be linked to Reich's interest in another diaspora, that of Africa. Reich himself studied drumming techniques in Ghana. *Drumming*, especially, is often said to have been heavily influenced by Reich's apprenticeship in Ghana (see Lannes). Yet at times Reich has downplayed the "ethnic" in his music, whether in terms of its relation to his Jewish identity or his African influences: "[A]ll music is 'ethnic' because everybody comes from an ethnicity. They may not perceive that, because when you look at a distance at Africa—that is, the Africa of the past—you think of drums" (qtd. in Vorda, 14). In their treatment of African American cultural material and politics, therefore, both *Come Out* and *It's Gonna Rain* might be understood as diasporic pieces as well (the latter being a reference to the deluge in the Hebrew Bible on the part of an African American preacher). And in *The Cave* the Jewish and African diasporas intersect in the third act when an African American woman living in Texas is asked to discuss Hagar and responds, "When I think of Hagar, as a black female, I really think of myself" (48).

Furthermore, I think it is possible to connect the political content of Reich's music in terms of its expression of diasporic identity with what I have been calling his compositional techniques. In his essay "Music as a Gradual Process," he outlines what he finds to be the most important of these "perceptible processes," writing, "I want to be able to hear the process happening throughout the sounding music" (34). The title of this essay is perhaps the best indication of the way he conceives of making audible to the listener the very process of musical development: "To facilitate closely detailed listening a musical process should happen extremely gradually" (34). Perhaps the clearest example of making this "gradual process" audible is *Pendulum Music* (1968), for which two "or more microphones are suspended from the ceiling by their cables so that they all hang the same distance from the floor and are all free to swing with a pendular motion" ("Pendulum" 31). All are pulled back, released in unison, and allowed to swing freely. As they drift out of and back into sync, "a series of feedback pulses are heard which will either be all in unison or not depending on the gradually changing phase relations of the different mike pendulums" (31). Indeed, in "Music as a Gradual Process," one example Reich gives of his title concept bears a remarkable resemblance to *Pendulum Music:* "Performing and listening to a gradual musical process resembles . . . pulling back a swing, releasing it, and observing it gradually come to rest" (34). On the one hand, the term *gradual process* most frequently refers to music as an audible text whose structure unfolds in a way that the listener can hear: "We all listen to the process together since it's quite audible, and one of the reasons it's quite audible is because it's happening extremely gradually" ("Music" 35). On the other, Reich occasionally uses this term to describe not the performance of the musical text but its composition (at least in the sense of the conception of process music): "What I'm interested in is a compositional process and a sounding music that are one and the same thing" (35).

Pendulum Music, like *It's Gonna Rain* and *Come Out* before it, is thus characterized by "gradually shifting phase relations" ("Phase" 38). In all three, because "the process of phase shifting [is] gradual enough, . . . minute rhythmic differences . . . become clearly audible" (38). But only *It's Gonna Rain* and *Come Out* involve "identical tape loops moving out of phase with each other" (Drumming" 66). If I insist on these earlier pieces, it is because Reich himself has described how his early experimentation with electronic music paved the way for compositional strategies that could also be performed by musicians on more traditional instruments ("First" 54). *Drumming* (1971) is one such piece. It consists of a series of repeated measures with no time signature, the first of which contains only a simple eighth note following four quarter rests and followed by an eighth rest and a quarter rest. Subsequent measures gradually add notes one at a time to create more and more complex rhythms. As rhythm and, in the case of marimba parts, melody evolve, instruments in this piece shift in and out of phase. Thus the gradual phase-shifting process that was first only obtainable electronically has been transferred here to music composed and performed more conventionally, a technique that also produced such works as *Piano Phase* (1967) and *Violin Phase* (1967).

On the one hand, Reich has said that he abandoned this compositional technique ("Clapping" 68) and even stated that the entire essay "Music as a Gradual Process" does not apply to his works after 1972. On the other, I would argue that the relation between videotaped interviews and instrumental and vocal music in *The Cave* nonetheless makes audible the process of composition because the transposition of the "music" from spoken interviews (like the taped voices of *It's Gonna Rain* and *Come Out*) into music composed for singing voices and musical instruments is so clear. It is for this reason that I would propose that *The Cave*, like the works that Reich acknowledges himself to be examples of "music as a gradual process," be characterized (in line with narratives studied in previous chapters) as an allegory of its own composition and therefore an allegory of listening to the very process of its composition and performance.[6] For a work to be understood as an allegory of "reading" in the de Manian sense (with the difference here that "reading" encompasses listening in the case of musical works), it must also be "readable" as narrative. While a work by Reich such as *The Cave* might more easily be understood as narrative (because of the biblical and Qur'anic narratives it relies on), works such as *Drumming* and *Pendulum Music* are perhaps more difficult to understand as such. Even works like *Come Out* and *It's Gonna Rain* seem to create rhythm *at the expense of* the narrative context in which the voice recordings at the root of their composition were made. Indeed, minimalist music in general has often been characterized as nonnarrative in addition to repetitive.

But one of the ideas that a so-called new musicology has brought to musical analysis is an understanding of all nonprogrammatic (or "absolute") music (music like most symphonies and concertos that are not attached to stories as, say, an opera, ballet, or overture to a play would be) as narrative.[7] In fact, one of the insights of new musicologists like Susan McClary is the potential relevance of poststructuralist thought such as deconstruction to the study of music.[8] Certainly Reich has understood his own music, even when less or not at all programmatic, as telling a kind of story, and the story is that of the composition of the very music that is being played. As the music composes then decomposes itself (e.g., sections in *Drumming* slowly return to the same simple rhythm with which they began), Reich's allegories of listening become narratives of their own deconstruction, just as *The Cave* deconstructs the very Jewish/Arab binary (or the "fateful" Israeli/Palestinian/American "triangle," to repeat Chomsky's expression) that the Cave of Machpelah is used to root in the traditions of the various Abrahamic religions, and by deconstructing this binary he goes to even greater lengths to highlight the political paradox of roots narratives (in this case that of Zionism) than any of the other roots narratives considered here have done thus far. And as an allegory of listening, *The Cave* draws attention to the narrative of its own composition even as, in a self-referential way, it highlights the "composition" of roots as a narrative that paradoxically creates its own beginning as effect not cause.

Furthermore, I would argue, it is not a coincidence that the new musicology overlaps with an emerging queer musicology. McClary appears as an important name in both these trends, as well as that of feminist musicology. In *Feminine Endings: Music, Gender, and Sexuality*, for example, she even uses a once common musical term (an ending was considered "feminine" if it occurs on an unstressed and therefore "weak" beat) to theorize the gendered implications of closure along the lines discussed in chapter 3. Similarly, the queer possibility of the musical text arises in *The Cave* with Reich and Korot's inclusion among the interviewees featured in the third act of Lisa Rogers, a "[g]raduate of the Episcopal Theological Seminary of the Southwest, and program director of Out Youth Austin, a lesbian and gay youth peer support group" (29). In response to the question "Who is Hagar?" Rogers responds, "She gets kicked out. . . . The first single mother" (48). By suggesting a queer role for Hagar in the third act, "set" in the United States, a place within both Jewish and Palestinian diasporas, Reich and Korot offer diaspora as a place for the potential queering of both Jewish and Muslim identifications with Hagar. (Although Israeli interviewees distance themselves from Hagar, Palestinian ones do identify with her and American interviewees whose biographies suggest a Jewish identity are much more sympathetic.) Again, highlighting the political and narrative paradoxes in *The Cave* also involves the sexual paradox.

Memmi's Queer Zionism

As for Hagar, she also figures prominently in the fictional work of Jewish Tunisian writer Albert Memmi. His second, partially autobiographical novel *Agar* (French for Hagar) carries her name and tells the story of a French-educated Jewish Tunisian doctor who has married a French Catholic woman whom he brings back to live in Tunisia where he opens a medical practice. Given Memmi's later pro-Zionist essays, it might seem odd that, through this title, his autobiographical protagonist would allude to his own *French* wife through the mythical mother of all Arabs, including Palestinians. In one of these essays, *Liberation of the Jew*, Memmi writes, "The Diaspora must cease to be a Diaspora" (286), thereby placing his hope for Jewish liberation in the realization of the Zionist project through the modern state of Israel. Memmi would later confirm his assertion of the Israeli state as the essence of Jewishness: "Israel is the heart and the head. Israel is now our heart of hearts . . . but the Diaspora is the great, suffering body" (*Jews* 67; 2nd ellipsis Memmi's). Through a mind/body binary, Memmi presents diasporic identities as degraded and inauthentic, as the corporeal supplement to a Jewish essence (and this in spite of his conscious decision to remain in diaspora throughout his life).

This understanding of Jewishness stands in stark contrast to anti-Semitic racializations of Jews as pure embodiment (see Gilman), but is Memmi's project the only possible route to Jewish liberation? For those for whom diaspora *is* the "essence" of Jewish identity, would Memmi's project not signify annihilation? Memmi himself states that "the existence of a Jewish nation will at last permit the disappearance of Jewishness" (*Liberation* 301). According to Ammiel Alcalay, state Zionism is founded on precisely such a desire: "Official discourse spoke matter-of-factly of the 'elimination of the Diaspora,' a slogan that even slipped into the 'elimination of the Jews'" (221).[9] When Memmi writes, "[T]he Jew has to find a *total solution*" (*Liberation* 277), he not only suggests the disturbing implications of the "disappearance" he envisions but also conjures up (in the English version at least) a resonance with the final solution.

Yet, whereas Memmi understands returning to Israel as a remedy for the uprootedness that characterizes his vision of diaspora, in this section I seek out alternative returns within Memmi's work itself. Memmi did not come to his explicitly pro-Zionist position right away. He was first known for his theorization of the situation of the colonized, his anti-colonial writings, and his support for *Arab* nationalism. His first essays are directly related to his first, semiautobiographical novel—*La statue de sel* [*The Pillar of Salt*],[10] to which *Agar* might be read as a sequel even though its characters have different names and the narrator's profession has changed. In the first novel, a kind of Bildungsroman, Memmi revives

Jewish identity through a different kind of narrative, one that plants its roots not in Palestine but in a predominantly Arab North Africa. In direct opposition to the passages from Memmi's essays cited above, and with what Ella Shohat calls "the Zionist rejection of the Diaspora" (272), Memmi's novels retrieve a biblically based model of Jewish identity in which diaspora and connection with a homeland are not at odds.[11] In a later interview, Memmi would redeploy the same heart/mind rhetoric he used to describe Israel: "Many of my readers . . . themselves have a Hara in their hearts and minds" (*Terre* 12). Here, however, he reverses his previous associations, so that the Hara—Tunis's Jewish quarter— becomes the heart and reason of Jewish identity. This statement conjures up the ghosts that haunt Memmi's Zionism, ghosts of the very diaspora he has condemned to death.

Whereas Memmi's return to a collective past in the Hara might at first seem to parallel Zionist narratives that claim to return the Nation of Israel to its prediaspora origins, by reading Memmi's first novel against his later Zionist essays, one can revive the ghosts of a diasporic body left to die in the latter.[12] And this body returns with its Jewishness inscribed onto the site of the circumcised penis, a site of both a difference from and connection to the Arab world of which Memmi is a part. If Alcalay describes a body of Arab Jewish texts from Israel in which the promised land has become a land of uprootedness and broken promises, Memmi's early fiction reroots Jewish identity in a Hara of the mind, where the Arab/Jew opposition is deconstructed as in Alcalay's reconception of Mediterranean culture. Traditionally, the circumcised penis is a sign of man's alliance with God; it is thus the place where a phallocentric genealogy is inscribed onto the male body, making him a member of the Nation of Israel. (As Howard Eilberg-Schwartz writes, "[O]ne must have a member to be a member" [*Savage* 145].) Yet this site on which patriarchy is founded nonetheless signifies the potential for its undoing, for circumcision also threatens to negate the masculinity that undergirds the Zionism on which the Israeli state is founded. By reviving the emasculated diasporic penis, therefore, *The Pillar of Salt* reroutes Jewish identity through alternative origins, which will also serve here as my point of departure for some reflections on the emerging field of queer diaspora studies.

Memmi's novel can thus be situated in relation to a body of work on Jewish masculinity. In *The Jew's Body*, for example, Sander Gilman examines anti-Semitic constructions of the Jewish male body as degenerate, castrated, and (through the antifeminist notion of femininity as lack)

feminized. Conversely, without embracing the anti-Semitic feminiza-
tion of Jewish men, both Daniel Boyarin and Eilberg-Schwartz seek to
reclaim this alternative masculinity in an avowedly feminist recuperation
of a more traditional Jewish masculinity from biblical and rabbinic sources. Both have also described circumcision as a key component of this
alternative masculinity (see Boyarin, "This"; Eilberg-Schwartz, *God's Phallus*). Boyarin describes circumcision as making the Jewish man "open to
receive the divine speech and vision of God" ("This" 495). Since "God
is the husband to Israel the wife" (97), according to Eilberg-Schwartz,
"men may meet God only as women. And circumcision makes them
desirable women" (174).

Daniel Boyarin discusses more recent implications of the anti-Semitic
view of Jewish masculinity as defective in *Unheroic Conduct: The Rise of Heterosexuality and the Invention of the Jewish Man* as regards the consolidation
of Zionism in nineteenth-century Europe. To assert Israel as a nation of
manly men among nations of men, a repudiation that finds its epitome
in Max Nordau's "Muscle-Jew," this consolidation required a repudiation
of the Jewish man abjected as feminine by anti-Semitic discourses. For,
inasmuch as the Zionism that led to the Israeli state claims to return the
Nation of Israel to the promised land, it is not merely a return to roots;
it is also a narrative of progress, of gendered progress (see also Biale
176–203). Although Boyarin is careful to limit his findings to Ashkenazi
traditions and warns against seeing a continuity in the parallel between
ancient and rabbinic writings on the one hand and pre-nineteenth-
century northern European Jewish cultures on the other, his conclusions
are nonetheless relevant for understanding Memmi's relation to Zionism. Given that the Zionist state establishes an Ashkenazi hegemony at
the expense of Arab Jews, the diasporic male body in Memmi's early fiction, without explicitly resisting the Zionist masculinization that finds its
epitome in Max Nordau's "Muscle-Jew," nonetheless returns to haunt it.

Agar details the conflicts between the new wife and her husband's
family, and the key event in these tensions is the decision about whether
to circumcise their first son. Indeed, nearly all of the second half of the
novel results from their disagreements about circumcision. Eventually,
the narrator comes to agree with his wife's opposition to circumcision
(required in the absence of a religious marriage if the son is going to
inherit according to Jewish family law), but in the end a circumcision is
performed for medical reasons. The novel ends with the wife pregnant
for a second time and planning to leave her husband and have an abortion. In short, circumcision is divisive in *Agar*, even though the biblical

character named in its title has a circumcised son (at least in the Islamic tradition) just like Abraham's wife Sarah. In *The Pillar of Salt*, however, circumcision connects Tunisians *across* confessional divides. Within this novel, whose narrative is framed as a looking back (its narrator Alexandre Mordekhaï Benillouche remembers his childhood as he is sitting for an exam), there is a particular chapter that consists of looking back within the looking back: "Au kouttab" [At the *Kouttab* School] begins as Alexandre, at this point a high school student, witnesses a peculiar scene in a streetcar. A grocer from the island of Djerba (known for its historically large Jewish population) singles out a two-year-old Muslim boy for teasing after inquiring whether he is circumcised.[13] When the boy's father says no, the grocer attempts to "purchase" the boy's penis at higher and higher prices and, after a series of more and more adamant refusals, reaches into the boy's pants and pretends to snatch his penis without paying. In this lesson of phallic privilege, the little boy fights off the aggressor and defends his penis against the threat of castration.

Even as the game begins, the narrator identifies with its victim across ethno-confessional lines:

> Visiblement, il connaissait la scène, déjà on lui avait fait la même proposition. Moi aussi, je la connaissais. Je l'avais jouée dans le temps, assailli par d'autres provocateurs, avec les mêmes sentiments de honte et de concupiscence, de révolte et de curiosité complice. Les yeux de l'enfant brillaient du plaisir d'une virilité naissante et de la révolte contre cette inqualifiable aggression. (186)

> [Quite obviously, the boy knew this whole routine and had already heard the same proposition before. I too, knew it all, and had myself played the game some years ago, attacked by other aggressors and feeling the same emotions of shame [and sexual excitement, of revolt and complicitous curiosity]. The child's eyes sparkled with the pleasure of his awareness of his own growing virility, and with the shock of his revolt against such an unwarranted attack. (167)]

This identification is so strong that the narrator experiences a physical sensation in his penis, which he takes to be the same as what the little boy is feeling:

> Lorsque l'enfant hurla, je sentis mon sexe frémir à l'appel brusquement resurgi du fond de mon enfance. . . . Oui, je le connais bien ce

frisson désagréable et voluptueux. Avant d'aller à l'école primaire, je fréquentais un kouttab. (188)

[When the boy in the streetcar screamed with fear, I felt my own [sex] quiver as if in response to a [call surging] suddenly from the depths of my own childhood. . . . Yes, I know well that unpleasant but voluptuous [shiver]. Before going to grade school, I used to go to the *kouttab*. (169–70)]

This sensation functions as a sort of Proustian madeleine that revives an identical feeling from his much earlier past, thereby bringing an entire scene into the present. One day at the *kouttab*, or Hebrew school, after the rabbi leaves the room, a class of boys decides to stage a circumcision ceremony.

They choose the smallest among them to be circumcised, and yet again, Memmi's narrator identifies with the frightened victim, so totally in fact that he experiences the very same fear:

Mais le risque m'avait lié à la victime, avait déclenché en moi les affres du calvaire. Je ressentais l'angoisse du tout petit tremblant, porté sur les épaules du surveillant comme un agneau de sacrifice. (191)

[But the mere threat had bound me closely to the victim and [set off inside me] all the terrors of a real calvary. I could feel the anguish of the small boy who, all trembling, was now being carried, like the sacrificial lamb, on the shoulders of our [monitor]. (172–73)]

Since the boy is already circumcised, the excitement that drives their play-acting is, to a great extent, the tension and fear that the boy might "really" be "circumcised" again, which would necessarily involve the removal of something other than a foreskin:

Mon cœur battait de peur et d'émotion confuse. Qu'allait-il lui arriver ? Allaient-ils vraiment lui couper le membre ? J'en avais une douleur vague et cependant non désagréable au bas-ventre. (192)

[My heart beat faster, under the pressure of fear and [embarrassed] emotion. . . . Were they really going to cut off his penis? The mere thought of it gave me a vague but not unpleasant pain in my [groin]." (173)]

He again experiences this identification as a physical sensation at the site of his own penis, which tingles with excitement.

This scene ends climactically, and quite literally so, since the narrator describes his own reaction as an explosion of jouissance:

> Ce fut physiquement intolérable, et je me sentis défaillir lorsque la main droite du sacrificateur, armée du rasoir, descendit lentement vers le petit bout de chair blanche qui émergeait entre l'index et le majeur de sa main gauche.
>
> Brusque fut la délivrance, explosèrent d'un seul coup ma peur, ma honte, ma jouissance, mon dégoût et l'insupportable tension du silence angoissé de tous : à bout de nerfs, la victime venait d'éclater en sanglots. (193)

> [It was physically intolerable, and I felt truly faint when the High Priest's right hand, armed with a razor, came slowly down toward the tiny bit of white flesh that [protruded] between the index and the second finger of his left hand.
>
> But my sense of having been liberated was sudden, and all my fear vanished explosively, together with my shame, my [jouissance], my disgust, and the unbearable tension that was born of the anguished silence of all of us: unable to stand it any longer, the victim had just burst into tears. (174–75)]

These passages could serve as textbook examples of what Boyarin has called "Jewissance," a pleasure that comes from "an extraordinary richness of experience and a powerful sense of being rooted somewhere in the world, in a world of memory, intimacy, and connectedness" (*Unheroic* xxiii). Jewissance à la Memmi is much more concrete than Boyarin's pleasures of the mind and of being a member of a collective identity; Memmi's Jewissance is a physical pleasure emanating *from* his member:

> Je ressentais dans mon sexe cette peur voluptueuse se traduire en frissons électriques. Comment oublierais-je cette complicité ? Oui, je participais à la cérémonie, à la pâture collective, ancestrale. (193)

> [[In my sex, I felt this voluptuous fear translate into electric shivers.] How shall I ever forget my complicity? Yes, I was playing my part in the ceremony, in the ancestral and collective ritual that was food for the mind. (174)]

In fact, Memmi's Jewissance is jouissance in *all* the meanings of the word: *il jouit de sa judéité.* That is, he enjoys, benefits from, and relishes in his Jewishness, which also brings him sexual ecstasy. In this passage, at least, the liberation of a particular Jew ("my sense of having been liberated") takes on quite different contours from those outlined in *The Liberation of the Jew.* Furthermore, his penis not only makes him quintessentially Jewish, but it also connects him to other penises, those of other Jewish men. Although his circumcised penis inserts him into a phallic understanding of Jewish identity, however, the circumcision that writes this Jewishness onto his penis also signifies his emasculation: "J'avais mal au bas-ventre, au même point, comme si le couteau allait me blesser" (193) ["[M]y groin ached[, at the same spot,] as if the knife were about to wound me" (174)]. And, although the narrator shares this threat, the possibility of castration is an inextricable component of his physical pleasure.

Yet, whereas his circumcised penis is supposedly what defines him as Jewish, that is, as not Christian or Muslim, it actually gives him an *intimate* connection with those from whom he is supposed to be different. The most intimate connection is reserved for the Muslim penis, which tingles in complete sync with the narrator's own (at least as the two are brought together in the mnemonic space of his mind). For identification with/through the penis is a tactile process: "Pourrai-je jamais oublier l'Orient alors qu'il est greffé dans ma chair, qu'il me suffit de me toucher pour vérifier sa marque definitive ?" (188) [Will I ever be able to forget the Orient, since it is grafted into my flesh, and it is enough to touch myself to verify its definitive mark?]. And we remember that it is indeed by touching the uncircumcised penis that the Djerbian (and through him, the other men present) participates in a collective experience of circumcision. In the space of the streetcar, "Toutes les races se trouvaient représentées" (185) ["All the races of our city were represented" (166)]: "Décidément, nous nous sentions en famille, entre Méditerranéens" (187) [Decidedly, we felt like family, among Mediterraneans]. This rhetoric of kinship unites Jewish, Muslim, French, Bedouin, Sicilian, and Djerbian, and it is precisely this genealogy, this "Orient . . . grafted into my flesh," that marks his penis not only with Jewish difference but also as being in relation with non-Jewish Mediterraneans. The streetcar thus serves as a metaphor for a diasporic Jewish identity, for in it Alexandre experiences his Jewissance as he and his fellow travelers (get in) touch (with) their penises along the shared routes to their identities rooted in collective memories. The streetcar scene might therefore be read as a circle jerk in which Memmi's narrator only gets in touch with his Jewishness by figuratively touching other penises.

In a later chapter, this figurative contact is literalized in Memmi's characterization of the homoerotic nature of a specifically Mediterranean sexuality:

Jamais je n'avais pu accepter les jeux sexuels des garçons. Je refusai avec mépris et scandale lorsqu'on m'apprit qu'un grand élève s'offrait pour caresser précisément et jusqu'à la jouissance tous ceux qui le désiraient. Mes camarades organisaient ces parties de plaisir collectif dans un terrain vague non loin du lycée. Ils s'alignaient, paraît-il, le dos au mur et Giacomo passait devant chacun, à tour de rôle. Dans la salle des surveillants d'internat, j'étais le seul à refuser de raconter mes aventures, le seul à ne pas évoquer, à ne pas décrire avec complaisance les attributs féminins et masculins, mille fois par jour. Je trouvais cette promiscuité de fort mauvais goût et d'ailleurs je n'avais rien à raconter. (257–58)

[I had never been able to [approve of] the sexual games of boys. When I was told that one of the older pupils offered to caress, with enough skill to cause an orgasm, anyone who wished, I refused with scorn and horror. My comrades organized these parties of collective pleasure out on a vacant lot not far from the school. Apparently, they all lined up with their back[s] to the wall and Giacomo passed [in front of them] one by one. I was the only one in the [lounge for the boarders' monitors] not to talk of my adventures or to describe with [self-indulgence] the sexual attributes of men and women a thousand times a day. To me, such promiscuity was [in very bad taste]; besides, what had I to tell? (239–40)]

The very passage that admits the homoerotic nature of this community of men bound through the connections they feel in their penises serves to deny the narrator's participation in its homoeroticism. Yet Alexandre certainly knows a lot about something he has supposedly never done, enough to repeat in great detail descriptions of that from which he pretended to recoil in horror.

In a previous reading of these and other passages from *The Pillar of Salt*, I situated these erotic scenarios from Alexandre's past within the novel's narrative of colonial assimilation and alienation.[14] There I understood Memmi's denial of being implicated in the "parties of collective pleasure" as part of a narrative of sexual development that parallels the civilizing process of Alexandre's colonial assimilation. As Memmi's narrator leaves behind the dark continent of a primitive past, of a childhood marked as polymorphously perverse, he comes closer to achieving the goal of French education for the colonized. Yet *The Pillar of Salt* quite clearly details the price of such an assimilation—alienation—and in the end its narrator rejects French civilization altogether when he fails to hand in the exam he has been taking (or more accurately not taking, since he was remembering his childhood instead). Because he ends up rejecting his previous rejection of the "Orient" (itself a colonial construct), this second rejection logically entails a reversal of his rejection of "Oriental sex" in the above passage. The very narrative structure of the novel, therefore, brings the remembered childhood into conflict with its framing (the French educational system and its civilizing mission), brings the queerness of the past into conflict with the present. In other words, the novel not only represents queer childhood episodes but also offers a narrative structure for queering the present by returning *to* the past and returning the past to the present.

In that earlier reading, I stressed the implications of this queer haunting for *Tunisian* nationalism, since the Jewish presence revived in *The Pillar of Salt* comes to contest a politics of purity that would define the Maghrebian nation as Arab and Muslim. This questioning of the nation was *also* a queering because the multiple connections of the rhizomatic origins of Tunisian identity were not just homoerotic (in a way whose denial can so easily slide into homosociality) but homoerotic in a way that involved the emasculation of any homosociality that might result in a justification of male privilege. It was the return of a preheterosexual childhood (preheterosexual because it was prior to a mature adult sexuality—even an "indigenous" one—and, since childhood allegorizes the precolonial, prior to the heterosexuality imposed by colonialism) that made this ghosting queer.

My point in this section has been to carry out a parallel reading of Memmi in relation to Zionism, in relation to Israeli as opposed to Tunisian nationalism. For, inasmuch as the Zionism that led to the Israeli state claims to return the Nation of Israel to the promised land, it is not merely a revival of the past or a return to roots; it is also a narrative of progress, of gendered progress, one that requires the masculinization of its men in relation to (other) European nations. No matter how many Zionist essays Memmi pens, the emasculated "Oriental" penis of his first novel will always stand in contrast to the gendered politics of Zionism described by Boyarin and resisted by both Daniel and Jonathan Boyarin in their more explicitly anti-Zionist writings. This rather queer penis may also provide one way to understand the potentially queer role of diaspora within what James Clifford calls "a *diasporist* anti-Zionism," of which, for him, the Boyarins and Alcalay serve as prime examples ("Diasporas" 326). In their jointly authored "Diaspora: Generation and the Ground of Jewish Identity," Daniel and Jonathan Boyarin propose an alternative "genealogy" of Jewish identity, one based on diaspora as a counter to Zionism. In direct opposition to the passages from Memmi's essays that begin this section and with what Ella Shohat calls "the Zionist rejection of the Diaspora" (272), they retrieve a biblically based model of Jewish identity in which diaspora and connection with a homeland are not at odds.

In the specific context examined by Gopinath in *Impossible Desires* (as I discuss in the introduction to this volume), nation and diaspora are seen as much more compatible (at least in the hegemonic models of diasporism she critiques) than within Zionist discourses. Gopinath's retrieval of queerness within diaspora thus leads directly to a queering of the nation. It is probably the case, however, that diaspora haunts the nation differently for Zionism, which actually envisions the elimination of diaspora. One can thus not only locate queerness within the diaspora but also understand diaspora as having a queer relation to the Israeli nation.[15] In contrast to Gopinath's project, rather than queering the Israeli state, retrieving the Jewish diaspora as queer in Memmi's fiction contributes to an imagining of the undoing of Zionism as a political project by allowing the rhizomatic connections of diaspora to return in the process of returning to origins in a homeland of the mind. Memmi thus allows us to carry forward Gopinath's queering of diaspora by allowing us to tease out the queer potential of the very concept of diaspora itself.

While Memmi's revival of his penis relies on the same phallic genealogy Helmreich alludes to in his etymological definition of *diaspora* as the spreading of seed/sperm, his Jewissance entails spilling his seed rather differently. Indeed, it is not through heterosexual reproduction that he plants the seeds of a Zionist state; rather, the promised land flows forth like milk and honey every time he touches himself "to verify [the] definitive mark [of the Orient]." Jonathan and Daniel Boyarin retrieve an antimasculinist diasporic anti-Zionism by performing "the double mark of the male Jew," that is, their circumcision and head covering, thereby undoing the body/mind opposition Memmi's Zionism relies on ("Self-

Exposure" 16–22). Yet, whereas they write (about) their penises, Memmi has a wank. Indeed, for Memmi "l'alliance avec Dieu était sexuelle" (190) [the covenant with God was of a sexual nature (171)]. But instead of getting in touch with *God* as he touches himself, Memmi touches (the penises of) fellow Arabs. The home of Jewish identity is thus not a state that pushes out the Other; rather Muslim and Jewish penises rub together, acknowledging that they share an alliance with God signed by Abraham. The Nation of Israel that comes into being through a kind of circle jerk with (other) Arabs makes for a rather queer Zionism, which is more like no Zionism at all. Unlike the tree of begats recited in *The Cave*, a homoerotic affiliation counters the models of filiation on which the Zionist roots narrative is founded. If there are few examples of more violent effects of the political paradox of roots, the sexual paradox in Memmi's fictional work may be mined to challenge the politics of his essays.

Indeed, Memmi shows us that the very narrative structure on which Zionism relies offers a strategy for its undoing. The very gesture of looking back is evoked by the novel's title; *The Pillar of Salt* is a biblical reference to Lot's wife, who—disobeying God's command not to look back on a burning Sodom—turns into a pillar of salt. Memmi explicitly connects his fate to hers:

> [J]e meurs pour m'être retourné sur moi-même. Il est interdit de se voir et j'ai fini de me connaître. Comme la femme de Loth, que Dieu changea en statue, puis-je encore vivre au-delà de mon regard? (368)

> [I am dying [from] having turned back [on my]self. It is forbidden to see oneself, and I have [finished knowing] myself. [Like Lot's wife, whom God turned into a pillar of salt, can I still live beyond my gaze]? (335)]

Since Memmi looks back on himself as Lot's wife looked back on Sodom, he equates his own past with Sodom. Furthermore, since Memmi's use of the verb *to know* recalls the very reason for Sodom's destruction— "[T]he men of Sodom, compassed the house round. . . . And they called unto Lot, and said unto him, Where *are* the men which came in to thee this night? bring them out unto us, that we may know them" (Gen. 19.4–5)—"knowing" could be read here in the biblical sense. Lot declines to let the men of Sodom "know" his guests and offers up his own daughters instead. In contrast, Memmi opts to know himself by getting in touch with other Mediterraneans. When knowing oneself is the equivalent of touching oneself (which is the equivalent of touching the penises of other Jews and Arabs), the mind/body binary on which Memmi founds his explicitly Zionist position begins to collapse as surely as the city of Sodom. As with the Hara, however, there will always be a Sodom of the mind. "Next year in Jerusalem," then, becomes the equivalent of "Tonight in Sodom," as Zion surges from every wank in a certain street-car of the mind, a streetcar named desire.

Derrida's Queer Root(s)

The queering of diaspora through the pleasure derived from emascula-tion that Memmi feels at the site of his circumcision is taken a step fur-ther by Jacques Derrida. Like *La statue de sel,* "Circumfessions"—a sort of footnote running the entire length of Geoffrey Bennington's "Derrida-base," both of which together constitute their jointly authored *Jacques Derrida*—returns Derrida to the moment of his circumcision with the result that his circumcised penis becomes a figure for his Jewish Algerian roots. Unlike the numerous representations of circumcision in Franco-Maghrebian fiction that return to circumcision in memory only to bring it back as trauma, however, Derrida's discussion evokes a "Jewissance" that parallels Memmi's. Reading Derrida's penis through the model provided by Memmi, then, allows us to understand that when Derrida's penis enters his writing it stands as a site for his emasculation consistent not with the erection of phallogocentrism but with its deconstruction. Of Derrida's autobiographical texts, "Circumfessions" lavishes the most attention on his own penis (or root) and the circumcision of that penis as a figure for his Jewish Algerian origins (or roots). Written around his penis, these origins are also doubly circumscribed by seemingly oppos-ing limits, the limits of both identity and its deconstruction. By focusing on the homoerotics that arise when Derrida's penis enters his writing, this section brings his autobiographical writing into contrast with decon-struction and argues that this contradiction is at the heart of a queering of identity, for which deconstruction might be read as an allegory. Once autobiography intrudes into Derrida's deconstructive writing, decon-struction turns out to have been, in part, about identity all along.

On several occasions in this study, I have already considered Derrida's deconstruction of origins in *Of Grammatology.* By asserting their *après-coup* constitution, Derrida implies that searching for and then "finding" one's roots does not consist of returning to preexisting origins; rather the very return posits them *after the fact* as if they existed prior to it. At first glance, this deconstruction of origins (a critical component of the deconstruction of essence since Derrida's earliest writings) might seem contrary to the articulation of identity through narrative returns to origins or roots. If the notion of roots literalizes identity's essence as an organic attachment to its origins in a material, geographic site, for Derrida a metaphysical search for origins is actually a writing of origins as fiction (in short what I have called the narrative paradox). Yet Derrida increasingly wove an important autobiographical thread into writings like "Circumfessions" and *The Monolingualism of the Other* with the result that, in spite of his deconstruction of origins, origins keep coming back in the form of narrative returns to his Jewish Algerian roots. Derrida's later texts (and their deployment of the autobiographical) therefore offer rich pre-texts for unraveling the ties that bind a metaphysics of origins to accounts of identity as rootedness, as well as a strategy for dealing with a rooted identity that resists such an unraveling.

In "Circumfessions," Derrida returns to his Algerian childhood by reading Saint Augustine's *Confessions*. Writing his own autobiography by reading the autobiography of another, Derrida gives the queering of identity a literal component in two explicit mentions of homosexuality. In one passage, Derrida queers his North African literary forebear: "[J]'ai la vision de sA, lui aussi, en petit Juif homosexuel (d'Alger ou de New York), il a tout refoulé, se convertit en somme assez tôt en don Juan chrétien par peur du sida" (161) [I have the vision of SA, too, as a little homosexual Jew (from Algiers or New York), he has repressed everything, basically converts himself quite early on into a Christian Don Juan for fear of AIDS (172)]. Here, through his Berber pre-text, Derrida returns to a pre-Muslim, pre-French Algeria, thereby *un*converting Saint Augustine and recasting his Christianization as repression. In addition, he could be said to equate queering with rendering Jewish. In another passage, this queering extends to Derrida himself:

> [M]on homosexualité impossible, celle que j'associerai toujours au
> nom de Claude, les cousins-cousines de mon enfance, ils débordent
> mon corpus, la syllabe CL, dans *Glas* et ailleurs, avouant un plaisir
> volé, ces raisins par exemple sur le vignoble du propriétaire arabe,
> de ces rares bourgeois d'El-Biar. . . . [D]epuis je suis les confessions
> de vol au cœur des autobiographies, la ventriloque homosexuelle, la

dette intraduisible, le ruban de Rousseau, les poires de sA. (150–51)

[M]y impossible homosexuality, the one I shall always associate with the name of Claude, the male and female cousins of my childhood, they overflow my corpus, the syllable CL, in *Glas* and elsewhere, admitting to a stolen pleasure, for example those grapes from the vineyard of the Arab landowner, one of those rare Algerian bourgeois in El-Biar. . . . [S]ince then I have followed the confessions of theft at the heart of autobiographies, homosexual ventriloquy, the untranslatable debt, Rousseau's ribbon, SA's pears. (159–60)]

Derrida's reading of Saint Augustine thus occurs as a homosexual encounter that equates reading with queering, both of which are also the means by which the autobiographical subject identifies with his pretext and becomes (one with) it.

Furthermore, these two queerings occur through several returns: to an Algerian childhood episode of stealing; and to Derrida's own previous writings, namely, *Glas,* in which, as we shall see, he lavishes much attention on penises and erections. By extension, in mentioning Rousseau's theft of a ribbon, he not only inserts himself into a genealogy of autobiographical forebears (from Saint Augustine's *Confessions* to Rousseau's to his own), but he also recalls his own reading (and queering) of Rousseau in *Of Grammatology,* his reading of Rousseau's confessions of masturbating. If Derrida can transform the autobiographies of others into his own, if queering Saint Augustine is simultaneously a self-queering, then reading Rousseau masturbating is a way of masturbating (with) him. This practice of reading (as) a sexual act would thus be the "homosexual ventriloquy" that consists of making his pre-texts speak or, further, throwing his voice to fool us into believing that they are the ones that are speaking instead of Derrida.

In addition to these explicit mentions of homosexuality, *Jacques Derrida* carries out another, more subtle queering of Derrida in a photo of Bennington standing behind Derrida, who is sitting at a computer. The caption to this photo reads, "Carte postale ou tableau vivant . . . 'prétexte dérobé pour y inscrire ma propre signature derrière, dans son dos'" (15) ["Post Card or *tableau vivant* . . . 'a hidden pretext for writing in my own signature behind his back'" (11)],[16] thereby asserting a visual parallel between this photo and the eponymous image of *The Post Card,* an illustration taken from a "*Fortune-telling book* du XIIIe siècle (*Prognostica*

Socratis basilei)" (68) [13th century *Fortune-telling book* (*Prognostica Socratis basilei*) (61)] by Matthew Paris.[17] This image represents Plato standing behind Socrates as if the latter is taking dictation from the former in an inversion of the conventional wisdom regarding which philosopher is transmitting the other's thoughts in writing. It is undoubtedly this inversion between teacher and student—an inversion of the conventional primacy of the spoken word over writing—that first attracted Derrida to this image, but he goes on to push this inversion toward queerer limits by sexualizing the "postcard":

> [J]e vois Plato bander dans le dos de Socrate et l'ubris insensée de sa queue, une érection interminable, disproportionnée, traverser comme une seule idée la tête de Paris et la chaise du copiste avant de glisser doucement, toute chaude encore, sous la jambe droite de Socrates, en harmonie ou symphonie de mouvement avec ce faisceau de phallus, les pointes, plumes, doigts, ongles et grattoirs, les écritoires même qui s'adressent dans la même direction. . . . Il plonge sous les vagues que font les voiles autour des fesses dodues, tu vois le double arrondi, assez invraisemblable, il plonge droit, rigide, comme le nez d'une torpille, pour électrocuter le vieux et l'analyser sous narcose. . . . Tout cela, que je ne sais pas ou ne veux pas voir encore, revient aussi du fond des eaux de ma mémoire, un peu comme si j'avais dessiné ou gravé la scène, depuis le premier jour où, dans un lycée d'Alger sans doute, j'ai entendu parler de ces deux-là. (*La carte postale* 22–23)

> [I see *Plato* getting an erection in *Socrates*' back and see the insane hubris of his prick, an interminable, disproportionate erection traversing Paris's head like a single idea and then the copyist's chair, before slowly sliding, still warm, under *Socrates*' right leg, in harmony or symphony with the movement of this phallus sheaf [this bundle of phalluses], the points, plumes, pens, fingers, [finger]nails and *grattoirs*, the very pencil boxes which address themselves [rise up to one another] in the same direction. . . . It plunges under the waves made by the veils around the plump buttocks, you see the rounded double, improbable enough, it plunges straight down, rigid, like the nose of a stingray to electrocute the old man. . . . All of this, that I do not know or do not yet want to see, also comes back from the bottom of the waters of my memory, a bit as if I had drawn or engraved the scene,

from the first day that, in an Algiers *lycée* no doubt, I first heard of those two. (*Post Card* 18)]

By reading the elongated object protruding from beneath Socrates' leg as Plato's penis, Derrida suggests that the latter is fucking the former between the legs. Socrates is thus taking more than dictation, Plato giving more than the spoken word. *Platon prend Socrate, qui lui donne son cul.* Or, we could say, Plato gives it to Socrates, who in turn takes it (between the legs).[18] Yet even the text that *Jacques Derrida* sends us back to (*The Post Card*) sends us back even further to Derrida's Algerian adolescence (the kind of looking back that turns one into a pillar of salt) as if a return to his Jewish Algerian roots were inseparable from his reflections on the possibility of two of his philosophical pre-texts and forebears engaging in intercrural intercourse.

Derrida's queer reading of the give-and-take between Socrates and Plato in *The Post Card* returns in *Jacques Derrida* to inflect his relation with his translator and commentator. By reading the above passage from *The Post Card* into the photo in *Jacques Derrida*, we could say that Bennington gives it to Derrida, who in turn takes it (up the ass). This photo thus turns Bennington into Derrida's top just as Derrida's autobiographical reflections are positioned at the bottom of the page. We could also say that, as Derrida's autobiography undergirds Bennington's account of his life's work, the top becomes an allegory of the bottom. Perhaps I, too, become Derrida's top in my reading of his work. Or is it deconstruction that is constantly being not undergirded but undermined, screwed, that is, by the insertion of the autobiographical (penis)? "Circumfessions" is thus not only the text in which Derrida most literally inserts his penis and his autobiography into his writing; it is also the text in which the penis of another is inserted into him. To read Derrida, to turn him into the pre-text for (in this case, queer) theorizing is also to penetrate him (i.e., to sodomize as well as understand him).

If we might also read the particular give-and-take I have just described as a queering of Derrida's writings on the gift, one text, in particular, seems to give more than others: *Glas*, in which each numbered page consists of two columns (each containing multiple subcolumns or inserts). The one on the right, devoted to Jean Genet, offers the most explicit penises, which should not surprise given their abundance in Genet's own writings. The left-hand column is devoted to the Hegelian dialectic and Hegel's reflections on the relation among

Christianity, the family, civil society, and the state. According to Derrida, claims to truth in Hegel's narrative of progress from Judaism to Christianity rely on the bourgeois family and religion, and Hegel's reflections on religion and the dialectic depend on the notion that Christianity represents the fulfillment or teleology of Judaism (like the synthesis, or *Aufhebung*, of the dialectic) in which the three terms of the lifting up become a kind of Holy Family: "*Aufhebung* au sein du christianisme d'abord, puis *Aufhebung* du christianisme, de la religion absolue **relevée** dans la philosophie qui en aura été la vérité" (H99) [*Aufhebung* first in the heart [*sein*] of Christianity,[19] then *Aufhebung* of Christianity, of the absolute revealed religion in(to) philosophy [of the absolute religion raised up or highlighted within philosophy that will have been its truth] (H70)].[20]

In fact, Derrida's deconstruction of Truth as both Christianity and heterosexuality occurs precisely through a sexualization of *Aufhebung*:

> [L]e procès de la copulation vise à conserver cette différence tout en l'annulant.
> Il la **relève** : l'*Aufhebung* est très précisément le rapport de la copulation à la différence sexuelle.
> On ne peut comprendre la **relève** en général sans la copulation sexuelle, ni celle-ci en général sans la **relève**. (H156)

> [Copulation relieves [highlights/raises up] the difference: *Aufhebung* is very precisely the relation of copulation and the sexual difference.
> The relief in general cannot be understood without sexual copulation, nor sexual copulation in general without the relief. (H111)][21]

Passages such as these serve to associate the lifting or raising up of *Aufhebung* with erection; indeed, Derrida turns the *Aufhebung* that is Christianity back against Christianity to get a rise out of it. In fact this rise occurs in part by turning the Last Supper into the scene[22] of a homosexual orgy in which penetration is again sexual as well as epistemological:

> La pénétration identificatoire de Jésus en ses disciples—Jean d'abord, le disciple chéri—, du Père en Jésus et à travers lui en ses disciples— Jean le premier—, subjective en un premier temps, puis objective, redevient subjective par l'ingestion. La consommation intériorise, idéalise, **relève** . . . . Pourvu qu'il nomme, qu'il engage un discours, le mouvement de la langue est analogue à la copulation dans la Cène.

Tout cet analogon ne se forme, ne **tient debout** et ne se laisse saisir que sous la catégorie des catégories. Il se **relève** tout le temps. C'est une *Aufhebung*. (H96–97)

[Jesus' identifying penetration in his disciples—first John, the beloved disciple; the Father's in Jesus and through him in his disciples—John first; subjective in a first time, then objective, becomes subjective by ingestion. Consum(mat)ing interiorizes, idealizes, relieves [uplifts]. . . . Provided it name, it engage a discourse, the movement of the tongue [and language] is analogous to the copulation at the Last Supper scene.

This whole analogon takes form, stands up, makes sense [*tient debout*] [holds up], and lets itself be grasped only under the category of categories. It relieves itself [lifts itself up] all the time. It is an *Aufhebung*. (H69)]

Derrida here reverses/inverts Hegel's heterodialectical understanding of Christianity, thereby deconstructing the Christianity/Judaism distinction, turning Judaism against Christianity in order to queer the latter. In fact, if Derrida refers to absolute knowledge throughout *Glas* as "*Sa*" (*Savoir absolu*), this abbreviation inverts the capitalization of the abbreviation for Saint Augustine in "Circumfessions" (*sA*) much as he turns *sA* into an invert and a Jew. In addition, through both *Sa/sA*'s relation to the homonym *ça* (the id), Derrida further sexualizes knowledge as penetration. In Saint Augustine (*sA*), we also see *Sa* as an inverted truth, the truth inverted, inversion as ~~Truth.~~

From *Aufhebung* as erection, Derrida proceeds through the French colloquial term for having an erection, *bander* (more accurately "to get a hard-on"), to multiple parallels with Genet's penises and Hegel's erections. The strongest of these parallels is found in Derrida's own writing on both Genet and Hegel, which takes the form of two bands of text. In fact, Derrida suggests rather strongly that content shapes the form of *Glas*, which itself becomes a kind of double hard-on: "il **bande** double" (G280) [he bands erect double (G201)], "DOUBLE **BANDE** . . . **Bande** contre **bande**" (G92) [DOUBLE BAND(S). . . . Band contra band (G66)]. We might then read this *double bande* as not only a visualization of the Hegelian dialectic but also its queering, since the erection of Christianity as Judaism's *Aufhebung* is literalized on the page and forced to rub against Genet's erect penises in a kind of theoretical *frottage* or dry humping. In addition, Hegel's synthesis (Christianity) becomes just another thesis for which Genet's penises serve as the antithesis in a queering of the Hegelian dialectic.

Furthermore, as if the mechanics of this theoretical maneuver needed a little greasing up, Derrida inserts some lubrication through one of Genet's fetish objects, the tube of Vaseline described in *Journal du voleur* (20–24) [*The Thief's Journal*]. Derrida glorifies this object—"La langue (française) doit donc chanter, fêter le petit tube de vaseline" (G226) [The (French) tongue then ought to sing, to fete the little tube of vaseline (G162)]—and sexualizes it even beyond Genet's own allusions to its potential sexual uses: "Et le crachat dont s'enduirait le mât glissant devient très vite, la plume est trempée dans une glu très fluide, de la vaseline. Et même, sans avoir à forcer, un tube de vaseline goménolée" (G200) [And the spit with which the gliding mast would be smeared becomes, very quickly—the pen is dipped into a very fluid glue—some vaseline. And even, without forcing, a tube of mentholated vaseline (G143)]. As if the tube of Vaseline were insufficient, Derrida even adds a little spit to the mixture as his pen becomes a penis (as does Plato's in *The Post Card*). Furthermore, this pen(is) needs its own lubrication: "Essayez donc avec le tube de vaseline . . . avant le début du livre" (G201–2) [[S]o try with the tube of vaseline . . . before the beginning of the book" (G143–44)]. And if, in *Glas*, writing is equated with the insertion of a penis (the literal subject of "Circumfessions"), by turning the pages of *Glas* the reader rubs erection against erection, an act facilitated by the textual lubrication provided by Derrida (and Genet). In other words, the Vaseline does more than provide the textual lubrication to ease the turning of pages in *Glas* in order to rub erection against erection; it also eases the insertion of Derrida's own penis in the form of *Glas*'s most prominent autobiographical references.

One of these references is a passage over two pages long in which Derrida describes an Algerian synagogue in which the Torah is brought out from behind curtains:

> La Thora porte robe et couronne. Ses deux rouleaux sont ensuite écartés comme deux jambes, elle est soulevée à portée de bras et le sceptre du rabbin suit approximativement le texte **dressé**. Les **bandes** dont il était entouré avaient d'abord été défaites et en général confiées à un enfant. (G335)

> [The Torah wears a robe and a crown. Its two rollers are then parted [*écartés*] like two legs; the Torah is lifted to arm's length and the rab-

bi's scepter approximately follows the upright [erect] text. The bands in which it was wrapped had been previously undone. (G240)]

Derrida also speaks of the rabbi "raising the two parted columns" [**élever** les deux colonnes écartés] and states, "Il fallait ensuite, le texte sacré, l'enrouler et **bander** de nouveau" [Afterwards, they had to roll up the sacred text and wrap [*bander*] it all over again (G336 for the French, G241 for the English)]. Here Derrida thus compares the doubly erectile structure of *Glas* to the two rollers of the Torah. Or, conversely, we could say that he uses the form of *Glas* to sexualize, read queer, the Torah, and vice versa as well, since we could also read this passage as converting the erect bands into spread legs.

In spite of the implied homoeroticism of bringing so many penises into contact, there is a way in which Derrida's predilection for the penile in *Glas* is not queer. It is by no means the only text in which he displays an affinity for penises; almost all his writings have something to do with penises since, with only a few exceptions, all the writers he has written about presumably have or had one. That he would come to focus on his own in a few texts might thus come as no surprise. For a writer who has consistently aspired to a deconstruction of phallogocentrism, and who sounds its death knell in *Glas*—"Glas du phallogocentrisme" (G315)—his writings *could* be read as phallocentric. Could he then be claimed to reinforce the very phallogocentrism he claims to deconstruct? But to do so in the case of *Glas* would be to equate the penis with the phallus (which of course cannot be completely separated from it) and therefore to circumvent further dislodging the phallus from its supposed corporeal referent. Or by literalizing the phallus as erect penises, which he then brings together to rub against one another in homosexual contact, does Derrida use a male queering to deflate the phallus and the phallogocentrism that is Christianity? Indeed, bringing penises together in *Glas* brings about a perversely emasculating effect.

We see this effect in the above description of the Torah, which transforms two erections into opened legs, legs opened not to the penetration of heterosexual coitus but to the pointed finger of the scepter used to read a sacred text that cannot be touched by human hands.[23] This sex change occurs in a number of other passages in *Glas* as well, for no sooner does Derrida erect penises (and textual columns) than he begins to cut them down:

Si j'écris deux textes à la fois, vous ne pourrez pas me châtrer. Si je délinéarise, j'**érige**. Mais en même temps, je divise mon acte et mon désir. Je—marque la division et vous échappant toujours, je simule sans cesse et ne jouis nulle part. Je me châtre moi-même—je me reste ainsi—et je "joue à jouir." (G91)

[If I write two texts at once, you will not be able to castrate me. If I delinearize, I erect. But at the same time I divide my act and my desire. I—mark(s) the division, and always escaping you, I simulate unceasingly and take my pleasure nowhere. I castrate myself—I remain(s) myself thus—and I "play at coming" [je "joue à jouir"]. (G65)]

In his discussion of Genet, Derrida stages a castration that is not one, a castration that then has to rub against his association in the opposite column of circumcision with castration:

La circoncision est une coupure déterminante. Elle permet de couper mais, du même coup, de rester attaché à la coupure. Le Juif s'arrange pour que le coupé reste attaché à la coupure. Errance juive limitée par l'adhérance et la contre-coupure. Le Juif n'est coupant que pour traiter ainsi, contracter la coupure avec elle-même. . . . À cette castration symbolique sur laquelle glisse le discours hegelien, Abraham associe l'endogamie. (H58)

[Circumcision is a determining cut. It permits cutting but, at the same time and in the same stroke [du même coup], remaining attached to the cut. The Jew arranges himself so that the cut part [le coupé] remains attached to the cut. Jewish errance limited by adherence and the countercut. The Jew is cutting only in order to treat thus, to contract the cut with itself. . . . With this symbolic castration that Hegelian discourse lightly glides over, Abraham associates endogamy. (H41)]

Here Derrida establishes an analogy between the cutting of circumcision (and the castration associated with it) and Abraham's cutting himself off from his original people to wander elsewhere and found a new nation. Jewish identity, cut into the member of the male members of the group, depends on an attachment to circumcision/castration: "Ça **bande**, la castration. L'infirmité elle-même se panse à **bander**" (G193) [It (Ça) bands erect, castration. Infirmity itself bandages itself [se panse] [thinks itself/is thought] by banding erect" (G138)]. Circumcision/castration is thus a kind of pharmakon that marks Jewish identity as wounded while healing the very wounds it produces; it is the cut that separates Jews from Gentiles and that binds [bande] (at least male) Jews together.

In "Circumfessions," circumcision will, furthermore, become a source of jouissance:

> [L]a jouissance suprême pour tous, d'abord pour lui, moi, le nourrisson, imaginez l'aimée (me) circoncisant elle-même, comme faisait la mère dans le récit biblique, provoquant lentement l'éjaculation dans sa bouche au moment où elle avale la couronne de peau saignante avec le sperme en signe d'alliance exultante, ses jambes ouvertes, les seins entre les miennes, . . . se passant les peaux de bouche à bouche comme une bague. (202–3)

> [[T]he supreme enjoyment for all, first of all for him, me, the nursling, imagine the loved woman herself circumcising (me), as the mother did in the biblical narrative, slowly provoking ejaculation in her mouth just as she swallows the crown of bleeding skin with the sperm as a sign of exultant alliance, her legs open, her breasts between my legs, . . . passing skins from mouth to mouth like a ring. . . . (217–18)]

Here the jouissance results from heterosexual (yet Oedipal) fellatio, though one that is paradoxically based on the emasculation of a circumcision associated with castration. This curious obsession with bloody fellatio is articulated though a chain of associations, the first with a traditional aspect of the circumcision ceremony: "[T]ant de mohels des siècles durant avaient pratiqué la succion, ou *mezizah*, à même le gland, y mêlant vin et sang, jusqu'à-ce que la chose fût abolie à Paris en 1843 pour raison d'hygiène " (68–69) [[S]o many *mohels* for centuries had practiced suction, or *mezizah*, right on the glans, mixing wine and blood with it, until the thing was abolished in Paris in 1843 for reasons of hygiene" (69)]. Derrida further associates *mezizah* with the biblical story of

> Zipporah, celle qui répara la défaillance d'un Moïse incapable de circoncire son propre fils, avant de lui dire "Vous m'êtes un époux de sang" devait manger le prépuce alors sanglant, j'imagine en le suçant d'abord, ma première cannibale aimée, l'initiatrice à la porte sublime de la fellation. (68)

> [Zipporah, the one who repaired the failing of a Moses incapable of circumcising his own son, before telling him, "You are a husband of blood to me," she had to eat the still bloody foreskin, I imagine first by sucking it, my first beloved cannibal, initiator at the sublime gate of fellatio. (68)]

By characterizing his mother as Zipporah's descendant, Derrida provides a matrilineal alternative to the genealogy inscribed onto the Jewish penis, which connects men to their fathers, circumcised, like them, in a chain leading all the way back to Abraham.[24]

Derrida's roots are thus cut into his root, which is the site of a sexual pleasure that Daniel Boyarin calls "Jewissance" (xxiii):

> [L]e mélange sur cette cène incroyable du vin et du sang, le donner à voir comme je le vois sur mon sexe chaque fois que du sang se mêle au sperme ou à la salive de la fellation, décrire mon sexe à travers des millénaires de judaïsme. ("Circonfessions" 145)

> [[T]he mixture on this incredible [last] supper of the wine and blood, let people see it how I see it on my sex each time blood is mixed with sperm or the saliva of fellatio, describe my sex throughout thousands of years of Judaism. ("Circumfessions" 153)]

Having one's freshly circumcised penis sucked by the moist lips of the (ancestral) mother connects one to previous penises similarly sucked in a kind of communion (and of making the Last Supper Jewish—which of course, as a Passover seder, it already was). The recuperation of castration in an Oedipal relation with the mother, of course, need not result in a decentering of phallogocentrism or even masculinity; castration founds the very masculinity it threatens in Freudian models of gendered development. Derrida, however, emasculates quite differently by turning the penis into an orifice through another complex chain of significations. Already in *Glas*, therefore, Derrida offers his own version of an anti-Oedipus in that, in spite of his desire for the mother, the emasculation that this desire entails undoes what Deleuze and Guattari call the "triangle papa-maman-moi" (*L'anti-Œdipe* 60), but as always, contra Deleuze, this Derridean deconstruction of Oedipus nonetheless retains a love for what it deconstructs.

In *Glas*, the reversibility of sex is part of the cutting down of erections: "Elle [l'erion] entoure le cou, le con, la verge, l'apparition ou l'apparence d'un trou en **érection**, d'un trou et d'une **érection** à la fois, d'une **érection** dans le trou ou d'un trou dans l'**érection** : elle entoure un volcan" (G93) [The golden fleece surrounds the neck, the cunt, the verge [the penis], the apparition or the appearance of a hole in erection, of a hole and an erection at once, of an erection in the hole or a hole in the erection (G66)]. Like the castration that is not one, this erection that is not one further complicates any association one might make between Derrida's cutting and the castration foundational to Freudian masculinity. Whereas Freudian castration cuts men off (separates them) from women by also cutting the latter (defining them as castrated, as being not-men), Derrida's castration, as will become even clearer below, carries out a deconstruction of sexual difference. Further distinguishing Derrida from Freud is the jouissance the former derives from self-castration. In "Circumfessions," it is circumcision itself that, while cutting the penis, removes an orifice that nonetheless remains attached. In turn, Derrida turns the foreskin, a kind of ring, into a wedding ring (*alliance* in French), marking the alliance of Jewish men with God and their covenant with him. In *Glas*, this ring is sexualized and becomes a site of sexual penetration:

> Le présent de la coupe qui rend possible la copulation dans l'alliance, ce présent n'est pas donné, il n'est pas présent. Il ne se présente que dans l'attente d'un autre accouplement qui viendra remplir, accomplir (*vollenden*) celui qui s'annonce ou s'entame ici. (H96).

> [The present of the cup that makes copulation possible in the covenant [alliance], that present is not given, is not present. It presents itself only in the expectation of another coupling that will come to fulfill, accomplish (*vollenden*) what is announced or broached/breached here. (H68)]

This ring is even described through imagery strongly suggesting a sphincter:

> L'anneau est trop serré. N'abandonnons pas. Ce que je cherche à écrire—gl— . . . c'est ce qui se passe, plus ou moins bien, par la stricture rythmée d'un anneau. Essayez, un jour anniversaire, de pousser une bague autour d'un style **érigé**, outré, tendu. (G153–54)

> [The annulus [or ring] is too tight [*serré*]. Let us not give up. What I am trying to write—gl—is . . . what passes [or happens], more or less well, through the rhythmic strict-ure of an annulus. Try, one anniversary day [or birthday], to push a ring around an erected, extravagant, stretched style [or stylus]. (G109)]

This eroticization of the foreskin even inflects Derrida's relation with Bennington. Although Derrida characterizes the text he offers Bennington as uncircumcised—"de tout ce que G. peut attendre de moi, un écrit soi-disant idiomatique, inentamable, illisible, non circoncis, tenu non plus à l'assistance du père, dirait Socrate" (181) [everything G. can be expecting of me, a supposedly idiomatic, unbroachable, unreadable, uncircumcised piece of writing (194)]—the content of that text is his own autobiography, given to Bennington for incorporation into *Jacques Derrida*. Derrida gives himself over as text in a gift, most literally, of his penis, or perhaps its removed foreskin. This ring, sacrificed to seal an alliance with God, becomes a wedding ring (*alliance*) offered to Bennington.

One might think that all this cutting and bleeding would be enough to make most men go limp, but the loss of erection—like the loss that is castration—nonetheless keeps what is cut off:

> Il tourne en dérision tout ce qui se dit au nom de la vérité ou du phallus. Il joue l'**érection** dans l'être à poil de son écriture. La dérision ne fait pas simplement tomber l'**érection**, elle la garde mais en la soumettant à ce dont elle la garde, déjà, la fêlure du nom propre. (G96–97)

> [The *erion* [or golden fleece] derides everything said in the name of truth or the phallus, sports the erection in the downy being [*l'être à poil*] of its writing. Derision does not simply make the erection fall; it keeps the erection erect but does so by submitting the erection to what it keeps the erection from, already, the crack of the proper no(un) [*du nom propre*]. (G69)]

And, according to Derrida at least, this unbinding (*débander*) of penises challenges the phallus as opposed to upholding it (and holding it up). In other words, Derrida *erige* (or erects) in *Glas pour débander* or to make his theoretical writing lose the very erections he inserts into it by turning each of them into an "**érection** débandée" (H165). In addition, this cutting down or turning off of erections is not simply one specific example among many of what deconstruction can accomplish through the insertion of penises—including Derrida's own—into his writing; it describes the act of deconstruction itself. For it has often been pointed out that etymologically *deconstruction* and *analysis* ("to loosen again" or "untie again") are quite close. From *Glas* we can also say that the action designated by the verb *débander* (which also carries the additional sense of loosening bands or ties) could, like *analysis*, be used to name deconstruction. The cutting down of erections, like the cutting of penises that is circumcision, therefore allegorizes deconstruction. In fact, if in *Glas* Derrida suggests replacing essence or being with hard-ons—"je propose qu'on essaie partout de remplacer le verbe *être* par le verbe **bander**" (G186) [I propose that one try everywhere to replace the verb *to be* with the verb *to band erect* (G133)]—the term *débander* becomes an equivalent of the analysis of essence and therefore, again, of deconstruction.

And it is not only in its bringing down of erections that Derrida challenges the phallogocentric; deconstruction could be said to become an equivalent of queering in what Derrida calls "[é]nantiose homosexuelle" (H314), a homosexual putting into opposition that understands the two elements of a binary as a homosexual couple:

> Et si elle **relève** la différence, l'opposition, la conceptualité elle-même, est homosexuelle. Elle commence à le devenir quand *les* différences sexuelles s'*éffacent* [sic] et se déterminent comme *la* différence. (H312)

> [And if the sexual difference as opposition relieves [raises up] difference, the opposition, conceptuality itself, is homosexual. It begins to become such when the sexual differences efface themselves and determine themselves as *the* difference. (H223)]

Derrida then allows this homosexual couple to mate: "[L]a copule couple, accouple la paire, resserre dans le même ligament (**Band**) (H94) [[T]he copula couples, mates [*accouple*] the pair, draws closer in the same ligament (*Band*) the thing and the attribute thus becoming party again to *Sein* (H67)]. The copula (i.e., the verb *to be*) binds (*bande*) what it couples; by making this erection literal, Derrida unbinds (*débande*) and undoes the essentialized ties signified through the copula. If his reading of Hegel teases out the heterosexuality of Truth and the dialectic, the going limp that happens once Hegel's erections touch Genet's penises results in a queering of all these terms and, in the case of Christianity, a reversal of Hegel's narrative of religious progress, a reversal that renders it Jewish. Since Derrida constantly associates the *double bande* with the double bind—what better definition for the aporia, that figure for an irresolvable question or problem of the sort Derrida so fondly rests his gaze upon—the double band and the *double bande* that is *Glas*, the rubbing of Genet's penises and Hegel's erections, is a visualization of not only a queering of the dialectic but also a deconstructivist understanding of binaries that quite literally involves a queering, a very male queering admittedly, but one that is then emasculated.

In "The Lesbian Phallus and the Morphological Imaginary," Judith Butler theorizes, through readings of several texts by Freud and Lacan, the installment of the penis in the imaginary as an erotogenic site. The penis is projected onto a bodily surface made whole via a chain of signification originating in the gaping hole of a toothache:

> Freud's discussion began with the line from Wilhelm Busch, "the jaw-tooth's aching hole," a figure that stages a certain collision of figures, a punctured instrument of penetration, an inverted vagina dentata, anus, mouth, orifice in general, the spectre of the penetrating instrument penetrated. Insofar as the tooth, as that which bites, cuts, breaks through, and enters is that which is itself already entered, broken into, it figures an ambivalence that, it seems, becomes the source of pain analogized with the male genitals a few pages later. This figure is immediately likened to other body parts in real or imagined pain, and is then replaced and erased by the prototypical genitals. This wounded instrument of penetration can only suffer under the ideal of its own invulnerability, and Freud attempts to restore its imaginary power by installing it first as prototype and then as originary site of erotogenization. (61–62)

It is through this process, which requires the denial or erasure of the signifying chain leading back from the penis to a gaping hole that the penis becomes phallic. Derrida's textual penises, however, which are also at least in part autobiographical, openly acknowledge and eroticize their gaping wounds, still fresh with blood. His body is "in pieces," as Butler might say (83); it conjures up the specters of its wounds.

With so many penises on the pages of Derrida's writing, one might wonder whether, instead of deconstructing phallogocentrism, as I have suggested, these penises reinforce a phallic from which they cannot be dissociated (see Gallop). While my comments on Derrida's penises might seem at first glance to contradict feminist critiques of such understandings of castration, it is my hope that they will instead contribute to a response to second-wave feminist Germaine Greer's call, first made about forty years ago but arguably still relevant today: "[W]omen must humanize the penis, take the steel out of it and make it flesh again"

(315).[25] I also hope that my comments here might contribute to a feminist writing about the penis, as well as to the already rich engagement with Derrida on the part of a number of feminists.[26]

Derrida's penis is therefore haunted, and in *The Post Card*, it also haunts:

> P.S. Je les ai encore surchargées de couleurs, regarde, j'ai maquillé notre couple, tu aimes ? Tu arriveras sans doute pas à déchiffrer le tatouage sur la prothèse de plato, cette troisième jambe de bois, ce membre-fantôme qu'il se réchauffe sous le cul de Socrates. (71)

> [P.S. I have again overlooked them with colors, look, I made up our couple, do you like it? Doubtless you will not be able to decipher the tattoo on *plato*'s prosthesis, the wooden third leg, the phantom-member that he is warming under *Socrates*' ass. (64)]

Cut off from its biological roots, the penis can circulate; by cutting it off, Derrida transforms it into a dildo. This dildo, like the numerous penile pre-texts he plays with (Rousseau's in *Of Grammatology*, Genet's in *Glas*, Plato's in *The Post Card*), is an avatar of Derrida's autobiographical penis in "Circumfessions," a fictional penis or root that stands in for Derrida's fictional roots. In *Glas* this prosthetic penis, a "prothèse qui **bande** toute seule" (G194) [prosthesis that bands erect all alone (G139)], also stands up to the erection of the Hegelian dialectic: "[T]oute thèse est (**bande**) une prothèse" (G235) [[E]very thesis is (bands erect) a prosthesis (G168)]. The subtitle of *Monolingualism of the Other—The Prosthesis of Origins*—further associates this dildo with roots. Because in French the Greek prefix *pros-* becomes *pro-*, the title not only transforms Derrida's root(s) into a dildo; it also names the deconstructivist understanding of origins as a fiction that involves putting (*thesis*) them forth (*pro-*), putting them in front (where the penis presumably is on the male body), putting them at the beginning in an acknowledgment of the narrative paradox of roots narratives.

The *après-coup* construction of origins with which this section begins puts in front only by looking back (through the return to origins that is the roots narrative), similar to the looking back named in Memmi's title: "Je ne suis accessible, lisible, visible que dans un rétroviseur" (*Glas* G117) [I am accessible, legible, visible only in a rearview mirror (G84)]. And if what is in front is such an obsession in "Circumfessions," *Glas, The*

Post Card, and *Monolingualism*, Derrida derives great pleasure from putting it in back, in the/his behind. For it is from behind that Plato sticks his pen(is) into Socrates' "inkwell":

> Il est trop evident, je reprends tes mots comme toujours, que S. ne voit pas P. qui voit S., mais (voilà le vrai de la philosophie) seulement *de dos*. Il n'y a que du *dos*, vu de *dos*, dans ce qui s'écrit, voilà le dernier mot. Tout se joue en *retro*, et *a tergo*. . . . Tout au plus, trempant sa plume ou plus voluptueusement l'un de ses doigts dans ce qui fait office d'encrier (ci-contre, j'ai découpé pour toi le calame et l'orifice dudit encrier . . .). (55)

> [It is too obvious, to use your words as always, that S. does not see P. who sees S., but (and here is the truth of philosophy) only *from the back*. There is only the *back*, seen from the back, in what is written, such is the final word. Everything is played out in *retro,* and *a tergo* . . . . At the very most, dipping his pen, or more sensuously one of his fingers, into that which has the office of inkwell (attached, I have cut out for you the calamus [le calame] and the orifice of said inkwell . . .) (48)]

It is by becoming behind and bottom that Derrida inserts his pro(s)thetic root(s) into his corpus:

> [T]out est toujours attaqué *de dos,* écrit, décrit par derrière. A tergo. Je suis *déjà* (mort) signifie que je suis *derrière*. Absolument derrière, le Derrière qui n'aura jamais été vu de face, le Déjà que rien n'aura précédé, qui s'est donc conçu et enfanté lui-même, mais comme cadavre ou corps glorieux. Être derrière, c'est être avant tout—en rupture de symétrie. Je me retranche—derrière—je saigne au bas de mon texte. (G117)

> [[E]verything is always attached *de dos, from the back,* written, described from behind. *A tergo.* I am *already* [déjà: also J.D.] (dead) signifies that I am *behind* [derrière].[27] Absolutely behind, the *Derrière* that will have never been seen from the front, the *Déjà* that nothing will have preceded, which therefore conceived and gave birth to itself, but as a cadaver or glorious body. To be behind is to be before all—in a rupture of symmetry. I cut myself off, I entrench myself—behind—I bleed [*je saigne*] at the bottom of my text. (G84)]

Like "Socrates [qui] a ses règles" (*Carte postale* 145) [*Socrates* [who] is having his period" (*Post Card* 133)], Derrida transforms that centuries old anti-Semitic trope of the menstruating Jewish man (itself often associated with the blood of circumcision) into a queer figure for deconstruction. The wound of Jewish identity that heals nonetheless keeps bleeding as a sign of the covenant (*alliance*) that ruptures the ring of the an(nul)us. By taking (it up the ass, offered up as a sacrifice), Derrida gives us what is potentially the most explicit definition of what it might mean to use *queer* as a verb. And if *queer* is often considered to be that which challenges identity, Derrida's articulation of deconstruction *as a queering* nonetheless retains a sexualized identity whose root(s) is/are the site of a "Jewissance," the pleasure of a deconstructivist analysis that unties, questions, and cuts down (*débande*) the very identity it erects.

If the roots narrative of Edmond Jabès—whose intersecting diasporas Derrida shares to a certain extent (as examined in the previous chapter)—can be characterized as Zionist, in its acknowledgment of the narrative paradox it is indeed a queer Zionism. Is it a coincidence that Jabès's *Book of Questions* preceded Derrida in questioning rootedness as signified by a site of origins? This shared critique extends into the realm of political discourse in Jabès's diasporist understanding of the expression "people of the Book," by which "the Book" becomes both the homeland of the diaspora and the promised land to which return narratives can make "territorial" claims. Derrida would echo this queering of Zionism in his reading of Jabès, in which he also writes, "Le retour alors ne reprend pas possession. Il ne se réapproprie pas l'origine" (*L'écriture* 430) [The return . . . does not retake possession of something. It does not reappropriate the origin" (*Writing* 295)].[28] I suggest that this sentence be read as rejecting Zionist territorial claims. In his quite literal queering of the narrative paradox, therefore, Derrida reveals, like Reich and Memmi, the structural violence inherent in the political paradox of Zionism as a roots narrative.

Furthermore, a comparison between Memmi's and Derrida's looking back and the queer South Asian diaspora that Gopinath theorizes (as discussed in the introduction to this volume) highlights a certain instability with regard to the relation between roots and diaspora. Some diasporic discourses presume stable roots that can ground a stable identity. Others promote diaspora as a destabilization of any roots that might ground identity in a homogenized community whose purity could thereby be policed. The "overlapping diasporas" of the Jewish Maghreb thus constitute an ideal site for bringing queer diasporas like the one Gopinath theorizes into comparison while nonetheless retaining careful attention to the specificities of individual diasporic cultures. In carrying out such a comparatist practice, one is better positioned to seek answers to a number of questions that might be considered fundamental to any attempt to define the field of queer diaspora studies. Where is the *queer* in queer diaspora or roots? Does one have to queer roots in order to queer diaspora? or vice versa? Does the one necessarily lead to the other? Will queering diaspora entail queering roots in every diasporic context? Is either diaspora or roots inherently queer in relation to the other?

One of the reasons why Derrida and Jabès—like Memmi, Sapho, and Condé—can be said to queer both roots and diaspora, is that they all bring the narrative paradox out of the closet. Yet, if this were the only reason, *queer* here would only be queer in a rather abstract way, far too removed from the critique of sexual normativity that has proved to be the strength of queering as an analytical move. Like Condé, Sapho, and Memmi, however, in queering roots and diaspora, Derrida outs not only the narrative paradox but also the sexual one, both of which are just as intertwined in Derrida's writing as in Condé's mangrove. If Helmreich understands diaspora as an *in*semination whose root is the penis qua phallus, Derrida might be said to offer an alternative understanding best characterized as a *dissemination*, another key term within Derrida's understanding of writing:

> [L]a multiplicité numérique ne survenant pas comme une menace de mort à un germe antérieurement un avec soi. Elle fraye au contraire la voie à "la" semence qui ne (se) produit donc, ne s'avance qu'au pluriel. Singulier pluriel qu'aucune origine singulière n'aura jamais précédé. Germination, dissémination. Il n'y a pas de première insémination. La semence est d'abord essaimée. L'insémination "première" est dissémination. Trace, greffe dont on perd la trace. (*La dissémination* 337–38)

> [[N]umerical multiplicity . . . serves as a pathbreaker for "the" seed, which therefore produces (itself) and advances only in the plural. It is a singular plural, which no single origin will ever have preceded. Germination, dissemination. There is no first insemination. The semen is already swarming. The "primal" insemination is dissemination. A trace, a graft whose traces have been lost. (*Dissemination* 304)]

Derrida thus scatters his seeds not in service of the reproduction of heteronormative models of homeland, diaspora, and the relation between the two but to sow a diasporic model of identity through a queer return to roots in writing. Along with the death knell of phallogocentrism that tolls in *Glas*, the key concept of dissemination in Derrida's writing might be read as a queerer model of diaspora than what Helmreich offers. When read alongside Derrida's treatment of his body in its more material manifestations, the penis that has been instituted as a kind of root for diaspora—that which disseminates it—turns out to be a cultural artifact that can be written in multiple ways, some of which consist of cutting into the very "thing" that is written. Commonly considered to be the origin or root of masculinity, its writing/cutting can also sever the very link it is usually considered to institute.

If Derrida's earliest writings carry out a deconstruction of origins, therefore, his more recent autobiographical writing literalizes those origins as his own Jewish Algerian roots. If de Man characterizes every narrative as an allegory of reading that is also an allegory of its own deconstruction, Derrida has instead inverted the de Manian hierarchy by retrospectively providing the more literal autobiographical narratives that allegorize his earlier, more abstract deconstruction of origins. Derrida's queer roots thus appear as having already been deconstructed; they disseminate impossible origins and can be planted only in diaspora. Derrida's own rites of return thus take us back not only to his Jewish Algerian roots but also to the Jewish roots of diaspora as a concept. These roots help us to queer diaspora in part by understanding it as a deconstructivist dissemination that is both theoretical and literally sexual. Yet the heteromasculinist associations behind the literal image that figures diaspora as a sowing of seeds are nonetheless resisted in a manner consistent with the diasporic tradition of the emasculated Jewish man described by Daniel Boyarin and Eilberg-Schwartz, in which Jewish, queer, and diasporic are as inextricably linked as the roots of a mangrove.

CHAPTER 5

The Seduction of Roots and the Roots of Seduction

✦ ✦ ✦

Israeli independence, or the founding of the Jewish state in 1948, is known among Palestinians as Nakba, the disaster or catastrophe. Conversely, disaster in the form of the Holocaust constitutes a key event in Zionist foundationalist discourses alongside the more triumphalist implications of the notion of an independence struggle. Similarly, in *My Father and I: The Marais and the Queerness of Community*, David Caron describes the role that what he calls "the inaugural function of disasters" (11) plays in "the realization of the community" (8). In his compelling example of personal or autobiographical criticism, Caron theorizes how inaugural disasters help define the communities that coexist in (or at least that, across historical time, have shared) the Parisian neighborhood named in his title: the Holocaust for the Marais's Jewish community and the AIDS pandemic for its gay community. The connections between these two communities are played out in relation to "the founding failure" (139) that, according to Caron, characterizes his relationship with his Hungarian-born Jewish father as they stroll together through two different Marais (different because seen through different eyes, experiences, and histories). From the individual failure that defines his familial relation to the inaugural disaster that founds communities on the scale of an urban neighborhood, we can further extend this understanding of "a founding disaster" (8) to the national level at the roots of both Palestinian and Israeli identities.

Indeed, "the inaugural function of disasters" extends even beyond the borders of the nation altogether for diasporic peoples, be they Jewish (because of dispersal) or African (because of the slave trade). Armenian diasporic identity likewise rests on a "founding disaster." In 1915 when, during World War I, as the Ottoman Empire was approaching its demise, forced migration and accompanying massacres and starvation resulted in the death of about a million Armenians. These events, widely recognized as genocide, resulted in a dispersal that has long constituted one of the most conventionally accepted instances of the phenomenon of diaspora. Consideration of the Armenian case has also furnished diaspora studies with an important example. The prominent diaspora studies scholar of Armenian descent, Khachig Tölölyan was the founding editor of *Diaspora*, and he has frequently drawn on the Armenian diaspora for his contribution to the definition of diaspora studies as a field. And, while the Armenian diaspora may seem to have fewer implications for postcolonial studies than the other diasporas considered in this volume, the Armenian diaspora's historical origins in the rush to replace the Ottoman Empire upon its breakup on the part of European powers (which would impose mandates and the like in its former territories) make postcoloniality more relevant to understanding the effects of Turkish independence than it might seem at first.

The genocide that founded the Armenian diaspora is also key to understanding the films of the Canadian director of Armenian descent Atom Egoyan. Most explicitly, *Ararat* (2002), made almost twenty years after Egoyan's first commercially released feature-length film, extensively tells the story of the Armenian genocide. *Calendar* (1993) is likewise partially set in historical Armenia, across whose landscape are scattered the remnants of ancient churches that seem abandoned, perhaps because of the displacement of their original congregations. This chapter also argues that founding failures characterize the more familial narratives of Egoyan's earlier films. Some of these—like his first two, *Next of Kin* (1984) and *Family Viewing* (1987), as well as *The Adjuster* (1991)—have explicitly Armenian characters and are thus situated within the Armenian diaspora in Canada. Indeed, in these films, family narratives have been frequently read as allegories of both the Armenian diaspora's history and diasporic identity (just as the "founding failure" of Caron's relationship with his father comes to allegorize the more collective inaugural disasters he weaves into his cultural study). Furthermore, Egoyan always situates the question of identity within the structure of family genealogy in his films.

Yet for Egoyan, kinship is always invented, performed; indeed, it is frequently by highlighting instances in which affiliation takes precedence over filiation in family structures or by populating his invented families with non-repronormative relations that Egoyan queers the kinship unit of the (mostly) heterosexual family that roots Armenian identity in diaspora. This queering then functions at the allegorical level as a queering of diaspora itself. Furthermore, even films like *Speaking Parts* (1989) and *Exotica* (1994), which do not have explicitly Armenian characters, can be read through his narratives about Armenian families or national history to tease out the ways in which they reflect on the queer roots of Armenian diasporic identity. As such Egoyan's films contradict the restrictive definition of *diaspora* that Tölöyan articulates in "The Contemporary Discourse of Diaspora Studies" by arguing, "It is helpful to distinguish [diaspora] from a dispersion that is the consequence of individual and chain migration, motivated by economic reasons; in such communities, nostalgia can be strong, but commemoration and collective mourning are less prominent" (649). Tölöyan maintains that a broader understanding of the concept of diaspora that has developed within diaspora studies is problematic, and one casualty of his stricter definition is the concept of queer diaspora: "When . . . queer communities . . . are . . . labeled diasporas, the struggle to maintain distinctions is lost" (648–49). Yet this definitional exclusion of the notion of queer diaspora fundamentally misunderstands the critical work that this term has enabled in queer diaspora studies, which, contra Tölöyan, does not define *queer diaspora* as "queer communities" that constitute diasporas in and of themselves but as, at the very least, queerness within the very communities he accepts as diasporas or, more significantly, as the queer relation between these communities and their roots or even as the critical queering of the very concept of diaspora.

It is through his characters' relation to founding familial failures and the inaugural disaster of the Armenian genocide (as well as the way in which the one allegorizes the other) that Egoyan contradicts Tölöyan's heteronormative understanding of diaspora by queering Armenian diasporic identity in relation to its roots. In an interview, Egoyan stated, "There's a group of analysts in Toronto who have looked at all my films. They've told me that from their point of view, all my films deal with a process called 'faulty mourning'—when a patient builds up a ritual of mourning which only accentuates and exaggerates the sense of loss which they think they're dealing with" (Rayns 8). Emma Wilson, however, literally questions the desirability of successful resolution when it comes to mourning or the possibility of a "cure" for faulty mourning and writes instead of "the pleasure of this faulty mourning" (34–35). She further elaborates, "Faulty mourning may be Egoyan's subject, but what is difficult to determine is how far, for Egoyan or his viewer, this process is at fault. Questioning this may lead us to a different reckoning with Zoe's role in *Exotica*" (33). In his book-length study of Egoyan's career, Jonathan Romney does likewise in his discussion of the film *Exotica*:

> There is, of course, another ritual concerned, like striptease, with laying bare, and similarly informed by the understanding that the desired object of revelation may never be wholly uncovered or exorcised. Francis's private sessions with Christina are nothing if not a course of psychoanalysis. Zoe tells Francis, "We're here to entertain, not to heal," yet this seems a misunderstanding of the club's real function, and indeed of cinema's function as Egoyan conceives it. Rather than provide passive entertainment, Egoyan's work has an inherent psychoanalytic drive: we not only analyse a film but become its analysands, our own neuroses and perversions exposed, if not necessarily healed, by the fiction. . . . Francis's "therapy" is not necessarily directed towards an end: it has become self-sufficient, an addictive ritual. It seems a perversion of his grief. (118)

Yet, while this passage focuses on the murder of one character's daughter in *Exotica*, it might also be used to characterize personal loss in other films and, indeed, the more collective losses represented in *Ararat* and *Calendar*. In other words, in Egoyan's films psychoanalytic narratives of loss and trauma become allegories of collective experiences of loss and trauma as constitutive of Armenian diasporic identity.

In Egoyan's films, in other words, the loss of roots—never successfully mourned but carefully cherished in an eroticized melancholia—becomes seductive in and of itself. If Egoyan disseminates meaning in his filmic explorations of diasporic identities, this very Derridean *dis*semination (i.e., precisely not the *in*semination that might accompany coming stories and "happy endings") conjures up the ghosts that are the phantom pains left after the amputation of/from one's roots. Melancholia, therefore, not mourning, becomes a pleasure in Egoyan because its happy ending is denied (and here "happy ending" should be read in its multiple meanings, as both successful resolution and the orgasm sometimes provided as closure to a massage), and this questioning of the happy ending serves a narrative function similar to the challenges to closure examined in chapter 3. Egoyan thus leads his viewers away from such endings, leads them astray or seduces them in the etymological sense of the word *seduction*. His particular acknowledgments of the narrative paradox, in fact, exploit the *après-coup* structure that, as we shall see in the psychoanalytic writings of Jean Laplanche and Jean-Baptiste Pontalis, characterizes the function of seduction as the root of sexuality. If seduction provides a narrative structure to their theorization of fantasy, Egoyan offers roots narratives in which origins are the *après-coup* products of similarly seductive fantasies.

Furthermore, just as a number of Reich's pieces make audible the process of their own composition, Egoyan's eclectic editing techniques make visible the very process of "piecing together" (as on the editing board) the filmic narrative. Lest some find my readings of Egoyan's films overly literary, I point out that these readings focus on their narrative *structure* in its specifically *filmic* manifestations, since this is what most characterizes the filmmaker's innovation as an auteur. For, as we shall see, Egoyan's characteristic editing technique involves intercutting scenes from many moments along his narrative's chronological trajectories, thereby leaving viewers to piece together this narrative gradually by themselves, a cinematographic practice he himself characterizes as seductive. Egoyan, furthermore, combines this approach to montage with a multiplicity of metacinematic references that far prefigure the shift from film studies to screen arts (a shift made necessary in part by the increasing obsolescence of celluloid film as the medium on and by which films are "filmed," produced, reproduced, distributed, and projected or otherwise screened). Such references deconstruct the filmic text into its visual and sound components, blur the distinction between film as a medium and its alternatives (like magnetic video- and audiotape, social media, closed-circuit surveillance footage, television footage, and live performance), and highlight the technologies that permit the consumption of film (such as projectors and screening rooms), as well as that of alternative media (VCRs, answering machines, tape recorders, and the telephone). Further uses of mise-en-abyme—like film-within-the-film, filming of a film-within-the-film, the material film and videotape as physical objects—as well as metavisual references to home movies, paintings, and photographs and photography, some of which are to the extradiegetic (snow, horizontal and vertical roll, freeze frame, rewinding, and the jarring inclusion of a bit of laugh track within a narrative film), draw attention to the filmic gaze, especially in relation to other visual-culture practices. Other references to various technologies of desire (telephone sex, sex via live video feed, pornography, strip club performances, and prostitution) highlight the fact that narrative cinema itself is one such technology. Combining all these references with a blurring of the distinction between flashback and other forms of analepsis contributes to what one might call an allegory of watching as viewers observe the very processes by means of which the filmic narrative is constructed.

Rooted in Genocide

Ararat is comprised of several interrelated narratives, which Egoyan intercuts within the montage of the film as a whole. The narrative of the Armenian genocide is recounted in classic film-within-the-film in the form of a historical epic directed by the fictional Edward Saroyan (played by the well-known French-language singer of Armenian origins, Charles Aznavour). *Ararat* also tells the story of the making of this film, for which Ani (played by Egoyan's wife, Arsinée Khanjian, whom he has cast in almost all his films) has been hired because she is an art historian who specializes in the work of Armenian-born artist Archile Gorky. Gorky's supposed childhood experience of the genocide is incorporated into Saroyan's film (with the child Gorky being played by Garen Boyajian), and scenes of Gorky (played as an adult by Simon Abkarian) in New York while painting *The Artist and His Mother* are also interspersed throughout *Ararat* (fig. 1). The family narratives of Ani and Ali (Elias Koteas), the gay, half-Turkish actor cast as the villain in Saroyan's epic, constitute two additional narrative threads that make up *Ararat*. Raffi (David Alpay), Ani's son from a first marriage to an Armenian militant killed by the police during his participation in an attempt to assassinate a Turkish diplomat in Canada, is hired to run errands for Saroyan and is in a sexual relationship with Celia (Marie-Josée Croze), his stepsister from Ani's marriage to a second, late husband. *Ararat* as a whole is framed by yet another fragmented narrative, which occurs after most of the events of the film (we learn at the end that it coincides with the premiere of Saroyan's film): Raffi's experience of going through customs after a trip to historic Armenia (now partly in Turkey). Because of the fragmentation of its narrative threads, however, it would be difficult to describe *Ararat* as structured as a more conventional flashback. Indeed, Ali's "family" narrative crosses several of these threads. His lover Philip (Brent Carver) is a

Fig. 1. Arshile Gorky (c. 1902–48). *The Artist and His Mother* (1926–c. 1936).
Oil on canvas, 60 × 50 1/4 in (152.4 × 127.6 cm). (Whitney Museum of
American Art, New York; gift of Julien Levy for Maro and Natasha Gorky in
memory of their father 50.17; © 2015 The Arshile Gorky Foundation/The
Artists Rights Society (ARS), New York; Digital Image © Whitney Museum of
American Art.)

guard at the museum hosting a Gorky exhibit (the occasion of a lecture by Ani), and Philip's father David (Christopher Plummer) is the customs officer who interrogates Raffi.

Just before *Ararat*'s final credits, the following message appears onscreen: "The historical events in this film have been substantiated by holocaust scholars, national archives, and eyewitness accounts including that of Clarence Ussher." Egoyan himself has used public speaking engagements in the aftermath of *Ararat*'s release to assert the veracity of the Armenian genocide, a veracity often denied or at the least diminished by the Turkish Republic (Egoyan, "In Other Words"). Ussher's account is taken from *An American Physician in Turkey* (1917), with Ussher played by Bruce Greenwood in Saroyan's film (and, by extension, Egoyan's). The young Gorky also becomes a fictional character in Saroyan's film; he participates in the Armenian resistance against Ottoman forces in the Battle of Van and is one of the boys whom Ussher asks to relay a message to US or other western consulates about the impending massacre.[1] Indeed, Ani explicitly relates Gorky's self-portrait to the Armenian genocide: "His experience as a survivor of the Armenian genocide is at the root of [the painting's] power. With this painting, Gorky had saved his mother from oblivion, snatching her out of a pile of corpses to place her on a pedestal of life."[2] Ani also uses this painting, which is unusually representational in the context of Gorky's mostly abstract life work, to connect Gorky to his roots by characterizing it as "the only image that exists of the artist in his native land." Finally, by incorporating the session in which the photograph (fig. 2) on which the painting is based into the narrative of the Battle of Van, Saroyan reinforces its supposedly referential nature.

In spite of such claims to veracity, however, Egoyan's film also suggests that the relation of this founding violence to the contemporary diasporic Armenian identity is of a fictional nature. Is it a coincidence, for example, that Gorky took great pains to hide his Armenian origins once he was in America?[3] Furthermore, Ani is most noticeable during scenes of filming the film-within-the-film for the challenges she poses to its accuracy. In the following exchange between her and Saroyan, for example, she goes to the heart of his film's eponymous point of identification, the mountain that represents, more than anything else, a diasporic identification with a lost homeland:

ANI: You wouldn't be able to see Mt. Ararat from Van.
SAROYAN: I thought it would be important.

Fig. 2. Gorky and his mother in Van City, Turkey, 1912. (Photo courtesy of Dr. Bruce Berberian.)

ANI: But it's not true.

SAROYAN: It's true in spirit.

When he justifies the liberties he has taken with Armenian geography by staking a claim to "poetic license," she asks in reply, without the slightest hint of irony or sarcasm, "Where do you get those?" He has just admitted, in fact, "Everything you see here is based on what my mother told me." The eponymous mountain is thus marked as having a fictional relationship with the imaginary cultural geography of an Armenian homeland; it appears as a figment of what is almost a childhood fairy tale. And, given that the title of Egoyan's film names this imaginary Ararat rather than the real one, his very title marks *Ararat* as a fictionalized account of the relation between genocide and diasporic identity.

Footage of the *actual* Ararat, however, is what Raffi supposedly brings through customs in canisters he claims cannot be opened because their exposed film has not been developed. In response to the customs officer's numerous questions, Raffi explains why such footage is necessary for Saroyan's film by first claiming that it is intended for migration scenes to which images of human actors will be added digitally. When customs officer David does not understand why Raffi could not get permission from Turkey to send such footage through a bonded agent, the latter carefully explains the historical significance of the film (not to mention the genocide it represents) in relation to Armenian identity; Raffi, in other words, gives him a lesson on the politics of an Armenian diasporic identity rooted in a genocide denied by Turkey. Yet what at first seems to be a plausible narrative on Raffi's part starts to break down in subsequent fragments of this narrative thread as he must change his story in response to David's unmasking of its contradictions and the increasingly tenuous nature of Raffi's connection to *Ararat*'s production. As Raffi's story unravels, he goes on to claim that he encountered a film crew shooting a commercial whose cameraman loaned him his camera. Raffi then bribed a Turkish soldier to take him up a military road to Ararat. When David asks, "Did he ask you to do him a favor in return?" Raffi responds that the cameraman asked him to bring the film canisters back to Canada and that he had simply accepted as truth the cameraman's assertion that they contained only film. It finally turns out not only that the footage was not really needed for the film but also that Saroyan's film is already complete, which means that any footage Raffi carries can no longer be incorporated into the film-within-the-film.

In short, just like the fictional and geographically inaccurate Ararat of Saroyan's film, the validity and veracity of the supposed footage of the *actual* Ararat, symbol of Armenian roots, is undermined in Egoyan's film. In fact, when Raffi calls Ani from customs, she tells him in Armenian that she will say whatever he wants. She is willing to lie, in short, which only adds to the web of lies around the "real" Ararat. In a final shot of this narrative thread we see an open canister containing heroin. Is this heroin, then, a metaphor for the roots narrative fabricated in the film-within-the-film, a kind of "opium for the masses"? Does Egoyan suggest that Saroyan's kind of story about Armenian origins inevitably involves the kind of fabrication Sapho exposes in *Un mensonge*? In one scene between Raffi and David, the latter is quite open about the patience with which he waits for potential drug smugglers to defecate their stash, for the truth to come out, as he puts it, the truth that comes out as shit! This is not the most reverent of associations with what Raffi claims is in the canisters—images of the beloved symbol of the Armenian homeland first of all, then, with more distressing political-ethical implications, proof of the Armenian genocide. In fact Raffi is delayed at customs in part because of Celia's police record as a marijuana grower and drug dealer, and, as it turns out later in the film, it was a friend of hers who entrusted him with the canisters.

Celia's character is even more important in *Ararat*'s challenges to truth claims regarding the roots of Armenian identity. And first and foremost among these are her pesky challenges to Ani's reading of Gorky's place in the Armenian diaspora. Fairly early in the film, Celia disrupts Ani's lecture on Gorky, in part by bringing up the name change that helped conceal his Armenian origins. Yet, whereas Ani reads the mother's gaze in the portrait as a challenge to her husband to return to Armenia from the United States, where he was at the time, Celia interjects an alternative connection with the Armenian genocide by suggesting that Gorky's father may have known that Armenians were about to be massacred (hence his move to America to prepare a new life for them there) and that the photo on which the painting is based was sent to him from Armenia as proof that they were still alive. In a later scene during which Ani reads from her published study in conjunction with an exhibit that includes Gorky's self-portrait with his mother, Celia again challenges Ani's reading of the painting and finally attempts to take a knife to the painting. And, in parallel with Ani's reading of Gorky's painting, Egoyan's film brings Gorky himself back from the dead in one of the many narratives that Egoyan intertwines and intercuts with Ani's family drama, the film-within-the-film, and the making of the film-within-the-film. That

Gorky shows up at the premiere of the film-within-the-film blurs the distinction between Saroyan's film and Egoyan's and thus between fact and fiction within the fictional world of *Ararat*.

In her opposition to Ani's readings, however, Celia does not seek to replace a family narrative with a collective one (or vice versa) or to deny autobiographical or Armenian diasporic readings of Gorky's work; indeed, she suggests that Ani is reading her own life story into Gorky's painting by accusing Ani of confusing Gorky's father with her first dead husband. Ani counters by suggesting that Celia is the one reading her own life story into Gorky's work; because Gorky committed suicide (see Spender, *From a High Place* 306–72), she assumes that her father must have done so as well. (At first Celia insists that Ani pushed her father off a cliff and then that he committed suicide by jumping off because of Ani. In Ani's version, he simply fell, although she later admits that she was not actually looking when the fall occurred. Her version, however, is given the weight of truth in a flashback or analepsis to this fall.) In short, Egoyan's most individualized personification of diasporic identity in relation to the Armenian genocide is also the object of sharp disagreements over family tragedies that occurred in Canada. Furthermore, these family disputes extend into Raffi's attempts to understand the meaning of his father's death and therefore of his own place in the history of the Armenian diaspora due to how impossible it is for him to live up to his father's heroic martyrdom in the struggle to reestablish an Armenian homeland. For example, whereas Raffi's father was a terrorist, he can refer to his father as a freedom fighter according to Celia; as she says to Raffi, even though she is likewise haunted by "the ghost of the father, my father, not yours; yours died like a hero." That Raffi is in a relationship with his stepsister, which Ani characterizes as incestuous, further complicates the family tree that allegorizes collective identity, even more so since Celia is not Armenian but French Canadian; normally, neat lines of linear descent structure genealogy, but here incest tangles up these lines by requiring the representation of multiple connections between the same individuals.

The familial narratives of *Ararat* are most literally queered, however, in David's gay son Philip, whose sexuality he at first has difficulty accepting. Indeed, David has no problem suggesting to his grandson that Phillip's lover Ali does not believe in the same God Christians do (a blatantly racist misunderstanding of Islam). As in the case of Ani's family drama, therefore, there is much tension in this family as well. This tension, however, looks well on its way to being resolved at the end of the film when

David tells Philip about his interview with Raffi, conducted on his last day of work before retirement. David describes, in what we are led to believe is an unusual moment of openness for David when it comes to his son, allowing Raffi to pass through customs in spite of the fact that one of his canisters contained drugs. David explains that he did not believe Raffi was lying: "The more he told the closer he came to the truth." "What came over you?" Philip asks. "You did, Philip," responds his father, highlighting the generosity of accepting Raffi's account as truth regardless of evidence to the contrary and in spite of other indications in *Ararat* that Armenian roots are a fabrication. As in Sapho and Haley, therefore, narratives of origins may be fictional but they nonetheless establish and tell the truth about roots. In Egoyan's case, however, this truth is inserted into a kind of queer family romance (see Munro, "Queer") in which David identifies the Armenian Raffi, returning from his homeland, with his gay, presumably Anglo-Canadian son. As we shall see below, such family romances characterize even the earliest of Egoyan's films, which will offer pre-texts for further theorizing the relation between family stories and diasporic roots narratives.

David's newfound family romance, in fact, turns out to be related in multiple ways to the other aspects of the story of the Armenian genocide. His son's lover Ali is cast as the villain in Edward Saroyan's film, Cevdet Bey (written Jevdet Bay in the credits), Bey being the governor of Van province who oversaw the treatment of the Armenian population during the genocide. Once shooting is completed, Edward thanks Ali in a polite but distant manner, and here is where Egoyan places denials of the genocide in Ali's mouth. Ali first wonders whether he was cast in this role because he is half Turkish. Then there ensues a discussion about whether Edward wonders whether a genocide actually happened. When Edward answers "I'm not sure it matters," Ali explains that he thinks there might have been a reason why the Ottomans felt threatened by the Armenian population, that killing is a standard occurrence during times of war. Charged with driving Ali home and bewildered by Edward's failure to refute Ali's objections, Raffi continues the discussion and explains that, prior to seeing the violent scenes starring Ali, he could not imagine what would make him want to commit murder as his father had done. Raffi thus comes to feel at home in his Armenian family tree by hating a fictionalized historical character to the point of almost hating (indeed perhaps being willing to kill) the actor who played him. He sarcastically thanks the half-Turkish Ali for this gift almost as if Armenia has Turkey to thank for its diasporic identity.

In a dinner conversation following a lecture on *Ararat* at the Univer-

sity of Michigan (Egoyan, "In Other Words"), after overhearing a reference on my part to being gay, Egoyan stated that making Ali gay was his
way of complicating the Turkish villain (and his reluctance to recognize
the Armenian genocide); it was thus a way to "soften" the character of
Ali and the Turkish/Armenian opposition. While problematic (because
of the long-standing association of softness with homosexuality, for the
"colonization" here of gayness for its liberalizing potential in making a
political point, and for the way gayness is projected onto a Turkish character where it runs less of a risk of "infecting" Armenianness as defined
in opposition to Turkishness), this comment nonetheless suggests that
Egoyan considers queerness central to his film's representation of diasporic identity. Also in this conversation he engaged with two Turkish
colleagues, Aslı Iğsız and Aslı Gür, about their reaction to the film, the
very ones who had initiated Egoyan's visit to begin with due to the way his
films (as opposed to when he is speaking in more straightforward genres)
complicate not only official Turkish histories of the Republic but also
the very Turkish/Armenian opposition at the heart of official versions of
both Turkish and Armenian identities. Egoyan was curious as to what a
"Turkish reaction" to his film might be like, and Aslı Igsız surprised him
by arguing that she found David to be the most important character in
her opinion because he is precisely the character who provides the model for a Turkish need to listen to the Armenian version of the genocide.

I added that I also found him to be the queerest character in his central role within the queer family romance that I have argued is the key
to understanding the film as a narrative about diasporic identity whose
roots are queer. For in "adopting" Raffi as a kind of queer son, he also
renders the very national borders his job requires him to police more
porous, more open to "infection" by the very drugs he is supposed to
keep out. In accepting his own son's gayness, in other words, he opens
up his own Anglo-Canadian identity to a rhizomatic connection to the
Armenian diaspora as he simultaneously forces Raffi to acknowledge the
fictions (and even lies) on which his own Armenian identity is founded.
Through David, therefore, more so than through Ali, the Armenian diaspora comes to have a queerer relation to its own roots in *Ararat*.

Perverting Roots

Ararat is not Egoyan's only explicit filmic representation of an Armenian
homeland. About half of his earlier *Calendar* (1993) was filmed in Armenia. Egoyan had even received a grant from the Soviet Union to make

this film when Armenia was still a Soviet republic (which it no longer was by the time Egoyan got around to making the film). In *Calendar*, an Armenian Canadian couple undertake a trip to Armenia so that the husband (played by Egoyan himself) can photograph historic churches for the eponymous calendar. On the surface, the film's trajectory is thus a return to roots. Yet the photographer's wife (played by Khanjian) must serve as her husband's interpreter because he cannot speak the language of his ancestors and has therefore, to a certain extent, forgotten his roots.[4] The driver hired by the couple (Ashot Adamian) is, as it turns out, a wealth of historical knowledge about the churches. In the beginning, the wife translates his historical commentary, in which the photographer seems mildly interested. He is less interested, however, in the role the churches have played in Armenian history, and therefore what they represent for his own identity, than in their image, their commercial value as simulacra.

The driver is perplexed by the photographer's lack of interest in getting close to the churches (he always photographs them from a certain distance): "If you had seen someone else's photographs of these places, you wouldn't have wondered like what it must be inside, what it would look like inside?" The photographer responds, "No, I would just think they were very, very beautiful places, and I'd think they were very, very well composed, beautifully lit and very seductive." Bit by bit, the wife pays less and less attention to her husband and more and more to the driver. To a certain extent, this estrangement is first brought about by the photographer, who frequently asks them to remove themselves from his field of vision so he can get a good shot of the church. She also translates less and less of her conversations with the driver. (Since the film has no subtitles, the non-Armenian spectator is placed in the same position as the photographer.)[5] The husband is bothered by their constant conversation, which he cannot penetrate, but by the time he realizes that he is being excluded it is too late; his wife has been seduced by the driver (by her roots in a sense), for whom she leaves her husband (who returns to Canada alone).

In addition to being seduced by the churches as simulacra, however, the photographer is seduced by his roots in another way, also different from his wife's seduction. Intercut with the "Armenian" narrative is a series of somewhat erotic encounters with "exotic" women in his Toronto apartment. The calendar, prominently visible on the wall, marks the "Canadian" narrative as subsequent to the "Armenian" one, and we see the photographs that make up the calendar one by one, month by month, in order from January to December. The calendar thus structures the two parallel narratives—both the series of events that occur in the photographer's Toronto apartment and the series that occurs at least as far back as during the previous year—and we know this because the order in which the churches are photographed in the Armenian narrative is the same order in which they appear in the calendar.[6] In the Toronto narrative, furthermore, another parallel gradually emerges. (The encounters are not always represented in toto, which makes figuring out the plot, at least at first, an interpretive endeavor as in many other Egoyan films.) At a certain point during the "dates" the photographer has in his apartment, the women ask to make a phone call, which always occurs in a language the photographer cannot understand. The erotic tone of each conversation leads the photographer (and the spectator) to understand that the person at the other end of the line is a man (husband? boyfriend?) to whom she owes a primary allegiance.[7] During these conversations, the photographer writes what at first seems to be an endless letter to his wife after having refused to answer her numerous phone calls and messages.

When an agent leaves a message on his machine confirming the choice of the next woman and her language and outfit, we understand that these women are being paid to "entertain" the photographer. But why is the "entertainment" consistently cut short? As this incident repeats itself over and over, something begins to seem fishy; no one has luck this bad! Finally the spectator hears what the woman hears on the other end of the line—a dial tone! The entertainer or actress is thus performing the role she has been hired to play and not trying to escape an encounter she has begun to find uncomfortable.[8] In other words, the photographer gets off, so to speak, on having his desire to get off frustrated; he gets off on *not* getting off. If the "actresses" are read as escorts, therefore, Egoyan frustrates the closure male orgasm seems to provide at first in *Un mensonge* and suggests that all origins are not only fictions but also sources (and products) of perverse desire, the most basic of which is Egoyan's casting of his real-life wife as the character who leaves him for someone more "authentically" Armenian. *Calendar*, then, one of Egoyan's most explicit films about his own origins, is also a story about the failure of coming stories. If male ejaculation supposedly brings closure to heterosexual intercourse and gives it meaning, therefore, Egoyan refuses this closure. In a certain sense then, the narrative of roots can never have closure, just as the seduction of roots remains ultimately uncontrollable. For Egoyan, however, this seems to be a positive thing.

Like *Ararat, Calendar* is composed not only of two parallel narratives but also of multiple media. In addition to the photographs that make up the calendar and the answering machine recordings, portions of the Armenian narrative are made up of videotaped (as opposed to filmed) footage, presumably taken by the photographer, who watches this footage in this apartment after his return. He frequently rewinds this footage, which takes up the full screen, and this rewinding is shown complete with "snow" and horizontal roll, as if the film *Calendar* itself is being projected in reverse (a kind of looking back that, like Memmi's *Statue de sel*, parallels the return to roots narrated by the film). In one scene in which the photographer watches this video footage we see his bare torso and legs. Is he masturbating?[9] If so the parallel between his breakup in Armenia and the scenes played by women hired to leave him becomes even stronger. In his Toronto apartment, therefore, the photographer not only watches and rewatches his rejection, but he also repeats this loss of desire with the women he hires. One possible way to watch the film is therefore that of experiencing being dumped in real time or even slow motion. (When is the agony of being dumped *not* experienced as if in slow motion?!) In their multiple stagings with hired women, therefore, the photographer's "dates" repeat the loss of his wife to a man to whom she spoke in a language the photographer cannot understand. This repetition also imbues the calendar images with the affair about to happen. In *Calendar*'s Toronto narrative, therefore, the photographer's failed marriage stands in ruin much like a number of the churches he has photographed, ruins that stand as traces of the violence depicted in *Ararat*, even if only through the medium of a fictional epic film.

For while following his wife and the driver with a video camera in Armenia, the photographer speaks of "our history of each other," as if the story of the couple's shared past in Canada might be read as paralleling a more collective history. Yet the photographer is most marked by his lack of connection with the collectivity that he supposedly shares with his wife. "You make me feel like a stranger," he says at one point while watching video footage and writing his letter, "We are both from here yet being here has made me from somewhere else." Thus, instead of strengthening their connection as Armenian Canadians, the return to roots actually leads to their "separation" (as both physical distance and the prelude to a divorce). When read "back" through *Ararat*, then (and yes, I am suggesting that the "looking back" that makes *Calendar* an allegory of reading or watching itself can also be used as a method for "reading" Egoyan's complete works as a coherent corpus), the montage or intercutting between the two parallel narratives also establishes a parallel between the photographer's loss of his wife and the loss of an Armenian homeland. Rewinding videotape, then, constitutes a meta-cinematic reference to the filmic narrative's numerous analepses and, furthermore, corresponds to the photographer's looking back (again, as in Memmi) to a desire lost in his homeland, to the lost love of his wife, which then allegorizes the loss at the heart of his diasporic identity. In other words, the repetition of sexual loss, played out as having one's loved one seduced and led astray, thus becomes an allegory for the loss of an Armenian homeland, the loss of connection with the roots of diasporic identity.

Instead, in its ruins is left family as diaspora, as in the following description, by Caron, of the relation between homosexuals and their families:

> [T]he first conscious image of oneself that young homosexuals often "make" *as homosexuals* is one of failure and separation from the family, a domestic fall from grace in which we realize that we were not exactly made in our parents' image. This "extant shortcoming"—in effect the departure point of the queer diaspora—generates the first instance of gay shame and, from then on, posits identification as difference *from* the family rather than as sameness *with* the family. The memory of our separation from the familial Eden and subsequent isolation remind us that there hasn't always been community and that, therefore, there may not always be community. An identity thus defined by its own negation through an identification mediated by difference cannot produce communities simply on the basis of a shared positive trait. It doesn't *ground* communities so much as disseminate them on a free-floating diasporic model of out-of-placeness and out-of-timeness, in which the self can only be comprehended through its contact with others and experience its selfness as otherness. (148)

In other words, there is something diasporic about a queer relation to family and the "out-of-placeness and out-of-timeness" that characterize communities imagined, indeed "disseminated," to use Caron's word, through this relation. This "out-of-placeness and out-of-timeness" might also describe the narrative structure of most Egoyan films. Resolution occurs not through a progression of events ordered in a cause-and-effect order but with the viewer finally putting together the pieces of the plot; resolution occurs not with a successful completion of mourning but with an entrenchment of melancholia, queerly embraced as a state of being in diaspora.

In other words, diasporic Armenian identity founded on an obsession with loss comes to have sexual implications in *Calendar*. These implications have normative implications in the wife's choice of the driver over her husband. For in the Armenian narrative the driver suggests to the couple that if they had children they would have had a reason to live in Armenia, and he thereby proposes a heteronormative explanation for the connection between diaspora and its roots: the childless couple has not yet chosen to pass down their Armenian roots to offspring and therefore has not (yet) reproduced diasporic identity. The wife's choice might thus be read as a heterosexual embrace of the authenticity of bearing Armenian-speaking children in a common homeland. Whereas his estranged wife chooses heterosexual roots over diaspora, however, the photographer eroticizes his loss and ultimately replaces his roots with a diasporic family romance in reverse (reverse because it is the potential parent, not the child, who fantasizes about adoption). In a hokey sentimentality (as hokey as the heterosexual ending of *Un mensonge*), the photographer "adopts" an Armenian child (cue in late-night infomercials starring Sally Struthers here).[10] For a small monthly donation, he receives photos and video footage. In the end, the letter to his wife is replaced with a letter to this adopted child, who thereby replaces his wife in an alternative and diasporic family romance.

The Roots of Seduction

Understanding *Calendar* (and through it *Ararat*) as a peculiar kind of family romance (structured by haunted genealogies) will, as we shall see, allow us to go farther back in Egoyan's corpus to read his earliest films as diasporic even when they have no obvious connection to the Armenian diasporic identity. But I would first like to consider at greater length the role of seduction in *Calendar* (specifically) and the queer role that seduction might play in roots narratives more generally. In *Calendar* both the photographer and his wife are seduced by their Armenian roots, each in his or her own way; both are led astray, the wife from her husband and the photographer from his roots. In the work of Jean Laplanche and Jean-Baptiste Pontalis, however, seduction is at the root of even normative sexuality. In "Fantasme originaire, fantasmes des origines, origines du fantasme" (1964) [Primal Fantasy, Fantasies of Origin, and the Origins of Fantasy (my translation)], they articulate a psychoanalytic model that explains the connections among roots, fantasy (and therefore fiction), and seduction. This essay, which might be seen as a part of their collaborative work *Vocabulaire de la psychanalyse* (1967) [*The Language of Psycho-Analysis*], offers only a glimpse of a particular understanding of seduction, which would become *central* to Laplanche's work after his collaboration with Pontalis ended. Indeed, in *New Foundations for Psychoanalysis* (1987), seduction, though understood quite differently from Freud, becomes *the* foundation for psychoanalysis. Since roots narratives share the narrative structure of seduction and since seduction is itself a particular kind of roots narrative, Laplanche and Pontalis suggest a way to understand how the fictionality of roots, when not denied as in more conventional narratives of origin, might nonetheless lead us astray (*seduce* us, in the etymological sense of the word), away from the paths or routes of patrilineal descent and heterosexual couplings.

In spite of Freud's abandonment of his seduction theory over a hundred years ago, in the work of Laplanche and Pontalis, seduction continues to be considered the origin of sexuality. In their return to Freud "in their own manner" (an expression they use to distinguish their return from Lacan's), they have read much of Freud's writings as roots narratives. Freud was obsessed with and seduced by fantasies and myths of origin—the *roots* of symptoms, the primeval origins of circumcision and the Oedipus complex, the primal scene as the origin of the individual, castration as the origin of sexual difference, and, in his early writings, seduction as the origin of sexuality. If Haley seduced so many viewers into searching for their own roots, considering psychoanalytic models of the origins of sexuality allows us to reconceive the role of seduction in the originating "lie" or fiction of roots. In this chapter, I am not interested in psychoanalyzing roots narratives but rather in examining what psychoanalysis can tell us about their narrative structure. In roots narratives, I have suggested throughout this study, origins are written *après coup*. The *après coup* is also a central concept for Laplanche and Pontalis because it sums up the narrative structure of seduction. Seduction is rewritten as an origin only after the fact through a retroactive fantasy (or fiction). Furthermore, given the structural parallels between psychoanalytic myths of the origins of subjectivity and roots narratives of the origins of identity, the trope of seduction constitutes an important nexus for theorizing the relations between queer subjectivities and identities and the individual's affective relation to his or her roots. When I speak of *my* roots as a way of describing who *I* am, I am not just articulating an identity but a means of embodying that identity; I am imbuing my identity with subjectivity. Roots narratives are therefore about not only identity but also subjectivity.

In their essay on fantasy, Laplanche and Pontalis (re)read the historical moment in the development of psychoanalysis between 1895 and 1897, the latter being the date when Freud is usually said to have abandoned his seduction theory. Originally, in Laplanche and Pontalis's understanding of Freud, seduction actually consists of two events:

> In the first scene, called "seduction scene," the child is subjected to a sexual approach from the adult . . . without arousing any sexual excitation in himself. . . . As for the second scene, which occurs after puberty, it is, one might say, even less traumatic than the first: being non-violent, and apparently of no particular significance, its only power lies in being able to evoke the first event, retroactively, by means of association. It is then the recall of the first scene which sets off the upsurge of sexual excitation. ("Fantasy" 9)

The sexual nature of the first scene is the retroactive fantasy of a postpubescent subject who cannot *remember* it as such. Since the "subject" who lived the first scene was a presexual subject incapable of understanding the sexual implications of the event, the first event is actually written for the first time *après coup*, after the second scene. In fact, to a certain extent, this (re)writing also writes (as a fiction) the sexual subject who finds his or her origins in seduction.

Faced with the alarming possibility that so many fathers were actually molesting their daughters, Freud abandoned the "reality" of the first scene, which he then converted into fantasy. Laplanche and Pontalis, however, see a paradox there:

> [A]t the very moment when fantasy, the fundamental object of psychoanalysis, is discovered, it is in danger of seeing its true nature obscured by the emphasis on an endogenous reality, sexuality. . . . We have indeed the fantasy, in the sense of a product of the imagination, but we have lost the structure. Inversely, with the seduction theory we had, if not the theory, at least an *intuition* of the structure. (14)

Many cited this abandonment as itself a kind of origin within psychoanalysis, for it marks "the beginning of psychoanalysis as a science, a therapy, and a profession" (Masson xix). According to this view, only when Freud abandoned his seduction theory was he able to "discover" the importance of fantasy life and the Oedipus complex.

From a feminist perspective, of course, abandoning the seduction theory is problematic since it denies the "reality" of sexual abuse suffered by female patients. But as Laplanche and Pontalis point out in *Language*, "Right up to the end of his life, Freud continued to assert the existence, prevalence and pathogenic force of scenes of seduction actually experienced by children" (406). They thus define *seduction* as a "[r]eal or phantasied scene in which the subject, generally a child, submits passively to the advances or sexual manipulations of another person—an adult in most instances" (404). And in *New Foundations* Laplanche would distance himself even further from Freud's understanding of seduction: "I am, then, using the term *primal seduction* [*séduction originaire* in the original] to describe a fundamental situation in which an adult proffers to a child verbal, nonverbal and even behavioural signifiers which are pregnant with unconscious sexual significations" (126; 125). Seduction thus has much larger implications in terms of a child's gaining access to the adult world and becoming a sexual subject. In what he calls a "general theory of seduction," Laplanche "regard[s] 'primal seduction' as including situations and forms of communication which have nothing to do with 'sexual assault.' The *enigma* is in itself a *seduction* and its mechanisms are unconscious" (128). Whereas one might discern an Oedipal structure in the western family tree, then, in Laplanche's view of seduction both Oedipus and castration become secondary stages of primal seduction (149).

Although seduction theory presupposed an innocent child initiated into sexuality by an adult or older child, after the abandonment of seduction theory, sexuality was seen as developing naturally from inborn instincts. These instincts are not entirely biological as they are related to what Freud called *Urphantasien*, or "primal fantasies" (*fantasmes originaires* in French), that is, fantasies that take us back to the origins of humanity, fantasies whose origins are found not in the lived experience of the fantasizing subject but in the collective experience constituted by the history of human civilization (e.g., in the way the Oedipus complex reenacts the primal horde's murder of a original father). Primal fantasies (as opposed to Freud's seduction theory) are more like roots narratives à la Haley in that they seek out prehistoric anthropological origins of psychoanalytic phenomena. In addition, since "the origin of the fantasy is integrated in[to] the very structure of the original [or primal] fantasy" ("Fantasy" 18), origins are a creation of narrative and do not preexist it. Laplanche and Pontalis end their essay on fantasy with a discussion of autoeroticism, in a perverse move that resembles Derrida's in *Of Grammatology*, where masturbation—supposedly "ce dangereux supplément qui trompe la nature" [that dangerous supplement that cheats and fools nature (my translation)]—actually becomes central, thereby making (heterosexual) coitus a supplement to masturbation. Freud himself argued that fantasies of seduction cover up autoerotic activity in the first years of childhood, and Laplanche and Pontalis see it as crucial to the origins of the sexual subject in fantasy. But the *queering* that goes on here is more than a decentering of heterosexuality; it also has implications vis-à-vis a related disruption of narrative.

"Narrative, like genealogy," writes Peter Brooks, "is a matter of patronymics" (302). If we think back to many of the grand fictional narratives of the nineteenth century (*Les Rougon-Macquart* first comes to mind), we begin to understand how closely narrativity and genealogy are related. In the example of Zola, narrative structure depends and is modeled on genealogy. Each character's character (*le caractère du personnage*) depends on his or her placement within the family tree (which conveniently folds out like a centerfold in the Pléiade edition), and "reading for the plot" (Brooks) requires retracing this family tree just as it does in the fiction of Glissant and Faulkner (as described in chapter 1). In "The Aetiology of Hysteria," one of his most elaborate articulations of seduction (though limited to hysterical symptom formation), Freud traces a link between seduction and the family tree through a description of tracing backward (in analysis) from hysterical symptoms to their origins through a chain of connected memories:

> [T]he chains of memories lead backwards separately from one another; but . . . they ramify. From a single scene two or more memories are reached at the same time, and from these again side-chains proceed whose individual links may once more be associatively connected with links belonging to the main chain. Indeed, a comparison with the genealogical tree of a family whose members have also intermarried, is not at all a bad one. Other complications in the linkage of the chains arise from the circumstance that a single scene may be called up several times in the same chain, so that it has multiple relationships to a later scene, and exhibits both a direct connection with it and a connection established through intermediate links. In short, the concatenation is far from being a simple one; and the fact that the scenes are uncovered in a reversed chronological order . . .

certainly contributes nothing to a more rapid understanding of what has taken place.

If the analysis is carried further, new complications arise. The associative chains belonging to the different symptoms begin to enter into relation with one another; the genealogical trees become intertwined. (198)

So, while the task of psychoanalysis is to create a narrative linking hysterical symptoms to their roots, in the psyche of the hysteric and in the text he or she produces in conversation with the analyst, linear narrative is complicated. If one could qualify the resulting narrative structure as being hysterical, then Freud is certainly the hysteric here since the narrative structure of this passage mimics those of the patients' stories that he is describing.

At this point, one can only speculate as to how much the necessity of abandoning this rather un-Oedipal family tree in order to theorize the more modern nuclear family lay at the root of Freud's abandonment of seduction theory. It is in this hysterical structure (pre-Oedipal in the historical sense), in this unconventional family tree, that we might find an alternative narrative structure for writing origins. As we saw in the first chapter, *Traversée de la mangrove*'s family trees and narrative structures (intertwined no less than in Zola's oeuvre) constitute a tangle of "messy" roots remarkably similar to Freud's hysterical family tree. In its disruption of linear narrative, Condé's mangrove leads us astray, seduces us. The example of intermarriage in Freud's family tree here also resembles the glitch that Raffi's relationship with Celia introduces into Ani's family structure. Since seduction always occurs *après coup*, it is both a cause (because written as origin) and an effect (because its effect has always already occurred and might therefore be more accurately described as a cause). Condé's rhizomatic story line(s)—simultaneously plural and singular—therefore impel(s) us to rethink origins as being as much an effect of identity as its cause. Likewise, if we take Laplanche and Pontalis one step further and understand seduction as being not only the root of sexuality and subjectivity, but also both an origin and an effect of roots, a queer understanding of roots emerges that can lead to radically different family trees.

As described above, seduction is a major theme of Egoyan's work. He has also described it as one way of thinking of the narrative structure of his films. Sylvain Garel compares the structure of Egoyan's 1991 film *The Adjuster* to a puzzle that is gradually put together (43). In an interview,

Egoyan also described this film (like his previous ones) as an attempt to seduce differently:

> I believe that one of the great advantages of the feature-length film is the ability to play on expectations. During the first twenty minutes, it is very difficult to understand what's going on, to know whether there is a narrative. At the same time, I know that the spectator expects to be told a story. Between fulfillment and this expectation a tension is thus created, which is very important for me. Among my films' audiences, there are many people who are seduced by this tension, but there are also those who reject it. (Rouyer 25)

Whereas "most films attempt to seduce in the very first minutes" (Egoyan, qtd. in Garel 43), Egoyan's deferral of the conclusion to his films' coming stories puts spectators in the position of the photographer in *Calendar*; if they are to get off, it will have to be on not getting off. Seduction, here, leads the spectator astray by leading him or her away from linear narrative by means of a narrative structure that mixes up causes and effects and requires spectators to write for themselves a narrative that matches effect with cause, thereby creating their own origins. This understanding of seduction as narrative structure therefore strengthens the link between the narrative and sexual paradoxes in the allegory of watching that is Egoyan's films, which also allegorize the relation between psychoanalytic models of seduction and film by which film spectatorship becomes one mode of writing the fiction of roots as fantasy.

In her own reading of Laplanche and Pontalis, Judith Butler describes fantasy as follows:

> There is, then, strictly speaking, no subject who has a fantasy, but only fantasy as the scene of the subject's fragmentation and dissimulation; fantasy enacts a splitting or fragmentation or, perhaps better put, a multiplication or proliferation of identifications that puts the very locatability of identity into question. In other words, although we might wish to think, even fantasize, that there is an "I" who has or cultivates its fantasy with some measure of mastery and possession, that "I" is always already undone by precisely that which it claims to master. ("Force" 110)

In addition to Butler's understanding of fantasy "as the scene of the subject's fragmentation," we might also draw attention to her suggestion of fantasy as fantasy *of* an "I" or subject, particularly one with a rooted identity, which would then be precisely the roots narrative *as fantasy*. Such a fantasy would then be, in a rather de Manian fashion, an allegory of fantasy as the fantasy that simultaneously deconstructs what it fantasizes: the subject of a rooted identity. Egoyan's films, I am arguing, are precisely the visualization of such fantasies.

Indeed, through the very repetition of loss performed by the actresses/escorts in *Calendar*, the loss of homeland as allegorized by the loss of a heterosexual attachment to homeland is constituted as a kind of primal scene (being dumped *at* and rejected *by* one's roots), which then becomes its own kind of origin. That is, after all, what primal scenes do: they are constituted as origins *après coup*. It is a cliché of a certain kind of nationalist discourse that being detached from one's homeland, either in diaspora or by having one's homeland colonized, is akin to prostitution. Indeed, in *Calendar*'s Toronto narrative, a neighbor takes one of the actresses/escorts to be the photographers wife. Leaving him for the driver is thus his "real" wife's *Pretty Woman* story. By being married to her in diaspora, one might say, the photographer has prostituted his Armenian identity and turned his wife into a kind of prostitute. He does not, however, seek to connect with his roots in any sexually normative way but rather does so by indulging in his perverse relation to the loss of roots with an excessive jouissance, itself rooted in the rejection of the kinds of coming stories examined in chapter 3 and Memmi's and Derrida's challenges to masculinity discussed in chapter 4.

Egoyan's Porn Diaspora

A number of Egoyan's earlier films also deal with a kind of personal loss on the part of explicitly Armenian characters and likewise become allegories for the loss of an Armenian homeland. In *The Adjuster* (1991), for example, it is the job of the eponymous insurance agent, Noah Render (played by Koteas), to help people through the loss of their homes after a fire. Noah puts all his clients up in the same motel and even has affairs with some of them while they await a settlement. His wife Hera (Khanjian) is an Armenian Canadian censor for the Ontario Film Classification Board (see McSorley 60), who pirates copies of the porn and horror films she is hired to classify and shows them to her sister Seta (Rose Sarkisyan), who can only speak Armenian. In an obvious parallel with *Calendar*, therefore, *The Adjuster* eroticizes loss, and the latter more explicitly queers this eroticization on one occasion especially, when Noah has sex with a male client named Matthew (Raoul Trujillo), who owned a home with his lover Larry (Stephen Ouimet). The eponymous character's name is, as well, a reference to the biblical Noah, who, we remember, landed on Ararat with his ark. The connection between the eponymous character of *The Adjuster* and the biblical narrative of Noah's ark has not been lost on critics. In the book-length work on this film in the University of Toronto Press's Canadian Cinema series, Tom McSorley writes, "Like almost all the characters on this Noah's 'ark,' Noah himself is unknowable" (55). (The ark, here, is the hotel where he puts up his clients.) He thus connects *The Adjuster* with *Ararat*, and a story line from the latter was deleted that would have explicitly queered the deluge narrative even further. In the first scene of this narrative fragment, David gives his grandson Tony (Max Morrow) a hand-carved model of Noah's ark as a birthday present. As the latter rehearses the biblical narrative of loading the ark with animals two by two, one of each sex, Tony wonders, "So Noah didn't take any gay animals?" In another deleted scene, as Tony's gay father Phillip is recovering after being stabbed in Celia's attack on the Gorky painting, Phillip reads his boyhood children's version of the same deluge narrative, a version that includes a pair of unicorns. And, as if this detail alone were not enough to make Noah's ark gay(!), Phillip explains that he always found this version comforting. Pointing out that both have "horns," Phillip suggests that they might also both be male.

Furthermore, like *Ararat, The Adjuster* represents the making of a film within a film, for which Noah lets out his family's home, the model home in a housing development that never happened. The filmmaker, a homeless man named Bubba cruised and cleaned up by a bored, wealthy, and sexually active woman, Mimi (Gabrielle Rose), gradually destroys the home/film set in the process and ends up setting it on fire, presumably along with himself.[11] In a flashback/memory Noah has while watching his home go up in flames at the very end of the film, the spectator finally learns that Hera is also a former client of Noah's who lost her previous husband in a house fire. Noah has put his family up at the same motel to avoid the inconveniences of the filming, and we see his family leaving him in frustration, also at the end of the film.[12] Figuratively, then, his family goes up in flames as well. Since Hera has a baby in her arms in the flashback, we finally learn that her son Simon (Armen Kokorian) is not Noah's biological child but rather a kind of adopted son. Noah's eroticization of loss thus accompanies his own kind of family romance based on rescuing those in need of succor.

He is, in other words, a paternalistic and patriarchal figure, one with colonial overtones, such as those echoed in an image that figures on a poster for the film (as well as the box cover for its videotape version), the image of Noah wearing only a towel around his waist (like a loincloth) and shooting an arrow with a bow. In another scene in which he engages in archery, Hera says of Simon, "He wants to know if you're an Indian." Noah replies, "What if I say yes?" When Hera responds, "He'll believe you," Noah answers, "Yes." The colonial reference to the displacement of indigenous Americans by European settler colonialism in the New World (paradoxically figured through "playing Indian" or "going native") is reinforced by the billboard advertisement for the housing development that serves as his target. The failed development, for which the billboard stands as a reminder, thus suggests a colonial project of "development" in ruins and places the narrative of *The Adjuster* within a colonial narrative of progress (like *Calendar*'s references to the adopted Armenian girl, from a "developing" country). Another allusion to settler colonialism may be teased out of the impending promise of an insurance settlement, for which all the creatures in "Noah's ark" are waiting. As the film proceeds, however, this settlement seems continually deferred in a frustration of desire (of everyone's but Noah's), which foreshadows the elaborate ritual of desire being frustrated in *Calendar*.

The frustration of desire is most literally eroticized in the censoring of pornography that occurs at Hera's workplace. When a coworker, Tyler (Don McKellar), blows the whistle on her piracy, her supervisor, Bert (David Hemblen), thanks her for bringing into the open what no one else is willing to admit, that their job is sexually stimulating. Hera counters that she records these films not for sexual use but to share her work with her sister so that the latter can understand what she does for a living. Hera remembers doing the same as a schoolgirl to teach Seta what she had learned earlier each day. As the older sister, Seta was unable to attend school as Hera later would. "That's how things are where I am from," Hera explains. In this somewhat veiled reference to their diasporic existence as Armenian Canadians, the connection in diaspora between Hera and Seta is provided by the sharing of pornography.

In the director's commentary to the DVD version of *Calendar*, Egoyan explains that he was led to understand that one particular conversation an escort has on the phone in a language the photographer cannot understand is pornographic. Pornography also replaces diasporic memory in Egoyan's earlier film *Family Viewing*. It is only by watching home videos that Van (Aidan Tierney), the protagonist of *Family View-*

ing, whose very name references the same Armenian city that serves as the setting for the film-within-the-film in *Ararat*, can still remember his happy childhood before his Armenian mother (Rose Sarkisyan) left his Anglo-Canadian father Stan (David Hemblen). Yet Van discovers that his father is videotaping sex with his live-in lover Sandra (Gabrielle Rose) over the home movies of Van and his mother and grandmother Armen (Selma Keklikian). Since memory here is inseparable from video representations of it, Stan's erasure of the home videos also erases Van's childhood memories. Since these tapes constitute the only remaining trace of Van's childhood ability to speak Armenian, their erasure also constitutes the effacement of his roots along with their replacement with pornography.

In *Calendar*, we remember, sex is mediated though a wide range of media: the wife's voice on the answering machine, the escort-service agent's recorded messages, the photographs that constitute the calendar, the home videos that the photographer and his wife made of their trip to Armenia. These, along with the more conventionally filmed narratives in Armenia and the Toronto apartment (conventionally filmed but less conventionally edited through intercutting) make up the material film of *Calendar* (itself structured like a calendar). This mixed media, in fact, is typical of Egoyan's films, for representation in *Family Viewing* also occurs through a variety of media: the telephone technology that allows phone sex, videotapes produced by hotel surveillance cameras, the television programming Armen is constantly watching, the videotapes of Stan and Sandra having sex, Van's early childhood memories preserved on videotape (memories made possible because Stan worked for one of the first companies to distribute VCRs), and the surveillance videos of Van made by a private investigator hired by Stan. What little connection Van has with his father comes from watching TV and videos with him and Sandra; a common experience of watching television thus stands in for kinship structure. At one point, as Van is watching TV just before he is about to kiss Sandra, the narrative that is supposed to be the "true" story of the film (as opposed to sequences shown in the film *as* video representations) is freeze-framed. Then there is applause, as if the film itself were a sitcom with laugh track, and the film is rewound complete with horizontal interference. Snow and rewinding, as in *Calendar*, interrupt the film at other points as well, thereby explicitly representing the family plot that constitutes the film's narrative as no less of a *mediated* representation.

Although it seems at first that *Family Viewing* will explore a quasi-

Oedipal relationship between Van and Sandra, as it turns out Van will make alliances within his family tree along markedly *un*-Freudian lines; when necessary, he will even invent it anew. It thus comes as no surprise that, instead of investing himself in his nuclear family, Van devotes most of his attention to Armen, who, neglected by other members of the family, is now suffering from a loss of speech in a rest home. Since we hear her speaking Armenian in the home movies, this aphasia also allegorizes a loss of the Armenian language in diaspora. While visiting Armen at the home, Van meets Aline (Khanjian) who also visits her mother (Jeanne Sabourin). Aline is a phone sex worker, and Stan and Sandra are among her clients. While she is away servicing a client in Montreal, her mother dies, and Van switches the bodies in order to write his father out of his alternative family and constitute a new one with Armen and Aline.

Film critic Amy Taubin writes, "The phrase 'family viewing' evokes both the 6 pm–8 pm broadcast time slot and a funeral parlor ritual" (28). Both meanings are combined as Van puts the "biological" family to death in so many ways. The family (Stan and Sandra) with whom he has experienced several family viewings of TV in the evening is killed off, as he fakes Armen's death and films Aline's mother's funeral so Aline can watch it. (Aline's mother's family viewing is thus only accessible to her on videotape, which replaces the experience of attending her own mother's funeral. For Egoyan, therefore, even when the death of a family member is "real," it can lead to fictional family viewings.) In essence, the death of her "biological" family allows Van to replace her "real" mother with Armen. In the end, Stan, who was previously indifferent to his son's maternal kin, can only catch glimpses of this family on video surveillance tapes, which constitute, to a certain extent, a parallel to the tape of Aline's mother's funeral; Stan's family is falling apart before his eyes, and there is nothing he can do about it. When Stan initiates an investigation to find out why Aline was placing flowers on what was supposed to be Armen's grave, videotapes maintain (or at least attempt to maintain) paternal authority and, therefore, kinship structure through surveillance. But is Van's relationship with Armen any less mediated by videotape? At the end of the film, as Van and Aline find Armen in her new shelter, a surveillance camera figures prominently. Thus no family— not even an alternative one—escapes the mediation of surveillance.

Part of the film's constantly running television shows is a series of Discovery-Channel-type nature documentaries. Stan wonders one day, after reflecting on one of these shows, why humans have not lost their nails, which no longer seem to serve any biological or evolutionary purpose. After Van manages to convince him to visit Armen for her birthday in spite of his reluctance, she scratches his face and proves that nails can still be useful for human survival. Whereas evolution is usually considered to be a scientific account of the human "family" tree, one existing independent of representation, *Family Viewing* demonstrates that television biologizes genealogy as something natural and attempts to cover up the ways it constructs sexuality as biological rather than cultural. According to *New York Times* film critic Caryn James, Egoyan has "come to see the camera as an insidious voyeur's tool, a barrier to communication, the *root* of many evils" (13; emphasis added). In his more scholarly article, "Video as Accessible Artifact and Artificial Access," Timothy Shary similarly misses the point: "[W]hatever access [Egoyan's characters] do attain to their past, to their identity, or to the unknown, is constantly undermined by their continuing dependency on images" (26). Van's family is obviously a dysfunctional one, and its reliance on video mediation emphasizes the breakdown of human-to-human connection within the family. But is there a family that is not dysfunctional? Is the functional family itself not a fiction? Critics like James and Shary (and they are not alone) seem to think that the families Egoyan represents are dysfunctional because they are abnormal in their contamination by videos and other media, which in this case are in part pornographic. A careful reading of Egoyan's films, however, demonstrates that "biological" families are no more authentic, no less mediated through video representation, no less fictional than "made-up" ones. Every family, in short, is a family romance in the Freudian sense. If Deleuze devoted an entire chapter to Nietzsche's powers of the false in his work on cinema (*Cinéma II*, 165–202), here we see these powers laid bare.

After Van replaces the videotaped home movies with blank cassettes to preserve his childhood memories, Stan discovers the exchange and is upset about it. This detail suggests that it is not just the making of sex tapes that turns him on but also the erasure of his son's childhood spoken in Armenian. In one videotaped scene, Van as a young boy (Vasag Baghboudarian) sings an Armenian song to his father, who responds by asking him to sing a song in English. Stan's relation to his own son, therefore, allegorizes an assault on diasporic connections to Armenian roots. This assault takes on additional sexual implications when Van and Armen, watching home videos together, discover footage of Van's mother mostly undressed and tied up while engaging in sadomasochistic sex with Stan. This clip provides one possible explanation for Van's mother's leaving the family and foreshadows the scene of bondage and sexual violence depicted in *Ararat*'s film-within-the-film as a part of the Armenian genocide, which, according to Lisa Siraganian, constitutes a kind of primal scene (130).

The assault on Van's Armenian identity intensifies when he removes Armen from the rest home after faking her death. Stan—who previously showed no interest in her and, in fact, neglected her—becomes obsessed with finding out what Van is up to, perhaps because she represents Van's only remaining connection to his Armenian identity. Stan hires a private detective and places Van and Aline (with whom he and Armen begin to live after removing the latter from the rest home) under surveillance, videotapes of which are edited into the film. Each time Stan gets close to uncovering their ruse they move Armen to another location until they finally escape Stan's Anglo and Anglicizing gaze by dressing Armen up as a "bag lady," faking her discovery in a closed wing of the hotel where they are working at the end of the film after Aline has quit her job as a sex worker, and having her taken in by social services. Video surveillance thus seems to be detrimental to safeguarding a diasporic identity throughout most of the film, but this danger is turned back on the Anglo gaze when Stan is caught on surveillance in despair after failing to uncover "the crime" his son is engaged in. In a final scene, we also see a surveillance camera in Armen's final shelter as a new kind of family is reunited. Aline and Van walk in to see Armen smiling while sitting with her daughter. The new family is thus constituted by ridding the patricentric one of its Anglo father. And if Aline is read as Armenian (she is not identified ethnically, and there are some indications that she could be French), this family romance is written in an invention of its Armenianness.

The Family Romance of Armenian Identity

Romney also describes *Family Viewing* as a family romance (44). According to him, Egoyan's first feature-length film, *Next of Kin*, constitutes a family romance as well, albeit in a variation on the Freudian understanding of the concept:

> Above all, Peter's story exemplifies the "family romance," Freud's term for the fantasy by which a child rejects its real parents, fancying itself to be a step-child or adopted (Peter's surname is "Foster") and its true parents to be socially elevated, typically royalty. But *Next of Kin* inverts the Freudian scenario: here the impersonator is the child,

234 · QUEER ROOTS FOR THE DIASPORA

replacing the real son in his parents' affections. And where Freud refers to idealised parents of "high social standing," Peter's adoption of working-class Armenian immigrants chimes with a western middle-class fantasy of ethnic authenticity—a dream of belonging to a culture more rooted, more marked by social oppression and bearing more conspicuous signs of identity than the WASP bourgeoisie. (26)

In *Next of Kin*, about a teenage boy, Peter (Patrick Tierney), undergoing therapy with his parents, each group session is videotaped so that family members may later watch them individually.[13] Peter's parents have initiated this family therapy because they think "he doesn't want to work, has no pride, and pretends that he is someone else all the time." Yet, in spite of the fact that he has no friends, he assures everyone that he is not lonely, which may suggest that he is not maladjusted or psychologically underdeveloped or damaged but merely not conforming to his parents' (and perhaps society's) normative expectations. In short, maybe it is the family (and Family as norm) that is "sick" not Peter. When his mother describes catching him in his room in the act of pretending, she suggests that "making believe" is for Peter a pleasure as guilty as that of masturbation.

One day at the practice, Peter checks out the wrong tape and watches it instead of giving it back. The tape is a recording of the sessions of members of an immigrant Armenian family, who, in their early days of hardship in Canada, gave their son Bedros (of Peter's age) up for adoption. Claiming that he needs some time on his own, Peter requests a getaway trip, and the therapist supports this request in the interest of furthering Peter's development and independence. Yet, as in a Derridean understanding of masturbation (most literally Rousseau's) in *Of Grammatology*, "making believe" (producing fantasy in the sense elaborated by Laplanche and Pontalis) will replace reality; the supplement, that is, will displace what it is considered to supplement when Peter presents himself as the long-lost Bedros, thereby inventing for himself not only a new kinship unit (as in the film's title) but also new roots. But is there a family that is not such an invention? The film suggests, in other words, that fictive roots may be no different from "true" ones. When Peter first meets his Armenian family, a discussion ensues as to whether he resembles his grandfather or uncle more. Genetics (the "science" of origins) also turns out to be a fiction in *Next of Kin*.

In fact the introduction of a fictional son even strengthens kinship ties within the biological family, as Peter mends the dispute between his Armenian "father" George (Berge Fazlian) and his "sister" (Khanjian), a rupture that allegorizes the schism between "tradition" and modernity, Armenia (roots) and Canada (diaspora). During a surprise birthday party given for him by his "adoptive" Armenian family, Peter makes an impromptu speech:

> In a way, it's a pity that you're born into a family. If you're raised with a group, you're obliged to love them, and that really denies you the possibility of getting to know them as people outside of that group. Now, in a way that means you can never really love your family. And that's because you're denied the freedom that's required to make that sort of commitment, I guess what you would call the freedom of choice.

Peter is arguing here for a family based on affiliation as opposed to filiation, a family that would be an "imagined community" that can serve as an allegory for the diasporic community imagined through the "adoption" or invention of roots by means of fictive narrative practices. The kinship structure alluded to by the film's title is therefore one constructed through fictional narratives.

The expression "next of kin" is usually used when settling an estate after the death of a family member; in *Next of Kin*, however, because in deciding to remain with "his" Armenian family he kills off his biological one, so to speak, in order to consolidate his invented family, the Freudian family romance, in short, becomes "real." In telling his Armenian family that the family that adopted him (in "reality," his biological family) has been in an automobile accident, as their son (i.e., "next of kin") Peter imagines a kind of death for his parents. His adoptive family becomes his "next (of) kin" as they inherit sole custody of him. Since the roots of the filmmaker are those not of the boy but of the adopted family, Egoyan suggests that his "real" family narrative is also a family romance in the Freudian sense. In fact he goes so far as to suggest that psychoanalysis itself is a kind of family romance. At one point during the film Peter says in a kind of interior monologue (i.e., a voice-over), "I envy therapists. It must be really exciting getting involved with another family, trying to solve their problems." The film reinforces the notion that analysts engage in family romances when two therapists conversing in an elevator speak of each other's analysands as their wives and husbands with second-person possessive adjectives. The analysand, here, becomes the "next of kin" of the analyst who inserts him- or herself in the patient's kinship structure. The patient seduces the analyst, in other words, into a fictional family (romance).

In film after film, Egoyan has explored the relation between origins— often his own—and desire, especially perverse desire. Film after film explores the relationship among kinship, sexuality, and Armenian diasporic identity, whose roots he queers by making them up through inventing such unconventional kinship structures. As Egoyan's roots are often intertwined with, and indeed even invented through, sexual fantasies (including pornographic ones), we could even say that for him all roots are necessarily sexual fantasies, sexual fantasies whose *après-coup* structures (as described by Laplanche and Pontalis) also structure the roots narratives as a whole. In short, the narrative and sexual paradoxes become almost indistinguishable in Egoyan's case. In the final section of this chapter, I consider what the eroticization of a loss that is more explicitly linked with a loss of direct connection with Armenian roots (or with their replacement in a family romance) might tell us about Egoyan's films that seemingly have little or nothing to do with the Armenian diaspora.

Allegories of Loss

A number of Egoyan's non-Armenian films focus on such losses or disasters. In *The Sweet Hereafter* (1997), for example, a lawyer, Mitchell (Ian Holm) visits a small town to explore the possibility of a class-action lawsuit in the aftermath of a school-bus accident that killed almost every child aboard. In the end, Nicole (Sarah Polley), the surviving girl who would have been a key witness, lies in her description of the accident and ruins the possibility of a lawsuit. In one of the film's final scenes, Mitchell runs into the school-bus driver, Delores (Gabrielle Rose), who is now working for airport transportation. Delores smiles, indicating that she has recovered not only from her injuries but also from her loss. Nicole says in a voice-over:

> As you see her two years later, I wonder if you realize something. I wonder if you understand that all of us, Delores, me, the children who survived, the children who didn't, that we're all citizens of a different town now, a place with its own special rules and its own special laws, a town of people living in the sweet hereafter, where waters gushed and

fruit trees grew and flowers before the fairy hew and everything was strange and new. Everything was strange and new.

Loss therefore results in a kind of idyllic paradise, a kind of Eden. And standing up to Mitchell and her own father (ignoring loss, in other words) is what allows Nicole to recover from an incestuous relationship with the latter.

In another example, *Felicia's Journey* (1999), Egoyan takes allegories of loss out of the Canadian context altogether by telling the story of a young Irishwoman, Felicia (Elaine Cassidy), who has set off to England in pursuit of the fantasy that her beloved still loves her and will marry her when he learns that she is bearing his child. He has told her that he left for England in search of work, but he has actually betrayed his nation by joining the British army. Interestingly, Felicia's fantasy, which is merely one of conforming to the rules of heteronormativity, becomes the most perverse of all because she persists in spite of mountains of evidence that she is being naive. Along the way, she is helped by a man, Joseph Hilditch (Bob Hoskins), who gets off by offering succor to girls down on their luck. He deals with the loss of his mother (and that of the idyllic childhood he never had with her) by investing in the mother-to-be that is Felicia, in whom he kills off the mother by facilitating her abortion before attempting to kill her. At first he seems like an incredibly nice man, but as spectators begin to understand the videotapes he has secretly made of these girls the violent nature of his desire becomes obvious: he turns out to be a serial killer.[14] So the normal, in *Felicia's Journey*, turns out to be a perversion, and the pervert easily masquerades as normal.[15]

In a third example, *Adoration* (2008), a French teacher, Sabine (Khanjian), assigns a translation of an account of a thwarted terrorist bombing of a flight between Toronto and Israel. One student, Simon (Devon Bostick), completes the assignment by reading his own family history into the narrative. In the fictional version, his pregnant Anglo-Canadian mother Rachel (Rachel Blanchard) takes the flight alone to visit the family of her Palestinian husband Sami (Noam Jenkins) in Bethlehem to be joined by him later. He has placed a bomb in her luggage without her knowledge and without the thwarting of this attempt by Israeli security, Simon would have never been born. As we gradually learn, Simon's mother and father died in a car accident that his maternal grandfather Morris (Kenneth Welsh) claims was caused on purpose by the father whom he characterizes as a terrorist. Simon has been interviewing Morris on his deathbed, and the latter maintains his racist position that Sami must have been a terrorist because of his ethnicity until the very end, but we finally learn that Sami had an eye condition that should have prevented him from driving at night. He was forced to do so because Rachel got drunk at a family dinner due to racist comments her father made to Sami. We also learn that Sami was married to Sabine when he first met Rachel, for whom he left his first wife. Simon's fictional story of averted loss (which causes many tempers to flair on Internet live-stream video chat rooms) also provides a surrogate for Sabine's loss of a beloved husband, and the film ends as Simon becomes a part of her life in a different family structure based entirely on affiliation, in another of Egoyan's many family romances in short.

But of all his films about loss, I would suggest that *Speaking Parts* (1989) and *Exotica* (1994) might most productively be read as allegories of Armenian diasporic identity. In both, as in *Calendar* and *The Adjuster*, diaspora is also pornographic. *Speaking Parts* is about a woman, Clara (Gabrielle Rose), whose brother died because he gave her one of his lungs. Her memory of him is represented onscreen through the videos of him she watches at "the mausoleum with video monitor memorial plaques" (Klawans 15); as in many Egoyan films, the medium of video-tape is thus strongly connected to the themes of memory and return to the past. Clara has written a book about her brother's death, which is itself being made into a movie. As part of the production process, she is staying in a chic boutique hotel where Lance (Michael McManus), a struggling actor, works on the cleaning staff and doubles as a gigolo *between* the sheets when he is not changing them. When Gabrielle meets him, he reminds her so much of her brother that she supports him for the role of her brother in the film. They also have an affair, which contin-ues through "live-feed, closed-circuit sexual intercourse" (Klawans 15), or what one might call video sex. She is, to a certain extent, having sex with her dead brother. This video mediation is further complicated by Lisa (Khanjian), also a hotel employee, who is obsessed with Lance. She persists in her obsession in spite of his very cold shoulder and feeds it by renting videos of movies in which he has played small roles (including porn videos), roles that are *not* "speaking parts."

Exotica is set largely in a strip club owned by Zoe (Khanjian). As in *Speaking Parts*, therefore, the pornographic gaze is inseparable from the character played by Egoyan's "real-life" wife, which therefore disrupts any autobiographical contextualization of his diasporic identity within a heteronormative kinship unit. The strip club, also named Exotica, is the place where Francis (Bruce Greenwood) goes to deal with the loss of his daughter from a murder for which he was a suspect. Christina (Mia Kushner), his former babysitter, is a stripper who works at Exotica and gives Francis regular table dances, which foster a fantasy, indeed a family romance, on his part that she can somehow replace his daughter. (Her stripper getup is that of a schoolgirl.)

Like the photographer in *Calendar*, Lisa in *Speaking Parts* gets off on not getting off. Lance and Gabrielle get off on being physically separated, on facing obstacles to getting off, which can then be mediated though film (or the live video feed that serves as a metacinematic reference to it). In short, their video sex is a mise-en-abyme of the spectator's scopophilic gaze cast so longingly on the character played by an Armenian actress desiring someone else's loss, which remains inaccessible to her. The film also stages a failure of heterosexuality in the very same character of Lisa, who questions marriage and quite literally so. When she discovers that her video store's employee Eddy (Tony Nardi) tapes special events such as weddings and orgies on the side, she insinuates herself into his work and ruins a wedding. During her own interview with the bride, Lisa reveals the stupidity of marriage through a giggling newlywed incapable of articulating the reason she has espoused the institution of marriage:

LISA: What do you see in Ronnie?
TRISH: What?
LISA: What do you see in Ronnie? When you look at him, what are you looking at?
TRISH: (*perplexed*) Him.
LISA: Did it come easy?
TRISH: What?
LISA: His love?
TRISH: (*giggling*) I'm not quite sure if I get what . . .
LISA: Have there been times when it didn't seem so . . . certain?
TRISH: No, I . . .
LISA: I mean, these things are pretty delicate, aren't they? There's no telling what could happen. One of you begins to have second thoughts and the whole thing can crumble away. And then what? (114–16)[16]

When Lisa suggests that the new husband might not love his wife forever, the bride breaks down: "Why should I even think about it?" (120), she says as she bursts into tears. With the slightest questioning, the ideal of marriage "crumbles away." Unlike Lisa, Toni understands that if he is to continue in his job of enshrining others' memories of marriage as happy ones (and of marriage as the "happy ending" to a love story) he must lie. Before accompanying Toni on a gig, Lisa watches a video in which he tells his patron, "I can honestly say that this is the best wedding I've ever taped." When Lisa asks, "Is that true?" he responds, "Of course not. You've seen one, you've seen 'em all" (78). *Speaking Parts* therefore suggests that (heterosexual) marriage is an institution whose foundation is based on lies in much the same way that Sapho's *Un mensonge* reveals the heterosexuality of origins to be a lie.

Lance finally gets the speaking part that has always alluded him, but Clara is gradually pushed out of the production process as her autobiographical role of sister is turned into that of a brother, and her story, she feels, is cheapened by being framed as a talk show episode. She fails to cope with her loss and commits suicide on the film set. Lisa, however, finally gains access to the object of her desire, since the film ends with her kissing Lance. Yet how "real" can we understand this ending to be? Having lived out her fantasies about Lance by watching his nonspeaking parts, she experiences the boundary between video and reality being blurred (as borders are so often crossed in Egoyan's films) in the last video we see her watching. She sees what resembles surveillance footage of Lance, the hotel manager, and the body of the female guest/client who has committed suicide because her love for Lance was unrequited, and in a *Poltergeist*-like moment, Lisa is able to talk to Lance through the television screen that separates them. He asks for her help, but she does not know how to cross the border between her reality and his, a boundary represented by the television screen.

While *Speaking Parts* might be considered figuratively queer in its challenge to heteronormative kinship structures, *Exotica* literally has a gay character, Thomas (Don McKellar), a pet shop owner who illegally smuggles rare birds into Canada. His illegal job involves sneaking across borders in a manner similar to Raffi's experience with contraband in *Ararat.* Like the airport scenes in so many of Egoyan's films, especially those of Raffi at customs in *Ararat,* the opening scene of Thomas's arrival portrays the policing of borders as one customs official trains another in how to stop contraband from entering the country. On his way home from the airport, the man with whom he is sharing a cab offers him ballet tickets in lieu of his share of the fare. Thomas offers the second ticket to a man whose crotch and thighs he eyes during "The Montagues and the Capulets" movement of Prokofiev's *Romeo and Juliet.* After not following through on his invitee's subsequent advances, he later repeats this scene by restaging it (as the photographer repeats his own primal scene in *Calendar*). He ends up bringing a subsequent invitee home, but the latter turns out to be one of the customs officials who found him so suspicious at the film's beginning. When Thomas wakes up there is a message on his answering machine explaining why the incubating eggs smuggled into Canada are now missing. His trick from the previous evening handed them over to the unit that takes care of contraband exotic animals, probably by giving them to a zoo. He has lied to his supervisors, probably to avoid reporting Thomas, and states that he would like to see Thomas again.

Thomas's queer potential, however, is not confined to this particular narrative thread but also crosses its own kind of border into the strip club as a self-exoticizing diasporic space, first of all in the parallel that the film establishes between Exotica and the pet shop. Zoe inherited Exotica from her mother, and Thomas inherited the pet shop from his father. Zoe lives in a kind of tent inside Exotica with her tropical bird, and sounds in this space resemble those we hear in the pet shop. Editing frequently intercuts directly between the two spaces, and, as Romney writes, "*Exotica* is itself a dense jungle, its narrative an intricate network of hidden roots and interconnections" (110). Furthermore, Zoe's space in the club functions as "a panopticon," which "recalls . . . the . . . customs office . . . , where two inspectors watch [Thomas] behind a one way mirror" (Wilson 32). When the hirsute Thomas is making out with his trick, the latter remarks, "It's like petting a gorilla." Thomas responds, "I got it from my mother, I mean my mother's side of the family. That's where you inherit hair patterns." Way too lanky to be a "bear" (more common—as an animal—in more temperate and colder climes), he can only be a gorilla (more common in tropical regions). Like Zoe, in other words, he has inherited something exotic from his mother. As it turns out, Francis (an auditor for Revenue Canada who has been inspecting Thomas's books) has suspected the smuggling operation all along. After being tricked by Eric (Koteas), Christina's ex-boyfriend and Exotica's deejay and announcer, into touching Christina, with the result that he is barred from Exotica permanently, Francis blackmails Thomas into handing over his gun and going into Exotica wired and undercover to discover Christina's reaction to Francis's expulsion. Thomas is tasked with requesting a table dance in order to touch Christina and get kicked out in the same manner. The gay-owned pet shop therefore crosses over into the heterosexual strip club; like contraband, queerness is smuggled

across the boundary between gay and straight into Exotica. Although
one should be careful not to conflate the jungle motifs of Exotica with
the orientalist discourse theorized by Said, both deal in the exotic, and
Exotica becomes, to use Said's expression, "a living tableau of queerness"
(*Orientalism* 103).

For it is during this table dance that Thomas (and, through the mic
wired to him, Francis) discovers that Francis's need for Christina, his
need to protect her as he could not protect his daughter, is mutual; she
describes their "special type of relationship" and confides that she needs
him for certain things just as he needs her. A rather queer kind of family
is consolidated at this point. Francis cannot follow through on his intention to kill Eric, who finally seems to give up on Christina (whom he met
as part of the search for Francis's daughter). Zoe, pregnant through a
contract with Eric, will bequeath her legacy (a strip club) in a rather
queer alternative to the driver's notion of what a baby could give the
photographer and his wife in *Calendar*. Instead of rooting *Calendar*'s couple in a homeland, Zoe's baby reproduces a porn diaspora. Francis himself has reproduced his dead daughter's "babysitter" with Tracey (Sarah
Polley), who ostensibly comes over only to house sit. Tracey's question,
"Do you think this is normal, what we do?" (which might be applied
to Egoyan's entire oeuvre), highlights the perverse fantasies that Francis has articulated around his daughter's death. Tracey's father Harold
(Victor Garber), Francis's brother, was having affair with Francis's wife,
who was killed in the same car accident that disabled Harold (hence the
police's suspicion that Francis may have killed his own daughter upon
discovering that Harold might actually be her biological father).[17] Tracey
discontinues her services at the end, which may suggest that Francis's
faulty mourning has finally resulted in a resolution to the mourning process or a cure.

Other parts of the ending, however, until which we must wait to
learn about Harold's affair, contradict such a normative resolution. In
fact much of the ending simply returns to a time prior to the death of
Francis's daughter as Francis is taking Christina home in the exact same
way we have seen him taking Tracey home throughout the film. The
younger Christina notes, "I was just thinking . . . about the way you talk
about Lisa. You get so excited. It's nice." He remarks that Christina and
Lisa really listen to each other. Christina had become a kind of adoptive member of the family, in other words, a family she has come to idealize. In other words, the end of *Exotica* only serves to emphasize the
"founding disaster" that is the destruction of this idealized family, not

to mark the successful mourning of the loss in which it resulted. Tracey may have removed herself from Francis's perverse jouissance in indefinitely prolonging his faulty mourning, but he no longer has access to his "therapy," for which the "analyst" pole dances and the "analysand's" lap replaces the analyst's couch. This therapy may have reached its "happy" end, but hardly because the "talking cure" has been a success.

Like the photographer's eroticized restaging of loss in *Calendar* and Clara's live video sex with a surrogate for her dead brother in *Speaking Parts*, Francis allegorically translates the loss of rootedness at the origins of diaspora into the roots of desire. Like the families invented through fantasy in *The Adjuster*, *Next of Kin*, and *Family Viewing*, Francis's strip club family, with all its queer intrusions, allegorizes the crossing of national and cultural borders entailed in diasporic migration. And, like the unmasking of the eroticized fictionality of the fetish of inaugural disaster in *Ararat*, Francis's acknowledgment of his perverse attachment to his own familial loss in no way results in its mourning. Ends may indeed "come" in Egoyan's films, but they come without narrative closure, without a reattachment of the Armenian diaspora to its roots, without the retracing of a heteronormative family tree that might structure a return to Armenian origins. *Je sais bien . . . mais tout de même.*

CHAPTER 6

Booger Hollar and Other Queer Sites

Ghosts in the Family Tree

✦ ✦ ✦

Off the beaten path about three miles from where I grew up in Stan-ly County, North Carolina, a one-lane wooden bridge crosses Big Bear Creek at a site locals call Booger Hollar (fig. 3). If you drive onto this bridge at night, turn off your car and headlights, and roll down the win-dows, it is said that you can hear ghosts—or boogers as we call them—wailing down the creek (see Boyd, J.). Upon crossing the more traveled Saint Martin Church Road (which connects Albemarle, the county seat, and the town of Oakboro), Booger Hollar Road becomes Efird Road, Efird being my maternal grandmother's maiden name (figs. 4–5). In 1822 our forebear Jacob Efird founded the Lutheran church now sit-uated at this crossroads. In *The History and Genealogy of the Efird Family* (1964), Oscar Agburn Efird asserts that Jacob Efird is the ancestor of all living Efirds and the first of his family—which probably emigrated from Germany to America with the Pennsylvania "Dutch"—to hold a family meeting and a vote to simplify their German family name Ehrenfried into one more easily spelled and pronounced by Anglo-Americans. So just down the hill from the precise location where my family history can be mapped onto the topography of the county of my birth, and where a number of distant relatives are buried, boogers await anyone willing to listen for them. But who are the dead who return on a nightly basis to remind the living of their (former) presence? Could they be connected to my family tree? Could they occupy a place in it?

244

Fig. 3. Booger Hollar, North Carolina. (Photos by Jarrod Hayes.)

Fig. 4. Booger Hollar, North Carolina. (Photos by Jarrod Hayes.)

Fig. 5. Booger Hollar, North Carolina. (Photos by Jarrod Hayes.)

Fig. 6. Oakboro, North Carolina. (Photos by Jarrod Hayes.)

I only discovered Booger Hollar's connection to my family tree once this project was well under way, a connection that has forced me to think of the relation between identity and genealogy in queer ways, even though genealogy is usually structured along kinship lines defined through heterosexual reproduction. Booger Hollar itself also has a long history as a *heterosexual* make-out spot; I have heard guys boast of "parking" with girls on a farm road, now blocked off, whose entrance is only a few hundred yards from the bridge. Indeed, my first attempt to photograph the bridge was foiled by a teenage couple embracing on the large rock to the left of it. Signs of this heterosexuality are physically inscribed onto the bridge itself in the form of graffiti. On some missions, I was able to photograph hints of lesbian love, again in the form of a graffito (figs. 7–8). I would suggest, however, that Booger Hollar's queer meaning does not depend on its hospitableness to same-sex desire. Although the goings-on to which these inscriptions allude might provide a less unearthly explanation of the wailing just described, it is the more supernatural version that nourished my childhood, along with ghost stories attached to other sites as well. For crossing the bridge at Booger Hollar entails traveling a distance much greater than the span of the bridge; it involves traveling back through time, a digression, if you will, much like the one that the more strong-of-heart take when they pause there on journeys long and short or even drive out of their way to determine for themselves whether they can hear these boogers.

I have come to this reading of Booger Hollar in conjunction with two North Carolina novels, one familiar, Thomas Wolfe's *Look Homeward, Angel*, the other perhaps less familiar, *Dream Boy*, by the gay novelist Jim Grimsley. Wolfe's novel is a haunted one; even the living, including its protagonist Eugene Gant, are frequently described as ghosts. And, like those in my reading of Booger Hollar, these ghosts are related to a particular vision of its characters' family tree. Furthermore, defined in matrilineal not patrilineal terms, Eugene's position in this family tree is explicitly described by other family members as queer (in the sense of eccentric). In contrast, *Dream Boy* is also haunted by the ghosts of repressed family secrets. Its ghosts are queer in a more contemporary sense (i.e., related to nonnormative sexualities and desires). Grimsley's novel tells the story of Nathan, the son of an abusive alcoholic father, and of his love affair with Roy, a farmer's son and school-bus driver. The final part, over a third of the entire novel, describes a camping trip the two go on with Roy's straight buddies, Burke and Randy. During this trip, the boys also visit a plantation house haunted by the ghost of a decapitated master.

Fig. 7. Booger Hollar, North Carolina. (Photos by Jarrod Hayes.)

Fig. 8. Booger Hollar, North Carolina. (Photos by Jarrod Hayes.)

This haunted house, however, is home to a *variety* of ghosts, ghosts representing sexual secrets and histories of family violence in addition to the history of slavery and racial terror. Whereas, at first glance, Booger Hollar, *Look Homeward, Angel*, and *Dream Boy* may seem to be haunted by very different ghosts, a hauntological reading, to borrow Derrida's term, one that allows the ghosts of each of these three topoi or texts to haunt the others, can reveal the hidden similarities lurking behind the differences. If, according to Abraham and Torok, ghosts represent repressed family secrets, and according to Derrida, a disavowed alterity, I shall argue that, by conjuring up a history of violence at least partially forgotten, such a reading brings a repressed past back to queer the present.

In this, my final chapter, I return home, to a certain extent, to my own roots. It is also the chapter that drives home the affective pull of my roots in a very personal way. I am struck now that, as a graduate student when personal or autobiographical criticism was an area of exploration on the part of a number of my feminist mentors, I was never able to completely pull off acts of personal criticism myself. Even works begun at the intersection between my intellectual inquiries and my own life story always seemed to benefit when the autobiographical was expunged and I made my work conform to the more conventional academic essay. Yet, for some reason, the personal or autobiographical has managed to cling to my readings of Wolfe and Grimsley, and one of my goals in this chapter is to explore the implications of the affective pull of roots and what life writing enables in this project. In chapter 4, I considered Derrida's use and deconstruction of the autobiographical; here I point toward a theorization of the role of the autobiographical within queer affect theory.

Looking for Ghosts

Haints, boogers: I am never quite sure when it is appropriate or necessary to translate such words from my mother tongue. If conversations with nonsouthern acquaintances are any indication, *booger* is not obvious to most speakers of English; most understand it to mean "nose boogers." Though *booger* has an approximate equivalent in Standard Written English—*bogey*—a booger is not the same as the bogey in *bogeyman,* a word also used in Southern English, though pronounced slightly differently (as in *boogey* or *booger man*). As I grew up using the word, a booger can be any ghost of malevolent intentions. Yet I was well into adulthood before I had the slightest idea of how *booger* might be spelled. In fact, it was when I began to revisit Booger Hollar for this project that I first saw the word in writing on a road sign. I can remember when such roads never had signs or when only "locals" in the most restricted sense (i.e., those living within, say, a half-mile radius of a given site) could name a particular rural road. In some cases, there were even disagreements over the names of roads. Because of its boogers, however, and the more earthly teenagers who haunted its most famous attraction, Booger Hollar Road was more widely recognized, even if those who knew of it probably would not have been able to agree on a spelling. Yet, regardless of how widely a road name was used, oral culture had a monopoly over such naming until 1981, when all the roads in Stanly County were given official names to permit the numbering of rural homes in order to ensure timely ambulance service to remote areas. At that time, the name Booger Hollar took on its present written form.

When I tell southerners from elsewhere about this place, and especially when I show them pictures of the road sign, I am usually treated to a knowing grin. Many are amazed that this word can be written on signposts and maps. My own first attempts to photograph the signs were frustrated by the fact that, twenty years after the first signs were erected, they were still being stolen at such a rate that they could not be replaced fast enough. The pleasure of seeing in writing a word many associate with an exclusively oral language, especially a language so often scorned, is undoubtedly part of this desire to "reappropriate" the written word by confiscating the few material "signs" of its existence. My own pleasure at seeing the word in writing elicited not a desire to break the law but rather a reflection on how the sign itself broke certain rules of Standard English. *Hollar* has a perfectly exact standard equivalent—*hollow*, as in "The Legend of Sleepy Hollow" (Irving)—and the association between the two would come easily for most southerners. I was thus a bit surprised that the signs did not read "Booger Hollow." It came as no surprise, however, that *booger* would be phonetically transliterated as opposed to mistranslated into Standard English as *bogey*; *Bogey Hollow* seems so laughable to me that I would have been deeply disappointed had I discovered that the county officials who held the public forums to settle on these road names had even considered such a ridiculous option. If *booger* resists translation into Standard English, this resistance has also infected *hollar*, a perfectly translatable word; it seems almost as if the ghostly boogers have extended their haunting to the very language used to name them. I guess Standard English is not the only official language of Stanly County after all.

I was curious, however, as to how Booger Hollar *became* official, so curious that I devoted the afternoon of 3 August 2004 to another kind of digression in order to track down any possible record of how a word as unwritable as *booger* made its way onto the most official manifestations of the language of the state. The archives at the local public library offered only the year during which the official naming occurred. A trip to the county commissioners' office in the county courthouse revealed that these years' records had long been banished to "the vault" in the basement. When found, the minutes simply referred me to the planning department's records, which were back upstairs, right next door to the county commissioners' office where I had started. After a bit of searching, Stanly County planner Linda Evans pulled a folder of aged yellow notepad papers out of a filing cabinet and, among these, found the minutes of the Stanly County Planning Department meeting of 12 February 1981. They simply state, "Proposed Little Creek Rd. Objections and discussion were heard. Officially named Booger Hollar Rd." Unaccustomed, no doubt, to requests for these *particular* public documents, Evans offered, without being prompted, much information about the process of officializing road names. I could still vaguely remember the public forums held to solicit input from ordinary folk, but Evans added to this knowledge by telling me about a man and woman who spent several days riding all over the county to come up with the names that were originally proposed. But Little Creek Road? How could anyone familiar with the area propose such a banal name for a road everyone knew as Booger Hollar? Did they not speak to the residents living near Booger Hollar? Perhaps more perplexing is the fact that anyone would take the time to attend an evening meeting to object to a proposal for naming a rural road that is only 2.3 miles long. It was yet another digression in their busy lives, no doubt, one not unlike the digression that usually must be taken to visit Booger Hollar.

Furthermore, what kind of objections were heard at the meeting in question? While I can appreciate the thought of good country folk rising up against this assault on their oral culture by officialdom, a more likely scenario involves local residents showing up to add a family name to an unnamed road and thus being able, by accident, to object to a name they were unaccustomed to using for *another* road. Efird Road, for example, was not the first suggestion either; rather, Battle Road was initially proposed. One can only presume that distant relatives were there to object to the official proposal and stamp the family name onto official county geography at the very place where it could continually be haunted.

Could they have also been the ones to push for Booger Hollar's reinstatement? Road names such as Richard-Sandy Road serve as evidence that those with the incentive to have a road named after themselves often did so without objections (fig. 6). (And this name, a more formal equivalent of the "so-and-so loves so-and-so" inscriptions at Booger Hollar only a few miles away, officializes heterosexual naming in a way graffiti on the bridge never could.)[1] But what else was discussed at the forum? A spelling? When Evans asked me why I was interested in the minutes, I commented on the name Booger Hollar and its spelling. She replied by stating that the Planning Department was required to spell names as they were written in the minutes. Was she suggesting that Booger Hollar might be a misspelling? What constitutes a misspelling in the case of a word that only exists in spoken language?

Booger has no entry in the *Oxford English Dictionary* (*OED*), even though one can find many related words: *bogy*, *boggard*, *bogle*, all, like *bug*, "from Welsh *bwg* (= bug) 'a ghost'" (*OED* II, 626):

> **boggard¹, -art** . . . [A word in popular use in Westmoreland, Lancashire, Cheshire, Yorkshire, and the north midlands, and of occasional appearance in literature since *c* 1570. Evidently related to BOG-GLE, BOGLE, and BOG *sb.*²: if the status of the last-named were more assured, it would be natural to see in *bogg-ard* a derivative with the augmentative suffix -ARD; or if the occasional variant *buggard* could be assumed as the etymological form, it might stand in the same relation to BUG. See BOGLE.]
>
> **1.** A spectre, goblin, or bogy; in dialectal use, esp. a local goblin or sprite supposed to "haunt" a particular gloomy spot, or scene of violence. . . .
>
> **b.** *fig.* A bugbear, a source of dread. (II, 359)

Since the final *d* and *t* are interchangeable, it is not much of a stretch from *boggard* to *booger* in contexts like the ones in which Southern English is spoken and final dental consonants can be replaced with glottal stops. If "the occasional variant *buggard*" is used, it is even less of a stretch. In fact, the entry's use of *appearance* turns the word itself into an apparition with a shadowy past that cannot be determined with certainty, a word whose roots withdraw into the recesses of history. *Bogle* contains a definition that perfectly matches that of *booger*: "1. A phantom causing fright; a goblin, bogy, or spectre of the night; an undefined creature of superstitious dread. Also, applied contemptuously to a human being who is a 'fright to behold'" (II, 360). Southerners as well might sometimes say that so-and-so is as ugly as a booger or a haint. Although I finally found most of what I was looking for in the *OED*, my quest for these very specific etymological roots was delayed by boogers haunting the pages of that most venerated historical account of the English lexicon, boogers hiding this entry from me during my first visits to these pages of the *OED*, itself, then, a sort of Booger Hollar.

Furthermore, if one attributes the definition of *boggard* to *booger*, the lack of hints in local lore that Booger Hollar was the scene of any violence suggests that it owes its reputation to the fact that it is simply a particularly gloomy spot. But, to make it into ghost stories, even merely gloomy spots must have narratives attached to them or at least must gain a narrative as they enter a ghost story. Since boggards, like boogers, "'haunt' a particular . . . spot," their haunting of that place marks it as a peculiar site of memory, one where the past can be conjured up. But what kind of *violence* returns from night to night at Booger Hollar to remind the living of what they have repressed? Are the boogers at Booger Hollar related to my family tree? If so, does it mean that the family tree itself can be a site of violence? It is hard to think of a family tree as a place, even if its roots might be planted somewhere quite specific. The family tree visualizes a *structure,* that of kinship; but what kind of violence lurks within structures? And why must such violence be kept secret?

Family Romance as Ghost Story

If, as a site of memory, Booger Hollar recalls a family naming as not only a repressed secret but also a kind of violence that comes back to haunt, this site becomes haunted with latent meaning. If Booger Hollar is haunted as a place by "real" boogers (whatever spectral reality might be), if these real boogers serve as a figure for the linguistic haunting represented by the written form of Booger Hollar, Efird, too, is a haunted name, one containing the ghosts of all its previous versions. As place-names, Efird and Booger are thus intimately intertwined; as they share a single road, their signs face each other from opposite sides of Saint Martin Church Road. And, just as the etymology of *booger* was tricky to unravel, so, too, does the name Efird have a history whose digressions Oscar Agburn Efird took many pains to track down, a little over a decade before Haley's own return to roots. He provides a list of the many spellings of the name, spanning the decades from the day of Johann Georg

Ehrenfried's arrival in Philadelphia from Germany to the middle of the following century. Some of the listed versions follow:

Johann Gerg [*sic*] Ehrenfried. Signature to Oath of Abjuration on September 18, 1773.

Johann George Erndfried and wife, Catharine Barbara Erndfried. Baptismal record of daughter, Sara, April 6, 1777.

George Ernfreed. Tax listing in 1780.

George Ernfried. Military record, November 18, 1780.

Jacob Iffert. Land grant from the State of North Carolina, October 9, 1783.

George Ernfridt. Grantee in a deed in Easton, Pa., dated July 15, 1784.

George Ehrinfried. Military record, May 9, 1785.

George Earenfried. Tax listing in 1785.

Jacob Eafrit. United States census of 1790 for North Carolina.

Martin Eafert. Recital in a deed of purchase of land, November 17, 1792.

Jacob Iffret. Land grant from the State of North Carolina, June 30, 1797.

Jacob Eford. United States census of 1810 for North Carolina.

Martin Efferet. United States census of 1810 for North Carolina.

Jacob Eafort. Sponsor at baptism of Esther Eafort, daughter of George Eafort, at Bethel Lutheran Church, Stanly Co., N.C., August 22, 1819.

Jacob Euford. Grantee in land grant from the State of North Carolina, December 15, 1821.

Daniel Efird. Signature on marriage bond, July 9, 1827.

Daniel Eaford. Grantee in land grant from the State of North Carolina, December 4, 1829.

Adam Ephert. Delegate to Tennessee Lutheran Synod in 1842.

Jacob Iferdt. Signature to his will, December 3, 1842. (7–8)

According to Oscar Agburn Efird, the "memorable meeting of the clan," which "met together and agreed to simplify and anglicize the spelling of the name, and adopted the present spelling of *Efird*, . . . was probably about 1827, or before, because we find Daniel Efird, one of the parties to this agreement, signing his marriage bond <u>Daniel Efird</u> on July 9, 1827, in Cabarrus County, North Carolina" (6).

Oscar Agburn Efird explains the motivation behind the renaming as follows:

> The name <u>Ehrenfried</u> was difficult for anyone who was not a German or of German extraction to pronounce. . . . Outside the German communities in which they settled, these immigrants had to come in contact with the English tax collectors and many other public officials, as well as the numerous others with whom they transacted business.
>
> It is not difficult to visualize Jacob Ehrenfried, a son of Johann Georg Ehrenfried, who together with his father had migrated to North Carolina, busily engaged at work about his farm in Mecklenburg County, that portion now Cabarrus County, North Carolina, as a total stranger rode up to his home on a good sorrel horse with bulging saddle bags across the horse's back behind the saddle. Jacob was not alarmed, but very interested. The stranger got off his horse and tied it to a sapling, got writing material out of a saddle bag and approached the house. Jacob Ehrenfried met him at the door. The stranger introduced himself and informed him that he was the United States census taker, and asked Jacob what his name was. Jacob told him that it was "Air-en-freed." The census taker said, "What?" Jacob, experiencing the same thing that he had so many times before, probably tried to simplify it for him and said "Air-freed." The census taker thereupon wrote down <u>Eafrit</u> as it appears in the 1790 United States census of North Carolina, and secured the other information about his family contained therein. (5)

In this fictionalized account of family history, Oscar Agburn Efird invents details as specific as a sorrel horse, a sapling, and an imaginary tax collector. Yet Jacob, the hero of this story, was not alarmed. In spite of the fact that "other German names" were entered into the tax register in much the same way, and that Jacob lived within one of any number of "German communities," he confronts the census taker alone. And even though this passage hints that the necessity of renaming is tied to economic structures, it downplays any coercive aspect of economic pressures to Anglicize the family name. Oscar Agburn Efird reinforces the glorification of the ancestor as an American hero and exemplification of the American dream.

Yet the various spellings listed above tell the story not of an abrupt change but one of gradual evolution. Iffert, very similar to the final

orthography, appeared as early as 1783, and alternative spellings continued to appear after 1827, including one by the very same Daniel. Furthermore, Oscar Agburn Efird continues the story told by the list with
the following description of Lutheran Church records:

> In 1846, Simon H. Efird was a delegate from [Montgomery C]ounty.
> In 1847, Daniel Efirt was a delegate from the same county. In 1848,
> Adam Efert was assistant in ministerial services. In 1848, N. P. Ifert was
> a delegate. In 1848, Daniel Ifert was a ministerial student. In 1849,
> Adam Efird was pastor at Lexington, North Carolina. In the early
> days, the Lutherans spoke and conducted services in both German
> and English, and it is noted that in the German records the name is
> spelled Ifert, whereas in the English records it is spelled Efird. Consis-
> tently, from 1850 on, the name is spelled Efird in these minutes. (5)

Yet, since this very paragraph offers examples of four spellings not two,
its attribution of spelling to the records' language is contradicted by the
evidence that immediately precedes it. It is understandable that there
might be differences between signatures, church records in German and
English,[2] and government documents in English, but there is often as
much variation within each of these categories as between them.

Furthermore, there is no written evidence of the meeting at which
a collective decision was taken *on a specific date* to change the spelling
of the family name once and for all. The only evidence for the meeting comes from Laura Christine Efird, who "said that her father Martin Luther Efird, told her that he remembered when his father, Daniel,
his grandfather, Jacob, and his uncles, George, Martin, Jacob John, and
Solomon, met together and agreed to simplify and anglicize the spelling
of the name" (6). In most cases Oscar Agburn Efird is suspicious of oral
history (xvii), and this particular informant is notoriously unreliable (1),
believing, for example, that the family's heritage was Dutch, not German. What purpose, then, is served by hanging on to the aspect of family
oral tradition regarding a name-change meeting when Oscar Agburn
Efird's research has shown most of this tradition to be wrong, or at the
most to contain only a kernel of the version Oscar Agburn ultimately
settled on as truth?

The answer to this question, I think, can be found in the family
romance Oscar Agburn Efird attempts to create with his genealogical
history:

That these early forebears did an excellent job in simplifying and anglicizing the name cannot be gainsaid. This act of itself demonstrates so many dominant characteristics of them. These forebears had come from a cultural country into a new, undeveloped country expecting to hew a home out of the forest. They bore a name which was difficult for their English neighbors to pronounce. They had faith in themselves and in their adopted country, and anticipated its development and progress with the necessary business, religious and social contacts. This was why they adopted the present spelling of the Efird name. (6)

The version that Oscar Agburn Efird asserts as truth, therefore, allows him to present the change of name as a mark of the family's ingenuity. This narrative of an Old World family finding the American dream in the New World (published in the Cold War 1960s no less) transforms family romance into a story of Americanization. It does not matter that every other German family that moved to the area changed its name in a similar way (see Hammer 31–33; Sharpe and Pepper 39); Oscar Agburn Efird manages to present the Efird name change as a unique example of rugged individualism. The forebear had to be a hero, and this hero could be none other than Jacob Efird: "The fifth chapter gives a full account of Jacob Efird, the patriarch of the family, so as to place him on the high pedestal upon which he so justly belongs" (xviii). In fact, he goes to great lengths to create the fiction of noble origins by mentioning at great length "Ehrenfried, son of Herman, I, of the House of Franconia, was born A.D. 995 [who] became the third ruler of the Palatinate on the Rhine, Germany, A.D. 959" (4). He also details his interest in tracking down an Old World coat of arms (6). Nonetheless, Old World coats of arms can be replaced with a different kind of New World nobility, that of the self-made man, self-made here in part because self-named. In spite of the fact that Jacob had a father, who immigrated to America, "All persons who spell their name Efird are descended from Jacob Efird" (42), not Johann Georg Ehrenfried.

The economic pressures downplayed so as to romanticize this history of the family name, however, suggest a kind of violence (even if "only" symbolic) behind the requirement that Jacob Efird's last name be intelligible to the Anglo county officials who ensured that he would keep his claim to the land he worked. Casting aside the father's name was specific to the class to which my ancestors belonged as yeoman farmers. Only when a name has so little attachment to power can it be thrown away so easily. Yet might we not also think of abandoning the father's name as a kind of patricide? In addition to being part of my family's ancestral lands, then, could Booger Hollar also serve as a metaphor for my ancestors' ghosts? Could the secrets that Booger Hollar simultaneously guards and reveals be the name of my great-great-great-great-great-great-grandfather abandoned so long ago? In such a reading of Booger Hollar, although the Efird family has been assimilated into Anglo-American culture for over a hundred years, it might still be thought of as haunted by its origins and the migrations that resulted in its (re)naming. In that case, Booger Hollar, in its connection to my family name, might be thought of as a scene of violence done to a name, a proper name. The ghosts in the Efird family tree thus reveal the economic structures that discouraged resistance to Anglicization. These economic structures might be seen as related to systems or structures of violence that leave any number of ghosts in the written and oral cultures of North Carolina.

Wolfe's Ghosts

One cultural text thus haunted is Wolfe's *Look Homeward, Angel,* which tells the coming-of-age story of Eugene Gant, a delicate, lanky, lonely bookworm growing up during the first two decades of the twentieth century in the fictional city and state of Altamont, Catawba (which bears a striking resemblance to Wolfe's hometown of Asheville, North Carolina). This novel is also the story of a family, which is rooted in an introductory narration of the family tree whose members are racist and anti-Semitic, as is the narrator in all likelihood. In most ways, therefore, *Look Homeward, Angel* is far from queer, especially in terms of its racial politics. Eugene at times even waxes nostalgic on the institution of slavery, and African American characters are nothing more than stereotypes. Where the novel becomes a bit more interesting is in its description of the construction of white masculinity, which relies on a simultaneous abjection of black bodies and a seemingly contradictory objectification of black women's bodies as available sexual objects (in contrast with the defense of the purity of white femininity). So we can see that the novel's gender politics, especially as they relate to race, are disturbing as well. But the novel does interestingly describe coming to masculinity not as a natural occurrence but as a social prescription enforced through violence. And this is the dominant role that Eugene has more trouble playing.

Of the novel's characters, none is more ghostly than its protagonist Eugene. After he has taken on a paper route in the African American section of town, the novel describes his having to wake up at 3:30 each morning:

> Waken, ghost-eared boy, but into darkness. Waken, phantom, O into us. Try, try, O try the way. Open the wall of light. Ghost, ghost, who is the ghost? O lost. Ghost, ghost, who is the ghost? O whisper-tongued laughter. Eugene! Eugene! Here, O here, Eugene. Here, Eugene. The way is here, Eugene. Have you forgotten? . . . O lost, and by the wind grieved, ghost, come back again. (244–45)

Eugene is characterized as ghostly here perhaps because of his early morning drogginess, which somehow diminishes his presence among the living. However, given that *O Lost* was the original title of *Look Homeward, Angel*, this passage can be read as more central to Eugene's characterization in general.[3] Furthermore, the last sentence of this passage replicates word for word the last sentence of the prefatory paragraph (1), which by its very position calls the novel into existence. In other words, the novel itself characterizes narrative production as conjuring up ghosts.

In addition to being like a ghost, Eugene is also haunted. In the novel's final chapter, he has a conversation with his dead brother, who denies being a ghost:

> "Don't you remember? I tell you, you are dead, Ben."
> "Fool," said Ben fiercely. "I am not dead."
> There was silence.
> "Then," said Eugene very slowly, "which of us is the ghost, I wonder?" (516)

Yet Eugene, here, is less disturbed by this haunting than reminded of his own ghostlike quality. Indeed, Eugene is more likely to conjure up ghosts than attempt to conjure them away. At his brother Grover's deathbed after the St. Louis world's fair, Eugene has the following reaction: "[L]ike one who has been mad, and suddenly recovers reason, he remembered that forgotten face he had not seen in weeks, that strange bright loneliness that would not return. O lost, and by the wind grieved, ghost, come back again" (47). Like the novel itself, therefore, Eugene is a conjurer of ghosts, a ghost whisperer. Eugene, however, is not the center of every haunting staged by the novel; his father, Oliver Gant, has his own relation with ghosts: "The eyes of the gaunt spectre darkened again, as they had in his youth" (5). And it is through Eugene's father that the novel's ghosts first haunt the family tree. The family history that serves as the preface to Eugene's story recounts the story of his paternal forebears' migrations from Britain. Like the patronymic Efird, Gant has been modified from its original—Gaunt—as part of the Americanization of the family. In the above quotation, however, the abandoned name of the father returns in adjectival form, modifying the word *specter* and returning as a ghost of the abandoned patronymic to haunt the family tree.

Quare Wolfe

Although the genealogical narrative that serves as the introduction to Wolfe's novel traces a conventional family tree, Eugene Gant stands out as the most out-of-place person in the patrilineage. In contrast to the ghosts in the Efird family tree, however, it is Eugene's matronymic that comes back to haunt *him*. His sister taunts, "You little freak. You nasty little freak. You don't even know who you are—you little bastard. You're not a Gant. Any one can see that. You haven't a drop of papa's blood in you. Queer one! Queer one! You're Greeley Pentland all over again" (198).[4] (Greeley Pentland was his mother's youngest brother.) Of course *queer* is used here in a very different way from more contemporary uses, as the novel itself indicates in an explicit definition: "His family felt obscurely that he was an eccentric—'queer,' they called it—and of an impractical or 'literary' turn" (501). (As a literary critic, I have always felt a special affinity with this particular characterization of the literary as queer!) To emphasize this specificity of Wolfe's use of the word *queer* and to distinguish this usage from its more contemporary meanings, I would suggest that it be pronounced as my parents would pronounce it: *quare*. In their usage, too, *quare* means "eccentric," or alternatively, "set in one's ways." Obviously there is an etymological link with the standard English word *queer*, but the two are not the same, especially in a post-ACT-UP! understanding of the word *queer*. (ACT-UP!, the AIDS Coalition to Unleash Power, was a militant AIDS activist group founded in the late 1980s.) *Quare* and *queer* are such different concepts for my parents that my father once thought he was teaching my queer lover (at their first meeting) something he might not otherwise know (as well as offering him some practical advice for living with someone as difficult as I) when he described me as also being *quare*. (Hopefully my lover had figured out that I was queer!) "He's so damn quare, sometimes you can't even talk to him," said my father, for whom *quare* means "ornery" in this context.

In "'Quare' Studies, or (Almost) Everything I Know about Queer Studies I Learned from my Grandmother," E. Patrick Johnson describes the very same word, though as part of a uniquely African American vernacular (in spite of his mention of an Irish precedent).[5] His own favorite memory of his North Carolina grandmother's use of the term *quare* is her expression "That sho'll is a 'quare' chile" (126), and he introduces the term as a response to the concerns of many African American critics who have rejected the term *queer* because of its predominantly white deployments. While sharing such concerns, Johnson seeks to recuperate the term in a model of queer studies that would situate sexual identities in relation to other categories such as race. To counter *queer*'s whitening tendencies, Johnson seeks "to *quare* queer—to throw shade on its meaning in the spirit of extending its service to 'blackness'" (Johnson and Henderson 7). In Johnson's vision, in short, a *quare* queer studies would also be antiracist.

Important in Johnson's strategy is a sometimes implicit, sometimes explicit connection between *queer* in the contemporary sense and the older *quare*. Such a connection might explain why southern lesbian feminists (or at least southern lesbians with lesbian feminist roots) might differ from their northern counterparts in embracing the term *queer*. Mab Segrest, for example, writes:

> One of the big secrets of Southern humor is eccentricity. If the tragic, grotesque tradition in the South peoples itself with freaks—outcasts punished because they act out the "abnormalcy" of everyone— another tradition coexists here. Southerners have a high tolerance of and appreciation for eccentricity, a knowledge in our heart of hearts that everyone is a little strange. It is from this playful, private sense of strangeness that people maintain sanity and protect one another from the life-destroying institutions and norms to which they give lip service. The eccentric knows the great comic truth: that all humans are peculiarly themselves and deserve the freedom to discover their own forms . . . I am coming to realize how much I am—always have been—queer-identified. Queerness is now becoming a high moral and aesthetic value in my system. (*My Mama's Dead Squirrel* 66)

In this passage, what my parents would call *quare* merges with the post-ACT-UP! *queer* in seemingly seamless ways.

Likewise, although at first glance Wolfe seems to restrict his usage of the word *queer* to the meanings of "odd" or "eccentric," other passages in *Look Homeward, Angel* suggest that *quare* and *queer* may not be as distant as my father's use of the words would lead one to believe. In fact at times Eugene's "quareness" comes dangerously close to threatening his heterosexual masculinity. In a passage prior to the one quoted above, Eugene's sister Helen taunts him in a similar way:

> You little freak—wandering around with your queer dopey face. Your're a regular little Pentland—you funny little freak, you. Everybody's laughing at you. Don't you know that? Don't you? We're going to dress you up as a girl, and let you go around like that. You haven't got a drop of Gant blood in you—papa's practically said as much—you're Greeley all over again; you're queer. Pentland queerness sticking out all over you. (117)

Quareness here is also associated with cross-dressing, so the passage suggests that, in addition to being eccentric, quares might be less than manly. Perhaps this is one reason why it so bothers Eugene to be called queer, more so than simply being called eccentric would seem likely to bother him: "Further, it annoyed and wounded him to be considered 'queer'" (492). In short, Eugene's quareness (and, I would argue, his queerness) comes from a "queer" genealogy, one that almost erases his being stamped with the Name-of-the-Father.

In other words, quareness haunts both the patrilineal family tree and masculinity, and thus it starts to look rather queer, especially when one considers the passage in which Eugene expresses a hint of erotic attraction to male bodies:

> He went to the movies only to examine the teeth and muscles of the hero; he pored over the toothpaste and collar advertisements in the magazines; he went to the shower-rooms at the gymnasium and stared at the straight toes of the young men, thinking with desperate sick pain of his own bunched and crooked ones. He stood naked before a mirror, looking at his long *gaunt* body, smooth and white save for the crooked toes and the terrible spot on his neck—lean, but moulded with delicate and powerful symmetry. (489; emphasis added)

And again we see the abandoned name-of-the-father return in this passage describing a homoerotic gaze.

Southern "Quare"

The importance of this connection between *quare* and *queer,* I would argue, extends far beyond Wolfe's novel to queer southern studies more generally. A lot of work in queer southern *history* has challenged the commonplaces in what one might describe as the master narratives of US lesbian and gay history. In *Men Like That: A Southern Queer History,* about gay life in rural Mississippi, John Howard emphasizes what he calls the three *R*s— race, religion, and the rural—to describe the specificity of southern queerness. The third *R* is perhaps the most crucial to challenging historical master narratives. His description of queer lives in the *rural* South is important because it challenges the essential link between the development of gay communities and urbanization that one sees in many lesbian and gay histories. As a few commentators have pointed out, much of lesbian and gay history is structured like a coming-out narrative. Coming out, as many understand it, would mean moving to a northern city. Queer southern histories, however, challenge this model of lesbian and gay identity.

In "Queering the South: Constructions of Southern/Queer Identity," Donna Jo Smith describes a paradox in relation to what the term *Queer South* conjures up for most non-Southern Americans: "One myth that is particularly southern *and* queer reflects the notion that it's harder to be queer in the South than in the rest of the nation. Southern and non-southern queers alike have internalized this myth to the degree that it has had a significant effect on southern queer experiences" (381). Smith also writes:

> For some, the notion of a "southern queer" is an oxymoron, conjuring up images of a drag queen with a pickup truck and gun rack or of a dyke with big hair and Birkenstocks. For others, the term *southern queer* is redundant: Since the South is already an aberration, what is a southern queer but deviance multiplied? In other words, did Truman Capote really need to tell the world that he was a pervert? After all, he was from south Alabama. (370)

Furthermore, Smith describes why it is important to resist these preconceived notions: "America has long projected its 'Queer Other' onto the

South. And in the national cultural imaginary, definitions of the southern are regularly utilized to maintain myths of American innocence. We should question this North/South binary opposition, because it maintains structures of power that oppress all historically marginalized groups" (378–79). In other words, "Queering the South" has implications that go beyond the borders of the South (if one can speak of the South as having borders). "Queering the South" not only challenges what it means to be southern, but it also challenges what we think it means to be queer in the South, as well as in the United States as a whole. It is not only that queerness makes the South more queer, but we might also think about how the South makes queerness more queer. Furthermore, Smith articulates an antiracist politics of queering the South by "dynamiting the rails," to use Patricia Yaeger's term (34), as well as by unmasking ways in which northern racism hides behind representations of an essentially racist South.

Grimsley's Queer Ghosts

Although Wolfe's novel recalls Eugene's haunted family tree, as well as his rather *quare* position within it, Grimsley's ghosts are more explicitly queer. As the four boys set off on the aforementioned camping trip, the novel explains, "The country thereabouts is haunted with memories of the courtship between the two boys" (110). Indeed, Nathan and Roy first make out in an old cemetery, where members of the Kennicutt family, former plantation owners, are buried. At one point, Roy also informs Nathan that the Kennicutts were "kin to [his] great-grandaddy" (27). Their making out among the remains of ancestors, therefore, queers the family tree in the more contemporary sense. In addition, during the camping trip the boys entertain each other with ghost stories. Roy "tells the story of the Devil's Stamping Ground, a place in the woods where the Devil comes to dance, you can see his hoofprints baked into the ground, and if you sleep too close to the circle, you're never seen again" (116). I, too, read of this story as a boy in books like Nancy Roberts's *An Illustrated Guide to Ghosts and Mysterious Occurrences in the Old North State*, which contains photos and a description of the "actual" Devil's Tramping Ground.[6] Within Grimsley's novel, as within its plot, ghosts often appear as always already citations of a previous ghost story, conjured up through narrative production in much the same way that Wolfe calls his characters to life from the dead pages of the book. In Grimsley as in Wolfe, therefore, ghosts appear primarily as characters in narrative.

The haunted plantation house Roy and Nathan visit is likewise not merely a site but also a story that precedes the visit, a story also related secondhand by Roy:

> My Uncle Heben says it was in a book about North Carolina ghosts. There was a picture of this house. The last full-blood Kennicutt who lived here got killed by one of his slaves, and they cut his head off. So he still walks around the place at night looking for his head." . . . But even so, the boys accept the facts as Roy presents them, that he has an Uncle Heben who once saw a picture of this house. That a head-less ghost is said to roam the grounds, in a story famous enough to have been published in a book. They will sleep tonight in sight of a haunted place. (136–37)

Although the novel does not explicitly say so, one might infer that the master of the haunted plantation fell victim to a sort of slave revolt. The master's ghost, then, returns to remind the living of this violence, and this haunted house, situated in the haunted landscape of a haunted nov-el, is a site where the past is conjured up as a ghostly presence. The ghost of the master decapitated by his slaves returns to remind the living of this violence, and the resulting haunting would be the memory of resistance to slavery kept alive. Ghosts thus serve as manifestations of history creep-ing into the present, histories of oppression and resistance.

On this former plantation, however, ghosts represent the haunting of more than dead individuals. Once inside the abandoned house, the boys see a ghost that produces additional meaning for Nathan:

> A figure in the door. A vaguer shadow. Someone stands there with his legs spread apart. He is sturdy, square-shouldered, like Nathan's Dad when he was younger, like Preacher John Roberts. Like Roy. He is familiar. He makes no sound. He is another blankness of the house, a ghost who could be anyone, living or dead. . . .
>
> And Dad's hand on Nathan's thigh.
>
> The unsteady voice in Nathan's ear whispering. *Do you remember what we did when you were a little boy?*
>
> While overhead the voice of the preacher sails like a wind of itself, *Do you remember what the Lord said unto Abraham?* (161–2).

It is thus through this haunting that the reader discovers that the abuse Nathan has suffered at his father's hands was sexual. Previous vague allusions then become clearer: "Sometimes the look in Roy's eyes reminds Nathan of his own father, of the look in his own father's eyes, but Nathan prefers not to think about that and shuts off the thought before it begins" (4). Or "An image of his father gives the fear. The image comes to Nathan from dangerous places, from territories of memory that Nathan rarely visits" (11).

After the ghost in the plantation house disperses the four boys, Roy and Nathan take advantage of being alone to have sex. When they are caught in the act by Randy and Burke, Roy runs away, and Nathan is raped and presumably killed by Burke (at first also thought to be a ghost). The ghost of the plantation house is also what connects Roy and Nathan's queer love to southern history. This haunting brings into association histories of paternal violence and racial terror as the present backdrop for homophobic violence. The haunted house, therefore, is home to a *variety* of ghosts, ghosts representing not only the history of slavery and racial terror but also sexual secrets and histories of family violence. This haunted site is thus the fertile ground for a very queer love that seems inseparable from the very violence that would prohibit it. As much as his rape by Burke, Nathan's love for Roy is haunted by memories of his father's abuse.

Hauntologies Familial and Collective

In *Dream Boy*, therefore, the political implications of two sorts of ghosts, the haunting associated with sexual secrets and that which represents the return of histories of racist violence, come into conflict, if, that is, one supports, as I do, solidarity between antihomophobic and antiracist criticism. While one might wish to conjure up the ghosts of repressed and marginalized sexualities, conjuring up the racializing violence from the past might have far less positive implications. How might one reconcile such contradictions? Is reconciliation the most productive way to negotiate them? How might ghosts in the family tree come to be seen as having a relation to those of more collective histories? The answers to these questions, I would suggest, might be worked out by turning to the work of the French-language, Hungarian-born psychoanalysts Nicolas Abraham and Maria Torok, who in *L'écorce et le noyau* (1978) [*The Shell and the Kernel: Renewals of Psychoanalysis*], describe the phantom as a manifestation of repressed family secrets (skeletons in the closet, we might say) and provide a means of expanding this relation between hauntology and genealogy.[7]

Abraham, often in collaboration with Torok, devoted much of his life's work to elaborating the interrelated theories of introjection, dual unity, the crypt, and the phantom, the concept of the crypt preceding that of the phantom in their work.[8] The most important distinction between the crypt and the phantom is that the crypt operates at the level of the individual subject whereas the phantom is not only intersubjective but also intergenerational: "The phantom which returns to haunt bears witness to the existence of the dead buried within the other" (*Shell* 175). The most practical elaboration of the crypt can be found in *The Wolf Man's Magic Word: A Cryptonomie* (1976), Abraham and Torok's reading of Freud's *History of an Infantile Neurosis*, the famous case of the Wolf Man. Here they define the crypt in the following way:

> The crypt works in the heart of the Ego as a special kind of Unconscious: Each fragment is conscious of itself and unconscious of the realm "outside the crypt." At once conscious and unconscious: This provides the explanation for the peculiarity of the *intra*symbolic and not *co*symbolic relationships of the *word*. (80)

Or, in *The Shell and the Kernel*:

> The crypt . . . is neither the dynamic unconscious nor the ego of introjections. Rather, it is an enclave between the two, a kind of artificial unconscious, lodged in the very midst of the ego. Such a tomb has the effect of sealing up the semipermeable walls of the dynamic unconscious. (159)

The existence of a crypt is most often signaled by a particular work or cryptonym that gives a peek at what is buried in the crypt. Put differently, the crypt represents a fake return of the repressed, a "false Unconscious: the crypt in the Ego—a false 'return of the repressed,' the action in the Ego of hidden thoughts from the crypt" (*Wolf Man* lxxi).

The encrypted secret par excellence is sexual and involves the "*cryptonymic displacement of a taboo word*" (*Wolf Man* 26), and it is this aspect of Abraham and Torok's theorization of the crypt that has made it attractive to literary critics who have used Abraham and Torok's meticulous analysis of word associations in their reading of Freud as a model applicable to other literary texts (see Rand's introduction and commentary in Abraham and Torok, *Shell*; Rashkin). It is also the crypt that, transmitted to the child by the mother as a result of the period of dual unity during which the child shares the mother's unconscious, results in the phantom. According to Abraham, therefore, not only does the phantom inhabit the family tree but the family tree also provides the structure that allows for the phantom's production. Or, as Nicholas T. Rand writes in his introduction to the English translation of the essay "Notes on the Phantom," "In Abraham's view, the dead do not return, but their lives' unfinished business is unconsciously handed down to their descendants" (Abraham and Torok, *Shell* 167). In this view, ghosts are the psychological manifestations of family secrets—hidden for generations—that return to haunt the present.

Although Abraham's collaborator Maria Torok has argued that "the diverse manifestations of the phantom, which we call *haunting*, are not directly related to instinctual life and are not to be confused with the return of the repressed" (*Shell* 181), we could say that ghosts represent the return of what *others* (namely, our ancestors) have repressed. So phantoms do return, *like* the repressed, thereby serving as a link between past and present in a familial context and resisting the erasure of past secrets from memory. As in the case with the crypt, the secret of illicit sexual relations (and their products) produce the most exemplary phantoms, Abraham and Torok suggest, so how might their sexual phantoms be used to theorize further the histories of violence that leave traces in so many of the ghost stories from my childhood? Illicit sexual relations, after all, are not necessarily more likely to be violent than licit ones.

On the one hand, one must be careful not to equate the phantom à la Abraham and Torok with the ghosts I have described in North Carolina culture: "[W]hat haunts are not the dead, but the gaps left within us by the secrets of others" (*Shell* 171). On the other, Abraham and Torok do occasionally associate metaphorical ghosts with more literal ones (if one can speak of literal ghosts): "The phantoms of folklore merely objectify a metaphor active in the unconscious: the burial of an unspeakable fact *within the love-object*" (172). And the literal (and literary) ghost that has most interested them is that of Hamlet's father in the same Shakespeare play that serves as one of Derrida's main pre-texts in *Specters of Marx*. Abraham even wrote a sixth act as an addition to Shakespeare's *Hamlet*, which (supposedly) lays Hamlet's ghost to rest by reestablishing the rule of the royal family in the person of Hamlet Jr. Yet it is in this sixth act that the role of the psychoanalyst with regard to phantoms becomes clear. In

Hamlet ghosts threaten the social order, and it is the duty of the psycho-analyst to restore that order by laying them to rest. By turning *Hamlet* into a detective story whose crime can be solved through cryptonymic analysis, Abraham reveals the secret that the ghost of Hamlet Sr., as a phantom in the psychoanalytic sense, appears (as in making an appear-ance) in order to hide: "[T]he duel alluded to by Horatio (1.1) between King Hamlet and King Forinbras was rigged and . . . King Hamlet, real-izing that Gertrude (not yet his wife) was in love with Fortinbras, killed the Norwegian ruler with a poisoned sword" (Rashkin 24). The role of the psychoanalyst is to silence ghosts; Abraham and Torok are thus anti-phantom in the sense that they seek to make phantoms disappear, to conjure them away.

One characteristic that unites Abraham and Torok with many other theorizations of haunting is a certain tendency toward metaphorization. Abraham and Torok's ghosts serve as *metaphors* of a prior repression, the traces of family secrets repressed by previous generations. With the exception of Morrison's *Beloved*, literal ghosts rarely haunt the pages of Chambers, Peterson, Gordon, or Abraham and Torok. But even Mor-rison's ghosts are products of literary invention. Can theorizations of haunting account for ghosts of a less metaphorical or less allegorical variety? Is it even possible to speak of a ghost whose haunting could be only literal? Abraham is interested in one more literal, though still lit-erary, ghost, but he can only lay Hamlet Sr.'s ghost to rest by raising another—that of Hamlet Jr.—kicking and screaming, if you will, from the dead. Although Hamlet rises from the dead in Abraham's version, he still thinks he is dead. If it is the work of ghosts to keep secrets—indeed to lie—in order to trick the living into turning them away from the path toward truth, toward resolution, toward laying these very ghosts to rest, how are we to know that the risen Hamlet is not yet another ghost conjured up to keep other secrets? How are we to know that Hamlet is not more than a mere representation in Gertrude's eyes of her desire for Fortinbras Sr.? How do we know that the ghost of Hamlet Sr. is not reproduced as the ghost of Hamlet Jr.? How do we know that he is not Fortinbras's bastard son? Ghosts that lie, in other words, are perhaps the only ones telling the truth.

The ghosts of this violence return until other readers produce politi-cal interpretations worthy of their hauntings, until they unlock their crypts, to use Abraham and Torok's analogy for the goal of a particu-lar model of psychoanalysis. In *The Writing of History*, Michel de Certeau describes history writing as necessarily involving the kind of silencing implied in such ghost stories: "Writing speaks of the past only in order to inter it. Writing is a tomb in the double sense of the word in that, in the very same text, it both honors and eliminates" (101). History is, to use another of Abraham and Torok's term, cryptophorous, and interment is a means of silencing. History, like the ego, then, has its crypts, wherein the secrets it cannot avow reside. At the political level, therefore, ghosts might be read as manifestations of repressed histories of violence and exploitation. As such, silencing such ghosts would only be to participate in the very violence that gave rise to them. This chapter thus attempts to reverse the metaphor that haunts Abraham and Torok. Whereas they think ghosts can be laid to rest, we can further theorize the intersection between Abraham and Torok, on the one hand, and de Certeau, on the other, by underscoring the importance of conjuring *up* ghosts, not conjuring them *away*. In other words, ghosts, even as defined psychologically by Abraham and Torok, can represent political secrets just as well as familial ones; in this sense, ghosts in the family tree are allegories of history, of what history has repressed. They are the repressed political secrets transmitted from generation to generation.

Abraham and Torok's talking cure of conjuring away phantoms is therefore ripe for deconstruction or, we might say, haunts deconstruction as much as the ghosts of Hamlet and Marx. For more connects Derrida to Abraham and Torok than their mutual interest in the ghosts of *Hamlet*. In addition to his introduction to their work, his analysis of Genet in *Glas* involves a kind of cryptonymic reading, which they develop in that book. With Derrida, then, we can read Abraham and Torok at yet another allegorical level; in fact, having queered Derrida in chapter 4, we can use him to queer Abraham and Torok in turn. When the ghost that represents the return of a repressed family secret is read not just as the particular secret of an individual family but also as the secret of the Family, those lurking within structures such as those of kinship and the family tree, haunting becomes more than a psychological phenomenon; it becomes an ideological one whose narrative form is that of allegory. Abraham and Torok's ghosts might thus be thought of not as an abnormality within a particular family but as products of a kinship structure that relies on the very abnormality it represses. One might even discern the seeds of this understanding of Family that queering Abraham and Torok gives access to in Derrida himself; it is, after all, the ghost of the father that haunts Derrida, the ghost of Hamlet's father and the spirit of Marx as a sort of forefather for deconstruction.

Queering the Ghosts of Racial Terror

When, in *Dream Boy*, Nathan's father shows signs of falling back into a pattern of abuse, Nathan hides in the cemetery, studies, and even sleeps there. It is easy to see how the ghostly memories of gay desire and love might constitute a queer haunting, even the southern comfort zone of a ghostly cemetery that protects Nathan from his father's violence. But the ghosts of slavery, paternal abuse, racial terror, how might they figure into a queer relation to the past? The answer to this question requires a brief and final detour back to Wolfe to understand the racial politics behind the construction of white heterosexual masculinity in opposition to its queer and racialized Others. By reading Grimsley and Wolfe against each other, then, we can also understand how Wolfe's ghosts are also conjurations of racial violence in a further queering of his family tree. In such a reading, the ghosts of the novel might thus be said to represent the others of white masculinity, ghosts that constantly haunt it, thereby recalling histories of racial terror and gendered violence.

The critical hubris I wish to embrace in such a return is indicated in/ by the title of Mab Segrest's *Memoir of a Race Traitor*. Like me, Segrest is white and southern; unlike me, she comes from a southern family with a pedigree, that is, with a "distinguished" and relatively complete genealogy. Yet this family tree has its own ghosts. A large part of her racial treason consists of bringing out of the closets of the past the history of her ancestors' participation in acts of racist violence. For example, she describes how her great-grandfather William Cobb "fought Osceola in Florida in the Seminole Wars" (101) and therefore participated in the Euro-American genocide of Native Americans, literal and cultural. Her grandfather "shot and killed Sammy Younge, a Black student activist" (2). She offers this second bit of her family's history of racist violence in the opening essay of the collection of her autobiographical essays on her experiences of anti-Klan organizing in North Carolina as a white southern lesbian: "Osceola's Head." Osceola, Segrest explains "became a leader in a guerrilla insurgency of Seminoles and escaped slaves" (4) who fought Andrew Jackson's troops in Florida until his capture. In the essay entitled "Robeson, Bloody Robeson" (103–32), Segrest links her great-grandfather's participation in the repression of Native American resistance to European colonization and genocide with the history of the Lumbee Indians in the North Carolina county named in the title. This essay details a long history of officially tolerated, if not sanctioned, violence against the Lumbee, as well as their rich and equally long history of resistance to this violence (including armed opposition to the Confederate army).

The title *Memoir of a Race Traitor* refers to reactions to her antiracist activism on the part of not only Klansmen but also some of her own kinfolk: "My Klan folk had me spotted: a race traitor. Even in this beginning, the 'I' of memoir betrays, when this story belongs to many people, many of whom in large ways or small do not agree about the facts I assemble, much less their interpretation" (4). And one of the key tropes that characterize her relation to her own whiteness is that of haunting. Indeed, ghosts are a metaphor she uses on several occasions. In spite of conjuring up ghosts of a violent past in order to conjure away such racism from her own conception of white lesbian feminist identity, haunting also plays a more positive role in asserting herself as a race traitor: "I had become a woman haunted by the dead. / I was haunted by people like Julian Pierce" (127).[9] But haunting is a metaphor for the memory of not just the targets of racist violence but also its perpetrators, and haunting even refers to her memories of her own mother, who had told Segrest stories that she came to consider potentially offensive to Segrest.

I would suggest that all family histories might be considered similarly haunted, that all roots are likewise haunted. Given that the US South is still haunted by its history of slavery, how does a southern white gay man reclaim origins in a way that does not glorify this history of racial violence? In *Slaves in the Family*, Edward Ball conjures up the ghosts of his family's history of owning slaves by debunking its oral tradition of remembering forebears as benign masters. In so doing, Ball uncovers not only histories of violence but also the interracial couplings that produced the distant African American cousins he discovered during the course of returning to his prominent Charleston roots. By bringing skeletons out of his family's closet, Ball has "blackened" his family tree of sorts, which earned him the anger of a large portion of (the white side of) his family. In contrast, many of Ball's African American relatives welcomed his efforts; indeed, as Haley *claimed* to have done, Ball was able to establish some of their family trees all the way back to an African ancestor pinpointed in a specific African region. These genealogical findings would have been inconceivable without the research of a large number of his African American cousins, research that had been, in large part, inspired by Haley.[10] No matter how many ghosts one finds in the family tree, conjuring them up does not repair the economic disparities that persist more than 145 years after abolition. But can they debunk the myths that have enabled these disparities to continue?

I find it hard to recognize myself in Ball's portrait of the South. In spite of his efforts to reveal the injustices of slavery, he is not immune to romanticizing his family's antebellum past, and his ability to rattle off the genealogies of white family members makes his writing more akin to European aristocratic genealogies than the history of my maternal grandmother and her Efird sisters. As I was growing up, the Efird dinner (our expression for the annual family reunion—my only family reunion—which occurred just before Christmas) was not only the occasion for eating the best southern food I have ever had; it also exemplified for me the meaning of *family*. My paternal grandparents (whom we only visited once a year just after Christmas, even though they lived only two and a half hours away across the South Carolina border) seemed distant in comparison. Indeed, my mother always punctuated the end of these visits with a familiar refrain: "I sure am glad we didn't raise our young'uns in South Carolina." Even the relatives on my maternal grandfather's side of the family (from whose lands came the small plot on which my parents built our first house) seemed like aliens for the most part. Home was the smell of southern cooking and the sound of my grandmother and her sisters chatting while their brothers remained silent. So strong were the kinship links that connected woman to woman among the Efirds that my grandmother's sisters-in-law were much more a part of the family than her brothers, even after these brothers died. Indeed, even after her sisters-in-law remarried, their new husbands were brought into the family. Though the most official version of the Efird family history traces its genealogy along patrilineal lines, when I was growing up, the Efird name was only significant as far as I could trace it back along matrilineal ones.

Remembering the Efird family tree as Ball remembers his constitutes for me a crucial component of queering the South, which should also bring to the fore a specific kind of glitch in African American family trees: the denial of a patronymic to slaves in the United States and the subsequent selection of one after abolition. Ball also counters the myth that most ex-slaves took their masters' names, at least in his family's context: "The Balls . . . thought the appearance of black families called Ball would diminish their status. An equal worry seemed to be that masters feared that darker families named Ball might be taken as sons and daughters of whites" (352). The miscegenation white Balls fear others would suspect had already been occurring for centuries, even if it had

274 QUEER ROOTS FOR THE DIASPORA

been concealed in a specific kind of closet central to southern constructions of race and sexuality. The Ball name, carefully preserved through centuries of genealogies, thus turns out to be just as haunted as the Efird name, though in its own way. Examining various family trees (including Haley's) in comparison therefore opens the doors of a variety of closets. Ball uncovers the story of a distant African American cousin who shot a man whose wife she was in love with (293). This story, carefully preserved by black oral tradition, comes into the white Ball family tree to queer it at the same time as it blackens it. How many other queer ghosts lurk within his family tree, ghosts whose stories he failed to tell? In a way, then, the fears that pursue Ball's white family members are literalized by the ghosts that haunt Wolfe's racist masculinities.

Season 3, episode 12, of the American version of *Who Do You Think You Are?* (2012) features Paula Deen and her teary reaction to the discovery that one of her ancestors was a pro-secessionist politician who owned thirty-five slaves. Situated in relation to the controversy of her use of the N-word, which resulted the following year in canceled shows and endorsements, this episode drives home the point that the notion of roots continues to be of contemporary concern and relevance. Yet it also serves to caution that uncovering ghosts of racial oppression in one's own (white) family tree does not necessarily lead to antiracist models of white identity. Indeed, read alongside Oprah's tears, discussed in the introduction to this volume, Deen's seem to repeat tragedy as a farce. Nonetheless, although the Efird family tree (especially my connection to it) and Eugene Gant's queer genealogy seem a far stretch from Paula Deen's and Edward Ball's family histories, I would argue that much can be gained by comparing them. Like Segrest's family tree, my own hosts its fair share of racial terrorists. Oscar Agburn Efird fondly speaks of the plantation of his grandfather and of the "tragedy" of its occupation by Union soldiers (vii). In the following passage, he even justifies certain past actions of the Klan:

> During reconstruction days, Reverend Adam Efird was a prominent advisor of the Ku Klux Klan in his community. Bruner Efird, son of Reverend Adam Efird, told his son, the author, a number of times how he, a mere boy five or six years of age, remembered that frequently, about twilight, groups of men wearing white sheets would ride to the grove in front of the house. Adam would go out and confer with them for some time and return to the home. Let neither his descendants, nor his relatives, nor his friends be dismayed at these incidents. At

that time, the Ku Klux Klan had among its leaders and members the best citizens of the white South, and was entirely different from the Ku Klux Klan of the present day. During Reconstruction Days in the South, law enforcement had broken down completely. In those days the Klan was necessary to protect the virtue of the white women from the recently freed slaves, and to protect the community and its property from the scalawags and carpetbaggers. (132)

The history of slavery thus haunts the present of Efirds whose ancestors did not own slaves in part because slavery was surely a factor in the accumulation of wealth that allowed Efirds of certain branches to profit from the labor of their distant relatives, as I discuss later in this chapter.

Wolfe's Queer Ghosts

But first, I would like to return to Wolfe one final time because, in a way, the fears that pursue Ball's white family members are literalized by the ghosts that haunt Wolfe's racist masculinities. Of all the parts of *Look Homeward, Angel*, none reveals the gendered politics of race and the racial politics of gender and sexuality more than chapter 22, which describes Eugene's experience as a newspaper delivery boy: "He was given the Niggertown route—the hardest and least profitable of all" (244). Before he even begins this route, he has heard talk from other paper boys about the difficulty of collecting money owed on subscriptions along it. For example, "Number 3 . . . had the Niggertown route" (138). Instead of collecting his money, however, Number 3 "takes it out in Poon-Tang. . . . A week's subscription free for a dose" (138). At another point, a boy with a grin on his face is accused, "You've been on a Poon-Tang Picnic in Niggertown" (145). Although *poontang*, is not a uniquely southern word, I encountered it far more frequently in the South of my boyhood, in which it was usually uttered in male homosocial settings because it was considered inappropriate in mixed company. This name for female sexual organs just as often refers metonymically to sexual acts committed with them, and although it did not imply a racial specificity in situations in which I heard it as a boy, in Wolfe's novel it is used almost exclusively in reference to black women in a way that reduces their femininity to sexual organs and acts as defined by white male access to them.

It is in this context that Eugene begins his paper route, work that requires him to rise early each morning. The description of waking so early (quoted above) is also where the novel connects white talk about black sexuality with the kinds of haunting I have described:

> Waken, ghost-eared boy, but into darkness. Waken, phantom, O into us. Try, try, O try the way. Open the wall of light. Ghost, ghost, who is the ghost? O lost. Ghost, ghost, who is the ghost? O whisper-tongued laughter. Eugene! Eugene! Here, O here, Eugene. Here, Eugene. The way is here, Eugene. Have you forgotten? The leaf, the rock, the wall of light. Lift up the rock, Eugene, the leaf, the stone, the unfound door. Return, return. . . . Brother, O brother! They shot down the brink of darkness, gone on the wind like bullets. O lost, and by the wind grieved, ghost, come back again. (244–45)

Even after he has left home for work, the novel describes "the ghostly ring of his own feet" (249). And in the following description of going along this paper route, this ghostly sleepiness is brought back to the question of black sexuality as he moves "past the stabled torpor of black sleepers, past all the illicit loves, the casual and innumerable adulteries of Niggertown" (247). It is not long, however, before interracial sex talk begins to include Eugene in its couplings, real or imagined. Coworker Jennings Ware, for example, offers advice concerning one of Eugene's new customers, whom the former labels "a High Yaller": "'She's a pretty good old girl,' he said. 'You've got a right to a few dead-heads. Take it out in trade'" (247).[11] The next customer Jennings talks about implicates Eugene as a potential sexual partner even further:

> "But, oh man" he said, after a moment. "If you want Jelly Roll you've come to the right place. I ain't kidding you!"
> "With—with niggers?" Eugene whispered, moistening his dry lips. Jennings Ware turned his red satirical face on him.
> "You don't see any Society Belles around here do you?" he said.
> "Are niggers good?" Eugene asked in a small dry voice.
> "Boy!" The word blew out of Jennings Ware's mouth like an explosion. He was silent for a moment.
> "There ain't nothing better," he said. (248)

While the other delivery boys treat such matters jokingly, even with pride, Eugene's reaction is one of abjection. And nowhere is this abjection more violently obvious than in the infamous "Jelly Roll" passage. It concerns Eugene's customer Ella Corpening, whom the novel describes as "a mulatto of twenty-six years, a handsome woman of Amazonian proportions, with smooth tawny skin" (251). When he goes to collect her subscription fees, she is unable to pay:

> "You come roun' in de mawnin'," she said hopefully. "I'll have some-
> thin' fo' yuh, sho. I'se waitin' fo' a white gent'man now. He's goin' gib
> me a dollah." . . .
> "What's—what's he going to give you a dollar for?" he muttered,
> barely audible.
> "Jelly Roll," said Ella Corpening.
> He moved his lips twice, unable to speak. She got up from her
> chair. "What yo' want?" she asked softly. "Jelly Roll?"
> "Want to see—to see!" he gasped. (252)

In typical Wolfe fashion, dialogue is transcribed here in a way that exaggerates differences in white and black vernaculars with deviations from the standard marked in a pronounced way in black speech even when almost identical ones in white speech are not.[12] Interestingly, in spite of the exaggerated deviation of black speech from the norm of literary English, it is Eugene who becomes inarticulate here. Nonetheless, once inside her house, he issues his requests:

> Far off, he listened to the ghost of his own voice.
> "Take off your clothes."
> Her skirt fell in a ring about her feet. She took off her starched
> waist. In a moment, save for her hose, she stood naked before him.
> Her breath came quickly, her full tongue licked across her mouth.
> "Dance!" he cried. "Dance!" (253)

Whereas the novel says of his pursuit of customers behind in their payments, "He sought these phantoms fruitlessly for weeks" (251), here *he* is the one who once again becomes ghostly, and this in an unbearable tension between desire and disgust. Furthermore, in spite of her compliance with his request, she does not offer herself up as spectacle before his gaze; rather, she draws him into *her* embrace to dance *with* him:

> Her powerful yellow hands gripped his slender arms round like brace-
> lets. She shook him to and fro slowly, fastening him tightly against her
> pelt.
> He strained back desperately against the door, drowning in her
> embrace.
> "Get-'way nigger. Get-'way," he panted thickly.

Slowly she released him: without opening her eyes, moaning, she slid back as if he had been a young tree. She sang, in a wailing minor key, with unceasing iteration:

"Jelly Roll! Je-e-e-ly Roll!"—

her voice falling each time to a low moan.

Her face, the broad column of her throat, and her deep-breasted torso were rilled with sweat. He fumbled blindly for the door, lunged across the outer room and, gasping, found his way into the air. (253)

He "drowns" in her embrace, which threatens to subsume him, and he responds to this embrace by pulling himself away violently as if the embrace were not merely physical but rather also threatened to dissolve his whiteness. He responds, in other words, by asserting her racial difference. In contrast with the curiosity he expresses after Jennings first uses the term *Jelly Roll*, faced with the actual possibility of interracial sex, Eugene recoils with revulsion even as Ella continues to taunt him.

"Jelly Roll," that object of fear and desire, like a "Poon-Tang Picnic," equates interracial sex with food. In fact, as a boy, I always assumed *poon* was an abbreviation of *pudding*, whose pronunciation (when pronounced with an elided *G* and a glottal stop instead of dental consonants) it resembles quite a bit. Web searches on the term, in fact, reveal that I am not alone in making this assumption. If for Julia Kristeva the experience of abjection involves an attempt on the part of the Self to expel what is actually an intrinsic part of the Self, if, as the expression goes, "you are what you eat," Eugene runs the risk here of becoming what he abjects and rejects, what he has almost "eaten" but instead expels from himself. Instead, the novel sublimates the object of his desire as he disseminates the printed word: "He knew all the sorrow of those who carry weight; he knew, morning by morning, the aerial ecstasy of release" (248). In this sexualized description of lightening his "load" of undelivered papers, he becomes "a lord of darkness" (248). Between Jennings's description of the availability of "Jelly Roll" and his own opportunity to taste it for himself, his sister Helen says, "What's wrong with him? Is it the Pentland crazy streak coming out?" (250). The near shattering of his white masculinity is thus associated with that queer/quare ghost in his patrilineal family tree, the one of his being "tainted" with a matrilineage that likewise threatens his right to the patronymic.

My point here is not to retrieve these passages (or even the novel as a whole) from accusations of racism. While it might be possible to engage in a debate about whether the novel shares its characters' racism, this is likewise not a debate I care to enter. (The slippage between the use of the N-word between dialogue and narration would make even this debate difficult.) Rather, along the lines of what has been called whiteness studies and the critical moves I would associate with critical race theory, I want to suggest that these passages in Wolfe might become fodder for a queer critique of southern white masculinity. Furthermore, the connection between *quare* and *queer* I have suggested is closely connected to the racial queering of white masculinity in Wolfe. This connection becomes more explicit in a passage that describes the aftermath of the guilt brought on by witnessing school buddies bullying a Jewish boy while his desire to conform (not to mention his lack of physical strength) prevented him from objecting:

> He never forgot the Jew; he always thought of him with shame. But it was many years before he could understand that the sensitive and feminine person, bound to him by the secret and terrible bonds of his own dishonor, had in him nothing perverse, nothing unnatural, nothing degenerate. He was as much like a woman as a man. That was all. There is no place among the Boy Scouts for the androgyne—it must go to Parnassus. (196)

In counterdistinction to other passages in which characters openly express their anti-Semitism, here Eugene becomes united with the object of his disgust much as he does in the "Jelly Roll" chapter. Only here, it is not just his Protestant whiteness that is questioned but also his masculinity.

The Ghosts of History

To allow Wolfe's queer ghost of racial violence to haunt my own family tree, I return one final time to the oral culture of Stanly County, North Carolina. As part of "rereading" my past through the ghost stories that nourished it, I also read for the first time a ghost story whose cast of characters includes an Efird family. "The Ghost of Jezebel" tells the story of Isaac Efird, a child laborer in a cotton mill who is chased by the ghost of a sheep murdered by his forebears (Morgan, "Ghost"). This varmint (as animal spirits are sometimes called) had killed Ishmael Efird (from an earlier generation) because he had been forced by his brothers to mistreat it as part of their own mistreatment of him. Through a bit of ingenuity, Isaac's family foils the varmint by tricking it into mistaking a dummy for Isaac, whose resemblance to Ishmael is what conjured up the ghost once again. When Jezebel butts the dummy into the water, thinking she has killed the one who wronged her, she is appeased and disappears forever.

I happened upon this story as upon a hidden treasure, not so different from the gold protected by ghosts in the stories of pirates who, in order to keep the location of their gold a secret, killed the associate(s) who helped them bury it. Yet I was still haunted by the question of the real. Was this a "real" nuclear family? I looked for it in *The History and Genealogy of the Efird Family*, but, while Old Testament names such as Ishmael and Isaac were quite common among Efirds, there was no Leyland Efird (Isaac's father in the story) in the family tree. Was the story an authentic product of local oral tradition? Like the other ghost stories discussed here, this one was collected by local journalist and amateur folklorist Fred T. Morgan. He published many of his stories in the county paper when I was a kid. Does the fact that I can remember some of them authenticate their circulation by means of oral transmission? Which comes first, here, the written version or the oral one? Were these even the most important questions to resolve? I came to bracket the question of the real as I learned (following Abraham and Torok) to do in the case of ghosts. Over the course of this project, folks back home have sometimes asked me whether I believe in ghosts, whether I think ghosts "really" exist. One of the advantages of Abraham and Torok's explanation is that it shifts the question of the real away from the ghost itself toward the ghostly *phenomenon* in the etymological sense of the work, that is, as an appearance, read apparition. When the more pertinent question becomes "Do folks 'really' see ghosts?" I think we have to agree that they do.

Ultimately, I came to realize that the "truth" told by "The Ghost of Jezebel" lies less in the accuracy of its representation of the Efird family tree than in its connection to the historical context in which the branches of this tree have unfolded. Isaac lives on what is locally known as a "mill hill," a "village" of houses for workers owned by the bosses as part of a system of economic exploitation that ensured obedience by granting bosses the power to evict their workers. My maternal grandmother and her sisters were the first generation (in their branch of the Efird family tree) to leave the farm and work in such textile mills. My mother's first years were spent in a house on a mill hill known as Wiscassett Hill. At the age of four, she was evicted with my grandparents because, although my grandmother was still employed by the mill, my grandfather had quit his job to start a business hauling brick and asphalt. Because "the man of the house" had betrayed his employer, the family no longer had the right to live there. The other mill hill in Albemarle, North Carolina, was formerly known as Efird Hill. In fact, the mill where Isaac Efird works in "The Ghost of Jezebel" is located on the property once owned by his great-grandfather, which suggests that his family must live on Efird or Wiscassett Hill as well. The "real" John Solomon Efird, his father Irenus Polycarp Efird, and J. W. Cannon (who founded Cannon Mills) opened Efird Mills, the first in Stanly County, in 1896. "J.S. Efird and J.W. Cannon started Wiscassett Mills in 1898" (Sharpe and Pepper 64; see also Efird 464). Jezebel's ghost returns to remind the living of the repressed memories of a son mistreated by his brothers, but because of its biblical references in the names of Isaac and Ishmael (as well as their diasporic implications), it also recalls the disinheritance of one son in favor of the other. Jezebel, then, is not just the ghost of a sacrificial sheep; she also tells the story of how one branch of the Efird family tree became part of the local ruling class by living off the labor of its "disinherited" brethren, such as the members of my grandmother's branch, a disinheritance conspicuously absent from the family history written by Oscar Agburn Efird.

Furthermore, Jezebel is not the only ghost that recalls this history of oppression. In "Ghostly Happenings at YMCA? Employees Learn to Accept 'Strange' Incidents" (2000), Morgan describes a series of unexplainable incidents occurring after hours at the Stanly County Family YMCA (formerly called the Wiscassett Memorial YMCA): loud crashes, an "errant elevator" (1A) that makes strange trips with no one inside to press the buttons, lights turning themselves on and off, the clothes dryer operating by itself, the turnstile clicking, footsteps, shadows, all without setting off the alarm as any late-night human intruder would. Employees have begun to refer to the author of these incidents as "Freddi, the friendly ghost" (3A). In his effort to explain the ghost story, Morgan relates the robbery and murder of L. W. "Dad" Watkins by John Gray and Carl Sweatte, who "hack[ed] off his head, arms, and legs . . . [and] placed these body parts in a burlap bag. . . . Later, they placed the burlap bag and its grisly contents in the hot furnace of the old Wiscassett School, which stood on the corner exactly where the older part of the Stanly County Family YMCA stands today" (3A).[13] I, however, would propose an alternative explanation. When I was a child, one summer at a day camp sponsored by the YMCA we were given the option of visiting the supposedly haunted upper floors of the YMCA building, which, we were told, was formerly a funeral parlor. I, of timid nature, opted out, but my pals were treated to a ghostly spectacle, performed no doubt by the camp counselors and/or other YMCA employees. I did tell my grandmother about this event, and when I got to the part about the YMCA being in a building formerly occupied by a funeral parlor, she had a rather strongly adverse reaction: she was a mill worker at Wiscassett when the YMCA was built, a funeral parlor never existed on that site, and their "donations" to the YMCA were deducted from their salaries without their consent. My own "ghost story" obviously conjured up the resentment still harbored thirty years after this extortion.

My reading of Freddi and Jezebel (like that of Booger Hollar) thus adds a layer of political meaning to Abraham and Torok's theorization of the phantom. It takes us from family past to economic history, indeed makes family genealogy an allegory of history *tout court*. Though tentative as an explanation, Morgan's narration of the murder of "Dad" Watkins is important because a ghost story that does not offer a cause or root of the symptom constituted by the ghostly phenomenon is somehow incomplete. The traditional ghost story thus explicitly contains its own interpretation at a certain level (the root of the haunting, the individual act of violence that returns with each apparition). Yet this explicitly articulated interpretation can itself be read as an allegory for more collective acts of violence. Sometimes this allegorical level is suggested literally in the ghost story. When Jezebel reappears, collective rumors point a finger at the company as bearing a certain responsibility: "Great alarm stirred the people. Couldn't the mill company do something? Couldn't the law do something?" (67). The use of free indirect discourse here obfuscates authorship of the assignation of blame in a stylistic parallel of the very keeping of secrets Abraham and Torok designate as the cause of ghostly phenomena. Furthermore, Jezebel is the name once used to refer to the archetypal promiscuous slave woman (see White 27–61). In addition to telling the story of class oppression within a single family tree, therefore, "The Ghost of Jezebel" also alludes to racial injustice and the history of slavery.

In fact, one might argue that "The Ghost of Jezebel" actually links the economic exploitation of the cotton mills to that of the institution of slavery. A familiar story about the rise of the New South (like a phoenix from its ashes), the story that emerges, for example, from a visit to the Museum of the New South in Charlotte, North Carolina, tells how, on the foundation of an agricultural society based on cotton raised and gathered by slaves, the Piedmont region of the middle South was industrialized through the development of the textile industry, which then provided the capital with which Charlotte became the banking center that it is today. Such museums frequently also promulgate another myth of the post-civil-rights-movement South, that it has risen above a dark past marred by racial violence to retain a distinctive regional identity not founded on nostalgia for antebellum institutions. The ghost of Jezebel, then, returns to remind us that there is more of a connection between Adam Efird (Oscar Agburn Efird's plantation- and slave-owning, Klan-supporting grandfather—personification of the Old South) and John Solomon Efird (the New South capitalist) than these myths would have us believe. In fact, John Solomon's father, Irenus Polycarp, owned a plantation as well, and the grist mill and cotton gin (which might be understood as the origin of his foray into textile manufacturing) were complementary ventures to that of running a plantation (Efird 464).[14] In fact, this plantation was only half a mile from the place where Booger Hollar Road becomes Efird Road.

As part of my rereading of ghost stories from my childhood, rediscovering once familiar stories, and discovering new ones for the first time, I found one even closer to home than Booger Hollar. "The Musical Ghost of Rocky River" tells the tale of Flaubert Greene, a musician who played at Rocky River Springs, a popular nineteenth-century resort for whose waters Aquadale, my hometown, was named. I visited the ruins of this resort as a child; they were only about half a mile from my house. The springs there, each high in its own mineral content, were believed to have therapeutic properties, but they went dry when greedy owners, desirous of filling swimming pools with their waters, used dynamite in the attempt to increase an insufficient natural flow. (This [hi]story itself comes back from my childhood as a morality tale with its own class implications.) Flaubert Greene, as the story goes, was inspired by voices coming from

the point where Alligator Branch empties into Rocky River. There the surface swirled and eddied over a suckhole with a depth that had never been probed. Early white settlers in the area said Indians claimed alligators and shad from the Atlantic Ocean, 175 miles away, once infested the creek and that an Indian maiden had drowned herself here in heartbreak for her slain lover. There was talk that the Indians gave some of their departed brethren a headstart toward the Happy Hunting Grounds via the suckhole.

Young people from the resort often hiked down the scenic trail to the Indian Hole. (Morgan, *Haunted Uwharries* 9–10)

After the musician becomes more and more obsessed with the musical inspiration flowing from this source, one day friends arrive too late to prevent him from being sucked into the hole himself. They hear the voice of his former beloved, who previously suffered the same fate. It is said that those with an ear for music can still hear the music of Flaubert Greene coming from Indian Hole.

Like Jezebel, the musical ghost of Rocky River also brings back not only the violence of an individual slaying but also that of the cultural and literal genocide committed by Europeans against Native Americans, a genocide that marks the very foundation of American nation build-ing. After all, stories about "Indians" constitute an important subgenre of ghost stories. Booger Hollar has taught me to understand such ghost stories as giving me access to another version of the history I learned through their more "official" counterparts. The fact that Anglo readers of these stories use them to satisfy an exoticist pleasure that associates Native American culture with the mysterious and (today) a New Age spir-ituality, the fact that Anglo tellers of the stories use them to reproduce denials of genocide in no way eliminates their allegorical significance. In the case of another important part of Grimsley's novel's haunted land-scape, for example,[15] the Indian Mound Roy shows to Nathan, the his-tory of violence goes back even further, situating human bondage in a territory expropriated through genocidal means at the very founding of America. They also make love on the Indian Mound, and memories of the latter haunt Nathan's day-to-day life: "In the submersion of home, Nathan returns again and again to the image of Roy's body on the Indian Mound, lost and bewildered under the power of Nathan's mouth" (44).[16]

When structures such as the family tree can be thought of as haunt-ed, and Booger Hollar can be read against the violence of heterosexual kinship structures, the definition of *heterosexuality* itself—which requires repressing its Other, sometimes with the use of physical violence—is haunted. From the histories of class and racial oppression allegorized in "The Ghost of Jezebel," we can then read it at a further allegorical level as telling a story about the violence inherent in the Family itself, Fam-ily being a key component of the institution of heterosexuality. Booger Hollar is a queer site, then, because it is here that the secret of Family, the violence on which the Family is founded, the violence that must be forgotten for the family to be institutionalized as a normative structure, returns to haunt. *Queer Roots* thus engages in a further queering of Der-ridean hauntology by conjuring up the haints that represent the violence kept out of the family tree as a representation of the kinship structuring the normative family. From the role of violence in ghost stories, we can thus return "real" ghosts, as well as the ghost of Marxist politics, to Derrida's hauntology.

As a child, "Don't let the boogers gitcha!" served as a more vivid equivalent of "Sleep tight, don't let the bed bugs bite!" The *OED* suggests that the two expressions might be etymologically connected, as *bug* and *booger* are.[17] For me, boogers could only come from one direction, the woods behind our house, the very woods I knew would take me to Rocky River Springs were I not afraid of getting lost and were there not more certain ways of getting there. In fact, during a brief period, I was visited at night by strange lights outside the window in my bedroom that looked out onto these woods. For a while, I left my curtains open so I could see them. Later I shut them to shut out the lights and finally shut out the memory of them, which returns only as I write these lines. As I have conceived and reconceived this project and worked toward its completion, the radical roots of *Queer Roots* have returned from my past like so many ghosts to haunt me once again. These ghosts, along with many others, have taken over this project as if this book, too, were a haunted house. I have made my peace with these haints, made my peace as many a proprietor of houses haunted has been forced to do. In fact, I have come to cherish the unsettling forces these hauntings arouse and become impassioned with unearthing the meaning they conjure up from the past. I thus end this chapter (and this book) by conjuring up Jezebel once again, Jezebel the essence (in the hauntological sense) of who I am.

Notes

✦ ✦ ✦

Introduction

Parts of the introduction, as well as other parts of the book, were previously published as "Queering Roots, Queering Diaspora." *Rites of Return: Diaspora Poetics and the Politics of Memory.* Ed. Marianne Hirsch and Nancy K. Miller. Copyright © Columbia University Press, 2011. Reprinted with permission of the publisher.

1. Cf. Axel, who adapts Anderson's concept to the key terms of diaspora studies.

2. For similar statements, see Haley, "Black History," "My Search," and "My Furthest-Back Person"; Fraser.

3. The concept of "structures of violence" is Spivak's and is related to what she calls *epistemic violence,* a term referring to "a complicity between violence and discourse," "the relationship between epistemological phenomena and other structures of violence," and even "the violence of writing" (*Post-colonial* 36).

4. Although he is not a "member" of the group that others and I call black British cultural studies, Clifford does carefully outline its importance in relation to diaspora studies.

5. In parallel with queer diaspora studies, a body of work has emerged that examines the gendered aspects of diaspora. See, for example, Jacqueline Nassy Brown's "Black Liverpool," which offers a preview of her *Dropping Anchor* and counters the male-only space of Gilroy's ship through the anthropology of a port where it dropped anchor, that port city being a space that includes both male sailors and the women they leave behind upon setting sail. See also Spivak, "Diasporas"; DeLoughrey; Gunning, Hunter, and Mitchell; Campt and Thomas.

6. A year after Gopinath's dissertation, Lawrence La Fountain-Stokes also used the term *queer diaspora* in his dissertation, "Culture, Representation, and the Puerto Rican Queer Diaspora," published in 2009 as *Queer Ricans: Cultures and Sexualities in the Diaspora.*

7. For other examples, see Manalansan; Braziel; Allen.

8. Gopinath refers to the collection in her dissertation as *Homosexuality in Motion: Gay Diasporas and Queer Peregrinations* (136n15).

9. For example, see Butler, K. A section in Safran is entitled "Diasporas in Comparison" (84–90), and the conclusion to Cohen contains a section entitled "Comparing Diasporas" (180–87).

10. *En retour,* the expression Spivak translates as "reciprocally," might also be translated as "in retrospect" (*De la grammatologie* 90).

11. What I mean by suggesting that western queers or queer theory could stand a little more queering will become clearer throughout the course of this study, but an important part of queering the supposedly already queer will involve challenging its western and Euro- or Anglocentric biases.

12. This conversation began in 1976 with Derrida's introduction to Abraham and Torok's *The Wolf Man's Magic Word: A Cryptonymy.* In 1977 Derrida continued with "Me—Psychoanalysis: An Introduction to the Translation of 'The Shell and the Kernel' by Nicolas Abraham."

13. I have Ross Chambers to thank for this point.

14. In addition to the writers discussed in this section, I would cite Ronell; Castle; Delvaux; Rayner; Cho; Rashkin.

15. See Heath 99. Spivak stated in "In a Word," "I don't know the Heath passage, so I can't contextualize that one" (154). Yet it is possible to map a chain of citations through which Heath's assertion is progressively attributed by association and retroactively to Spivak as well. In *Essentially Speaking* (1989), Diana Fuss would repeat Jardine's claims without questioning them: "One thinks of Stephen Heath's by now famous suggestion, 'the risk of essence may have to be taken' ('Difference' 1978, 99). It is poststructuralist feminists who seem most intrigued by this call to risk essence. Alice Jardine, for example, finds Stephen Heath's proclamation (later echoed by Gayatri Spivak) to be 'one of the most thought-provoking statements of recent date'" (18–19). Here Fuss appropriates Jardine's comment about Spivak echoing Heath as her own. Then, in the introduction to their collection *Displacement, Diaspora, and Geographies of Identity,* Smadar Lavie and Ted Swedenburg announce, "Here we take 'the "risk" of essence' (Fuss 1989: 1; 65)" (11), thereby making invisible the chain of citations that made Fuss's point possible (although the chain of citations leaves its trace in the embeddedness of the quotation within their quotation). I would argue that this chain of citations (and perhaps other ones similar to it) is partly what produced this understanding of strategic essentialism that cannot be found in Spivak.

16. For additional work on the queer implications of the work of Deleuze and Guattari, see O'Rourke; and esp. Cohen and Ramlow.

Chapter 1

Parts of previous versions of this chapter were published as two pieces: (1) "Looking for Roots among the Mangroves: *Errances enracinées* and Migratory Identities." *Centennial Review* 42.3 (1998): 459–74. © 1998 by Michigan State University; (2) "*Créolité*'s Queer Mangrove." *Music, Writing, and Cultural Unity in the Caribbean.* Ed. Timothy J. Reiss. Trenton, NJ: Africa World Press, 2005. 307–32. Reprinted with permission of the publishers.

1. *Tout Monde* also uses the word *rhizome* a number of times.

2. Other novels in this grouping include *Le quatrième siècle* (1964), *Malemort* (1975), *La case du commandeur* (1981), and *Mahogany* (1987).

3. Because of the inconsistency with which Ferguson translates *makoumè*, translations of *Eau de Café* are my own.

4. The pejorative French word *bicot* has no real English equivalent, referring as it does to North Africans. For these racist settlers, calling someone an Arab is more insulting than using a term that signals their descent from African slaves.

5. This version is taken from the 1967 translation (cf. n7).

6. Kobena Mercer pointed out this contradiction during his participation in a round table at the conference Black Nations/Queer Nations? on 10 March 1995.

7. In a more recent translation, Richard Philcox (Condé's husband and translator) renders the French of Fanon's original with the Creole word, thereby changing the language politics of the passage in French (157–58n44).

8. The Creole expression in this passage means "a little man."

9. Unless, that is, one considers the slight difference between her spelling, *makoumé*, and the more standard one for all French Caribbean Creoles, *makoumè*, to be a Frenchification.

10. Given the Caribbean storytelling convention of mocking the deceased at their own wakes by exaggerating their flaws, that the stories are told at a wake makes their veracity even more suspect.

11. This is my translation of the expression "la plante malfaisante de cette médisance" (Condé, *Traversée* 37), quoted above and rendered by Philcox in his translation of the novel as "[t]he poisonous plant of mischief" (20).

12. The last expression is difficult to translate. I have attempted to be as literal as possible while retaining the strong sexual connotations of the original.

13. A differing view of Creole's sexual vocabulary is given by Antilia in *Eau de Café*. "Ils nous ont métamorphosés en bourreaux de chaque mot, en contempteurs satisfaits de notre propre dire et nous n'avons rien fait, rien dit. 'Kal' (verge), 'Koukoun' (chatte), 'Bonda' (cul), 'Koké' (baiser): voilà ce qu'il en reste ! La tétralogie du foutre et de la merde. Le jargon néandertalien d'une grappe d'indigènes somptueusement fardés dans l'attente d'un enterrement de première classe" (286) [They have turned us into torturers of every word, into people contemptuous and complacent about what we say and we've done nothing, said nothing. 'Kal' (cock), 'Koukoun' (cunt), 'Bonda' (arse), 'Koké' (fuck): that's what's left! The tetralogy of fucking and shitting. The Neanderthal jargon of a cluster of natives, extravagantly made up in anticipation of a first-class burial" (216)].

14. Vaval is the personification of Carnival.

15. A *bwabwa* is a large puppet representing Carnival.

16. Literally "tool box," the *bwètzouti* is a sort of jack-of-all-trades. MacGyver would be a perfect example.

17. *Gôlbos* are people who think they are elegant but come off as rather ridiculous.

18. This figure can also be used as a sort of bogeyman to frighten children who misbehave.

19. A *bitako* is literally someone from an *habitation* or plantation.

20. Although the Créolistes use *matadô* as a synonym for *femme-à-graines* or *mâle-femme*, Guy Kabile translates it as "a stunningly beautiful Creole women" in this context.

21. Literally "smothering mosquitoes," *touféyenyen* is a dance in which the partners are extremely close.

22. I again thank Luc Boisseron, Guy Kabile, and Bénédicte Boisseron for their help in translating this passage.

23. Larrier describes as well the historical prohibition of the *laghia de la mort* (in which adversaries dance with "razors hidden between their toes to settle a score" [2]).

24. While *mon bougre* might very well be translated as "my friend," here the literal meaning of *bougre*, "bugger," is also applicable. "Poop-chute" would be a better translation of *trou-caca* than "arsehole."

25. Bothrops is also a genus of snake, one that includes the aforementioned *fer-de-lance* or lance head. A Brazilian species of this genus, the golden lance head, can even change its sex if a given population suffers from a lack of individuals of either sex.

26. Joséphine was born into a Martiniquan white Creole family of planters.

27. This term compares the one it names to a slave just off the boat from Africa.

Chapter 2

A previous version of this chapter appeared as "Queer Roots in Africa." *Topographies of Race and Gender: Mapping Cultural Representations.* Ed. Patricia Penn Hilden, Shari M. Huhndorf, and Timothy J. Reiss. 2 vols. Spec. issue of *Annals of Scholarship* 17.3/18.1–18.2/3 (2009): vol. 2, 151–82. Permission was granted by *Annals of Scholarship* to print a modified version of this essay.

1. For an analysis of the neocolonial implications of some of OutRage!'s actions, see Puar, *Terrorist* 17–23. On the colonial implications of Tatchell's politics, see Gunkel 72.

2. Mugabe has been in power since 1980 when the Zimbabwe African National Union-Patriotic Front (ZANU-PF) overthrew the white-controlled government of what was then Rhodesia.

3. In the year 2000, whites—who made up less than 2 percent of the population—still controlled more than half of Zimbabwe's arable farmland (Swarns, "West"), which indicates that, in spite of a black government, land distribution has changed little since independence. White farmers "have repeatedly promised and failed to deliver their own list of underused farms" for redistribution (Swarns, "Protest"), and Great Britain continues to withhold funds it promised to finance land reform until occupations of farmland end.

4. I would not wish to glorify the opposition, however, supported as it is by many white commercial farmers who support free-market economic policies at the expense of leaving colonial injustices uncorrected.

5. After initially agreeing with Mugabe on the topic of homosexuality, Tsvangirai has more recently come out in support of gay rights ("Zimbabwe's PM"; "Zimbabwean PM").

6. *Unspoken Facts* updates the book-fair controversy as follows: "At the next Book Fair in August 1996, the courts declared that GALZ was within its rights to have a stand, but a vigilante group led by prominent ZANU(PF) members nevertheless threatened to close it down by force. On hearing that the group was approaching to carry out this threat, and having already distributed their literature, GALZ representatives made a hasty 'tactical withdrawal.' This was followed by a strategic decision to keep a lower profile at subsequent Book Fairs until tempers cooled" (152).

7. See Epprecht, "Good God" 213. Mugabe himself is Shona.

8. See Epprecht, "Good God" 213–15 and "Unsaying" 631–32. On boy marriage in Zimbabwe, see also Antonio. Sometimes *ngotshana* (or its equivalents *ngochani*, *nkotshane*, and *inkotshane*, the last being a "colonial era spelling") is translated simply as "sodomy" or "homosexual" (Epprecht, *Hungochani* xi–xii).

9. See also Obbo (372), who nonetheless differs from O'Brien and Krige in pointing out that woman-woman marriage can provide a convenient structure for resistance to male domination.

10. On female husbands, see also Amadiume.

11. They are nonnormative, of course, with respect to both Europe and postinde-pendence African nationalism but quite often normative in a "traditional" context.

12. I thank Steve Bishop for passing along the text of this discussion to me.

13. Jean-Célestin Yamegni, "Re: Intolerance?" 7 July 1995. I identify the author of each statement (at least as it was given in the e-mail), the "title" as it appeared in the subject rubric, and the date on which the message was sent. Especially given the lack of orthographic consistency in this relatively early electronic exchange, I have chosen to provide only my translations.

14. Boubacar Bah, "La circoncision feminine," 21 Aug. 1995. The word *pederasty* was formerly used in "polite" French as a synonym of *homosexuality*.

15. Barry Mamadou Cellou, "Une Afrique pure," 21 Aug. 1995.

16. Jean-Célestin Yamegni, "Re: Intolerance? Dialogue," 7 July 1995.

17. Ken Bugul is the pen name of Mariètou Mbaye Biléoma; in Wolof, *ken bugul* means "nobody wants this one" (Azoda 1).

18. On male prostitution in Senegal, see also Davidson. On the *gôr-djiguen*, see also M'Baye.

19. Alioune Deme, "Re: Intolerance?" 6 July 1995.

20. "I did not tell them that I did research, or that I was looking for more than a leisurely time when I came" (162–63).

21. "In Dakar, I led a closeted life. I was very cautious, as I was aware of the strong sentiments against homosexuality in the city" (160).

22. Although she uses the French expression "homme-femme" instead of its Wolof original, Aminata Sow Fall makes a number of references to *gôr-djiguen* in her novel *Le revenant* [The One Who Returns/The Ghost]. For another contemporary study of men who have sex with men in Senegal, see Niang et al. This study also states that the term "*[g]orjigeen* is currently considered discriminatory and demeaning by MSM" (9). ("MSM" means men who have sex with men.)

23. On homoeroticism in Ghanaian boarding schools, see Ajen 130–31. Munro reads this novel as being more conflicted than I do ("Gender").

24. Desai's more recent essay (1997) and Hoad's even more recent book (2007) are discussed below.

25. Cf. Vincent O. Odamtten's much more positive characterization of the rela-tionship between Sissie and Marije (125–26). While avoiding western categories of sexual orientation altogether, he articulates a compassionate and embracing under-standing of the two women characters' relationship and encounter. Wilentz also offers a more nuanced reading of the encounter (84–85).

26. Hoad offers a much more detailed analysis of this incident and even gives four separate readings or narratives of it from four different standpoints (*African Intimacies* 1–20). The titles he gives to these analyses offer helpful indications as to the multiple ways in which the incident can be interpreted: "Frame 1: African 'Sodomy' as Incen-tive to the Taking Up of the White Man's Burden" (3), "Frame 2: African Corporeal Intimacies and the Production of the Metropolitan Homosexual" (7), "Frame 3: How 'African' Was 'African Sodomy'?" (10), and "Frame 4: 'African' 'Sodomy' as Primary Anticolonial Resistance" (12).

27. J. P. Thoonen's *Black Martyrs* (1942), an earlier account of the executions, also

carries the *nihil obstat* and *imprimatur*. Unlike its successor, however, it is vehemently anti-Protestant. In "The Purge of Christians at Mwanga's Court" (1964), J. A. Rowe describes how written histories of Mwanga's reign have "become heavily weighted towards issues involving the Christians" (57). On this incident, see also Hoad, "Arrested Development" 139–40; Epprecht, *Heterosexual Africa?* 42–43.

28. Hoad offers the clearest exception to this generalization (*African Intimacies*).

29. Cultural references suggest that he is American and, possibly, African American.

30. Godfrey A. Whyte, "Lifestyle choice," 11 July 1995.

31. Jean-Célestin Yamegni, "Re: Lifestyle choice," 12 July 1995.

32. Godfrey A. Whyte, "RE: Lifestyle choice," 12 July 1995.

33. Since this chapter was first written, in 2009, a new law against homosexuality was proposed in the Ugandan parliament that would even include the death penalty in some instances. On the climate surrounding this development, as well as the links between the US evangelical movement and Ugandan politicians, see Sharlet; "David Kato"; Tamale; Munro, "Queer Family Romance."

34. For a more recent expression of Soyinka's views on such matters, see his "Gays, Lesbians, and Legislative Zealotry," in which he condemns attempts to criminalize homosexuality. It should be noted, however, that this piece is not what one would call gay positive.

35. See, for example, Maugham-Brown 55–56; Early 170. Jeyifo writes of "the 'interpreters' and *other* finely drawn characters like Monica Faseyi, Joe Golder and Lazarus" (176; emphasis added).

36. Abodunrin, for example, speaks of Noah's being "driven to an untimely death by Joe Golder's homosexual lewdness" (162). Early speaks of "the morbid Joe Golder" (172) and "the pathetic insecurity of Joe Golder, a dislocated orphan of America, whose homosexuality aggravates his self-contempt for being only one-quarter black. An object of ridicule by the interpreters early in the novel . . . , Golder becomes a figure of stark misery after he precipitates Noah's death" (169–70).

37. Vignal's largely descriptive essay on representations of "homophilia" in African novels in both English and French classes Soyinka among his list of negative representations. I am not including him with Hoad here, since the latter does not argue that the novel itself is homophobic but rather that it criticizes Golder, and in a way that is not homophobic.

38. Although Vignal places *The Interpreters* on his list of homophobic novels, he does cite this passage (77–78). See also Hoad's (33, 41, 76) and Desai's (139) discussions of it.

39. Kleis and Abdullahi later elaborate on this list (44).

40. Cf. Gaudio's explanation of the terms used in this passage ("Male Lesbians" 308n7).

41. See also Gaudio's elaboration on this "assumption" ("Male Lesbians" 119). He also explains how encounters between men are facilitated in such heterosexual contexts (ibid.). See also his "Not Talking."

42. Cf. Hoad's analysis of this scene (44–45). He also provides the reference for Frederic W. Farrar's novel *Eric, or Little by Little!* mentioned in this passage.

43. My turn of phrase, here, "bottom reading," is inspired by Scott De Orio and Trevor Hoppe's webcast "The View from the Bottom" (http://www.youtube.com/user/theviewfromthebottom), which, as its title suggests, offers views on a variety of topics from this particular "position." See also Stockton.

44. On the "gender" of Yoruba divinities, see also Oyewumi, *Invention* 64, 136–42, 168–74.

Chapter 3

1. For Haley's response to the suits see his "There Are Days" (216).

2. The oral texts on which Haley based his assertion that Kunta Kinte was his forebear merely stated that "the oldest of [Omoro Kinte's] four sons, Kunta, went away from his village to chop wood . . . and he was never seen again . . ." (*Roots* 719; Haley's ellipses).

3. *Sarfate* is Hebrew for "France" or "French." Many thanks to Ryan Szpiech and Moulie Vidas for this information.

4. In particular, the director wanted to ridicule Alceste's proposal that Célimène marry him, an offer made on the condition that she accompany him in his retreat to the wilderness to escape the rest of society.

5. This Hebrew expression is used in French in a way that it is not in English.

6. The *Zohar* is also a text of ambiguous or contested origins. It claims to be a second-century text by the Rabbi Sim'on ben Yohai, and some would hold that this claim is accurate. Many thanks to Ryan Szpiech for this point.

7. In quotations from the *Zohar* and related texts, I have removed Hebrew letters and untransliterated words.

8. *Shekinah* and *Tif'eret* are the tenth and sixth *sefirot*, or divine entities.

9. Green offers a different chronology from the one my comments might imply: "The Torah given to Moses at Sinai was an embodiment of the primordial Torah, which existed with God before Creation and which He consulted in making the world" (*Guide* 122). Or the *Zohar* states, "When the blessed Holy One wished to fashion the world, all the letters were hidden away. For two thousand years before creating the world, the blessed Holy One contemplated them and played with them. As He verged on creating the world, all the letters presented themselves before Him, from last to first" (11). My comments, however, are meant as an argument less for synchronicity (God wrote the Creation as he wrote the Torah) than for a parallel. My reading here has in common with Green the possibility that God might be read as a manifestation of textual production; "author" and "text" can be reversible positions. My comments here are thus heavily influenced by Jabès, as will become clear below.

10. Throughout this chapter, quotations from Jabès's *Le livre des questions* are referenced as *LQ*. The volume numbers of the English translations correspond to the following titles: I, *The Book of Questions*; II, *The Book of Questions, II and III: The Book of Yukel, Return to the Book*; III, *The Book of Questions: Yaël, Elya, Aely*; and IV, *The Book of Questions: • El, or the Last Book*.

11. The seven volumes are entitled *Le livre des questions, Le livre de Yukel, Le retour au livre, Yaël, Elya, Aely*, and • (*El, ou le dernier livre*). And the four volumes of the English translation are entitled *The Book of Questions; The Book of Yukel, Return to the Book; Yaël, Elya, Aely*; and • *El, or the Last Book*. The more recent French edition combines the first three into a first volume and the last four into a second.

12. Glissant's neologism *tout-monde* is difficult to translate and often left in French in criticism written in English. *Tout* can mean "all," "whole," or "everything." *Tout le monde*, literally "the whole world," usually means "everyone." But hyphenated *tout-monde* conflates wholeness and worldness. Ly provides an interesting alternative— "Wholeland" (on this concept, see also his chapter 4).

13. By this I do not mean that finding one's roots should replace more material reparations.

14. The quotation is from Barthes's "Structure du fait divers" (192). The English translation reads as follows: "[T]he detective work consists in filling in, backwards, the fascinating and unendurable interval separating the event from its cause" (189).

15. I owe this understanding of the narrative structure of the detective novel in part to Christopher Prendergast's discussion of the French New Novel in a graduate seminar entitled Beginnings and Endings in Twentieth Century French Literature at the City University of New York's Graduate Center in 1990.

16. I first learned not only of this character but also of the novel itself from a paper read by Yvette Bénayoun-Szmidt at the annual Congrès Mondial of the Conseil International d'Études Francophones of 1996, held in Toulouse, France. For her reading of Sapho, see "De la contiguïté."

17. Of course, seeing in Genesis the origin of heterosexuality constitutes an anachronistic reading since heterosexuality did not exist at the time of its writing, which does not, however, hinder contemporary readings that use Genesis to attribute divine will to a certain kinship structure, as will become clearer below.

Chapter 4

Part of this chapter was previously published as "Circumcising Zionism, Queering Diaspora: Reviving Albert Memmi's Penis." *Wasafiri* 22.1 (2007): 6–11. © Taylor & Francis. Reprinted with permission of the publisher. The original version of this article may be found at http://www.tandfonline.com/doi/full/10.1080/02690050601097542.

1. In spite of the fact that Wright also points out, "If a man usurped the office of *mansa* [king] and required an elaborate lineage to help support his claim to rule, he simply got a *griot* to recite one" (211), his notion of a contaminated oral history fails to acknowledge the way griots write history as fiction in the way Law describes in the passage quoted in chapter 3.

2. Although recorded versions and the published libretto of *The Cave* carry Reich's name as the author/composer, sometimes it is referred to as both Korot's and Reich's work. I attempt to replicate that practice here, using only Reich when referencing the work as it appears in my "Works Cited" but both names when referring to the work in its multimedia entirety.

3. *Libretto* is a problematic term here, not only because *The Cave* can only problematically be labeled an opera but also because the spoken and/or sung words were not written down before *The Cave* was composed.

4. The transcript of this interview is included in the program notes published with the text of the opera that accompanies the CD recording, as well as with the text that was published separately (Reich and Korot, *Cave*). All page references are to this last version.

5. All quotations from the program notes and text of the opera are from the published text (Reich and Korot, *Cave*).

6. Sumanth Gopinath also links "music as a gradual process" to the character of a number of his pieces as "political allegories" (17, in web version) and argues for continuity between Reich's earlier "phase music" and more recent compositions like *The Cave* (22). He suggests, however, that more recent works move "toward an increasing political conservatism . . . and developing concern with the politics of Islamic fundamentalism" (22). It should be stated that, by including Jewish interviewees who

are not Israeli in Act I and only Muslim interviewees in Act II, Reich might be said to conflate the Israeli-Palestinian conflict with a Jewish-Muslim one.

7. McClary writes, "[W]e are now widely known (for better or worse) as 'the New Musicology.' My colleagues in this endeavor include (most prominently) Rose Rosengard Subotnik, Lawrence Kramer, Richard Leppert, Philip Brett, Gary Tomlinson, Richard Taruskin, Robert Walser, and—the godfather of us all—Joseph Kerman, whose calls for music criticism and attacks on the 'purely musical' date back several decades" (*Conventional* 2). To this list, one could add many more, not least of whom would be Carolyn Abbate, Leo Treitler, Ruth Solie, Suzanne Cusick, and Nadine Hubbs.

8. See also Subotnik.

9. The quotations are from Segev (117–18).

10. See Memmi's *The Colonizer and the Colonized*.

11. In fact, at the time of the novel's publication, the Jewish press condemned it for not being Zionist even as Arab critiques were saying the opposite (Dugas 50).

12. I use the expression "Nation of Israel" throughout this chapter in its biblical sense to distinguish it from the contemporary Israeli state.

13. In Tunis grocers were considered to come from Djerba in disproportionate numbers. *Djerbian*, here, could thus also be a synonym of *grocer*.

14. Hayes, *Queer Nations* 243–47, 253–55, 277–86.

15. My point is not that diaspora is necessarily antithetical to Zionism; the Israeli state receives much support from the diaspora. Rather, I am suggesting that the tensions between diaspora and Zionism might be mined to strengthen anti-Zionist positions.

16. The quotation within this quotation is from Bennington's last sentence (316; 292).

17. A reproduction of the "postcard" is also on the desk Derrida is sitting at in the photo.

18. The give-and-take dialectic works differently in the French and English sentences. In the French one—literally "Plato takes Socrates, who gives him his ass"—the top is the one who "takes."

19. Unless otherwise noted, any brackets containing an italicized French original are the translator's. Any nonitalicized text in brackets is an alternative translation of my own.

20. Page numbers from *Glas* are accompanied by an *H* or a *G* to indicate whether the quotations are from the Hegel or Genet column. In this particular passage, the translators seem to have mistaken the *relevée* of the original with *révélée*. In most cases, they translate *relever* as *relieve*, in the sense of relieving someone of their duties and responsibilities, as well as putting into relief (as in highlighting). This translation, however, removes the allusions to erections that Derrida makes in his discussion of *Aufhebung* in *Glas*, allusions I have attempted to highlight (**relever**) in my own alterations to his translations along with all the other French words that can signify erection. The boldface type used to do so in the French original is my own.

21. This passage is a good example of the shortcomings of Leavey and Rand's translation. Only as a noun does *la relève* refer uniquely to relieving (someone of their duties). Yet Derrida is associating *la relève* as feminine article plus noun with the same words as feminine direct object pronoun plus the third-person singular form of the verb in the present.

22. *La Cène* (a homophone of the French word for "scene") is French for "the Last Supper."

23. I would like to thank the late Lawrence R. Schehr for pointing out both the form of the scepter and its role in this passage.

24. Nancy K. Miller writes that the penis is "the place in which Jewish genealogy gets marked on the male body. A son is circumcised like his fathers before him" (*Bequest* 28).

25. Hélène Cixous would make a similar call, echoed by Alice Jardine in the late 1980s: "Men still have everything to say about their own sexuality" (Jardine 60). Cixous literally writes on "Circumfessions" by reproducing entire passages of it onto which she writes commentary by hand. Figuratively, therefore, she is writing *on* Derrida's penis.

26. For other feminist writings on the penis, see Nancy K. Miller's "My Father's Penis" and, although it is more about the phallus than the penis, Butler's "Lesbian Phallus."

27. These two sets of brackets are Leavey and Rand's.

28. In "The Legacy of Jean-Paul Sartre," Joseph Massad criticizes a lecture given by Derrida in Jerusalem for the double standard that its call for an end to violence on both sides and its recognition of a Zionist state implies, even as he acknowledges Derrida's opposition to the occupation and support of a Palestinian state. While I agree with Massad's reading of this particular text by Derrida, I think an anti-Zionist reading of Derrida must contextualize pronouncements such as this, made by a guest to his hosts, within the entire body of his work and its consistent deconstruction of concepts like what Derrida calls *élection* (the chosenness of the chosen people) without which Zionist roots narratives would lose their justification.

Chapter 5

1. While I have not found biographical confirmation of the latter detail, Spender's *Arshile Gorky* includes a "letter of recommendation to the American Consul in Tiflis, 1919" from Ussher regarding Gorky and several other boys (39).

2. Gorky's mother died of starvation in his arms after their forced migration.

3. Gorky was born Manoug Adoian. Egoyan's family's also changed its name from Yeghoyan. Recall the name change that Sapho's Alph undergoes as part of lying about his roots in chapter 3. The Efird family also changes its name in chapter 6 below.

4. Egoyan was born in Cairo, and his family immigrated to Canada when he was three. In contrast with the character he plays, although he "forgot" Armenian after he began school in Canada, he later relearned it. Khanjian (born in Lebanon of Armenian parents) immigrated to Canada when she was seventeen.

5. Egoyan himself makes this point in the director's commentary to the DVD release of the film.

6. Given the fragmented nature of the film's narrative structure, nothing requires that the Armenian narrative be told in chronological order. Since this narrative is also the narrative of the gradual rapprochement of the photographer's wife and the driver, however, the fragments of this narrative make the most sense when understood as being told in chronological order.

7. Egoyan confirms this point in his director's commentary to the DVD.

8. In his director's commentary, Egoyan explicitly refers to these women as "escorts." However, he excepts the first "date" from this category; in his explanation, the subsequent dates are with escorts paid to repeat the failure of the first date. I

would argue, however, that the film itself is less clear about the first date being an exception.

9. Because he is shot from behind over his right shoulder, his waist and groin are not visible.

10. While this turn of phrase might seem overly dismissive here, my argument is that it is no less so than in the film itself. Indeed, in his director's commentary to the DVD version of *Calendar*, Egoyan is even more dismissive of the very character he plays than I am in this chapter.

11. Bubba may actually just be performing as a homeless man (see McSorley 47–49). Nonetheless, in a fictional film (a performative genre after all), the distinction between "reality" and performance is a tenuous one.

12. McSorley suggests a different reason for their departure: "When Noah leaves in the middle of the night from his 'family's' room to have sex with a male client, Hera, Seta, and Simon are seen leaving by taxi without him" (44). The film, however, offers no evidence that Hera is aware of her husband's liaison with another man.

13. As Romney points out about *Family Viewing*, "Van is played by Patrick Tierney's younger brother Aidan" (44). Through casting, Egoyan thus creates a "kinship" between the two films.

14. A *New York Times* review of *Felicia's Journey* states that Joseph's videos are "either memories or actual tapes, the movie doesn't say" ("Way Too Trusting").

15. About Hilditch, Egoyan has stated, "[H]e's evil, kind of, but not" (qtd. in Jackson). He has also said, "I really saw *this* film, *Felicia's Journey*, as the heart of a child meeting the soul of a monster. Yet the heart of a child is also contained in the soul of that monster" (qtd. in McEwan 12).

16. All quotations from this film are from the published screenplay.

17. On the importance of perversion in *Exotica* and its relation to the family, see Schwartz (esp. 93–96).

Chapter 6

1. In spite of the gender ambiguity of *Sandy*, locals would know the heterosexual couple for which the road is named, at least for a couple of decades following the naming.

2. In *Rhinelanders on the Yadkin*, Carl Hammer Jr. explains the linguistic state of the Lutheran Church in North Carolina around the supposed time of the Efird name change: "Greater conservatism was shown by the Tennessee Synod. At its initial meeting in 1820, German was made the official language, and not until 1825 was the order given to publish the minutes in English also. At the following convention in 1826, the Rev. David Henkel was appointed interpreter for several ministers who understood no German. At the same time the following decision was reached: 'The business of the Synod shall be transacted in the German language during the first three days; afterwards the English language shall be used.' About 1825–1850, the real period of transition, there was a great demand for bilingual preachers" (96–97). Hammer is here comparing the Tennessee Synod to the North Carolina Synod from which the former split in 1820 (see also Morgan et al. 41–89). St. Martin's was founded after this split when "Rev. David Henkel held services . . . in the year 1822 in Jacob Efird's home and administered communion to thirty members" (Morgan, Brown, and Hall 322). David was the son of Paul Henkel, the first American-born Lutheran minister in North Carolina, and, along with his father and brother Philip, he pulled

out of the North Carolina Synod to found the Tennessee one (41–45): "Agreeable to all concerned, St. Martin's, in 1902, was transferred from the Tennessee Synod to the North Carolina Synod" (322). The two synods themselves rejoined in 1921 (91–97).

3. See Wolfe, *O Lost*, which offers the original text of his novel before the heavy editing (and cuts) of his editor Maxwell Perkins.

4. This taunt is repeated in a number of passages (see, e.g., 417).

5. The Irish precedent is referenced in Valente's title (Johnson 126).

6. Roberts describes this site as follows:

> Just off a country road near Harper Cross Roads is a perfect circle in the midst of the woods. It is 40 feet in diameter. Surrounded by pines, scrub oaks and underbrush, the circle itself is bare except for a type of wire grass.
>
> The narrow path around the edge of the circle brooks no growth of any kind. Sticks or other obstructions put in the path are never there in the morning.
>
> According to Chatham County natives, it is the Devil whose nightly presence discourages the growth of anything fresh and green and good. Round and round the well-worn path he paces, concocting his evil snares for mankind. (33)

See also Harden.

7. *L'écorce et le noyau* gathers a number of Abraham's essays with some by Maria Torok, as well as others they wrote together. Half of these essays are translated in *The Shell and the Kernel*, which also includes four uncollected essays by Torok.

8. Introjection is the "Process revealed by analytic investigation: in phantasy, the subject transposes objects and their inherent qualities from the 'outside' to the inside of himself" (Laplanche and Pontalis, *Language* 229). The concept of dual unity refers to the child's primary unity with its mother before individuation, when it shares its mother's conscious and unconscious without distinguishing between the two.

9. Pierce was a candidate for Superior Court judge who won his election even after being murdered, probably by racists.

10. Other relatives, however, such as Leon Smalls, were more critical: "Ed Ball was born with a silver spoon in his mouth and I was born into poverty. All of a sudden he is going to come forward and understand my situation and say 'sorry.' . . . A blank apology to 100,000 slaves. That is not enough" (quoted in O'Neill, D2).

11. *High Yaller* (Yellow) is a pejorative expression for a very light-skinned mixed-race person.

12. It should be noted, however, that the speech of black characters is not the only form marked with such difference. Only the speech of those who speak like Eugene and his family is spared. Other forms marked with differences from the standard include those of rural folk from areas surrounding Eugene's hometown ("hillbillies" or those referred to in the novel as "mountain grill") and, in subsequent novels, South Carolinians, New Yorkers, and Bostonians.

13. "It was during the 1930's [*sic*] that the Albemarle City Schools took over the Wiscassett and Efird mill schools. Wiscassett School, which burned in the 1940's [*sic*], was torn down when the YMCA was built on the site" (Sharpe and Pepper 96).

14. Furthermore, a 1930 city directory is entitled *Directory of Albemarle, N.C. and New Town, Efird and Wiscassett Hill and Kingville*, marginalizing the mill hills from the city proper and putting them in the same category as the African American neigh-

borhood Kingville, itself an effect of segregation. By 1937 *Baldwin's Albemarle North Carolina City Directory* had eliminated this distinction.

15. In this Anglo transmission of a supposedly Native American oral tradition—and the only transmissions to which I have ever been exposed have been Anglo, which is enough to make their "authenticity" suspicious—becomes one mode of "going native" (cf. Huhndorf).

16. An Indian mound is the remnant of a Native American earthen pyramid. The most studied complex of such "mounds" in North Carolina is located in Montgomery County, which is adjacent to the county where I grew up (see Coe).

17. The *OED* explains, "**bug** . . . *Obs.* or *dial.* . . . [ME. *bugge*, possibly from Welsh *bwg* (= bug) 'a ghost', quoted in Lhwyd's *Archæologia Brit.* (1707) 214, from the MS. Welsh Vocabulary of Henry Salesbury (born 1561). Owen Pugh has *bwg* 'hobgoblin, scarecrow'; but the word is apparently now known chiefly in its derivatives. When *bug* became current as the name of an insect (see BUG *sb.*²), this sense fell into disuse, and now survives only in the compound BUGBEAR. Cf. BOGY, BUGABOO" (II, 626).

Works Cited

✦ ✦ ✦

Abodunrin, Femi. "The Politics and Poetics of Otherness: A Study of Wole Soyinka's *The Interpreters.*" *Yearbook of English Studies* 27 (1997): 150–64.

Abraham, Nicolas. *L'écorce et le noyau.* With the collaboration of and other essays by Maria Torok. Paris: Aubier Flammarion, 1978.

Abraham, Nicolas, and Maria Torok. *Cryptonymie: Le verbier de l'homme aux loups.* Paris: Aubier Flammarion, 1976.

Abraham, Nicolas, and Maria Torok. *The Shell and the Kernel: Renewals of Psychoanalysis.* Ed., trans., and intro. Nicholas T. Rand. Chicago: U of Chicago P, 1994.

Abraham, Nicolas, and Maria Torok. *The Wolf Man's Magic Word: A Cryptonomy.* Trans. Nicholas Rand. Minneapolis: U of Minnesota P, 1986.

African American Lives. PBS Home Video. 2006.

African American Lives 2. PBS Home Video. 2008.

Aidoo, Ama Ata. *Our Sister Killjoy; or, Reflections from a Black-Eyed Squint.* Essex: Longman, 1977.

Ajen, Nil. "West African Homoeroticism: West African Men Who Have Sex with Men." Murray and Roscoe 129–38.

Alcalay, Ammiel. *After Jews and Arabs: Remaking Levantine Culture.* Minneapolis: U of Minnesota P, 1993.

Allen, Jafari S., ed. *Black/Queer/Diaspora.* Spec. issue of *GLQ* 18.2–3 (2012).

Amadiume, Ifi. *Male Daughters, Female Husbands.* London: Zed, 1987.

Anderson, Benedict. *Imagined Communities: Reflections on the Origin and Spread of Nationalism.* London: Verso, 1983.

Antonio, Edward P. "Homosexuality and African Culture." *Aliens in the Household of God: Homosexuality and Christian Faith in South Africa.* Ed. Paul Germon and Steve de Gruchy. Cape Town: Philip, 1997. 295–315.

Arens, W. *The Man-Eating Myth: Anthropology and Anthropophagy.* New York: Oxford UP, 1974.

Arnold, A. James. "Créolité: Cultural Nation-Building or Cultural Dependence?" D'haen 37–48.

Arnold, A. James. "The Gendering of Créolité: The Erotics of Colonialism." Condé and Cottenet-Hage 21–40.

Asante, Molefi Kete. *Afrocentricity*. Trenton, NJ: Africa World P, 1988.

Axel, Brian Keith. "The Diasporic Imaginary." *Public Culture* 14.2 (2002): 411–28.

Azodo, Ada Uzoamaka. "Mariètou Mbaye Biléoma: Eclectics and Pragmatism." Intro. to Azodo and de Larquier, 1–26.

Azodo, Ada Uzoamaka, and Jeanne-Sarah de Larquier, eds. *Emerging Perspectives on Ken Bugul: From Alternative Choices to Oppositional Practices*. Trenton, NJ: Africa World P, 2009.

Bâ, Mariama. *Un chant écarlate*. Dakar: Nouvelles Éditions Africaines, 1981.

Bâ, Mariama. *Scarlet Song*. Trans. Dorothy S. Blair. Essex: Longman, 1985.

Baldwin, James. *Another Country*. 1960. New York: Vintage, 1993.

Baldwin, James. *Collected Essays*. New York: Library of America, 1998.

Baldwin, James. "Encounter of the Seine: Black Meets Brown." 1950. *Notes* 84–90.

Baldwin, James. "Giovanni's Room." 1956. New York: Quality Paperback Book Club, 1993.

Baldwin, James. "Nobody Knows My Name." 1961. *Collected Essays* 137–290.

Baldwin, James. *Notes of a Native Son*. 1955. *Collected Essays* 5–136.

Baldwin, James. "Notes of a Native Son." 1955. *Notes* 63–84.

Baldwin's Albemarle North Carolina City Directory. Charleston, SC: Baldwin Directory Co., 1937.

Ball, Edward. *Slaves in the Family*. New York: Farrar, Straus and Giroux, 1998.

Barker, Francis, Peter Hulme, and Margaret Iversen, eds. *Cannibalism and the Colonial World*. Cambridge: Cambridge UP, 1998.

Barthes, Roland. *Le grain de la voix: Entretiens, 1962–1980*. Paris: Seuil, 1981.

Barthes, Roland. *The Grain of the Voice: Interviews, 1962–1980*. Trans. Linda Coverdale. New York: Hill and Wang, 1985.

Barthes, Roland. *Le plaisir du texte*. Paris: Seuil, 1973. Coll. Points.

Barthes, Roland. *The Pleasure of the Text*. Trans. Richard Miller. New York: Hill and Wang, 1975.

Barthes, Roland. *Roland Barthes par Roland Barthes*. Paris: Seuil, 1975.

Barthes, Roland. *Roland Barthes by Roland Barthes*. Trans. Richard Howard. New York: Hill and Wang, 1977.

Barthes, Roland. "Structure du fait divers." *Essais critiques*. Paris: Seuil, 1964. 188–97.

Barthes, Roland. "Structure of the *Fait-Divers*." *Critical Essays*. Trans. Richard Howard. Evanston, IL: Northwestern UP, 1972. 185–95.

Ben Joseph, Rabbi Akiba. *The Book of Formation (Sepher Yetzirah)*. Trans. Knut Stenring. London: Rider, 1923.

Bénayoun-Szmidt, Yvette. "De la contiguïté à l'espacement, de la fusion au schisme: Traversées interculturelles chez Elisa Chimenti et Sapho." *Colonizer and Colonized*. Ed. Theo D'haen and Patricia Krüs. Amsterdam: Rodopi, 2000. 451–66.

Bennington, Geoffrey, and Jacques Derrida. *Jacques Derrida*. Paris: Seuil, 1991.

Bennington, Geoffrey, and Jacques Derrida. *Jacques Derrida*. Trans. Geoffrey Bennington. Chicago: U of Chicago P, 1993.

Bernabé, Jean, Patrick Chamoiseau, and Raphaël Confiant. *Éloge de la créolité*. Paris: Gallimard, 1989.

Bernabé, Jean, Patrick Chamoiseau, and Raphaël Confiant. "In Praise of Creoleness." Trans. Mohamed B. Taleb Khyar. *Callaloo* 13.4 (1990): 886–909.

Besmer, Fremont E. *Horses, Musicians, and Gods: The Hausa Cult of Possession-Trance*. South Hadley, MA: Bergin and Garvey, 1983.

Biale, David. *Eros and the Jews: From Biblical Israel to Contemporary America.* New York: Basic Books, 1992.

Blackwood, Evelyn. "Cross-Cultural Lesbian Studies: Problems and Possibilities." *The New Lesbian Studies: Into the Twenty-First Century.* Ed. Bonnie Zimmerman and Toni A. H. McNaron. New York: Feminist P at the CU of New York, 1996. 194–200.

Blayney, Michael Steward. "*Roots* and the Noble Savage." *North Dakota Quarterly* 54.1 (1986): 1–17.

Boswell, John. *Christianity, Social Tolerance, and Homosexuality: Gay People in Western Europe from the Beginning of the Christian Era to the Fourteenth Century.* Chicago: Chicago UP, 1980.

Boyarin, Daniel. "'This We Know to Be the Carnal Israel': Circumcision and the Erotic Life of God and Israel." *Critical Inquiry* 18.3 (1992): 474–505.

Boyarin, Daniel. *Unheroic Conduct: The Rise of Heterosexuality and the Invention of the Jewish Man.* Berkeley: U of California P, 1997.

Boyarin, Daniel, and Jonathan Boyarin. "Diaspora: Generation and the Ground of Jewish Identity." *Critical Inquiry* 19.4 (1993): 693–725.

Boyarin, Daniel, and Jonathan Boyarin. "Self-Exposure as Theory: The Double Mark of the Male Jew." *Rhetorics of Self-Making.* Ed. Debbora Battaglia. Berkeley: U of California P, 1995. 16–42.

Boyarin, Jonathan. *Palestine and Jewish History: Criticism at the Borders of Ethnography.* Minneapolis: U of Minnesota P, 1996.

Boyarin, Jonathan. *Thinking in Jewish.* Chicago: U of Chicago P, 1996.

Boyd, Herb. "Plagiarism and the *Roots* Suits." *First World* 2.3 (1979): 31–33.

Boyd, Jason O. "The Tale of the Booger Hollar Bridge." *Stanly News and Press* 20 Aug. 2013: 1–2A.

Bravmann, Scott. *Queer Fictions of the Past: History, Culture, and Difference.* Cambridge: Cambridge UP, 1997.

Braziel, Jana Evans. *Artists, Performers, and Black Masculinity in the Haitian Diaspora.* Bloomington: Indiana UP, 2008.

Braziel, Jana Evans, and Anita Mannur, eds. and intro. *Theorizing Diaspora: A Reader.* Oxford: Blackwell, 2003.

Brooks, Peter. *Reading for the Plot: Design and Intention in Narrative.* Cambridge: Harvard UP, 1984.

Brown, Jacqueline Nassy. "Black Liverpool, Black America, and the Gendering of Diasporic Space." *Cultural Anthropology* 13.3 (1998): 291–325.

Brown, Jacqueline Nassy. *Dropping Anchor, Setting Sail: Geographies of Race in Black Liverpool.* Princeton: Princeton UP, 2005.

Buckley, Stephen. "Gambians Criticize Noted *Roots* Author." *Raleigh News and Observer* 20 May 1995: 13A.

Bugul, Ken. *The Abandoned Baobab: The Autobiography of a Senegalese Woman.* Trans. Marjolijn de Jager. New York: Lawrence Hill, 1991.

Bugul, Ken. *Le baobab fou.* Dakar: Nouvelles Éditions Africaines, 1984.

Burton, Richard D. E. "*Ki moun nou ye?* The Idea of Difference in Contemporary French West Indian Thought." *New West Indian Guide/Nieuwe West-Indische Gids* 67.1–2 (1993): 5–32.

Burton, Richard D. E. "Two Views of Césaire: *Négritude* and *Créolité.*" *Dalhousie French Studies* 35 (1996): 135–52.

Butler, Judith. *Antigone's Claim: Kinship between Life and Death.* New York: Columbia UP, 2000.

Butler, Judith. "The Force of Fantasy: Feminism, Mapplethorpe, and Discursive Excess." *differences* 2.2 (1990): 105–25.

Butler, Judith. "The Lesbian Phallus and the Morphological Imaginary." *Bodies That Matter: On the Discursive Limits of "Sex."* New York: Routledge, 1993. 57–91.

Butler, Kim D. "Defining Diaspora, Refining a Discourse." *Diaspora* 10.2 (2001): 189–219.

Butor, Michel. *L'emploi du temps.* Paris: Minuit, 1956.

Butor, Michel. *Passing Time.* Trans. Jean Stewart. New York: Simon and Schuster, 1960.

Camara, Laye. *Dramouss.* Paris: Plon, 1966.

Camara, Laye. *A Dream of Africa.* Trans. James Kirkup. London: Collins, 1968.

Camara, Laye. *L'enfant noir.* Paris: Plon, 1953.

Campt, Tina, and Deborah A. Thomas, eds. *Gendering Diaspora.* Spec. issue of *Feminist Review* 90 (2008).

Caron, David. *My Father and I: The Marais and the Queerness of Community.* Ithaca: Cornell UP, 2009.

Carrier, Joseph M., and Stephen O. Murray. "Woman-Woman Marriage in Africa." Murray and Roscoe 255–66.

Castle, Terry. *The Apparitional Lesbian: Female Homosexuality and Modern Culture.* New York: Columbia UP, 1993.

Cawelti, John G. *Adventure, Mystery, and Romance: Formula Stories as Art and Popular Culture.* Chicago: U of Chicago P, 1976.

Césaire, Aimé. *Cahier d'un retour au pays natal.* Paris: Présence Africaine, 1983.

Césaire, Aimé. *Notebook of a Return to the Native Land.* Trans. and ed. Clayton Eshleman and Annette Smith. Middleton, CT: Wesleyan UP, 2001.

Césaire, Aimé. *La poésie.* Paris: Seuil, 1994.

Chambers, Ross. *Room for Maneuver: Reading (the) Oppositional (in) Narrative.* Chicago: U of Chicago P, 1991.

Chambers, Ross. *Untimely Interventions: AIDS Writing, Testimonial, and the Rhetoric of Haunting.* Ann Arbor: U of Michigan P, 2004.

Chamoiseau, Patrick. *Chronicle of the Seven Sorrows.* Trans. and afterword Linda Coverdale. Lincoln: U of Nebraska P, 1999.

Chamoiseau, Patrick. *Chronique des sept misères.* Paris: Gallimard, 1986.

Chamoiseau, Patrick. "Reflections on Maryse Condé's *Traversée de la Mangrove.*" Trans. Kathleen M. Balutansky. *Callaloo* 14.2 (1991): 389–95.

Chamoiseau, Patrick. *Solibo Magnifique.* Paris: Gallimard, 1988.

Chamoiseau, Patrick. *Solibo Magnificent.* Trans. Rose-Myriam Réjouis and Val Vinokurov. New York: Vintage, 1997.

Chamoiseau, Patrick. *Texaco.* Paris: Gallimard, 1992.

Chamoiseau, Patrick, and Raphaël Confiant. *Lettres créoles: Tracées antillaises et continentales de la littérature—Haïti, Guadeloupe, Martinique, Guyane, 1635–1975.* Paris: Hatier, 1991.

Chauncey, George. "'What Gay Studies Taught the Court': The Historians' Amicus Brief in *Lawrence v. Texas.*" *GLQ* 10.3 (2004): 509–38.

Cho, Grace M. *Haunting the Korean Diaspora: Shame, Secrecy, and the Forgotten War.* Minneapolis: U of Minnesota P, 2008.

Chomsky, Noam. *The Fateful Triangle: The United States, Israel, and the Palestinians.* Boston: South End, 1983.

Cixous, Hélène. *Portrait de Jacques Derrida en Jeune Saint Juif.* 1991. Paris: Galilée, 2001.

Cleaver, Eldridge. *Soul on Ice.* New York: McGraw-Hill, 1968.

Clifford, James. "Diasporas." *Cultural Anthropology* 9.3 (1994): 302–38.

Clough, Patricia T. "The Affective Turn: Political Economy, Biomedia, and Bodies." *The Affect Theory Reader.* Ed. Melissa Gregg and Gregory J. Seigworth. Durham: Duke UP, 2010. 206–25.

Coe, Joffre Lanning. *Town Creek Indian Mound: A Native American Legacy.* Chapel Hill: U of North Carolina P, 1995.

Cohen, Jeffrey J., and Todd R. Ramlow. "Pink Vectors of Deleuze: Queer Theory and Inhumanism." O'Rourke.

Cohen, Robin. *Global Diasporas: An Introduction.* Seattle: U of Washington P, 1997.

Cole, Catherine M., Takyiwaa Manuh, and Stephan F. Miescher, eds. *Africa after Gender?* Bloomington: Indiana UP, 2007.

Condé, Maryse. *Crossing the Mangrove.* Trans. Richard Philcox. New York: Doubleday, 1995.

Condé, Maryse. "Order, Disorder, Freedom, and the West Indian Writer." *Yale French Studies* 83 (1993): 121–35.

Condé, Maryse. *Traversée de la mangrove.* Paris: Mercure de France, 1989. Coll. Folio.

Condé, Maryse, and Madeleine Cottenet-Hage, eds. *Penser la créolité.* Paris: Karthala, 1995.

Confiant, Raphaël. *Aimé Césaire: Une traversée paradoxale du siècle.* Paris: Stock, 1993.

Confiant, Raphaël. *L'allée des soupirs.* Paris: Grasset, 1994. Coll. Livre de Poche.

Confiant, Raphaël. *Eau de Café.* Paris: Grasset, 1991. Coll. Livre de Poche.

Confiant, Raphaël. *Eau de Café.* Trans. James Ferguson. London: Faber and Faber, 1999.

Confiant, Raphaël. *Le nègre et l'amiral.* Paris: Grasset, 1988.

Core, Philip. *Camp: The Lie That Tells the Truth.* New York: Putnam, 1984.

Courlander, Harold. "Kunta Kinte's Struggle to Be African." *Phylon* 47.4 (1986): 294–302.

Crosta, Suzanne. "Narrative and Discursive Strategies in Maryse Condé's *Traversée de la Mangrove.*" *Callaloo* 15.1 (1992): 147–55.

Crowder, Michael. *Pagans and Politicians.* London: Hutchinson, 1959.

Dadson, Philip. "Steve Reich in Conversation with Philip Dadson." *Music in New Zealand* 9 (1990): 28–33, 58.

Darnton, John. "Kunta Kinte's Village in Gambia Takes *Roots* Author to Its Heart." *New York Times* 14 April 1977: A1, 4.

Dash, J. Michael. *The Other America: Caribbean Literature in a New World Context.* Charlottesville: UP of Virginia, 1998.

"David Kato." *The Economist* 12 Feb. 2001: 96.

Davidson, Michael. "A 1958 Visit to a Dakar Boy Brothel." Murray and Roscoe 111–13.

de Certeau, Michel. *L'écriture de l'histoire.* Paris: Gallimard, 1975.

de Certeau, Michel. *The Writing of History.* Trans. Tom Conley. New York: Columbia UP, 1988.

Deleuze, Gilles. *Cinéma.* Paris: Minuit, 1983, 1985. 2 vols.

Deleuze, Gilles. "Philosophy of the *Série Noire.*" 1996. Trans. Timothy S. Murphy. *Genre* 34 (2001): 5–10.

Deleuze, Gilles, and Félix Guattari. *L'anti-Œdipe.* Vol. 1 of *Capitalisme et schizophrénie.* Paris: Minuit, 1972.

Deleuze, Gilles, and Félix Guattari. *Anti-Oedipus: Capitalism and Schizophrenia.* Trans. Robert Hurley, Mark Seem, and Helen R. Lane. Minneapolis: U of Minnesota P, 1983.

Deleuze, Gilles, and Félix Guattari. *Mille plateaux*. Vol. 2 of *Capitalisme et schizophrénie*. Paris: Minuit, 1980.

Deleuze, Gilles, and Félix Guattari. *A Thousand Plateaus: Capitalism and Schizophrenia*. Trans. Brian Massumi. Minneapolis: U of Minnesota P, 1987.

DeLoughrey, Elizabeth. "Gendering the Oceanic Voyage: Trespassing the (Black) Atlantic and Caribbean." *Thamyris* 5.2 (1998): 205–31.

Delvaux, Martine. *Histoires de fantômes: Spectralité et témoignage dans les récits de femmes contemporains*. Montreal: PU de Montréal, 2005.

Derrida, Jacques. *The Animal That Therefore I Am*. 2006. Ed. Marie-Louise Mallet. Trans. David Wills. New York: Fordham UP, 2008.

Derrida, Jacques. *Archive Fever: A Freudian Impression*. 1995. Chicago: Chicago UP, 1996.

Derrida, Jacques. *The Beast and the Sovereign*. 2008–2010. Ed. Michel Lisse, Marie-Louise Mallet, and Ginette Michaud. Trans. Geoffrey Bennington. Chicago: Chicago UP, 2009–11. 2 vols.

Derrida, Jacques. *La carte postale: De Socrate à Freud et au-delà*. Paris: Flammarion, 1980.

Derrida, Jacques. *De la grammatologie*. Paris: Minuit, 1967.

Derrida, Jacques. *La dissémination*. Paris: Seuil, 1972.

Derrida, Jacques. *Dissemination*. Trans. Barbara Johnson. Chicago: U of Chicago P, 1981.

Derrida, Jacques. *The Ear of the Other: Otobiography, Transference, Translation*. Ed. Christie McDonald. Lincoln: U of Nebraska P, 1985.

Derrida, Jacques. *L'écriture et la différence*. Paris: Seuil, 1967.

Derrida, Jacques. *États d'âme de la psychanalyse: L'impossible au-delà d'une souveraine cruauté*. Paris: Galilée, 2000.

Derrida, Jacques. *Glas*. Paris: Denoël/Gonthier, 1981. 2 vols.

Derrida, Jacques. *Glas*. Trans. John P. Leavey Jr. and Richard Rand. Lincoln: U of Nebraska P, 1986.

Derrida, Jacques. "Letter to a Japanese Friend." *A Derrida Reader: Between the Blinds*. Ed. Peggy Kamuf. New York: Columbia UP, 1991. 270–76.

Derrida, Jacques. "Me—Psychoanalysis: An Introduction to the Translation of 'The Shell and the Kernel' by Nicolas Abraham." *diacritics* 9.1 (1979): 4–12.

Derrida, Jacques. *The Monolingualism of the Other; or, The Prosthesis of Origins*. Trans. Patrick Mensah. Stanford: Stanford UP, 1998.

Derrida, Jacques. *Le monolinguisme de l'autre, ou la prothèse d'origine*. Paris: Galilée, 1996.

Derrida, Jacques. *Of Grammatology*. Trans. and intro. Gayatri Chakravorty Spivak. 1974. Baltimore: Johns Hopkins UP, 1997.

Derrida, Jacques. *Positions*. Paris: Minuit, 1972.

Derrida, Jacques. *Positions*. Trans. Alan Bass. Chicago: U of Chicago P, 1981.

Derrida, Jacques. *The Post Card: From Socrates to Freud and Beyond*. Trans., intro., and notes Alan Bass. Chicago: U of Chicago P, 1987.

Derrida, Jacques. *Psyche: Inventions of the Other*. 1987. Ed. Peggy Kamuf and Elizabeth Rottenberg. Stanford: Stanford UP, 2007.

Derrida, Jacques. *Résistances de la psychanalyse*. Paris: Galilée, 1996.

Derrida, Jacques. *Resistances of Psychoanalysis*. Trans. Peggy Kamuf, Pascale-Anne Brault, and Michael Naas. Stanford: Stanford UP, 1998.

Derrida, Jacques. *Specters of Marx: The State of the Debt, the Work of Mourning, and the New International*. Trans. Peggy Kamuf. New York: Routledge, 1994.

Derrida, Jacques. *Spectres de Marx: L'état de la dette, le travail du deuil et la nouvelle Internationale*. Paris: Galilée, 1993.

Derrida, Jacques. *Sur parole: Instantanés philosophiques.* Paris: de L'Aube, 1999.

Derrida, Jacques. "The Transcendental 'Stupidity' ('Bêtise') of Man and the Becoming-Animal According to Deleuze." Schwab 35–60.

Derrida, Jacques. *Writing and Difference.* Trans. and intro. Alan Bass. Chicago: U of Chicago P, 1978.

Desai, Gaurav. "Out in Africa." *Genders* 25 (1997):120–43. Hawley 139–84.

D'haen, Theo, ed. *(Un)writing Empire.* Amsterdam: Rodopi, 1998.

Directory of Albemarle, N.C., and New Town, Efird, and Wiscassett Hill and Kingville. Ed. A. Selders. N.pl.: A. Selders, 1930.

Drake, St. Clair. "Diaspora Studies and Pan-Africanism." Harris 451–514.

Duberman, Martin Bauml, Martha Vicinus, and George Chauncey Jr., eds. *Hidden from History: Reclaiming the Gay and Lesbian Past.* New York: Penguin, 1989.

Dugas, Guy. *Albert Memmi: Du malheur d'être juif au bonheur sépharade.* Paris: Nadir, 2001.

Dunton, Chris. "'Wheyting Be Dat?' The Treatment of Homosexuality in African Literature." *Research in African Literatures* 20.3 (1989): 422–48.

Dynes, Wayne R. *Homosexuality: A Research Guide.* New York: Garland, 1987.

Early, L. R. "Dying Gods: A Study of Wole Soyinka's *The Interpreters.*" *Journal of Commonwealth Literature* 12.2 (1997): 162–74.

Efird, Oscar Agburn. *The History and Genealogy of the Efird Family.* Winston-Salem, NC: Winston Printing, 1964.

Egoyan, Atom, dir. *The Adjuster.* Canada, 1991.

Egoyan, Atom, dir. *Adoration.* Canada, 2008.

Egoyan, Atom, dir. *Ararat.* Canada, 2002.

Egoyan, Atom, dir. *Calendar.* Armenia/Canada/Germany, 1993.

Egoyan, Atom, dir. *Exotica.* Canada, 1994.

Egoyan, Atom, dir. *Family Viewing.* Canada, 1987.

Egoyan, Atom, dir. *Felicia's Journey.* Canada, 1999.

Egoyan, Atom. "In Other Words: Poetic License and the Incarnation of History." Lecture, U of Michigan, Ann Arbor, 16 Oct. 2003.

Egoyan, Atom, dir. *Next of Kin.* Canada, 1984.

Egoyan, Atom. *Speaking Parts.* Toronto: Coach House, 1993. Published screenplay.

Egoyan, Atom, dir. *Speaking Parts.* Canada, 1989.

Egoyan, Atom, dir. *The Sweet Hereafter.* Canada, 1997.

Eilberg-Schwartz, Howard. *God's Phallus and Other Problems for Men and Monotheism.* Boston: Beacon, 1994.

Eilberg-Schwartz, Howard. *The Savage in Judaism: An Anthropology of Israelite Religion and Ancient Judaism.* Bloomington: Indiana UP, 1990.

Eisenger, Erica Mendelson. "The Adaptation of Detective Story Techniques in the French New Novel." PhD diss. Yale U, 1973.

Eng, David L. "Out Here and Over There: Queerness and Diaspora in Asian American Studies." *Social Text* 52/53 (1997): 31–52.

Eng, David L., and Alice Y. Hom, eds. *Q&A: Queer in Asian America.* Philadelphia: Temple UP, 1998.

Epprecht, Marc. "'Good God Almighty, What's This!': Homosexual 'Crime' in Early Colonial Zimbabwe." Murray and Roscoe 197–221.

Epprecht, Marc. *Heterosexual Africa? The History of an Idea from the Age of Exploration to the Age of AIDS.* Athens: Ohio UP, 2008.

Epprecht, Marc. *Hungochani: The History of a Dissident Sexuality in Southern Africa.* Montreal/Kingston: McGill Queen's UP, 2004.

Epprecht, Marc. "The 'Unsaying' of Indigenous Homosexualities in Zimbabwe: Mapping a Blindspot in an African Masculinity." *Journal of Southern African Studies* 24.4 (1998): 631–51.

Evans-Pritchard, E. E. "Sexual Inversion among the Azande." *American Anthropologist* 72 (1970): 1428–34.

Fanon, Frantz. *Black Skin, White Masks.* Trans. Charles Lam Markmann. New York: Grove, 1967.

Fanon, Frantz. *Black Skin, White Masks.* Trans. Richard Philcox. New York: Grove, 2008.

Fanon, Frantz. *Peau noire, masques blancs.* Paris: Seuil, 1952. Coll. Points.

Faulkner, William. *Absalom, Absalom!* 1936. New York: Random House, 1951.

Faulkner, William. *The Sound and the Fury and As I Lay Dying.* 1929, 1930. New York: Random House, 1946.

Faupel, J. F. *African Holocaust: The Story of the Uganda Martyrs.* New York: Kenedy, 1962.

Ferguson, Roderick A. *Aberrations in Black: Toward a Queer of Color Critique.* Minneapolis: U of Minnesota P, 2004.

Field, Douglas. "Looking for Jimmy Baldwin: Sex, Privacy, and Black Nationalist Fervor." *Callaloo* 27.2 (2004): 457–80.

Finding Oprah's Roots: Finding Your Own. PBS Home Video, 2007.

Fraser, C. Gerald. "Haley Is Hoping to Debate Reporter." *New York Times* 10 April 1977: sec. 1, 29.

Freud, Sigmund. "The Aetiology of Hysteria." 1896. *The Standard Edition of the Complete Psychological Works of Sigmund Freud.* Ed. James Strachey. London: Hagarth and the Institute of Psychoanalysis, 1962. Vol. 3. 187–221.

Freud, Sigmund. "Dreams and Occultism." 1932. *The Standard Edition.* Vol. 22. 31–56.

Freud, Sigmund. "Screen Memories." 1899. *The Standard Edition.* Vol. 3. 299–322.

Fuss, Diana. *Essentially Speaking: Feminism, Nature, and Difference.* New York: Routledge, 1989.

Gale, Matthew. *Arshile Gorky: Enigma and Nostalgia.* London: Tate, 2010.

Gallop, Jane. "Phallus/Penis: Same Difference." *Thinking through the Body.* New York: Columbia UP, 1988. 124–32.

Garel, Sylvain. "Atom Egoyan: Le cinéma comme obsession." *Cinéma* 478 (June 1991): 43–44.

Gates, Henry Louis, Jr. *Finding Oprah's Roots: Finding Your Own.* New York: Crown, 2007.

Gaudio, Rudolf P. "Male Lesbians and Other Queer Notions in Hausa." Murray and Roscoe 115–28.

Gaudio, Rudolf P. "Not Talking Straight in Hausa." *Queerly Phrased: Language, Gender, and Sexuality.* Ed. Anna Livia and Kira Hall. New York: Oxford UP, 1997. 416–29.

Gay, Judith. "'Mummies and Babies' and Friends and Lovers in Lesotho." *Journal of Homosexuality* 11.3/4 (1985): 97–116.

Genet, Jean. *Journal du voleur.* Paris: Gallimard, 1949.

Genet, Jean. *The Thief's Journal.* New York: Grove, 1964.

Gilman, Sander. *The Jew's Body.* New York: Routledge, 1991.

Gilroy, Paul. *The Black Atlantic: Modernity and Double Consciousness.* Cambridge: Harvard UP, 1993.

Gilroy, Paul. *"There Ain't No Black in the Union Jack": The Cultural Politics of Race and Nation.* Chicago: U of Chicago P, 1987.

Glissant, Édouard. *Caribbean Discourse: Selected Essays.* Trans. J. Michael Dash. Charlottesville: UP of Virginia, 1989.

Glissant, Édouard. *La case du commandeur.* Paris: Seuil, 1981.

Glissant, Édouard. *Le discours antillais.* Paris: Seuil, 1981.

Glissant, Édouard. *Faulkner, Mississippi.* Paris: Stock, 1996.

Glissant, Édouard. *L'intention poétique.* Paris: Gallimard, 1997.

Glissant, Édouard. *Introduction à une poétique du divers.* Paris: Gallimard, 1996.

Glissant, Édouard. *La Lézarde.* Paris: Seuil, 1958.

Glissant, Édouard. *Mahogany.* Paris: Seuil, 1987.

Glissant, Édouard. *Malemort.* Paris: Seuil, 1975.

Glissant, Édouard. "Migration, Memory, Trace: Writing in French Outside of the Hexagone." Keynote address. Conference. New York U. New York, 20 Apr. 2000.

Glissant, Édouard. *Ormerod.* Paris: Gallimard, 2003.

Glissant, Édouard. *Poetics of Relation.* Trans. Betsy Wing. Ann Arbor: U of Michigan P, 1997.

Glissant, Édouard. *Poétique de la relation.* Paris: Gallimard, 1990.

Glissant, Édouard. *Le quatrième siècle.* Paris: Seuil, 1964.

Glissant, Édouard. *Sartorius: Le roman des Batoutos.* Paris: Gallimard, 1999.

Glissant, Édouard. *Traité du tout-monde.* Paris: Gallimard, 1997.

Glissant, Édouard. *Tout-monde.* Paris: Gallimard, 1993.

Goddard, Keith. "Statement from GALZ Regarding London-Based Outrage's Attempted Citizen's Arrest of President Mugabe." 3 Nov. 1999. Circulated on <queerAfrica@queernet.org>. 3 Nov. 1999.

Goldberg, Jonathan. "Sodomy in the New World: Anthropologies Old and New." *Fear of a Queer Planet: Queer Politics and Social Theory.* Ed. Michael Warner. Minneapolis: U of Minnesota P, 1993. 3–18.

Gopinath, Gayatri. *Impossible Desires: Queer Diasporas and South Asian Public Cultures.* Durham: Duke UP, 2005.

Gopinath, Gayatri. "Queer Diasporas: Gender, Sexuality and Migration in Contemporary South Asian Literature and Cultural Production." PhD diss. Columbia U, 1998.

Gopinath, Sumanth. "Reich in Blackface: *Oh Dem Watermelons* and Radical Minstrelsy in the 1960s." *Journal of the Society for American Music* 5 (2001): 139–93. <http://dx.doi.org.proxy.lib.umich.edu/10.1017/S1752196311000022>. 21 June 2012.

Gordon, Avery F. *Ghostly Matters: Haunting and the Sociological Imagination.* Minneapolis: U of Minnesota P, 1997.

Gorer, Geoffrey. *African Dances: A Book about West African Negroes.* London: Faber and Faber, 1935.

Gorer, Geoffrey. *African Dances: A Book about West African Negroes.* New York: Norton, 1962.

Gould, Eric, ed. *The Sin of the Book: Edmond Jabès.* Lincoln: U of Nebraska P, 1985.

Green, Arthur. *A Guide to the Zohar.* Stanford: Stanford UP, 2004.

Greer, Germaine. *The Female Eunuch.* New York: McGraw-Hill, 1971.

Gregg, Melissa, and Gregory J. Seigworth, eds. *The Affect Theory Reader.* Durham: Duke UP, 2010.

Grimsley, Jim. *Dream Boy.* New York: Simon and Schuster, 1995.

Gross, Elizabeth. "Criticism, Feminism, and the Institution: An Interview with Gayatri Chakravorty Spivak." *Thesis Eleven* 10/11 (1984–85): 175–87.

Gunkel, Henriette. "Some Reflections on Postcolonial Homophobia, Local Interventions, and LGBTI Solidarity Online: The Politics of Global Petitions." *African Studies Review* 56.2 (2013): 67–81.

Gunning, Sandra, Tera W. Hunter, and Michele Mitchell, eds. *Dialogues of Dispersal: Gender, Sexuality, and African Diasporas*. Malden, MA: Blackwell, 2004.

Gutiérrez, Ramón A. "Must We Deracinate Indians to Find Gay Roots?" *Out/Look* 1.4 (1989): 61–67.

Haberman, Clyde. "Massacre at Hebron Exposes Anti-American Mood in Israel." *New York Times* 20 March 1994: sec. 1, 1, 14.

Haley, Alex. "Black History, Oral History, and Genealogy." *Oral History Review* 1 (1973): 1–25.

Haley, Alex. "My Furthest-Back Person—'The African.'" *New York Times Magazine* 16 July 1972: 13–16.

Haley, Alex. "My Search for Roots: A Black American's Story." *Readers Digest* April 1977: 148–52.

Haley, Alex. *Roots: The Saga of an American Family*. New York: Dell, 1976.

Haley, Alex. "There Are Days When I Wish It Hadn't Happened." *Playboy* March 1977: 115, 136, 212–16.

Hall, Stuart. "Cultural Identity and Diaspora." 1990. *Diaspora and Visual Culture: Presenting Africans and Jews*. Ed. Nicholas Mirzoeff. London: Routledge, 2000. 21–33.

Hammer, Carl, Jr. *Rhinelanders on the Yadkin: The Story of the Pennsylvania Germans in Rowan and Cabarrus Counties North Carolina*. 1943. 2nd ed. Salisbury, NC: Rowan, 1965.

Harcourt, Peter. "Imaginary Images: An Examination of Atom Egoyan's Films." *Film Quarterly* 48.3 (1995): 2–14.

Harden, John. *The Devil's Tramping Ground and Other North Carolina Mystery Stories*. Chapel Hill: U of North Carolina P, 1949.

Harris, Joseph E., ed. and intro. *Global Dimensions of the African Diaspora*. 1982. Washington, DC: Howard UP, 1993.

Hawley, John C., ed. *Postcolonial, Queer: Theoretical Intersections*. Albany: SU of New York P, 2001.

Hayes, Jarrod. "Idyllic Masculinity and National Allegory: Unbecoming Men and Anticolonial Resistance in Camara Laye's *L'enfant noir*." *Entre hommes: Francophone Masculinities in Culture and Theory*. Ed. Todd W. Reeser and Lewis C. Seifert. Newark: U of Delaware P, 2008: 224–50.

Hayes, Jarrod. *Queer Nations: Marginal Sexualities in the Maghreb*. Chicago: U of Chicago P, 2000.

Hayes, Jarrod. "Queer Resistance to (Neo-)colonialism in Algeria." Hawley 79–97.

Hayes, Jarrod, Margaret Higonnet, and William J. Spurlin, eds. and intro. *Comparatively Queer: Interrogating Identities across Time and Cultures*. New York: Palgrave Macmillan, 2010.

Heath, Stephen. "Difference." *Screen* 19.3 (1978): 51–112.

Helmreich, Stefan. "Kinship, Nation, and Paul Gilroy's Concept of Diaspora." *Diaspora* 2.2 (1992): 243–49.

Herskovits, Melville J. *Dahomey: An Ancient West African Kingdom*. 1938. Evanston, IL: Northwestern UP, 1967. 2 vols.

Herskovits, Melville J. "A Note on 'Woman Marriage' in Dahomey." *Africa* 10 (1937): 335–41.

Hewitt, Leah D. "Inventing Antillean Narrative: Maryse Condé and Literary Tradition." *Studies in Twentieth Century Literature* 17.1 (1993): 79–96.

Hillier, Paul. "'Some More Lemon? . . .': A Conversation with Steve Reich." *Contemporary Music Review* 12.2 (1995): 65–75.

Hoad, Neville. *African Intimacies: Race, Homosexuality, and Globalization*. Minneapolis: U of Minnesota P, 2007.

Hoad, Neville. "Arrested Development or the Queerness of Savages: Resisting Evolutionary Narratives of Difference." *Postcolonial Studies* 3.2 (2000): 133–58.

Hocquenghem, Guy. *Le désir homosexuel*. Paris: Fayard, 1972.

Hocquenghem, Guy. *Homosexual Desire*. Trans. Daniella Dangoor. Durham: Duke UP, 1993.

Houbein, Lolo. "*The Interpreters:* The Whole Soyinka?" *ACLALS Bulletin* 5.3 (1980): 98–111.

Hovis, George. "Wolfe's Racism Revisited: A Response to Robert H. Brinkmeyer Jr." *Thomas Wolfe Review* 34 (2010): 87–100.

Howard, John. *Men Like That: A Southern Queer History*. Chicago: U of Chicago P, 1999.

Howard, John, ed. *Carryin' On in the Lesbian and Gay South*. New York: New York UP, 1997.

Huhndorf, Shari H. *Going Native: Indians in the American Cultural Imagination*. Ithaca: Cornell UP, 2001.

Hurston, Zora Neale. *Their Eyes Were Watching God*. New York: Harper, 2000.

IGLHRC (International Gay and Lesbian Human Rights Commission). "Roundups of Gays Reportedly Have Begun in Uganda." Press release circulated on glas@post. cis.smu.edu. 1 Nov. 1999.

Integrity USA. "Integrity Announces Formation of Ugandan Chapter." Press release, 7 July 2000. <http://www.integrityusa.org/gc2000/press/7-7-00b.htm>. 16 Nov. 2000.

Irving, Washington. *The Complete Tales of Washington Irving*. Ed. and intro. Charles Neider. Garden City, NJ: Doubleday, 1975. 31–56.

Jabès, Edmond. *Bâtir au quotidien*. Vol. 3 of *Le livre des marges*. N. pl.: Fata Morgana, 1997. 3 vols.

Jabès, Edmond. *The Book of Margins*. Trans. Rosmarie Waldrop. Chicago: U of Chicago P, 1993.

Jabès, Edmond. *The Book of Questions*. Trans Rosmarie Waldrop. Vol. 1 of *The Book of Questions*. Middletown, CT: Wesleyan UP, 1976. 4 vols.

Jabès, Edmond. *The Book of Questions II and III: The Book of Yukel, Return to the Book*. Trans. Rosmarie Waldrop. Vol. 2 of *The Book of Questions*. Middletown, CT: Wesleyan UP, 1977. 4 vols.

Jabès, Edmond. *The Book of Questions:* • *El, or The Last Book*. Vol. 4 of *The Book of Questions*. Middletown, CT: Wesleyan UP, 1984. 4 vols.

Jabès, Edmond. *The Book of Questions: Yaël, Elya, Aely*. Trans. Rosmarie Waldrop. Vol. 3 of *The Book of Questions*. Middletown, CT: Wesleyan UP, 1983. 4 vols.

Jabès, Edmond. *The Book of Resemblances*. Trans. Rosmarie Waldrop. Hanover, NH: UP of New England/Wesleyan UP, 1990–92. 3 vols.

Jabès, Edmond. *Ça suit son cours*. Vol. 1 of *Le livre des marges*. N. pl.: Fata Morgana, 1975. 3 vols.

Jabès, Edmond. *Dans la double dépendance du dit*. Vol. 2 of *Le livre des marges*. N. pl.: Fata Morgana, 1984. 3 vols.

Jabès, Edmond. *Du désert au livre, suivi de L'étranger: Entretiens avec Marcel Cohen*. Pessac: Opales, 2001.

Jabès, Edmond. *L'ineffaçable, L'inaperçu*. Vol. 3 of *Le livre des ressemblances*. Paris: Gallimard, 1980. 3 vols.

Jabès, Edmond. *Le livre du dialogue*. Vol. 2 of *Le livre des limites*. Paris: Gallimard, 1984. 4 vols.

Jabès, Edmond. *Le livre du partage*. Vol. 4 of *Le livre des limites*. Paris: Gallimard, 1987. 4 vols.

Jabès, Edmond. *Le livre des questions*. Paris: Gallimard, 1963–73. 2 vols.

Jabès, Edmond. *Le livre des ressemblances*. Vol. 1 of *Le livre des ressemblances*. Paris: Gallimard, 1976. 3 vols.

Jabès, Edmond. *Le parcours*. Vol. 3 of *Le livre des limites*. Paris: Gallimard, 1985. 4 vols.

Jabès, Edmond. *Le petit livre de la subversion hors de soupçon*. Vol. 1 of *Le livre des limites*. Paris: Gallimard, 1982. 4 vols.

Jabès, Edmond. *Le soupçon, Le désert*. Vol. 2 of *Le livre des ressemblances*. Paris: Gallimard, 1978. 3 vols.

Jackson, Erik. "Head Trip: Director Atom Egoyan Travels a Dark Psychological Path in *Felicia's Journey*." *Time Out N.Y.* 11–18 Nov. 1999: 111.

James, Caryn. "New Role for the Movies: Peeping Tom." *New York Times* 21 March 1990: C13, 20.

Jardine, Alice. "Men in Feminism: Odor di Uomo or Compagnons de Route?" *Men in Feminism*. Ed. Alice Jardine and Paul Smith. New York: Routledge, 1987. 54–61.

Jeyifo, Biodun. *Wole Soyinka: Politics, Poetics, and Postcolonialism*. Cambridge: Cambridge UP, 2004.

Johnson, E. Patrick. "'Quare' Studies, or (Almost) Everything I Know about Queer Studies I Learned from My Grandmother." 2001. Johnson and Henderson 124–57.

Johnson, E. Patrick, and Mae G. Henderson, eds. *Black Queer Studies: A Critical Anthology*. Durham: Duke UP, 2005.

Kaplan, Aryeh, trans. and commentary. *Sefer Yetzirah: The Book of Creation*. York Beach, ME: Weiser, 1990.

Katz, David S. "Shylock's Gender: Jewish Male Menstruation in Early Modern England." *Review of English Studies* 50 (1999): 440–62.

Katz, Jonathan Ned. *The Invention of Heterosexuality*. New York: Dutton, 1995.

Kinkead-Weekes, Mark. "*The Interpreters*: A Form of Criticism." *Critical Perspectives on Wole Soyinka*. Ed. James Gibbs. Washington, DC: Three Continents, 1980. 219–38.

Klawans, Stuart. "Getting Inside the Head for a Portrait of Evil." Rev. of Atom Egoyan's *Felicia's Journey*. *New York Times* 21 Nov. 1999: 15, 24.

Kleis, Gerald W., and Salisu A. Abdullahi. "Masculine Power and Gender Ambiguity in Urban Hausa Society." *African Urban Studies* 16 (1983): 39–53.

Kramer, Jonathan D. *The Time of Music: New Meanings, New Temporalities, New Listening Strategies*. New York: Schirmer, 1988.

Krige, Eileen Jensen. "Woman-Marriage, with Special Reference to the Lovedu: Its Significance for the Definition of Marriage." *Africa* 44 (1974): 11–37.

Kristeva, Julia. *Pouvoirs de l'horreur: Essai sur l'abjection*. Paris: Seuil, 1980.

Kristeva, Julia. *Powers of Horror: An Essay on Abjection*. Trans. Leon S. Roudiez. New York: Columbia UP, 1982.

Kronick, Joseph G. "Edmond Jabès and the Poetry of Jewish Unhappy Consciousness." *MLN* 106 (1991): 967–96.

La Fountain-Stokes, Lawrence. "Culture, Representation, and the Puerto Rican Queer Diaspora." PhD diss. Columbia U, 1999.

La Fountain-Stokes, Lawrence. *Queer Ricans: Cultures and Sexualities in the Diaspora*. Minneapolis: U of Minnesota P, 2009.

Lamiot, Christophe. "A Question of Questions through a Mangrove Wood." *Callaloo* 15.1 (1992): 138–46.

Lannes, Sylvie. "*Coro* de Berio et *Drumming* de Reich: Deux compositions inté-
grant les *polyrythmies* africaines, comme expérience de renouveau." *Canadian
University Music Review/Revue de musique des universités canadiennes* 11.1 (1991):
101–27.

Laplanche, Jean. *New Foundations for Psychoanalysis.* Trans. David Macey. Oxford:
Blackwell, 1989.

Laplanche, Jean. *Nouveaux fondements pour la psychanalyse: La séduction originaire.* Paris:
PU de France, 1987.

Laplanche, Jean, and Jean-Baptiste Pontalis. *Fantasme originaire, fantasmes des origines,
origines du fantasme.* 1964. Paris: Hachette, 1985.

Laplanche, Jean, and Jean-Baptiste Pontalis. "Fantasy and the Origins of Sexuality."
Formations of Fantasy. Ed. Victor Burgin, James Donald, and Cora Kaplan. London:
Methuen, 1986. 5–34.

Laplanche, Jean, and Jean-Baptiste Pontalis. *The Language of Psycho-Analysis.* Trans.
Donald Nicholson-Smith. London: Hogarth, 1973.

Laplanche, Jean, and Jean-Baptiste Pontalis. *Vocabulaire de la psychanalyse.* Paris: PU
de France, 1967.

Larrier, Renée. *Autofiction and Advocacy in the Francophone Caribbean.* Gainesville: U of
Florida P, 2006.

Lavie, Smadar, and Ted Swedenburg, eds. *Displacement, Diaspora, and Geographies of
Identity.* Durham: Duke UP, 1996.

Law, Robin. Rev. of Alex Haley's *Roots. Oral History* 6.1 (1978): 128–34.

Lejeune, Philippe. *On Autobiography.* Ed. Paul John Eakin. Trans. Katherine Leary.
Minneapolis: U of Minnesota P, 1989.

Lewis, Earl. "To Turn as on a Pivot: Writing African Americans into a History of Overlapping Diasporas." *American Historical Review* 100.3 (1995): 765–87.

Leyland, Winston, ed. *Gay Roots: Twenty Years of Gay Sunshine—An Anthology of Gay History, Sex, Politics, and Culture.* San Francisco: Gay Sunshine, 1991.

Lionnet, Françoise. *Autobiographical Voices: Race, Gender, Self-Portraiture.* Ithaca: Cornell
UP, 1989.

Ly, Mamadou Moustapha. "Édouard Glissant in Theory and Practice: A Diasporic
Poetics of Politics." PhD diss. U of Michigan, 2014.

Malena, Anne. *The Negotiated Self: The Dynamics of Identity in Francophone Caribbean Narrative.* New York: Lang, 1999.

Manalansan, Martin F., IV. *Global Divas: Filipino Gay Men in the Diaspora.* Durham:
Duke UP, 2003.

Mannoni, Octave. "Je sais bien, mais quand meme. . . ." *Clefs pour l'imaginaire; ou,
L'autre scène.* Paris: Seuil, 1969. 9–33.

Massad, Joseph. "The Legacy of Jean-Paul Sartre." *Al-Ahram Weekly Online* 30 Jan.–5 Feb.
2003. <http://weekly.ahram.org.eg/print/2003/623/op33.htm>. 1 July 2009.

Masson, Jeffrey Moussaieff. *The Assault on Truth: Freud's Suppression of the Seduction
Theory.* New York: Farrar, Straus and Giroux, 1984.

Maugham-Brown, David. "Interpreting and *The Interpreters:* Wole Soyinka and Practical Criticism." *English in Africa* 6.2 (1979): 51–62.

M'Baye, Babacar. "The Origins of Senegalese Homophobia: Discourses on Homosexuals and Transgender People in Colonial and Postcolonial Senegal." *African
Studies Review* 56.2 (2013): 109–28.

McClary, Susan. *Conventional Wisdom: The Content of Musical Form.* Berkeley: U of California P, 2000.

McClary, Susan. *Feminine Endings: Music, Gender, and Sexuality*. Minneapolis: U of Minnesota P, 1991.

McCusker, Maeve. "De la problématique du territoire à la problématique du lieu: Un entretien avec Patrick Chamoiseau." *French Review* 73.4 (2000): 724–33.

McEwan, Nicole. "The Analyst: Filmmaker Atom Egoyan Talks with *Filmbill*'s Nicole McEwan about *Felicia's Journey* and the Nature of Choice." *Angelika Filmbill* 6.5 (1999): 10–14.

McFadden, Robert D. "Some Points of 'Roots' Questioned: Haley Stands by Book as a Symbol." *New York Times* 10 April 1977: sec. 1, 1, 29.

McGarry, Molly. *Ghosts of Futures Past: Spiritualism and the Cultural Politics of Nineteenth-Century America*. Berkeley: U of California P, 2008.

McKenzie, Peter. *Hail Orisha! A Phenomenology of a West African Religion in the Mid-Nineteenth Century*. Leiden: Brill, 1997.

McSorley, Tom. *Atom Egoyan's "The Adjuster."* Toronto: U of Toronto P, 2009.

Memmi, Albert. *Agar.* 1955. Paris: Gallimard, 1984.

Memmi, Albert. *The Colonizer and the Colonized*. Trans. Howard Greenfeld. New York: Orion, 1965.

Memmi, Albert. *Jews and Arabs*. Trans. Eleanor Levieux. Chicago: O'Hara, 1975.

Memmi, Albert. *Juifs et Arabes*. Paris: Gallimard, 1974.

Memmi, Albert. *La Libération du Juif*. Paris: Gallimard, 1966.

Memmi, Albert. *The Liberation of the Jew*. Trans. Judy Hyun. New York: Orion, 1966.

Memmi, Albert. *The Pillar of Salt*. Trans. Édouard Roditi. Boston: Beacon, 1992.

Memmi, Albert. *Portrait du colonisé, précédé de Portrait du colonisateur*. 1957. Paris: Gallimard, 1985.

Memmi, Albert. *La statue de sel*. 1953. Paris: Gallimard, 1966. Coll. Folio.

Memmi, Albert. *La terre intérieure: Entretiens avec Victor Malka*. Paris: Gallimard, 1976.

Mercer, Kobena. Contribution to a round table discussion at the conference Black Nations/Queer Nations? sponsored by the Center for Lesbian and Gay Studies, CUNY Graduate School, New York, 10 March 1995.

Mercer, Kobena. "Diaspora Culture and the Dialogic Imagination: The Aesthetics of Black Independent Film in Britain." 1988. Braziel and Mannur 247–60.

Mercer, Kobena. *Welcome to the Jungle: New Positions in Black Cultural Studies*. New York: Routledge, 1994.

Mercer, Kobena, and Isaac Julien. "Race, Sexual Politics, and Black Masculinity: A Dossier." *Male Order: Unwrapping Masculinity*. Ed. Rowena Chapman and Jonathan Rutherford. London: Lawrence and Wishart, 1988. 97–164.

Métreau, Joël. "L'honneur des makoumès." *Têtu* Sept. 1999. <http://www.têtu.com/archives/1999–09/2>. 13 Nov. 2004.

Miller, Christopher L. *Theories of Africans: Francophone Literature and Anthropology in Africa*. Chicago: U of Chicago P, 1990.

Miller, Nancy K. *Bequest and Betrayal: Memoirs of a Parent's Death*. 1996. Bloomington: Indiana UP, 2000.

Miller, Nancy K. "My Father's Penis." *Getting Personal: Feminist Occasions and Other Autobiographical Acts*. New York: Routledge, 1991. 143–47.

Mills, Elizabeth Shown, and Gary B. Mills. "The Genealogist's Assessment of Alex Haley's *Roots*." *National Genealogical Society Quarterly* 72.1 (1984): 35–49.

Mills, Elizabeth Shown, and Gary B. Mills. "*Roots* and the New 'Faction': A Legitimate Tool for Clio?" *Virginia Magazine of History and Biography* 89.1 (1981): 3–26.

Mogale, Israel. "Mugabe Repeats 'Gangster Gay' Claims." *Independent* (South Africa) 12 Nov. 1999. Circulated on glas@post.cis.smu.edu. 13 Nov. 1999.

Moore, David Chioni. "Revisiting a Silenced Giant: Alex Haley's *Roots*—A Bibliographic Essay and a Research Report on the Haley Archives at the University of Tennessee, Knoxville." *Resources for American Literary Study* 22.2 (1996): 195–249.

Moore, David Chioni. "Routes: Alex Haley's *Roots* and the Rhetoric of Genealogy." *Transition* 64 (1994): 4–21.

Morgan, Fred T. "Ghostly Happenings at YMCA? Employees Learn to Accept 'Strange' Incidents." *Stanly News and Press* 30 May 2000: 1A, 3A.

Morgan, Fred T. "The Ghost of Jezebel." *Haunted Uwharries* 66–71.

Morgan, Fred T. *Haunted Uwharries: Ghost Stories, Witch Tales, and Other Strange Happenings from North America's Oldest Mountains*. Asheboro, NC: Down Home, 1992.

Morgan, Fred T. "The Musical Ghost of Rocky River." *Haunted Uwharries* 8–14.

Morgan, Jacob L., Bachman S. Brown Jr., and John Hall, eds. *History of the Lutheran Church in North Carolina*. N. pl.: United Evangelical Lutheran Synod of North Carolina, n.d.

Morgan, Ruth, and Saskia Wieringa. *Tommy Boys, Lesbian Men, and Ancestral Wives: Female Same-Sex Practices in Africa*. Johannesburg: Jacana, 2005.

Morrison, Kathleen. "The Second Self as Vision of Horror in Wole Soyinka's *The Interpreters*." *Black American Literature Forum* 22.4 (1988): 753–65.

Morrison, Paul. "End Pleasure." *GLQ* 1.1 (1993): 53–78.

Morrison, Toni. *Beloved*. New York: Knopf, 1987.

Mudimbe, V. Y. *Entre les eaux*. Paris: Présence Africaine, 1973.

Muñoz, José Esteban. *Disidentifications: Queers of Color and the Performance of Politics*. Minneapolis: U of Minnesota P, 1999.

Munro, Brenna M. "Gender and Sexuality in African Fiction." *The Novel in Africa and the Atlantic World*. Ed. Simon Gikandi. Vol. 11 of *Oxford History of the Novel in English*. Oxford: Oxford UP. Forthcoming.

Munro, Brenna M. "Queer Family Romance: Writing the 'New' South Africa in the 1990s." *GLQ* 15.3 (2009): 397–439.

Murray, David Alexander Bruce. "'Martiniquais': The Construction and Contestation of a Cultural Identity." PhD diss. U of Virginia, 1995.

Murray, Stephen O., and Will Roscoe, eds. *Boy-Wives and Female Husbands: Studies of African Homosexualities*. New York: St. Martin's, 1998.

Niang, Cheikh Ibrahima, Moustapha Diagne, Youssoupha Niang, Amadou Mody Moreau, Dominique Gomis, and Mayé Diouf. *Meeting the Sexual Health Needs of Men Who Have Sex with Men in Senegal*. New York: Population Council, 2002.

Nicholls, David. "Transethnicism and the American Experimental Tradition." *Musical Quarterly* 80.4 (1996): 569–94.

Nobile, Philip. "Uncovering Roots." *Village Voice* 23 Feb. 1993: 31–38.

Obbo, Christine. "Dominant Male Ideology and Female Options: Three East African Case Studies." *Africa* 46.4 (1976): 371–89.

O'Brien, Denise. "Female Husbands in Southern Bantu Societies." *Sexual Stratification: A Cross-Cultural View*. Ed. Alice Schlegel. New York: Columbia UP, 1977. 109–26.

Odamtten, Vincent O. *The Art of Ama Ata Aidoo: Polylectics and Reading against Neocolonialism*. Gainesville: UP of Florida, 1994.

Ojo-Ade, Femi. "*The Interpreters*, or Soyinka's Indictment of the Ivory Tower." *Black American Literature Forum* 22.4 (1988): 735–51.

O'Neill, Helen. "Chains of Memory." *Ann Arbor News* 20 April 1998: D1–2.

O'Rourke, Michael, ed. "The Becoming-Deleuzoguattarian of Queer Studies." Spec. issue of *Rhizomes* 11/12 (2005–6). <http://www.rhizomes.net/issue11>. 11 June 2015.

Ottaway, Mark. "Tangled Roots." *Sunday Times* 10 April 1977: 17, 21.

The Oxford English Dictionary. 2nd ed. Prepared by J. A. Simpson and E. S. C. Weiner. Oxford: Clarendon, 1989. 20 vols.

Oyewumi, Oyeronke, ed. and intro. *African Women and Feminism: Reflecting on the Politics of Sisterhood*. Trenton, NJ: Africa World P, 2003.

Oyewumi, Oyeronke. *The Invention of Women: Making an African Sense of Western Gender Discourses*. Minneapolis: U of Minnesota P, 1997.

Patron, Eugene J. "Heart of Lavender." *Harvard Gay and Lesbian Review* 2.4 (1995): 22–24.

Patton, Cindy, and Benigno Sánchez-Eppler, eds. *Queer Diasporas*. Durham: Duke UP, 2000.

Peterson, Christopher. *Kindred Specters: Death, Mourning, and American Affinity*. Minneapolis: U of Minnesota P, 2007.

Phillips, Oliver. "Zimbabwe." *Sociolegal Control of Homosexuality: A Multi-Nation Comparison*. Ed. Donald J. West and Richard Green. New York: Plenum, 1997. 43–56.

Plumecocq, Michaël. "Entretien avec Patrick Chamoiseau autour de *Solibo Magnifique*." *Roman 20/50* 27 (1999): 125–35.

Puar, Jasbir K. "Queer Times, Queer Assemblages." *Social Text* 23.3/4 (2005): 121–39.

Puar, Jasbir K. *Terrorist Assemblages: Homonationalism in Queer Times*. Durham: Duke UP, 2007.

Puca, Antonella. "Steve Reich and Hebrew Cantillation." *Musical Quarterly* 81.4 (1997): 537–55.

Rashkin, Esther. *Family Secrets and the Psychoanalysis of Narrative*. Princeton: Princeton UP, 1992.

Rayner, Alice. *Ghosts: Death's Double and the Phenomena of Theater*. Minneapolis: U of Minnesota P, 2006.

Rayns, Tony. "Exploitations." *Sight and Sound* 5.5 (1995): 6–9.

Reich, Steve. *The Cave*. Video/text by Beryl Korot. 1993. New York: Nonesuch Records, 1995.

Reich, Steve. "Clapping Music." 1972. *Writings* 68.

Reich, Steve. "Different Trains." 1988. *Writings* 151–55.

Reich, Steve. "Drumming." 1971. *Writings* 63–67.

Reich, Steve. "First Interview with Michael Nyman." 1970. *Writings* 52–55.

Reich, Steve. "It's Gonna Rain." 1965. *Writings* 19–22.

Reich, Steve. "Music as a Gradual Process." 1968. *Writings* 34–36.

Reich, Steve. "The Phase-Shifting Pulse Gate—Four Organs—Phase Patterns—An End to Electronics." 1968–70. *Writings* 38–50.

Reich, Steve. "Pendulum Music." 1968. *Writings* 31–32.

Reich, Steve. "Two Questions about Opera." 1999. *Writings* 211–12.

Reich, Steve. *Writings on Music, 1965–2000*. Ed. and intro. Paul Hillier. Oxford: Oxford UP, 2002.

Reich, Steve, and Beryl Korot. *The Cave*. N. pl.: Hendon Music, 1993.

Reich, Steve, and Beryl Korot. "Thoughts about the Madness in Abraham's Cave." 1994. Reich, *Writings* 178–80.

Reid-Pharr, Robert F. "Tearing the Goat's Flesh." *Black Gay Man: Essays*. New York: New York UP, 2001. 99–134.

Reuter, Madalynne. "Two Writers Question the Originality of *Roots*." *Publishers Weekly* 2 May 1977: 20.

Roberts, Nancy. *An Illustrated Guide to Ghosts and Mysterious Occurrences in the Old North State*. 1959. Charlotte, NC: McNally and Loftin, 1967.

Romney, Jonathan. *Atom Egoyan*. London: British Film Institute, 2003.

Ronell, Avital. *Dictations: On Haunted Writing*. 1986. Urbana: U of Illinois P, 2006.

Roof, Judith. *Come as You Are: Sexuality and Narrative*. New York: Columbia UP, 1996.

Roscoe, Will. *Changing Ones: Third and Fourth Genders in Native North America*. New York: St. Martin's, 1998.

Roscoe, Will. *The Zuni Man-Woman*. Albuquerque: U of New Mexico P, 1991.

Rose, Willie Lee. "An American Family." *New York Review of Books* 11 Nov. 1976: 3–6.

Roumain, Jacques. *Gouverneurs de la rosée*. 1946. Paris: Temps Actuels, 1982.

Rouyer, Philippe. "Jeux de miroirs: Entretien avec Atom Egoyan." *Positif* Dec. 1991: 23–26.

Rowe, J. A. "The Purge of Christians at Mwanga's Court: A Reassessment of This Episode in Buganda History." *Journal of African History* 5.1 (1964): 55–71.

Safran, William. "Diasporas in Modern Societies: Myths of Homeland and Return." *Diaspora* 1.1 (1991): 83–99.

Said, Edward W. *Beginnings: Intention and Method*. 1975. New York: Columbia UP, 1985.

Said, Edward W. *Orientalism*. 1978. New York: Vintage, 1979.

Said, Edward W. *Peace and Its Discontents: Essays on Palestine in the Middle East Peace Process*. 1993. New York: Vintage, 1995.

Said, Edward W. *The World, the Text, and the Critic*. Cambridge: Harvard UP, 1983.

Sapho. *Un mensonge*. Paris: Balland, 1990.

Schnepel, Ellen M. "The Other Tongue, the Other Voice: Language and Gender in the French Caribbean." *Ethnic Groups* 10 (1993): 243–68.

Scholem, Gershom. *Kabbalah*. Jerusalem: Keter, 1974.

Schor, Naomi, and Elizabeth Weed, eds. *The Essential Difference*. Bloomington: Indiana UP, 1994.

Schwab, Gabriele. *Derrida, Deleuze, Psychoanalysis*. New York: Columbia UP, 2007.

Schwartz, Nina. "Exotic Rituals and Family Values in *Exotica*." *Perversion and the Social Relation*. Ed. Molly Anne Rothenberg, Dennis Foster, and Slavoj Žižek. Durham: Duke UP, 2003. 93–111.

Schwarz, K. Robert. "Steve Reich: Back on Track." *Ear* 14.2 (1989): 30–37.

Sedgwick, Eve Kosofsky. *Epistemology of the Closet*. Berkeley: U of California P, 1990.

Segal, Oren. "Imagining Independence Park." PhD diss. U of Michigan, 2012.

Segev, Tom. *1949: The First Israelis*. New York: Free P, 1986.

Segrest, Mab. *Memoir of a Race Traitor*. Boston: South End, 1994.

Segrest, Mab. *My Mama's Dead Squirrel: Lesbian Essays on Southern Culture*. Ithaca, NY: Firebrand, 1985.

Senghor, Léopold Sédar. *Anthologie de la nouvelle poésie nègre et malgache de langue française*. Paris: PU de France, 1948.

Sharlet, Jeff. "Straight Man's Burden: The American Roots of Uganda's Anti-gay Persecutions." *Harper's* Sept. 2010. <http://www.harpers.org.proxy.lib.umich.edu/archive/2010/09/0083101>. 30 April 2011.

Sharpe, Ivey Lawrence, and Edgar Fletcher Pepper III. *Stanly County USA: The Story of an Area and an Era (1841–1991)*. Greensboro, NC: Media P, 1990.

Shary, Timothy. "Video as Accessible Artifact and Artificial Access: The Early Films of Atom Egoyan." *Film Criticism* 19.3 (1995): 2–29.

Shenker, Israel. "Some Historians Dismiss Report of Factual Mistakes in 'Roots.'" *New York Times* 10 April 1977: sec. 1, 29.

Shepperson, George. "African Diaspora: Concept and Context." Harris 41–49.

Shohat, Ella. *Israeli Cinema: East/West and the Politics of Representation*. Austin: U of Texas P, 1989.

Siraganian, Lisa. "'Is This My Mother's Grave?': Genocide and Diaspora in Atom Egoyan's *Family Viewing*." *Diaspora* 6.2 (1997): 127–54.

Skaggs, Merrill Maguire. "*Roots:* A New Black Myth." *Southern Quarterly* 17.1 (1978): 42–50.

Smith, Donna Jo. "Queering the South: Constructions of Southern/Queer Identity." Howard, *Carryin' On* 370–85.

Smith, Michael S. "African Roots, American Fruits: The Queerness of Afrocentricity." *Outweek* 27 Feb. 1991: 30–31, 78.

Smyth, Heather. "'Roots beyond Roots': Heteroglossia and Feminist Creolization in *Myal* and *Crossing the Mangrove*." *Small Axe* 6.2 (2002): 1–24.

Sow Fall, Aminata. *Le revenant*. Paris: Nouvelles Éditions Africaines, 1982.

Soyinka, Wole. "Gays, Lesbians, and Legislative Zealotry." 24 Dec. 2012. <http://www.ynaija.com/wole-soyinka-gays-lesbians-and-legislative zealotry>. 18 Feb. 2013.

Soyinka, Wole. *The Interpreters*. London: Heinemann, 1965.

Spear, Thomas C. "Jouissances carnavalesques: Représentations de la sexualité." Condé and Cottenet-Hage 135–52.

Spender, Matthew. *From a High Place: A Life of Arshile Gorky—A Life in Letters and Documents*. New York: Knopf, 1999.

Spender, Matthew, ed. *Arshile Gorky: Goats on the Roof*. London: Ridinghouse, 2009.

Spivak, Gayatri Chakravorty. "Can the Subaltern Speak?" *Marxism and the Interpretation of Culture*. Ed. Cary Nelson and Lawrence Grossberg. Urbana: U of Illinois P, 1988. 271–313.

Spivak, Gayatri Chakravorty. "Diasporas Old and New: Women in the Transnational World." *Textual Practice* 10.2 (1996): 245–69.

Spivak, Gayatri Chakravorty. "In a Word: Interview." With Ellen Rooney. Schor and Weed 151–84.

Spivak, Gayatri Chakravorty. *The Post-colonial Critic: Interviews, Strategies, Dialogues*. Ed. Sarah Harasym. New York: Routledge, 1990.

Stockton, Kathryn Bond. *Beautiful Bottom, Beautiful Shame: Where "Black" Meets "Queer."* Durham: Duke UP, 2006.

Subotnik, Rose Rosengard. *Deconstructive Variations: Music and Reason in Western Society*. Minneapolis: U of Minnesota P, 1996.

Swarns, Rachel L. "Mugabe's Real Foes Aren't the Ones He Denounces." *New York Times* 30 April 2000: Week in Review 3.

Swarns, Rachel L. "Political Shift Seen in Zimbabwe Vote." *New York Times* 24 June 2000: A3.

Swarns, Rachel L. "Protest against Farm Squatters Stops Zimbabwe." *New York Times* 3 Aug. 2000: A3.

Swarns, Rachel L. "The West Sees One Mugabe, but Africa Sees Another." *New York Times* 6 Aug. 2000: sec. 4, 4.

Tamale, Sylvia. "Out of the Closet: Unveiling Sexuality Discourses in Uganda." Cole, Manuh, and Miescher 17–29.

Tatchell, Peter. "OutRage! Letter to British Prime Minister Tony Blair." 9 Nov. 1999. <http://www.outrage.org.uk/mugabe99a.htm>. 2 Feb. 2000.

Taubin, Amy. "Memoires of Overdevelopment." *Film Comment* 25.6 (1989): 27–29.

Taylor, Lucien. "Créolité Bites: A Conversation with Patrick Chamoiseau, Raphaël Confiant, and Jean Bernabé." *Transition* 74 (1998): 124–61.

Teal, Donn. *The Gay Militants.* New York: Stein and Day, 1971.

Teicher, Morton I. "Was Wolfe an Anti-Semite?" *Thomas Wolfe Review* 22.1 (1998): 24–37.

Teunis, Niels. "Homosexuality in Dakar: Is the Bed the Heart of a Sexual Subculture?" *Journal of Gay, Lesbian, and Bisexual Identity* 1.2 (1996): 153–69.

Thoonen, J. P. *Black Martyrs.* London: Sheed and Ward, 1942.

Tölölyan, Khachig. "The Contemporary Discourse of Diaspora Studies." *Comparative Studies of South Asia, Africa and the Middle East* 27.3 (2007): 647–55.

"Uganda, Martyrs of." *New Catholic Encyclopedia.* Vol. 14. San Francisco: Catholic U of America, 1967. 363.

"Uganda to Arrest Gays." *Chicago Sun-Times* 30 Sept. 1999: 22.

Unspoken Facts: A History of Homosexualities in Africa. Harare: Gays and Lesbians of Zimbabwe, 2008.

Ussher, Clarence D. *An American Physician in Turkey: A Narrative of Adventures in Peace and in War.* Boston: Houghton Mifflin, 1917.

Valente, Joseph, ed. *Quare Joyce.* Ann Arbor: U of Michigan P, 1998.

Vangroenweghe, Daniel. *Sida et sexualité en Afrique.* 1997. Trans. Jean-Marie Flémal. Brussels: EPO, 2000.

Veit-Wild, Flora, and Dirk Naguschewski, eds. and intro. *Body, Sexuality, and Gender: Versions and Subversions in African Literatures.* Vol. 1. Amsterdam: Rodopi, 2005.

Vicinus, Martha. "'They Wonder to Which Sex I Belong': The Historical Roots of the Modern Lesbian Identity." 1989. *The Lesbian and Gay Studies Reader.* Ed. Henry Abelove, Michèle Aina Barale, and David M. Halperin. New York: Routledge, 1993. 432–52.

Vignal, Daniel. "L'homophilie dans le roman négro-africain d'expression anglaise et française." *Peuples noirs, peuples africains* 33 (1983): 63–81.

Vorda, Allan. "Avoiding Boxes: An Interview with Steve Reich." *Cum notis variorum* 131 (1989): 13–16.

Waldrop, Rosmarie. "Mirrors and Paradoxes." Gould 133–46.

Wallace, Michele. *Black Macho and the Myth of the Superwoman.* London: Verso, 1990.

"Way Too Trusting of Kindly Strangers." Rev. of Atom Egoyan's *Felicia's Journey. New York Times* 12 Nov. 1999: B14.

Weil, Simone. *The Need for Roots: Prelude to a Declaration of Duties toward Mankind.* Trans. Arthur Wills. New York: Harper, 1952.

Welsing, Frances Cress. *The Isis (Yssis) Papers.* Chicago: Third World P, 1991.

Weston, Kate. *Families We Choose: Lesbians, Gays, Kinship.* 1991. New York: Columbia UP, 1997.

Wetherell, Iden. "Mugabe's Unholy War." *Southern Africa Report* 11.4 (1996): 13–14.

White, Deborah Gray. 1985. *Ar'n't I a Woman: Female Slaves in the Plantation South.* New York: Norton, 1999.

Wilentz, Gay. "The Politics of Exile: Reflections of a Black-Eyed Squint in *Our Sister Killjoy.*" *Emerging Perspectives on Ama Ata Aidoo.* Ed. Ada Uzoamaka Azodo and Gay Wilentz. Trenton, NJ: Africa World P, 1999. 79–92.

Wilson, Emma. "The Female Adjuster: Arsinée Khanjian and the Films of Atom Egoyan." *Cinema's Missing Children.* London: Wallflower, 2003. 28–40.

Wolfe, Thomas. *Look Homeward, Angel: A Story of the Buried Life*. 1929. New York: Simon and Schuster, 1957.

Wolfe, Thomas. *O Lost: A Story of the Buried Life*. Ed. Arlyn and Matthew J. Bruccoli. Columbia: U of South Carolina P, 2000.

Wolfe, Thomas. *Of Time and the River: A Legend of Man's Hunger in His Youth*. New York: Scribner, 1935.

Wolfe, Thomas. *The Web and The Rock*. 1939. New York: Signet, 1966.

Wolfe, Thomas. *You Can't Go Home Again*. 1940. New York: Signet, 1968.

Wright Donald R. "Uprooting Kunta Kinte: On the Perils of Relying on Encyclopedic Informants." *History in Africa* 8 (1981): 205–17.

Yaeger, Patricia. *Dirt and Desire: Reconstructing Southern Women's Writing 1930–1990*. Chicago: U of Chicago P, 2000.

Zaborowska, Magdalena J. *James Baldwin's Turkish Decade: Erotics of Exile*. Durham: Duke UP, 2009.

"Zimbabwean PM Morgan Tsvangirai Accused of 'Hate Speech' by Gay Rights Group." *Pink News*. <http://www.pinknews.co.uk/2013/03/08/zimbabwean-pm-morgan-tsvangirai-accused-of-hate-speech-by-gay-rights-group/>. 1 Jan. 2014.

"Zimbabwe's Mugabe Renews Attack in New Year Address." Circulated on glas@post. cis.smu.edu. 6 Jan. 2000.

"Zimbabwe's PM Morgan Tsvangirai in Gay Rights U-turn." *BBC News*. <http://www.bbc.co.uk/news/world-africa-15431142?print=true>. 1 Jan. 2014.

Zimmerman, Bonnie, and Toni A. H. McNaron, eds. *The New Lesbian Studies: Into the Twenty-First Century*. New York: Feminist, 1996.

The Zohar: Pritzker Edition. Trans. and commentary Daniel C. Matt. Intro. Arthur Green. Vol. 1. Stanford: Stanford UP, 2004.

Zola, Emile. *Les Rougon-Macquart*. 5 vols. Paris: Gallimard, 1960–67. Bibliothèque de la Pléiade.

Index

✦ ✦ ✦